Learning SAP Analytics Cloud

Discover, plan, predict, collaborate, visualize, and extend all in one solution

Riaz Ahmed

Packt>

BIRMINGHAM - MUMBAI

Learning SAP Analytics Cloud

First published: July 2017

Production reference: 2270717

Published by Packt Publishing Ltd.
Livery Place
35 Livery Street
Birmingham
B3 2PB, UK.
ISBN 978-1-78829-088-3

www.packtpub.com

Credits

Author
Riaz Ahmed

Reviewer
David Lai

Commissioning Editor
Merint Mathew

Acquisition Editor
Tushar Gupta

Content Development Editor
Tejas Limkar

Technical Editor
Dharmendra Yadav

Copy Editor
Manisha Sinha

Project Coordinator
Manthan Patel

Proofreader
Safis Editing

Indexer
Tejal Daruwale Soni

Production Coordinator
Deepika Naik

About the Author

Riaz Ahmed is an IT professional with more than 25 years of experience in the field. He started his career in the early 1990s as a programmer and has been employed in a wide variety of information technology positions, including analyst programmer, system analyst, project manager, data architect, database designer, and senior database administrator. Currently, he is working as the head of IT for a group of companies. His core areas of interest include web-based development technologies, business intelligence, and databases. Riaz possesses extensive experience in database design and development. He has worked intensively with almost all the major RDBMSs in the market today. During his career, he designed and implemented numerous databases for a wide range of applications, including ERP.

About the Reviewer

David Lai is a SAP Analytics and SAP BI consultant who specializes in data visualization, data analytics, and data warehouse architecture. He graduated with a degree in computer engineering from the University of Toronto. He has a passion for providing organizations with smart Business Intelligence solutions that encompass best practices and techniques.

David enjoys sharing his knowledge with the SAP community. He co-authored the book SAP BusinessObjects Dashboards 4.1 Cookbook and started a Business Intelligence blog (`http://www.davidlai101.com/blog`) in 2008, wherein he provides tips, tricks, and best practices on SAP-related material. He has also presented at several SAP conferences and provides SAP BI training to many clients.

David is the president of Xinfinity Solutions, where he and a team of highly skilled consultants provide Business Intelligence-related consulting services to a long list of satisfied clients in various industries.

www.PacktPub.com

For support files and downloads related to your book, please visit `www.PacktPub.com`.

Did you know that Packt offers eBook versions of every book published, with PDF and ePub files available? You can upgrade to the eBook version at `www.PacktPub.com` and as a print book customer, you are entitled to a discount on the eBook copy. Get in touch with us at `service@packtpub.com` for more details.

At `www.PacktPub.com`, you can also read a collection of free technical articles, sign up for a range of free newsletters and receive exclusive discounts and offers on Packt books and eBooks.

Mapt

`https://www.packtpub.com/mapt`

Get the most in-demand software skills with Mapt. Mapt gives you full access to all Packt books and video courses, as well as industry-leading tools to help you plan your personal development and advance your career.

Why subscribe?

- Fully searchable across every book published by Packt
- Copy and paste, print, and bookmark content
- On demand and accessible via a web browser

Customer Feedback

Thanks for purchasing this Packt book. At Packt, quality is at the heart of our editorial process. To help us improve, please leave us an honest review on this book's Amazon page at `https://www.amazon.com/dp/1788290887`.

If you'd like to join our team of regular reviewers, you can e-mail us at `customerreviews@packtpub.com`. We award our regular reviewers with free eBooks and videos in exchange for their valuable feedback. Help us be relentless in improving our products!

Table of Contents

Preface

SAP Analytics Cloud is a business intelligence, planning, and predictive cloud-based application that helps users blend data from different sources, create compelling data visualizations, run ad hoc reporting, and more. This book will demonstrate how SAP Analytics Cloud can help transform the way you discover, plan, predict, collaborate, visualize, and extend all in one solution. You will begin by being introduced to the SAP Analytics Cloud environment. From here, you will learn about the different models and understand the different capabilities with SAP Analytics Cloud, such as Predictive Analysis, BI, and Planning. Going further, you will learn how to create geomaps, charts, tables, and other objects. Using SAP Analytics Cloud, you will learn how to connect to SAP and non-SAP data sources. You will also learn how to analyze and blend small and big data on premise and in the cloud.

The book starts with the basics of SAP Analytics Cloud and exposes almost every significant feature that is necessary for a beginner. Packed with illustrations short descriptions, the book provides a unique learning experience.

Your exploration journey starts with the most basic introduction to SAP Analytics Cloud. In this introduction, you are briefed about the segments of the product, such as model, stories, Digital Boardroom. Then you are acquainted with the interface of the product (Home screen, Main Menu, and more). You then go to the hands-on side of the book, which starts with model creation. Next, you are guided on how to utilize a model to prepare different types of stories (reports) with the help of charts, tables, geomaps, and more. In the final chapters of this book, you will learn about Digital Boardroom, collaboration, and administration.

These are the objectives of this book:

- The first is self learning. The easy-to-follow visual instructions provided in this book help business users and report developers to create simple and complex stories quickly, all by themselves.
- The main objective of this book is to equip you with a solid understanding of what SAP Analytics Cloud contains so that you can effectively utilize the product.

- After completing the exercises provided in this book, you will have a clear understanding of the SAP Analytics Cloud platform. You will be able to create data models using different data sources, including Excel and text files, and will be in a position to present professional analyses using different types of charts, tables, and geomaps. You can share your stories with other team members or compile them in the SAP Digital Boardroom agenda for presentation to major stakeholders.

What this book covers

Chapter 1, *Getting Started with SAP Analytics Cloud*, provides a brief introduction to SAP Analytics Cloud platform and exposes its anatomy. In this chapter, you will get an overview of different SAP Analytics Cloud segments (models, stories, Digital Boardroom, and more), which are discussed in detail in subsequent chapters.

Chapter 2, *Models*, provides some basic conceptual stuff about models, such as analytics and planning models, measures, and dimensions. Models are the foundation of every analysis you create in SAP Analytics Cloud. You will create an analytics model in this chapter to get hands-on exposure to this segment of the application.

Chapter 3, *Planning Models*, provides details about planning models, which are models in which you work with planning features. A planning model is called a full-featured model because it is preconfigured with the time and categories dimensions for actual, budget, planning, forecast, and rolling forecast. It also supports multicurrency and offers security at both model and dimension levels to restrict access to specific values in the report to privileged users. It also comes with auditing features for traceability.

Chapter 4, *Creating Stories Using Charts*, discusses stories, which are used in SAP Analytics Cloud to present data graphically using charts, tables, geomaps, text, images, and shapes. In this chapter, there are some hands-on exercises to help you explore this significant segment of the application.

Chapter 5, *Extending Stories with KPI, Filters, and Other Handy Objects*, also relates to stories. Here, you will learn about key performance indicators (KPIs), add different types of filters to narrow the scope of you analysis, add reference lines, create linked analysis, add dynamic and static text, and a lot more.

Chapter 6, *Analyzing Data Using Geo Maps and Other Objects*, discusses the models that include latitude and longitude information and can be used in stories to visualize data in geomaps. By adding multiple layers of different types of data, you can show different geographic features and points of interest, enabling you to perform sophisticated geographic analysis. You will also learn how to add, delete, copy, and duplicate pages in your stories and how to provide them with expressive names. Adding comments, creating linked dimensions, predictive forecasting, and time calculation are also discussed in this chapter.

Chapter 7, *Working with Tables and Grids*, discusses tables and grids in detail. A table is a spreadsheet-like object that can be used to view and analyze text data. You will also learn about grid page, which is a type of page used to create analysis comprising text and formulas. Applying ranking to charts, applying filters to tables, setting visibility filters, using KPIs in tables, and creating blended tables are some of the topics covered in this chapter.

Chapter 8, *Collaboration*, highlights the collaboration features in SAP Analytics Cloud using which users can discuss business content and share information. These features include creating events and assigning tasks, commenting on a chart's data points, commenting on a story page, saving and sharing a story as a PDF, discussions, and sharing files and stories.

Chapter 9, *Digital Boardroom*, discusses the SAP Digital Boardroom, which is changing the landscape of board meetings. In addition to supporting traditional presentation methods, it goes beyond the corporate boardroom and allows remote members to join and participate in the meeting online. These remote participants can actively engage in the meeting and can play with live data using their own devices. The chapter will demonstrate how to create boardroom agenda and set up online meetings.

Chapter 10, *System Administration*, discusses how to make your SAP Analytics Cloud environment secure by creating users and setting their passwords, setting up teams, creating roles and setting permissions, monitoring users activities, data changes, and system performance. In the final section of this book, you will learn about system deployment in which you export and import system components.

What you need for this book

The most significant advantage of this platform is that you do not need to install or configure any software on your machine. A compatible web browser and a moderate Internet connection is all you need to access this application to create interactive dashboards in the cloud.

Who this book is for

This book targets IT professionals, business analysts, BI developers, managers, newcomers to SAP Analytics Cloud, and anyone who wants to learn from self-paced, professional guidance and needs a solid foundation in SAP Analytics Cloud.

Conventions

In this book, you will find a number of text styles that distinguish between different kinds of information. Here are some examples of these styles and an explanation of their meaning. Code words in text, database table names, folder names, filenames, file extensions, pathnames, dummy URLs, user input, and Twitter handles are shown as follows: "The `Bocage.xlsx` file is a simple Excel file being provided with this book for demonstration purpose."

New terms and **important words** are shown in bold. Words that you see on the screen, for example, in menus or dialog boxes, appear in the text like this: "select **Live Data Connection | SAP HANA**."

Warnings or important notes appear like this.

Tips and tricks appear like this.

Reader feedback

Feedback from our readers is always welcome. Let us know what you think about this book-what you liked or disliked. Reader feedback is important for us as it helps us develop titles that you will really get the most out of. To send us general feedback, simply e-mail `feedback@packtpub.com`, and mention the book's title in the subject of your message. If there is a topic that you have expertise in and you are interested in either writing or contributing to a book, see our author guide at `www.packtpub.com/authors`.

Customer support

Now that you are the proud owner of a Packt book, we have a number of things to help you to get the most from your purchase.

Downloading the example code

You can download the example code files for this book from your account at `http://www.p acktpub.com`. If you purchased this book elsewhere, you can visit `http://www.packtpub.c om/support`and register to have the files emailed directly to you. You can download the code files by following these steps:

1. Log in or register to our website using your e-mail address and password.
2. Hover the mouse pointer on the **SUPPORT** tab at the top.
3. Click on **Code Downloads & Errata**.
4. Enter the name of the book in the **Search** box.
5. Select the book for which you're looking to download the code files.
6. Choose from the drop-down menu where you purchased this book from.
7. Click on **Code Download**.

Once the file is downloaded, please make sure that you unzip or extract the folder using the latest version of:

- WinRAR / 7-Zip for Windows
- Zipeg / iZip / UnRarX for Mac
- 7-Zip / PeaZip for Linux

The code bundle for the book is also hosted on GitHub at `https://github.com/PacktPubl ishing/Learning-SAP-Analytics-Cloud`. We also have other code bundles from our rich catalog of books and videos available at `https://github.com/PacktPublishing/`. Check them out!

Downloading the color images of this book

We also provide you with a PDF file that has color images of the screenshots/diagrams used in this book. The color images will help you better understand the changes in the output. You can download this file from `https://www.packtpub.com/sites/default/files/downloads/LearningSAPAnalyticsClou d_ColorImages.pdf`.

Errata

Although we have taken every care to ensure the accuracy of our content, mistakes do happen. If you find a mistake in one of our books-maybe a mistake in the text or the code-we would be grateful if you could report this to us. By doing so, you can save other readers from frustration and help us improve subsequent versions of this book. If you find any errata, please report them by visiting http://www.packtpub.com/submit-errata, selecting your book, clicking on the **Errata Submission Form** link, and entering the details of your errata. Once your errata are verified, your submission will be accepted and the errata will be uploaded to our website or added to any list of existing errata under the **Errata** section of that title. To view the previously submitted errata, go to https://www.packtpub.com/books/content/support and enter the name of the book in the search field. The required information will appear under the **Errata** section.

Piracy

Piracy of copyrighted material on the Internet is an ongoing problem across all media. At Packt, we take the protection of our copyright and licenses very seriously. If you come across any illegal copies of our works in any form on the Internet, please provide us with the location address or website name immediately so that we can pursue a remedy. Please contact us at copyright@packtpub.com with a link to the suspected pirated material. We appreciate your help in protecting our authors and our ability to bring you valuable content.

Questions

If you have a problem with any aspect of this book, you can contact us at questions@packtpub.com, and we will do our best to address the problem.

1
Getting Started with SAP Analytics Cloud

SAP Analytics Cloud is a new generation cloud-based application that helps you explore your data, perform visualization and analysis, create financial plans, and produce predictive forecasting. It is a one-stop-shop solution to cope with your analytic needs and comprises business intelligence, planning, predictive analytics, and governance and risk. The application is built on the SAP Cloud Platform and delivers great performance and scalability. In addition to the on-premise SAP HANA, SAP BW, and S/4HANA sources, you can work with data from a wide range of non-SAP sources, including Google Drive, Salesforce, SQL Server, Concur, and CSV, to name a few. SAP Analytics Cloud allows you to make secure connections to these cloud and on-premise data sources.

This chapter is aimed at providing an overview of SAP Analytics Cloud and covers the following basics of the application:

- Anatomy of SAP Analytics Cloud
- Introduction to the Home screen and the main menu of the application
- A brief overview of data sources and models and ways to connect to different data sources
- A brief overview of visualization, collaboration, presentation, and application administration
- Finally, you will be guided to signing up for a free trial version to execute the exercises provided in this book

Anatomy of SAP Analytics Cloud

Models are the basis for all of your analysis in SAP Analytics Cloud. You can create planning and analytics models based on the cloud or on-premise data sources. Besides creating a simple analytics model, business analysts and finance professionals can quickly and easily build connected planning models to analyze data and then collaborate with each other to attain better business performance. After creating these models, you can share it with other users in your organization. Before sharing, you can set up model access privileges for users according to their level of authorization and can also enable data auditing. With the help of SAP Analytics Cloud's analytical capabilities, users can discover hidden traits in the data and can predict likely outcomes. It equips them with the ability to uncover potential risks and hidden opportunities.

Once you have created a model and set up appropriate security for it, you can create stories in which the underlying model data can be explored and visualized with the help of different types of charts, geo maps, and tables. There is a wide range of charts you can add to your story pages to address different scenarios. The intelligent charting feature of SAP Analytics Cloud proposes the ideal chart type based on data relationships. On your story pages, you can link dimensions to present data from multiple sources. Adding reference lines and thresholds, applying filters, and drilling down into data can be done on the fly. The ability to interactively drag and drop page objects is the most useful feature of this application.

The collaboration, alert, and notification features of SAP Analytics Cloud keep business users in touch with each other while executing their tasks.

In the past, board meetings were held in which the participants used to deliver their reports through their laptops and a bunch of papers. With different versions of reality, it was very difficult for decision makers to arrive at a good decision. With the advent of the SAP digital boardroom, board meetings have been revolutionized. It is a next-generation presentation platform, which helps you visualize your data and plan ahead in a real-time environment. It runs on multiple screens simultaneously, displaying information from different sources. Due to this capability, more people can work together using a single dataset that consequently creates one version of reality to make the best decision.

With the help of the administration and security features of the application, you can create users and set up teams, create new roles with different system access privileges and assign them to users, monitor the application usage, and use export and import utilities to deploy application content.

The following figure depicts the anatomy of SAP Analytics Cloud:

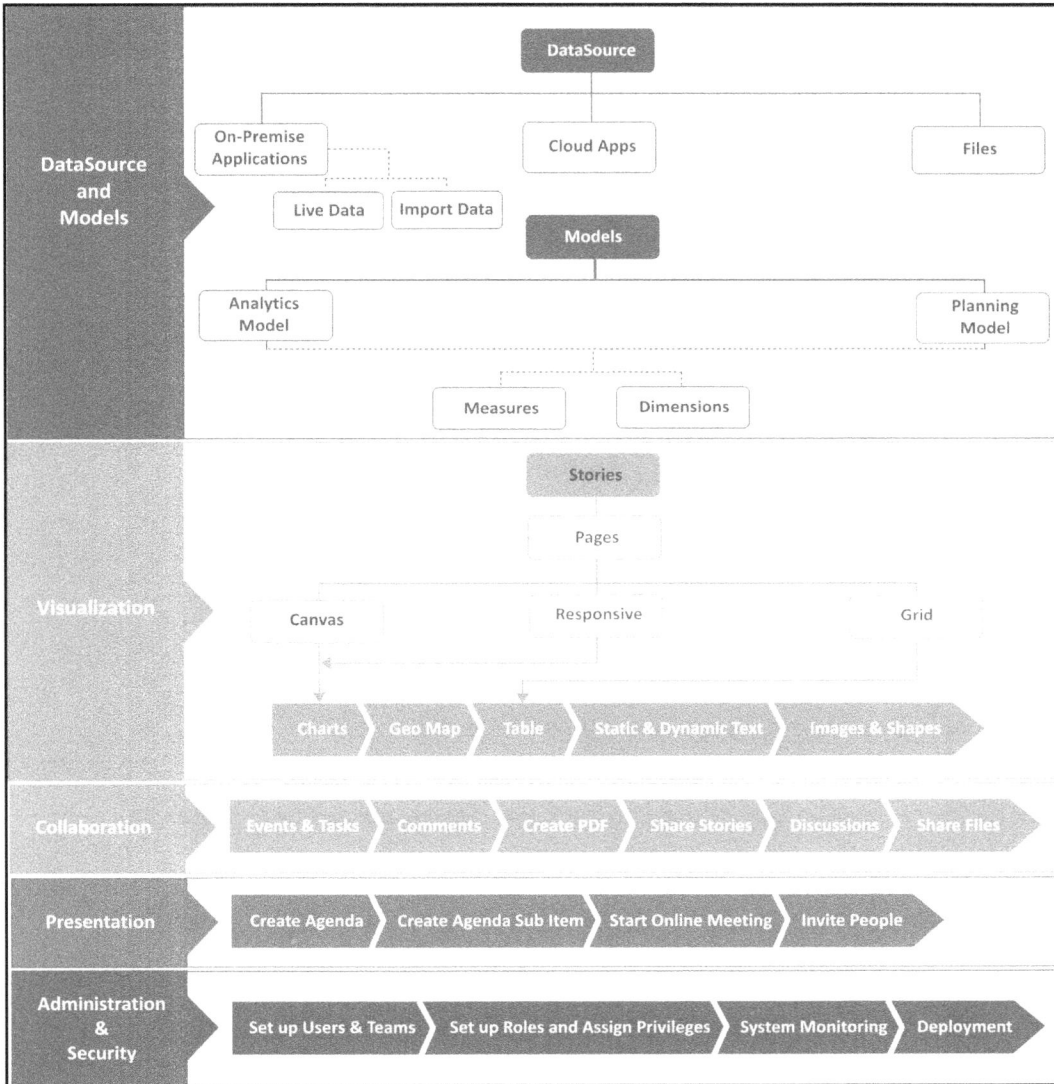

The Home screen

When you successfully log in to SAP Analytics Cloud, you are greeted with the **Home** screen. Note that the Home screen is private to every SAP Analytics Cloud user, so it can't be shared. Here are a few pointers to help you get acclimatized to the **Home** screen:

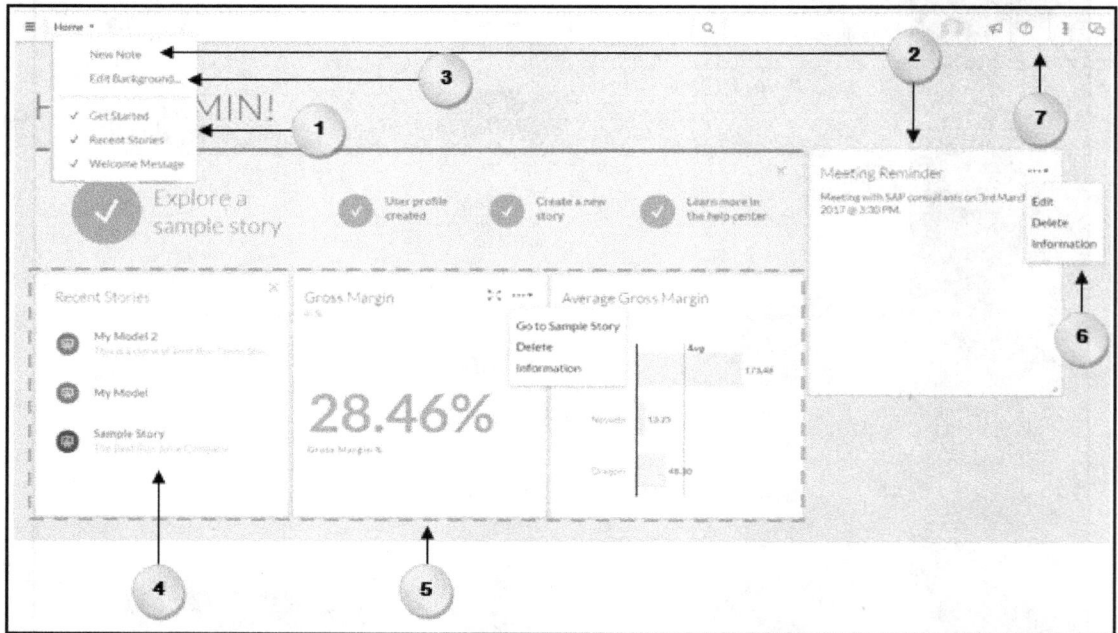

1. To remove the **Get Started** widget, the **Recent Stories** tile, or the **Welcome** message, go to the **Home** menu, and deselect the item you want to remove.
2. The **Home** screen also allows you to add useful reminders for upcoming events and personal notes.
3. Using the **Edit Background** option, you can customize the display background and add a logo to the **Home** screen.
4. The first tile titled **Recent Stories** lists the five most recent stories you have accessed.
5. Your recent stories and visualizations are displayed as tiles. You can pin additional tiles from your stories to the **Home** screen.
6. Click the ellipsis icon to modify or delete a note.
7. The toolbar appears on top of every screen. Using the icons on the toolbar, users can see their own profiles, view notifications, get online help, view the time panel, and collaborate.

The main menu

The following screenshot and bullets will help you understand the main menu better:

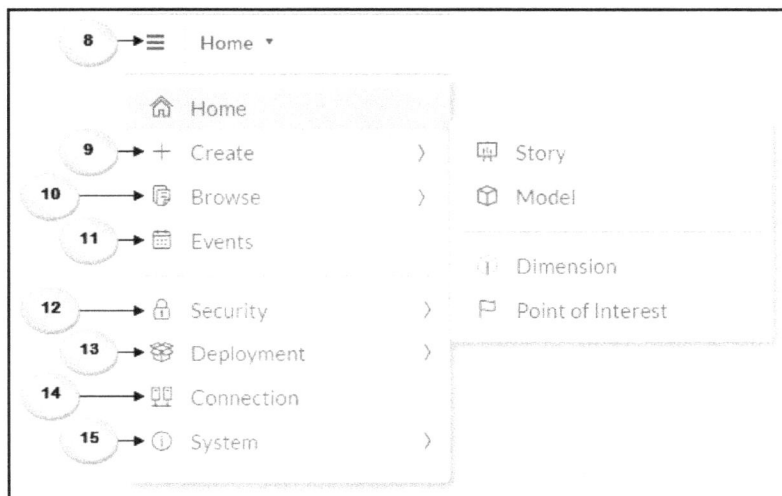

8. The main menu icon is your gateway to SAP Analytics Cloud. It provides you with all the options to get things done.

9. Click on **Create** to add new **Stories**, **Models**, **Process**, **Dimension**, **Currency**, and **Point of Interest**. Models are discussed in Chapter 2, *Models in SAP Analytics Cloud*, and Chapter 3, *Planning Model*, whereas you will create stories in *Chapters 4 to 7*. The Allocation option under the Process sub-menu is discussed in Chapter 3, *Planning Model*.

10. Select **Browse** to access existing **Stories**, **Models**, **Dimensions**, **Currencies**, **Point of Interest**, and **Files**. Files are discussed in Chapter 8, *Collaboration*.

11. The **Events** option opens the **Events** page, where you can manage your planning and analytic activities and assign tasks to other users. This subject is discussed in Chapter 8, *Collaboration*.

12. The options provided in the **Security** menu items lets you create and manage application users, teams, roles, requests, and monitor data changes and user activities. These options are discussed in Chapter 10, *System Administration*.

13. Deployment includes creation and management of export and import of application content. This subject is discussed in Chapter 10, *System Administration*.

14. Using the **Connections** menu item, you can create and maintain connections to remote systems. You can create connections to import data into SAP Analytics Cloud or create live data connections to SAP HANA. You will see some instances of establishing connections later in this chapter.

15. The **System** menu item includes the **Monitor**, **Administration**, and **Enabling SAML Single Sign-On** (**SSO**) options. Using these options, the system administrator monitors the system, reads system events and errors in the system log, and sets up SAML **Single Sign-On** (**SSO**) to work with SAP Analytics Cloud.

> Due to the frequent updates SAP makes to the application, the screenshots provided in this book might differ from yours.

Data sources and models

Before commencing your analytical tasks in SAP Analytics Cloud, you need to create models. A model is the foundation of every analysis you create to evaluate the performance of your organization. It is a high-level design that exposes the analytic requirements of end users. Planning and analytics are the two types of models you can create in SAP Analytics Cloud.

Analytics models are simpler and more flexible, while planning models are full-featured models in which you work with planning features. Preconfigured with dimensions for time and categories, planning models support multicurrency and security features at both model and dimension levels. Chapters 2 and 3 of this book are dedicated to these two models.

To determine what content to include in your model, you must first identify the columns from the source data on which users need to query. The columns you need in your model reside in some sort of data source. SAP Analytics Cloud supports three types of data sources: files (such as CSV or Excel files) that usually reside on your computer, live data connections from a connected remote system, and cloud apps.

In addition to the files on your computer, you can use on-premise data sources, such as **SAP Business Warehouse**, **SAP ERP**, **SAP Universe**, **SQL database**, and more, to acquire data for your models. In the cloud, you can get data from apps such as **Concur**, **Google Drive**, **SAP Business ByDesign**, **SAP Hybris Cloud**, **OData Services**, and **Success Factors**. The following figure depicts these data sources. The cloud app data sources you can use with SAP Analytics Cloud are displayed above the firewall mark, while those in your local network are shown under the firewall.

As you can see in the following figure, there are over twenty data sources currently supported by SAP Analytics Cloud. The methods of connecting to these data sources also vary from each other. Due to space constraint, it is not possible to outline every connecting method in this chapter. However, some instances provided in this chapter would give you an idea on how connections are established to acquire data. The connection methods provided here relate to on-premise and cloud app data sources. Considering the audience of this book who may not have access to these data sources, and to keep things simple, Chapter 2, *Models in SAP Analytics Cloud*, will guide them to create an analytics model in the trial version of **SAP Analytics** Cloud using an Excel file provided with this book.

> Due to relevance with the topic, the sub-sections that follow are added here to provide an overview of different types of connections you can establish in SAP Analytics Cloud to build your models.

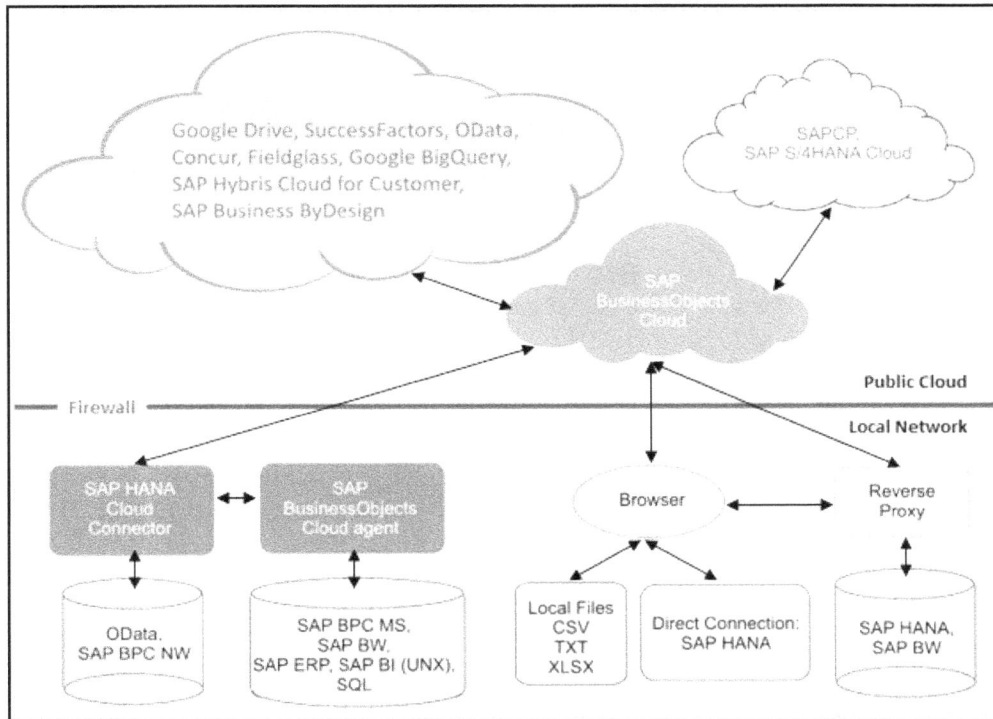

Create a direct live connection to SAP HANA

Execute the following steps to connect to the on-premise SAP HANA system to use live data in SAP Analytics Cloud. Live data means that you can get up-to-the-minute data when you open a story in SAP Analytics Cloud. In this case, any changes made to the data in the source system are reflected immediately. Usually, there are two ways to establish a connection to a data source--use the Connection option from the main menu, or specify the data source during the process of creating a model. However, live data connections must be established via the **Connection menu** option prior to creating the corresponding model. Here are the steps:

I. From the main menu, select **Connection**.

II. On the **Connections** page, click on the Add Connection icon (+), and select **Live Data Connection | SAP HANA**.

III. In the **New Live Connection** dialog, enter a name for the connection (for example, HANA).

IV. From the **Connection Type** drop-down list, select **Direct**. The **Direct** option is used when you connect to a data source that resides inside your corporate network. The **Path** option requires a reverse proxy to the HANA XS server. The **SAP Cloud Platform** and **Cloud** options in this list are used when you are connecting to SAP cloud environments. When you select the **Direct** option, the **System Type** is set to **HANA** and the protocol is set to HTTPS.

V. Enter the host name and port number in respective text boxes.

VI. The **Authentication Method** list contains two options: **User Name** and **Password** and **SAML Single Sign On**. The **SAML Single Sign On** option requires that the SAP HANA system is already configured to use SAML authentication. If not, choose the **User Name** and **Password** option and enter these credentials in relevant boxes.

VII. Click on **OK** to finish the process. A new connection will appear on the **Connection** page, which can now be used as a data source for models. The creation of the model is discussed in the next chapter. However, in order to complete this exercise, we will go through a short demo of this process here.

VIII. From the main menu, go to **Create | Model**.

IX. On the **New Model** page, select **Use a datasource**.

X. From the list that appears on your right side, select **Live Data connection**.

XI. In the dialog that is displayed, select the **HANA** connection you created in the previous steps from the **System** list.

XII. From the **Data Source** list, select the **HANA** view you want to work with. The list of views may be very long, and a search feature is available to help you locate the source you are looking for.

XIII. Finally, enter the name and the optional description for the new model, and click on **OK**. The model will be created, and its definitions will appear on another page. Refer to the next two chapters for further details on models.

Connecting remote systems to import data

In addition to creating live connections, you can also create connections that allow you to import data into SAP Analytics Cloud. In these types of connections that you make to access remote systems, data is imported (copied) to SAP Analytics Cloud. Any changes users make in the source data do not affect the imported data.

To establish connections with these remote systems, you need to install some additional components. For example, you must install SAP HANA Cloud connector to access SAP **Business Planning and Consolidation** (**BPC**) for Netweaver. Similarly, SAP Analytics Cloud agent should be installed for SAP **Business Warehouse** (**BW**), SQL Server, SAP ERP, and others. Take a look at the connection figure illustrated on a previous page.

The following set of steps provide instructions to connect to SAP ERP. You can either connect to this system from the Connection menu or establish the connection while creating a model. In these steps, we will adopt the latter approach.

I. From the main menu, go to **Create | Model**.

II. Click on the **Use a datasource** option on the choose how you'd like to start your model page.

III. From the list of available datasources to your right, select **SAP ERP**.

IV. From the **Connection Name** list, select **Create New Connection**.

V. Enter a name for the connection (for example, ERP) in the **Connection Name** box. You can also provide a description to further elaborate the new connection.

VI. For **Server Type**, select **Application Server** and enter values for **System**, **System Number**, **Client ID**, **System ID**, **Language**, **User Name**, and **Password**. Click the **Create** button after providing this information.

VII. Next, you need to create a query based on the **SAP ERP** system data. Enter a name for the query, for example, sales.

VIII. In the same dialog, expand the ERP object where the data exists. Locate and select the object, and then choose the data columns you want to include in your model. You are provided with a preview of the data before importing. On the preview window, click on **Done** to start the import process. The imported data will appear on the **Data Integration** page, which is the initial screen in the model creation segment and is discussed in subsequent chapters.

Connect Google Drive to import data

You went through two scenarios in which you saw how data can be fetched. In the first scenario, you created a live connection to create a model on live data, while in the second one, you learned how to import data from remote systems. In this section, you will be guided to create a model using a cloud app called Google Drive. Google Drive is a file storage and synchronization service developed by Google. It allows users to store files in the cloud, synchronize files across devices, and share files. Here are the steps to use the data stored on Google Drive:

I. From the main menu, go to **Create | Model**.

II. On the choose how you'd like to start your model page, select **Get data from an app**.

III. From the available apps to your right, select **Google Drive**.

IV. In the **Import Model From Google Drive** dialog, click on the **Select Data** button.

V. If you are not already logged into Google Drive, you will be prompted to log in.

VI. Another dialog appears displaying a list of compatible files. Choose a file, and click on the **Select** button.

VII. You are brought back to the **Import Model From Google Drive** dialog, where you have to enter a model name and an optional description.

VIII. After providing this information, click on the Import button. The import process will start, and after a while, you will see the **Data Integration** screen populated with the data from the selected Google Drive file.

Refreshing imported data

SAP Analytics Cloud allows you to refresh your imported data. With this option, you can reimport the data on demand to get the latest values. You can perform this refresh operation either manually or create an import schedule to refresh the data at a specific date and time or on a recurring basis. The following data sources support scheduling:

- SAP **Business Planning and Consolidation** (**BPC**)
- SAP **Business Warehouse** (**BW**)
- Concur
- OData services
- An SAP **Analytics BI platform universe** (**UNX**) query
- **SAP ERP Central Component** (**SAP ECC**)
- SuccessFactors HCM suite
- Excel and **comma-separated values** (**CSV**) files imported from a file server (not imported from your local machine)
- SQL databases

You can adopt the following method to access the schedule settings for a model:

I. Select **Connection** from the main menu. The **Connection** page appears. The **Schedule Status** tab on this page lists all updates and import jobs associated with any data source.

II. Alternatively, go to main menu | **Browse** | **Models**. The Models page appears. The updatable model on the list will have a number of data sources shown in the **Datasources** column. In the **Datasources** column, click on the **View More** link. The update and import jobs associated with this data source will appear. The **Update Model** and **Import Data** job are the two types of jobs that are run either immediately or on a schedule.

III. To run an **Import Data** job immediately, choose **Import Data** in the **Action** column. If you want to run an **Update Model** job, select a job to open it.

The following refreshing methods specify how you want existing data to be handled.

The **Import Data** jobs are listed here:

- **Update**: Selecting this option updates the existing data and adds new entries to the target model.
- **Clean and Replace**: Any existing data is wiped out and new entries are added to the target model.

- **Append**: Nothing is done with the existing data. Only new entries are added to the target model.

The **Update Model** jobs are listed here:

- **Clean and Replace**: This deletes the existing data and adds new entries to the target model.

- **Append**: This keeps the existing data as is and adds new entries to the target model.

The **Schedule Settings** option allows you to select one of the following schedule options:

- **None**: The import is performed immediately

- **Once**: The import is performed only once at a scheduled time

- **Repeating**: The import is executed according to a repeating pattern; you can select a start and end date and time as well as a recurrence pattern

IV. After setting your preferences, click on the Save icon to save your scheduling settings.

If you chose the **None** option for scheduling, select **Update Model** or **Import Data** to run the update or import job now.

Once a scheduled job completes, its result appears on the **Schedule Status** tab displaying any errors or warnings. If you see such daunting messages, select the job to see the details. Expand an entry in the **Refresh Manager** panel to get more information about the scary stuff. If the import process rejected any rows in the dataset, you are provided with an option to download the rejected rows as a CSV file for offline examination. Fix the data in the source system, or fix the error in the downloaded CSV file and upload data from it.

After creating your models, you access them via the main menu | Browse | Models path. The Models page, as illustrated in the following figure, is the main interface where you manage your models.

16. All existing models are listed under the **Models** tab. You can open a model by clicking on its name.
17. Public dimensions are saved separately from models and appear on the **Public Dimensions** tab. When you create a new model or modify an existing model, you can add these public dimensions.
18. If you are using multiple currencies in your data, the exchange rates are maintained in separate tables. These are saved independently of any model and are listed on the **Currency Conversion** tab.
19. Data for geographic locations, which are displayed and used in your data analysis, is maintained on the **Points of Interest** tab.

    The toolbar provided under the four tabs carries icons to perform common operations for managing models.

20. Click on the New Model icon to create a new model.
21. Select a model by placing a check mark (**A**) in front of it. Then click on the Copy Selected Model icon to make an exact copy of the selected model.
22. Use the delete icon to remove the selected models.
23. The **Clear Selected Model** option removes all the data from the selected model.

24. The list of data import options that are supported is available from a menu beneath the Import Data icon on the toolbar.

25. You can export a model to a `.csv` file once or on a recurring schedule using **Export Model As File**.

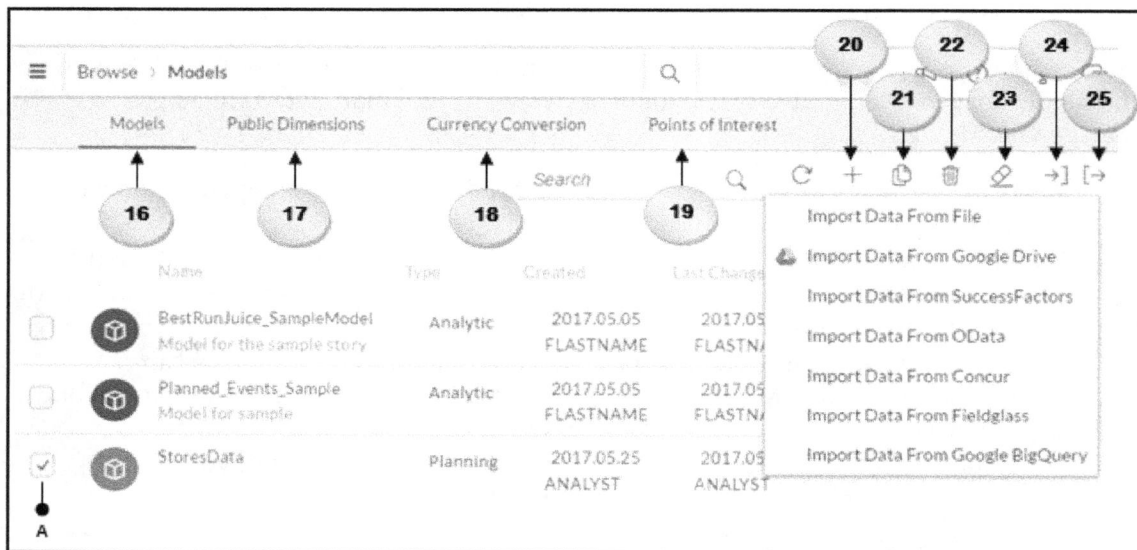

Visualization

Following are the important aspects of Visualization that are important for our discussion:

- **Stories**: After creating a model, you create stories to explore your model data. A story consists of one or more pages to present model data using objects such as charts, geomaps, tables, text, shapes, and images. To create a new story, you go to Create | Story from the main menu. You are asked to select one option from the provided four options that determine how you want to start your story. Usually, you start by adding a canvas page, where you put objects manually. For further details, see Chapter 4, *Creating Stories Using Charts*.

- **Charts**: SAP Analytics Cloud comes with a variety of charts, so choose the best chart type to present your analysis. You can add multiple types of charts to a single story page. You will learn how to add charts to your story pages in *Chapter 4* to *6*.

- **Geomap**: The models that include latitude and longitude information can be used in stories to visualize data in geomaps. By adding multiple layers of different types of data in geomaps, we can show different geographic features and points of interest enabling us to perform sophisticated geographic analysis. You will create geomaps in Chapter 6, *Analyzing Data Using Geo Maps and Other Objects*.

- **Table**: A table is a spreadsheet-like object that can be used to view and analyze text data. You can add this object to either canvas or grid pages in stories. Tables and grids are discussed in Chapter 7, *Working with Tables and Grids*.

- **Static and dynamic text**: You can add static and dynamic text to your story pages. Static text is normally used to display page titles, while dynamic text automatically updates page headings based on the values from the source input control or filter. You will add these two types of texts to your story page in Chapter 5, *Extending Stories with KPI, Filters and other Handy Objects*.

- **Images and shapes**: You can add images (such as your company logo) to your story page by uploading them from your computer. In addition to images, you can also add shapes, such as line, square, or circle, to your page. These topics are covered in Chapter 5, *Extending Stories with KPI, Filters and other Handy Objects*.

When you create a story, a new story with a default name appears on your screen, as illustrated in the following split screenshots:

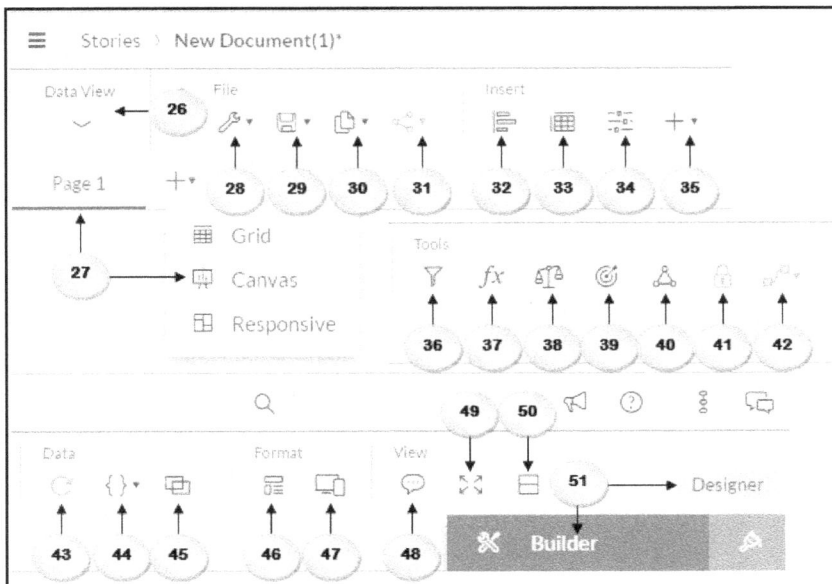

26. The **Data View** option lets you explore your model data. When you click on this option, the canvas hides, and two new panes appear on your screen, where you can see the measures and dimensions of your selected model. For further details, see in Chapter 2, *Models in SAP Analytics Cloud*, and Chapter 3, *Planning Model*.

27. You can create three types of pages in your stories: grid, canvas, and responsive. A grid is like an Excel sheet. You add a grid page and then add data by typing in numbers or pasting from another application or by adding a table based on an existing model. Grids and tables will be discussed in Chapter 7, *Working with Tables and Grids*. On canvas pages, you can lay out charts, tables, geomaps, images, and other objects to present your data. You will learn about the use of the canvas page in Chapter 4, *Creating Stories Using Charts*.

    The responsive page allows you to create flexible dashboards that can be presented on any screen size. This responsive page is a new enhancement to the application in which you can arrange your content in up to six lanes. The content is presented in order starting from the leftmost lane and ending at the rightmost lane. You can add or remove lanes using the options provided in the vertical toolbar, which is displayed to the right of every lane. Once you have added objects such as charts or geomaps to the responsive page lanes, click on **Device Preview** (**47**) to see how the page will look in different screen sizes. The page that appears lets you choose different screen sizes as follows: small 300 pixel wide displays, medium 768px, laptop 1366px by 768px, HDTV 1920px by 1080px, and 4K UHD 3840px by 2160px.

28. The **Edit Story** menu has two options: **Story Details** and **Preferences**. Clicking on the **Story Details** option presents a dialog where you can change the name of your story and provide a description, which is optional. The name you provide here appears on top of the screen beside the stories breadcrumb. Using the second option, you can change canvas and responsive page sizes and background colors. You can also set **Preferences** for your charts, geomaps, tables, and other elements in the **Story Preferences** dialog.

29. The Save icon also comes with a number of options. The **Save** option is generic and is used to save your story. Using the **Save As** option, you save a story with a different name. The **Save As** File option lets you save a story as a PDF file. The **Save As Template** option saves your story as a template, which can be used to create a new story.

30. The Copy and Paste icon carries utilities that you have already used in Windows applications. These utilities allow you to copy the selected object(s) to your clipboard, an existing story page, or to a new canvas. You can also duplicate the selected object(s) on the same canvas.

31. If you want to share your story with other users, click on the Share icon, and choose whether you want to share the story with all users or only selected users.

32. The **Chart toolbar** option adds a blank chart to the canvas. After adding a chart, use the **Designer** panel to format and manipulate the data in it.

33. This option is similar to the chart option and is used to add a blank table to the canvas. Again, using the **Designer** panel, you can set properties to show data in the new table.

34. Using the Input Controls, you define some values that act as variables in your calculations. By selecting values in an Input Control, a user can influence the result of a calculation without modifying the underlying data or formula. You will use input control in `Chapter 4`, *Creating Stories Using Charts*.

35. The Add icon lists additional objects, such as geomap, image, shape, text, RSS reader, web page, value driver tree, and symbols that you can add to your story page.

36. You can apply two types of filters: story filter and page filter. If you want to apply filters to all charts in a story, use the story filter. The page filter, as the name implies, can be applied to just one page in a story. See this topic in `Chapter 5`, *Extending Stories with KPI, Filters and other Handy Objects*.

37. Just link an Excel worksheet. You can also add formulas to a table element. The Formula Bar icon is used to see the formula you entered in a table cell. When you click on this icon, a **Formula Bar** appears under the page tab. You will use the Formula Bar in `Chapter 7`, *Working with Tables and Grids*.

38. If you use a measure in multiple charts in a story, the measure values are usually scaled differently on these charts, which makes it difficult to compare the values. Using the **Chart Scaling** option, you can scale these charts so that measures have the same scale across multiple charts.

39. The **Conditional Formatting** option is used when you want to highlight some key information, such as low sales. Thresholds are used to provide visual cues for your information. By defining thresholds on your objects, you can see at a glance what areas are performing well and what areas need improvements. **Conditional Formatting** will be used in `Chapter 4`, *Creating Stories Using Charts*.

40. You can add linked analysis to create interaction between charts within a story. When you establish a link and drill through hierarchical data or create filters, multiple charts in your story are updated simultaneously. This topic is discussed in `Chapter 5`, *Extending Stories with KPI, Filters and other Handy Objects*.

41. Using this icon, you can turn a table cell on or off. For example, if you enter a formula in a table cell and do not want other users to change it, click on the cell and then click on the lock icon. The value in the cell will freeze. To allow modification, click on the lock icon again to unfreeze the value.

42. The **Cell Reference** option creates a link between two cells to show the same value. For example, if you copy a value from a table cell and paste it to a cell in a grid that does not belong to a table, a cell reference is created. Any change you make to one cell is propagated to the other. Use the **Show/Hide** option to view cell references. To break the link between cells, select the reference cell in the grid, and then select Remove Reference.

43. Used to refresh table data.

44. When you use variables in a model and then use that model in a table, you are prompted to set values for the variables. The **Edit Prompts** option allows you to change a variable setting at any other time. When you click on this icon and select a model, you see the **Set Variables** dialog, where you can modify the values.

45. In your stories, you can display data from multiple models in a single chart by linking dimensions in those models. When you click on this icon, the **Link Dimensions** dialog box appears, where you specify the two models you want to link. This option is used in `Chapter 6`, *Analyzing Data Using Geo Maps and Other Objects*.

46. With the help of the **Layouts** option, you can apply formatting to your story by using a template, which provides predefined layouts and placeholders for objects to help you build a story.

47. After adding objects to a responsive page lanes, click on **Device Preview** to see how the page will look in different screen sizes.

48. You add comments to a story page to provide some vital information to other users. When you add a comment, other users can see and reply to it. The **Comment View** icon shows the number of comments to view. Hitting this icon shows the comment number at the top of the relevant page. Clicking on this number displays the comment. You will see **Comment View** in action in `Chapter 6`, *Analyzing Data Using Geo Maps and Other Objects*.

49. At any time while designing your story, you can click on the Present icon to see how your story will appear when it's presented or when users with view-only privileges view your story.

50. While working on charts in a story, you sometimes want to see the underlying data to evaluate the results being displayed on those charts. Selecting the chart and clicking on the Examine icon opens a table showing values that the chart is based on.

51. Use the **Designer** panel to format and manipulate the data in your canvas elements. The **Designer** panel consists of two tabs: **Builder** and **Styling**. On the **Builder** tab, you set the data source, measures, dimensions, colors, and more properties for the selected element. On the **Styling** tab, you specify properties such as background and font colors to change the physical appearance of the selected element.

You can access all of your saved stories via main menu | **Browse** | **Stories**. When you use this route, the **Stories** page, as illustrated in the following figure, comes up. The six tabs (**A**) under the **Stories** breadcrumb let you see all stories, public stories that are available to everyone, stories you created, other people's stories shared with you, sample stories, and your templates. Using the options provided on the toolbar (**B**), you can search for stories by name, refresh the stories list, create a new story, modify the name and description of an existing story, copy, delete, or share selected stories:

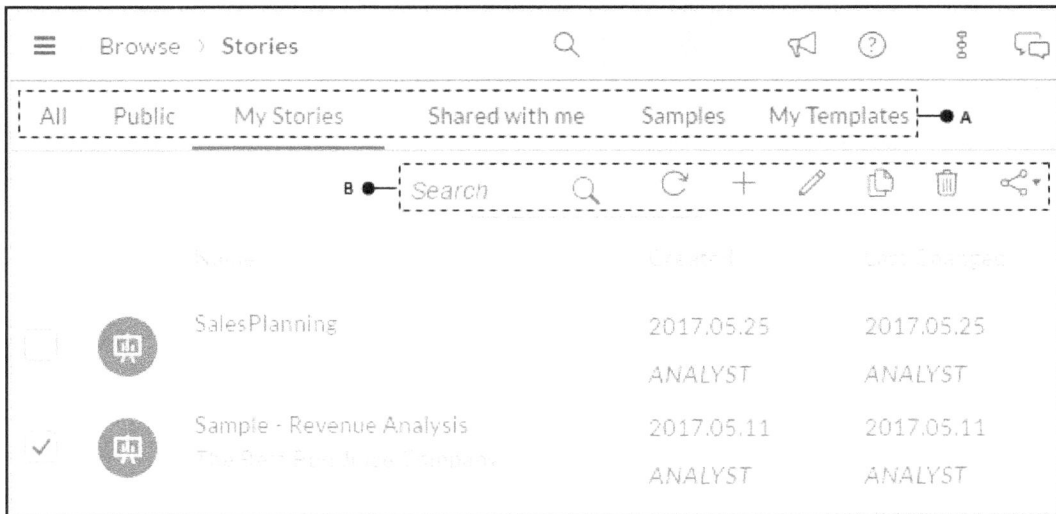

Collaboration

During the process of creating models and stories, you need input from other people. For example, you might ask a colleague to update a model by providing the first quarter sales data or request **Sheela** to enter her comments on one of your story pages. In SAP Analytics Cloud, these kinds of discussions come under the collaboration features of the application. Using these features, users can discuss business content and share information that consequently smoothed out the decision-making process. Here is a list of available collaboration features in the application that allow group members to discuss stories and other business content. All these features are discussed in detail in Chapter 8, *Collaboration*.

- **Creating a workflow using events and tasks:** The events and tasks features in SAP Analytics Cloud are the two major sources that help you collaborate with other group members and manage your planning and analytic activities. After creating an event and assigning tasks to relevant group members, you can monitor the task progress in the Events interface. Here is the workflow to utilize these two features:
  - Create events based on categories and processes within categories
  - Create a task, assign it to users, and set a due date for its submission
  - Monitor the task progress

- **Commenting on a chart's data point**: Using this feature, you can add annotations or additional information to individual data points in a chart. To see this feature in action, refer to the Pinning and Commenting on a Data Point section in Chapter 5, *Extending Stories with KPI, Filters and other Handy Objects*.

- **Commenting on a story page**: In addition to adding comments to an individual chart, you have the option of adding comments on an entire story page to provide some vital information to other users. When you add a comment, other users can see and reply to it. For further details, refer to the **Adding Comments** to a **Page** section in Chapter 6, *Analyzing Data Using Geo Maps and Other Objects*.

- **Produce a story as a PDF**: You can save your story in a PDF file to share it with other users and for offline access. You can save all story pages or a specific page as a PDF file. For more details, refer to the Save Story as a PDF section in Chapter 7, *Working with Tables and Grids*.

- **Sharing a story with colleagues**: Once you complete a story, you can share it with other members in your organization. You are provided with three options-- public, teams, and private--when you save a story. When you save your story in the public folder, it can be accessed by anyone. The **teams** option lets you select specific teams to share your story with. In the **private** option, you have to manually select users with whom you want to share your story. See in `Chapter 8`, *Collaboration* for further details on sharing stories.
- **Collaborate via discussions**: You can collaborate with colleagues using the discussions feature of SAP Analytics Cloud. The discussions feature enables you to connect with other members in real time. Refer to the Collaborate via Discussions section in `Chapter 8`, *Collaboration* for how to start discussions.
- **Sharing files and other objects**: The **Files** option under the **Browse** menu allows you to access the SAP Analytics Cloud repository, where the stories you created and the files you uploaded are stored. After accessing the **Files** page, you can share its objects with other users. On the **Files** page, you can manage files and folders, upload files, share files, and change share settings. This topic is also a part of `Chapter 8`, *Collaboration*.

Presentation

The ultimate purpose of creating a story is to present it to the concerned authorities--the higher management of an organization. SAP Analytics Cloud comes with a next-generation presentation tool called Digital Boardroom, which is changing the landscape of traditional board meetings.

SAP Digital Boardroom is a visualization and presentation platform that enormously assists in the decision-making process. It transforms executive meetings by replacing static and stale presentations with interactive discussions based on live data, which allows them to make fact-based decisions to drive their business. Here are the main benefits of the SAP Digital Boardroom:

- Collaborate with others in remote locations and on other devices in an interactive meeting room
- Answer ad hoc questions on the fly
- Visualize, recognize, experiment, and decide by jumping on and off script at any point

- Find answers to the questions that matter to you by exploring directly on live data and focusing on relevant aspects by drilling into details
- Discover opportunities or reveal hidden threats
- Simulate various decisions and project the results
- Weigh and share the pros and cons of your findings

The Digital Boardroom is interactive, so you can retrieve real-time data, make changes to the schedule, and even run through what-if scenarios. It presents a live picture of your organization across three interlinked touch screens to make faster, better executive decisions.

There are two aspects of Digital Boardroom with which you can share existing stories with executives and decision-makers to reveal business performance. First, you have to design your agenda for your boardroom presentation by adding meeting information, agenda items, and linking stories as pages in a navigation structure. Once you have created a digital boardroom agenda, you can schedule a meeting to discuss the agenda. In the Digital Boardroom interface, you can organize a meeting in which members can interact with live data during a boardroom presentation. In Chapter 9, *Digital Boardroom*, is dedicated to exposing this fascinating feature of SAP Analytics Cloud.

Administration and security

An application that is accessed by multiple users is useless without a proper system administration module. The existence of this module ensures that things are under control and secured. It also includes upkeep, configuration, and reliable operation of the application. This module is usually assigned to a person, who is called the system administrator and whose responsibility is to watch uptime, performance, resources, and security of the application. Being a multiuser application, SAP Analytics Cloud also comes with this vital module that allows a system administrator to take care of the following segments:

- Creating users and setting their passwords
- Importing users from another data source
- Exporting user's profiles for other apps
- Deleting unwanted user accounts from the system
- Creating roles and assigning them to users
- Setting permissions for roles
- Forming teams
- Setting security for models
- Monitoring users activities
- Monitoring data changes
- Monitoring system performance
- System deployment via export and import

Refer to `Chapter 10`, *System Administration*, where all these topics are covered in detail.

Signing up for the trial version

I know that most of you will purchase this book to evaluate SAP Analytics Cloud and will not have access to a live SAP environment. The good news for you is that you can explore the platform using most of the exercises provided in this book by signing up for a free thirty-day trial. Note that the trial version doesn't allow you to access all the features of SAP Analytics Cloud. For example, you cannot create a planning model in the trial version nor can you access its security and administration features. Execute the following steps to get access to the free SAP Analytics Cloud trial:

1. Put the following URL in your browser's address bar and press enter: `http://dis cover.sapanalytics.cloud/trialrequest-auto/`.
2. Enter and confirm your business email address in relevant boxes.
3. Select **No from the Is your company an SAP Partner?** list.

4. Click on the **Submit** button. After a short while, you will get an email with a link to connect to SAP Analytics Cloud.

5. Click the **Activate Account** button in the email. This will open the **Activate Your Account** page, where you will have to set a strong password. The password must be at least 8 characters long and should also include uppercase and lowercase letters, numbers, and symbols.

6. After entering and confirming your password, click on the **Save** button to complete the activation process. The confirmation page appears telling you that your account is successfully activated. Click on **Continue**.

7. You will be taken to the SAP Analytics Cloud site. The email you receive carries a link under SAP Analytics Cloud System section that you can use to access the application any time. Your username (your email address) is also mentioned in the same email along with a log on button to access the application.

Summary

The chapter provided a brief overview of the next generation cloud-based analytic application, which provides an end-to-end cloud analytics experience. SAP Analytics Cloud can help transform how you discover, plan, predict, collaborate, visualize, and extend all in one solution. In addition to on-premise data sources, you can fetch data from a variety of other cloud apps and even from Excel and text files to build your data models and then create stories based on these models. The ultimate purpose of this amazing and easy-to-use application is to enable you to make the right decision. SAP Analytics Cloud is more than visualization of data; it is an insight into action, it is the realization of success.

Fasten you seat belt and get ready to take a cloud tour. From the next chapter, you will be performing hands-on exercises to explore the exciting world of SAP Analytics Cloud, starting with models.

2
Models in SAP Analytics Cloud

In SAP Analytics Cloud, you create models that act as the basis for all data output. A model is a representation of the business data of an organization. It is a high-level design that exposes the analytic requirements of your end users. To determine what content to include in your model, you must first identify the columns from the source data on which users need to query. Then, to establish the role played by each column, identify whether it is a measure column or a dimensional attribute. We will be learning these attributes and many more steps that will assist us in creating and viewing models and other data filtration as well.

The following topics will be covered in the chapter:

- Introduction to models
- Understanding measures and dimensions
- Planning and analytical models
- Creating a new analytical model
- Viewing model details in the modeler interface
- Browsing models
- Viewing model data

Understanding measures and dimensions

You will see the terms "measures" and "dimensions" throughout this book. Every data column that you import from a source to build a model in SAP Analytics Cloud must be marked either as a measure or a dimension. Measures are the columns by which an organization gauges its business operations and performance, while dimension columns contain the data used to qualify the measures.

These terms can be further expanded as follows:

- **Measures**: Measures are those fields that can be measured, aggregated, or used for mathematical operations. Measures are typically calculated data, such as dollar value or quantity sold, and they can be specified in terms of dimensions. For example, you might want to determine the sum of dollars for a given product in a given market over a given time period.
- **Dimensions**: A business uses measures to evaluate performance by well-established dimensions, for example, by time, product, and market. Dimensions are usually those fields that cannot be aggregated. Dimensions contain values that describe business entities (such as time, product, customer name, region, country, city, address, and so on). Within a given dimension, there may be many attributes. For example, the time dimension can contain the attributes year, quarter, month, week, and day. These attributes are used to drill into and across dimensions to get more detailed views of the data.

In **relational database management systems** (**RDBMS**) terminology, tables at the one end of a join are treated as dimension tables, and tables at the *many* end of a join as measure tables. The following figure illustrates the many-to-one joins to a table carrying measure data. In this diagram, all joins have the crow's feet symbol (indicating the many side) pointing into the measure table:

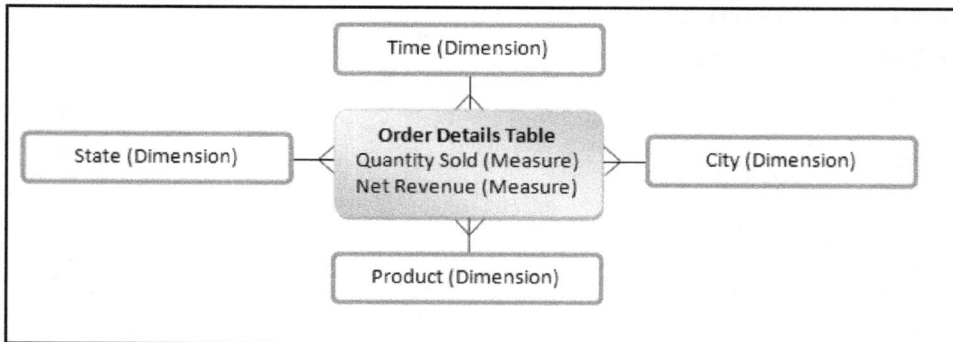

When you import data in SAP Analytics Cloud to create a model, it determines whether to consider a field as a dimension or a measure. By default, fields with all text values are determined as dimensions, and fields with numeric values are treated as measures.

Planning and analytical models

In SAP Analytics Cloud, you can create planning and analytical models. A planning model is a full-featured model, which comes with preconfigured time and categories dimensions for actual, budget, planning, forecast, and rolling forecast. A planning model also supports multicurrency and offers security at the level of both model and dimension to restrict access to specific values in the report to named individuals. It also comes with auditing features for traceability. The users who have planning privileges can create their own versions of model data, use allocation features, add new data to the model, and copy and paste data into the model.

In contrast, analytical models are simpler and more flexible general-purpose BI models. Analytical models are not preconfigured with categories for budget and forecast data.

In addition to these two models, you can connect to an SAP **high-performance analytic appliance** (**HANA**) database to import database views and create new models. You can create analytics models based on HANA views, which allow you to access dimensions from HANA. To create such models, the system administrator must first set up the HANA database. The analytic or calculation-type HANA views in the database can be imported to create new analytic-type models. A view can only be imported once; to re-import the view, delete the existing model from the Models list page, and then start the import process.

This chapter will teach you how to create a simple analytical model from an Excel file, while the planning model is the subject of `Chapter 3`, *Planning Model*.

Creating a new analytical model

Execute the following steps to create a new analytical model. The screenshot has numbered steps for sequence to be followed for creating an analytical model:

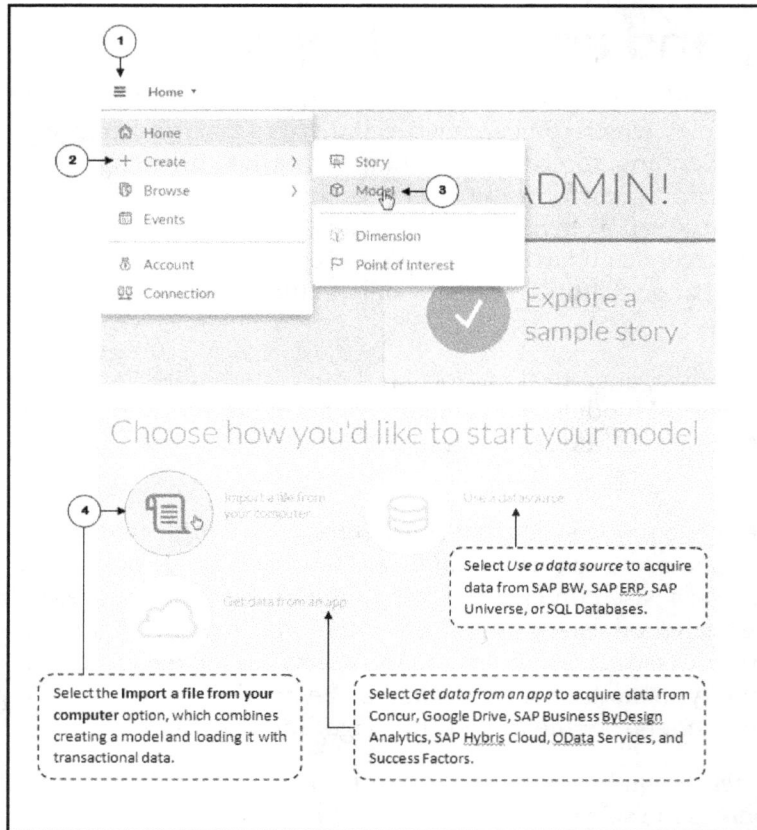

Selecting a source file

You can import data from an external file, such as an Excel spreadsheet or a comma-separated-values file, into a new model. If the data is saved in separate sheets in the Excel workbook, you will see a drop-down list from where you can choose which sheet to import:

Import Model From File

Source File

Select Source File

Bocage.xlsx

6 Then, select **Bocage.xlsx** file in the *Open* dialog box. The name of the selected file appears here. You can import data from an external file, such as an Excel spreadsheet or comma-separated-values (CSV) file, into a new model.

Import

Cancel

5 Click the **Select Source File** button.

7 Click the **Import** button to start the data import process.

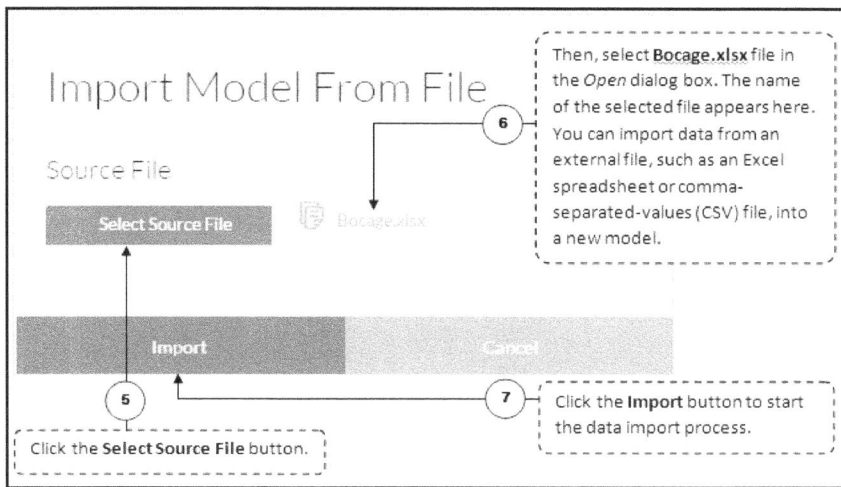

The source data must include columns that can be used to create dimensions in a new model, and it must also include transactional data (measures). The transactional data is not visible in modeler, only in the output that is generated.

You can connect to other systems to create a new model from an external source. To connect to such external sources, you have to select the use a datasource or get data from an app option. You can also create a model manually by setting up the dimensions individually and defining all the preferences and details of the model exactly as you require. You can create a model using the templates available in the planning wizard available within when you add a table to a story.

Note that some of these model creation options are not available in the trial version. So, in order to keep things simple, you are creating the model using an Excel file. The `Bocage.xlsx` file is a simple Excel file being provided with this book for demonstration purpose. It contains measures data (Quantity sold, Sales Revenue, Gross Margin, Discount, and Original Sales Price) to gauge the performance using date, state, city, store, manager, product, and category dimensions. In addition to measures and dimensions, the file has two columns (latitude and longitude) that will help you to visualize data in geo maps. This file can be downloaded from `https://github.com/PacktPublishing/Learning-SAP-Analytics-Cloud`.

Setting name, description, and other parameters for the model

After a while, you will see the **Data Integration** screen carrying the uploaded data in the **DataView** tab, as shown in the following screenshot:

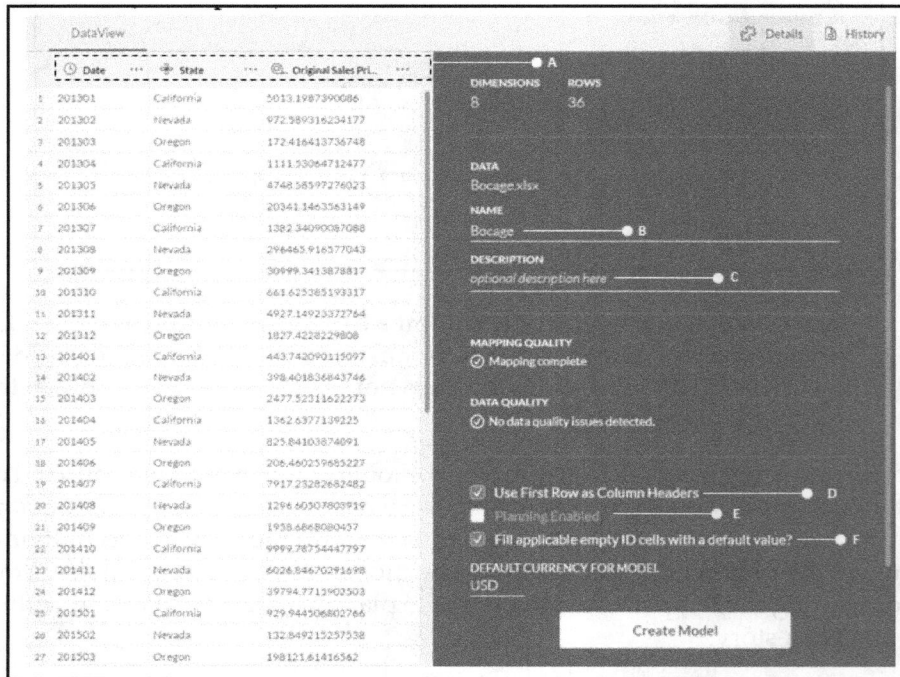

The initial column header names from the source data are shown together with symbols (**A**) to show the data type that has been recognized. The data columns in the source file are used to create dimensions and measures in the model. The import process analyzes the source data and creates an initial data view with proposed dimensions for the new model.

After this auto-mapping process, you can refine the proposal by specifying dimension types and fixing any data-quality problems, which you will do next. In the **Details** panel, review the model name (**B**), and change it if desired. You can also type the optional description (**C**). Specify whether you want to use the first row of the data as column headers (**D**), which you should in the current scenario. You can edit the column names by double-clicking on the column headers or by changing the column names in the **Details** panel. Specify whether you want the model to be **Planning Enabled** (**E**).

Specify whether you want empty ID cells (**F**) to be filled with automatically generated values. If you clear this check box, rows with empty ID cells will be omitted.

Setting dimension type

Once the data has been imported, you need to change some dimension types to ensure they deliver the result you intend to get from the model:

Click the **Date** column header. The column's detail will appear in the *Details* panel

If there are any messages in the Data Quality or Mapping Quality areas, you'll need to resolve those issues before creating the model.

Change the *Type* attribute of the *Date* column from *Dimension* to **Time.** Time specifies the smallest time period to be applied to the model. You can use year, quarter, month, or day. The Time dimension is a built-in dimension and it is created automatically with a model.

If not done automatically, change the *TIME FORMAT* to **YYYYMM** to match the source data.

Details Panel

The collapsible blue Details panel on the right of the screen is available to apply settings to each selected column. This panel has two views:

Model Info – shows general information about the import, including any mapping-quality or data-quality issues in the data.

Column – shows information for the currently selected column, and lists the attribute and dimension types that you can apply. If there are any data-quality issues in the selected column, specific information about them is shown here also.

Further refining of attributes can be achieved as described in the following screenshot:

After switching the *Type* attribute, the header icons of the two columns will also change.

Change the *Type* attribute of *Latitude and Longitude* columns from *Measure* to **Dimension**. You can add multiple dimensions of this type to a model. Note that the import process has already set the type of State, City, Store, Manager, Product, and Category columns to dimension.

Change the *Type* attribute of *Quantity sold* column from *Dimension* to **Measure**. In the initial data import, columns containing text are typically identified as Dimensions, and numeric data may be identified as Measures. Ensure that the *Type* attribute for Quantity Sold, Sales Revenue, Gross Margin, Discount, and Original Sales Price columns is marked as **Measure**.

Creating a location dimension

You can enrich the model by creating a location dimension using latitude and longitude columns in your dataset, which will enable users to visualize the data in geo maps. Here are the steps to create a location dimension:

Deleting unnecessary columns from the model

You should keep your model clean from unwanted data. In this step, you will remove a couple of redundant columns from the model:

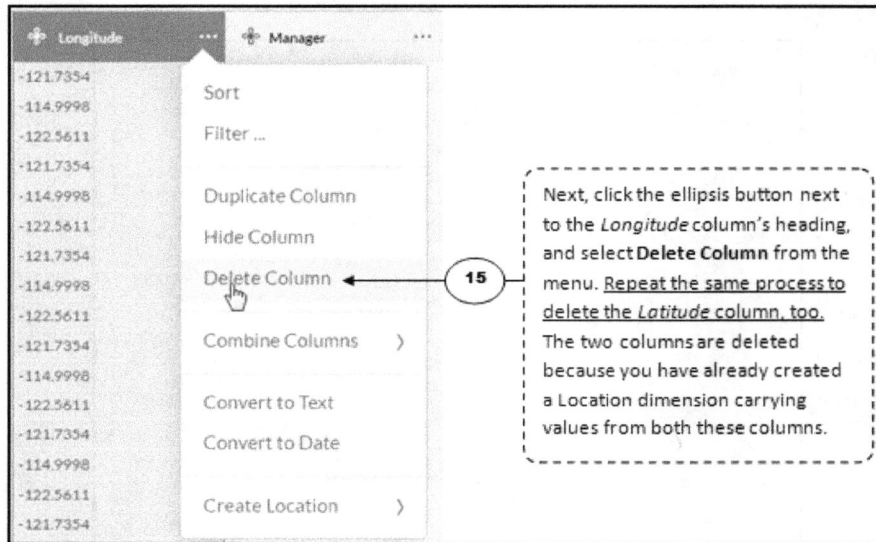

Creating a hierarchical relationship between two columns

Hierarchies are useful when there is a hierarchical relationship between two columns, such as category and product. Setting the columns up as a hierarchy allows us to drill up and down between the category and product values in charts. If hierarchical dimensions are included in a chart, you can drill up or down through dimensions to explore the data at different levels.

You use a dimension attribute called **Parent-Child Hierarchy (Parent)** to define a hierarchy for any generic dimension. For example, if your imported data contains two columns, **Country** and **City**, you can set the **Country** column to be the parent of the Country-City hierarchy.

In the current scenario, you will create a hierarchical relationship between the **Category** and **Product** columns available in the imported data:

The following step ensures that the **Category** column is marked as **parent** of the **Product** column:

Click the **Category** column and see that this column is marked as parent of the *Product* column.

20

Category ...	

Carbonated
Juices
Others
Carbonated
Juices
Others
Carbonated
Juices
Others
Carbonated
Juices
Others

MODEL INFO   COLUMN

▼ Modeling

COLUMN
Category

TYPE
Parent-Child Hierarchy (Parent)
✦ *Make this a Dimension*

PARENT OF DIMENSION
Product

⬅

After creating the model you will see this hierarchical relationship in the Modeler interface.

NAME
Bocage

DESCRIPTION
optional description here

MAPPING QUALITY
⊘ Mapping complete

DATA QUALITY
⊘ No data quality issues detected.

☑ Use First Row as Column Headers
☐ Planning Enabled
☑ Fill applicable empty ID cells with a default value?

DEFAULT CURRENCY FOR MODEL
USD

Create Model

21

Finally, click the **Create Model** button in the *Details* panel followed by another **Create** button that appears in a separate dialog box to complete the model creation process.

Viewing the model in the modeler interface

Once your model is created, you are taken to the modeler area with your new model appearing in the interface. It has a tab carrying two built-in dimensions (time and account) and five private dimensions (state, city, store, manager, and product), which are created using the source data file.

The time dimension

Click on the **Time** dimension tab (**A**). The **Time** dimension is built into analytical models that define the start and end dates of the plan's timeline and the smallest time units that will be used in the plan. The time dimension specifies the overall time frame for the model and also the granularity--the smallest time period down to which the data will be analyzed--for example, year, quarter, month, or day.

> Note that in the current scenario, the lowest granularity and the two date range filters are applied automatically based on the time granularity defined in the underlying model (see the **Date** column format in the Bocage.xlsx file).

These filters will ensure that only the details in the selected time period are visible, as is evident from the following screenshot:

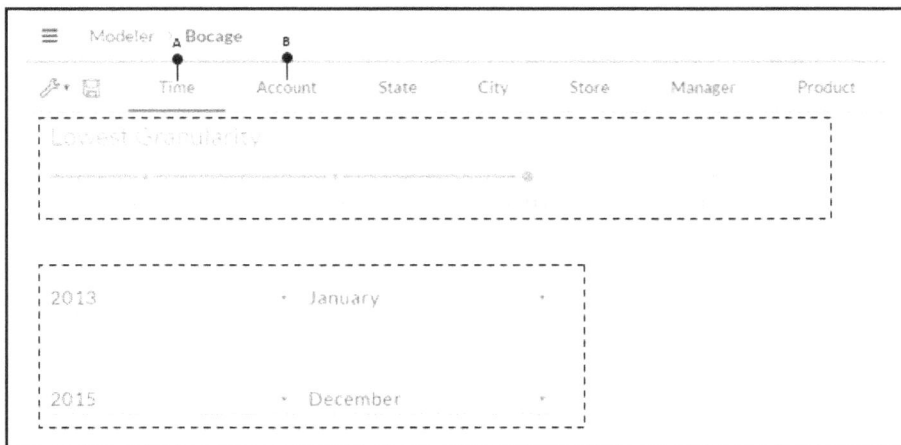

Account dimension

The **Account** dimension (**B**) is the main dimension of the model. The **Account** dimension defines the set of account members and the format of the account data. Each column that you mapped as a measure (**Quantity Sold**, **Sales Revenue**, **Gross Margin**, **Discount**, and **Original Sales Price** in the current scenario) will appear as members in the **Account** dimension. Models can have only one **Account** dimension. Unlike private dimensions, which have their values in different columns, data of the **Account** dimension members is not visible in the modeler. As you can see in the following illustration, the data you imported for some key-figure-based columns (**Sales Revenue**, **Gross Margin**, **Discount**, **Original Sales Price**, and **Quantity Sold**) is not visible:

In addition to the basic columns of **ID**, **Description**, and **Account** Type, a set of technical properties is automatically created when the dimension is first set up. You can hide these columns using the **Technical Properties** button on the toolbar, but they cannot be deleted. List boxes are available for most of the attributes of the account dimension to help you enter data. For example, you can set the **Currency** value for the four monetary columns to display a currency symbol after the numerical values. By default, **Aggregation Type** for all these account members is set to **SUM**, so you do not need to explicitly select this aggregation method here.

Private dimensions

Private dimensions exist only in the current model and don't appear in the public dimensions list. When you create dimensions while importing data from a file or from SAP Business Warehouse, SAP ERP, SAP Universe, or other databases, they are created as private dimensions. When you delete a model, private dimensions in that model are also deleted, but the public dimensions are not. All dimensions have, at minimum, both description and ID attributes. Typically, for each dimension, the imported data column is used as the dimension's description attribute. An ID column is then automatically generated for each dimension to contain the unique IDs of the rows:

Recall that in *creating a Location dimension* section at step 13, we set the **Store** column as its location identifier and specified the **Latitude** and **Longitude** columns. The model creation process accumulated all that information here under the **Store** tab, which will enable you to visualize the data in geomaps:

You created a hierarchical relationship between the **Category** and **Product** columns in steps 16 to 20. You can see that relationship under the **Product** tab. For example, the **Coconut Water** product has been linked to the **Others** category. The same hierarchical relationship is presented in the blue **Preview** panel on the right side:

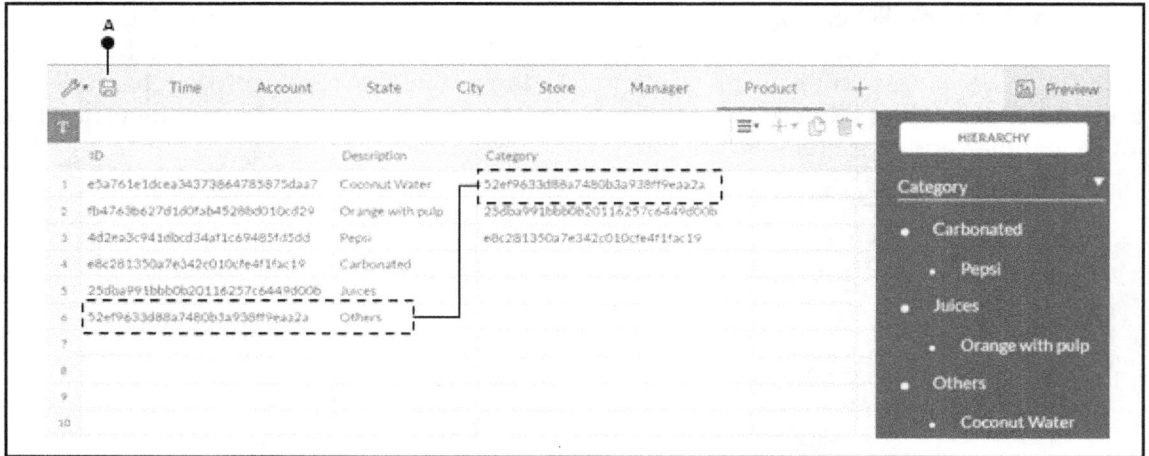

> When you make any changes to your model in the modeler (for example, changing filters in the **Time** dimension), click on the Save icon (A) to preserve your changes.

Browsing models

To see a list of existing models, click **Models** on the main menu icon and go to **Browse** | **Models**. You will be taken to the **Models** interface (illustrated here) with all your models listed:

The Models tab lists all your existing models. You can open a model by clicking the link text under the Name column.

Using these toolbar options you can create a new model, copy existing models, delete a model, clear all data from a model, and import data from different source.

Using this tab you can create your own public dimensions. Public dimensions are listed under this tab and can be shared between models, while private dimensions exist only in the current model. When you create a blank model, or create new dimensions in an existing model, you can choose whether the dimensions are private or public.

If your data consists of multiple currencies, exchange rates are maintained in separate tables under this tab independently of any model.

Points of interest are sets of geographical data that can be added to a geo map and analyzed with reference to business data from a model. Points of interest can show locations (such as store locations or event sites), lines (such as rivers, highways, or pipelines), and shapes (such as sales regions or electoral districts).

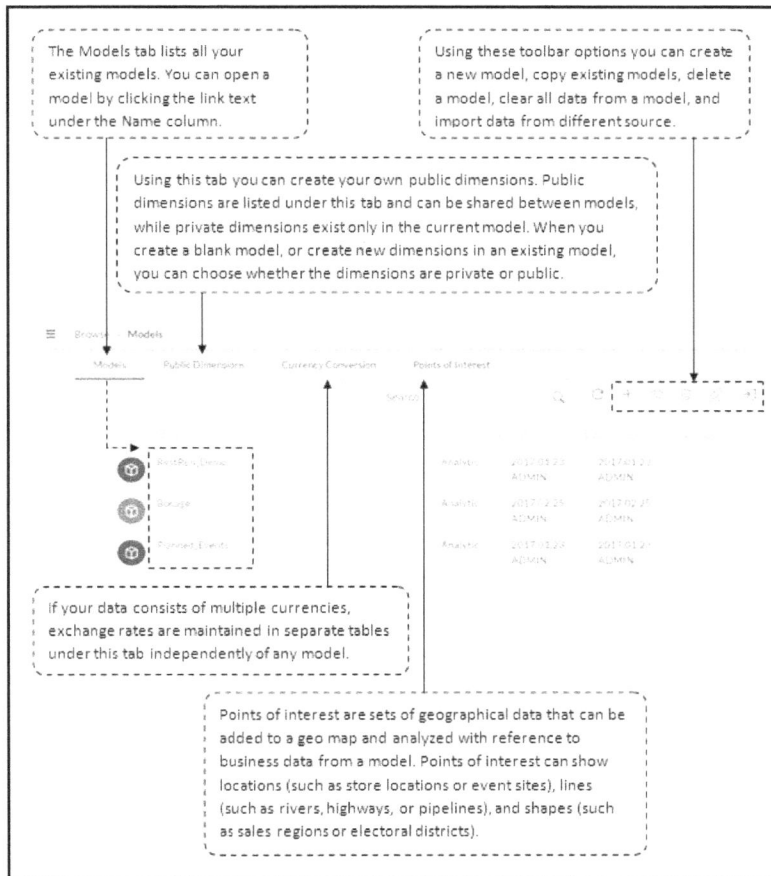

Copying a model

The copy option in the model's toolbar section is a very handy option to create a new model based on an existing model. It is illustrated in the following screenshot.

When you use this option to copy a model, the data and private dimensions are also copied to the new model. Public dimensions are referenced from the copied model. Note that you can use this option only for the models created in SAP Analytics Cloud version 2016.21 or later. Further, note that if a model uses a pool dimension (which is used for allocation), you cannot use the copy utility. Execute the following steps to make a copy of an existing model:

1. Go to main menu | **Browse** | **Models**.
2. Put a check mark in front of the model you want to copy. If the selected model is allowed to be copied, the Copy icon will be enabled.
3. Click on the Copy icon.
4. Enter a name for the new model and provide a description, which is optional.
5. Click on **OK** to make the copy.

Deleting a model

The delete icon on the toolbar lets you delete a model and all its data:

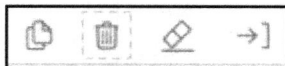

However, this option is available to user roles that have the privileges to delete models.

> Note that you cannot delete models that are currently in use. Stories are dependent on models, so if you try to delete a model used in a story, the name of the story is displayed and the delete operation is aborted.

Use the following set of steps to delete a model:

1. Go to main menu | **Browse** | **Models**.
2. Use the check box beside the model you want to delete. Note that you can select multiple models and delete them at once.
3. Click on the Delete icon on the toolbar.

Clearing model data

The **Clear Selected Model** option (represented with an eraser icon) on the toolbar is used to clear a selected model of all data:

Just like the **Delete** option, this one also requires the delete privileges on models. Here are the steps for this process:

1. Go to main menu | **Browse** | **Models**.
2. Select a model by checking its box.
3. Click the Clear Selected Model icon on the toolbar. You will see a hierarchy of members of each dimension in the model. Note that you can clear a model as a whole, individual dimensions, or selected dimension members. Select individual account members, or select all members of a branch at the top level.
4. Click on the **OK** button after making your selection to move on. A confirmation dialog box appears. Accept the confirmation to finish the process.

Viewing model data

As mentioned earlier, the data of the **Account** dimension members is not visible in the modeler. You can view this data in Stories, which is the subject of Chapter 4, *Creating Stories using Charts*. For the time being, you will create a temporary Story to see how the model data is reflected.

To view the model data, execute the following steps:

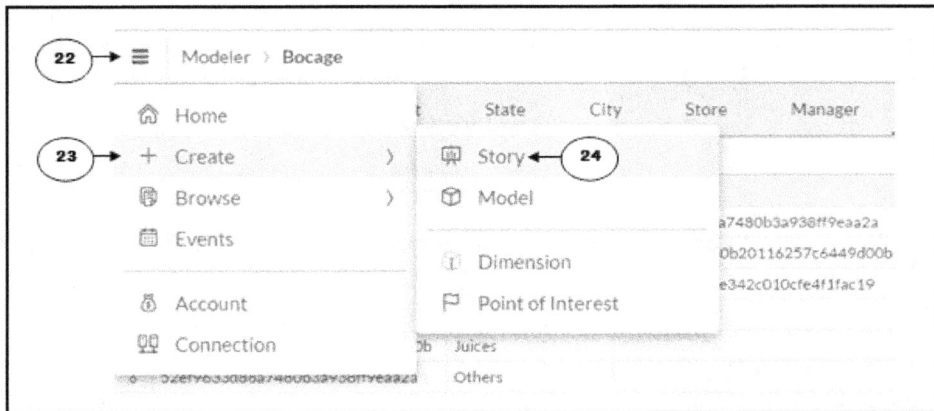

Upon clicking on the **Story** option, a wizard will initiate, and you will get the following screen:

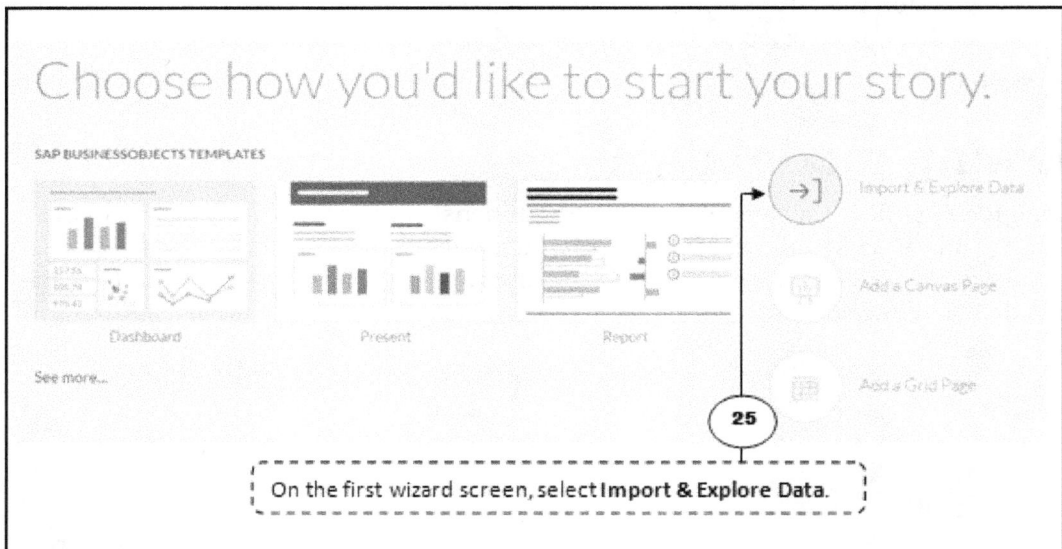

When you click on **Import & Export Data**, you get a **Choose how you'd like to add data** screen:

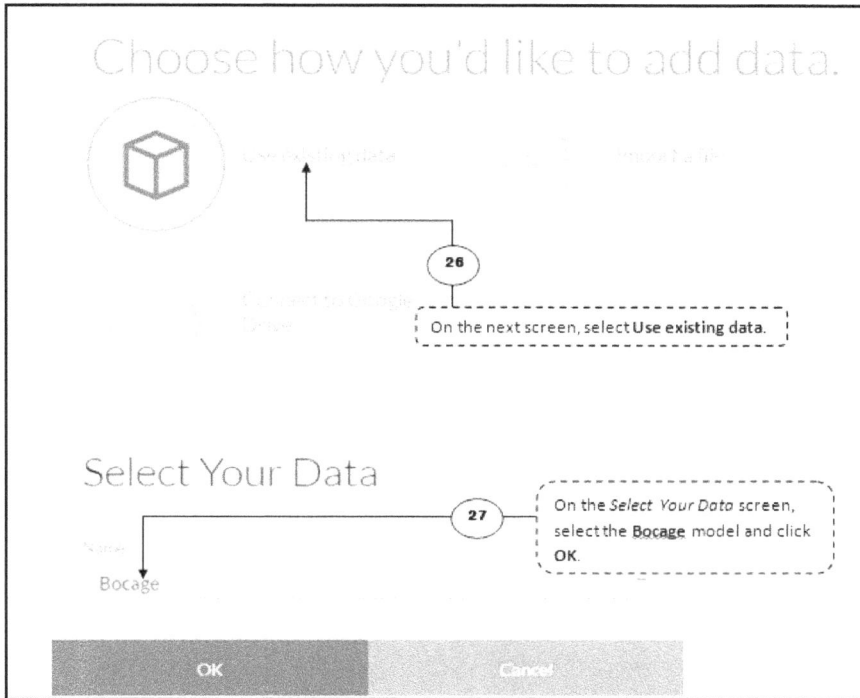

Proceed further with the steps displayed in the following screenshot to add dimensions:

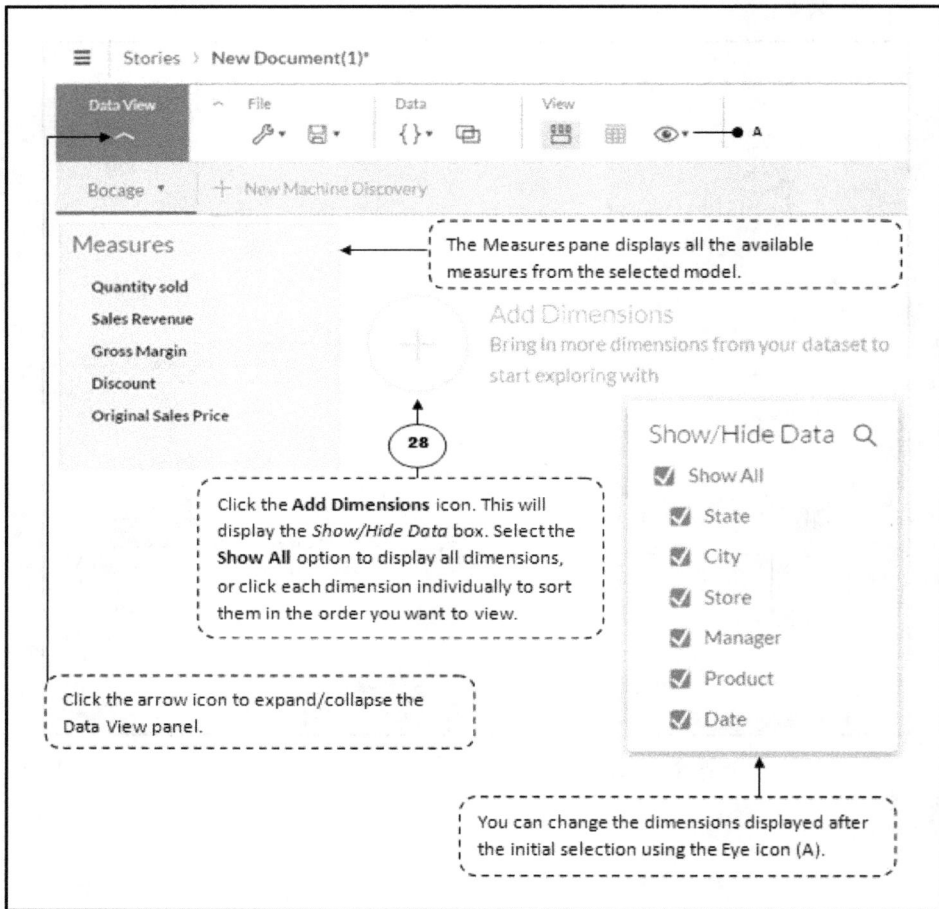

Viewing numerical data

We have the option of viewing numerical data. We can do this with the sequence described in the following screenshot:

Click the **Quantity sold** measure. The total value of this measure appears in the lower panel as a Numeric Point chart that you can reconcile with the source data in the Bocage.xlsx file.

Expand the **Date** node and select **Q1** under **2013**. Then, select **California** from the *State* pane. A Quantity Sold value of 1250 will appear in the lower pane. Open the source Excel file and match this figure in the second row under the *Quantity sold* column. Clicking the link "2 Filters applied" (A) will display the two applied filters.

Viewing data graphically

Graphical representation can provide a very clear picture of the data.
We can go about doing this with the sequence enumerated in the following screenshot:

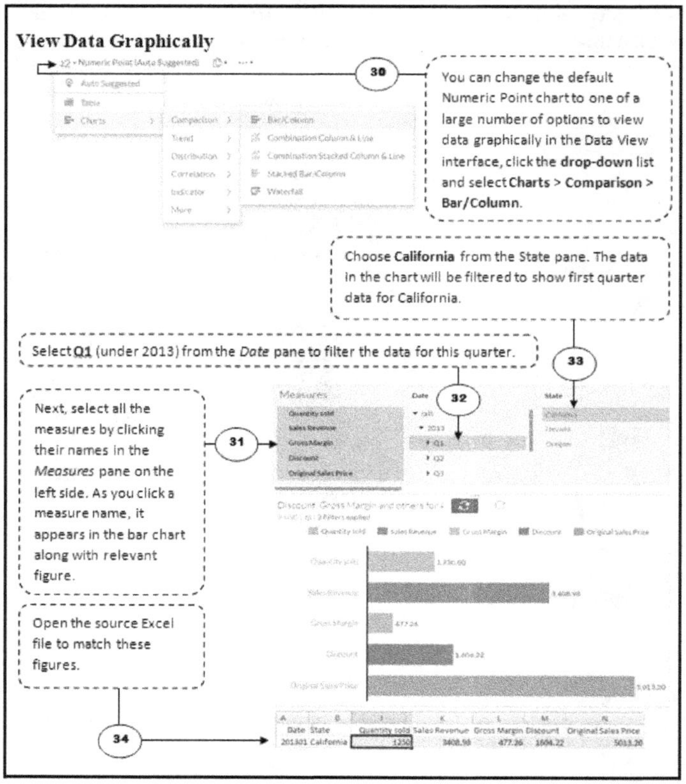

Now, click on the **California** state again to deselect it, and click on **Nevada** to select it. As you click this state's name, the graph is updated automatically to reflect **Nevada** state's figures that you can match with the source data. Repeat this step to see **Oregon** state's figures too.

Observe some more data filtration

Keep all the measures selected in the **Measures** pane (as depicted in the previous figure), and select **Q1** under **2013** in the **Date** pane. When you do not select any state, the result will resemble the output shown in the first column in the following screenshot. The result shows all cities, stores, managers, and products from all states. In the second column, you put a filter on the **California** state. When you choose this state, the remaining panes are filtered to display city, store, manager, and product related to **California** only. Similarly, the third and fourth columns display appropriate data for **Nevada** and **Oregon** states, respectively. This demonstrates the auto-filtration process of SAP Analytics Cloud, which is executed based on the source data.

State	State	State	State
California	California	California	California
Nevada	Nevada	Nevada	Nevada
Oregon	Oregon	Oregon	Oregon

City	City	City	City
Eugene	Los Angeles	Las Vegas	Eugene
Las Vegas			
Los Angeles			

Store	Store	Store	Store
Frills	Frills	Hudsons	InterMart
Hudsons			
InterMart			

Manager	Manager	Manager	Manager
David Curl	David Curl	Louis Wood	James Frank
James Frank			
Louis Wood			

Product	Product	Product	Product
▼ Carbonated	▼ Carbonated	▼ Juices	▼ Others
Pepsi	Pepsi	Orange with pulp	Coconut Water
▼ Juices			
Orange with pulp			
▼ Others			
Coconut Water			

Summary

This chapter provided hands-on exposure to creating an analytical model in SAP Analytics Cloud, which serves as the basis for all your analytical needs.

Here is the workflow to create a new analytical model from a file:

1. Import a source file.
2. Set name, description, and other parameters for the model.
3. In the initial data view, choose the dimension types for the dimensions in your new model.
4. Specify attributes for the dimensions.
5. Cleanse your data and fix any mapping or data quality problems.
6. If needed, create a location dimension to visualize the data in geo maps.
7. Delete the columns that you do not plan to use in your stories.
8. Create hierarchical relationships between columns.
9. Start the automatic creation of the model.

In the next chapter, you will go through the second type of model, that is, planning, which has categories for budgets, plans, and forecasts. It also comes with default time periods, which you can adjust to suit your data. It allows traceability via auditing features and provides strong security features to control user access privileges.

3
Planning model

This chapter is a continuation of the previous one in which you were briefed about the concept of models in SAP Analytics Cloud and got hands-on exposure to the analytics model. Here, you will get information about the second type of model, which is called the planning model. A planning model is a model in which you work with planning features. To remind you, a planning model is a full-featured model, which comes with preconfigured time and categories dimensions for actual, budget, planning, forecast, and rolling forecast.

A planning model also supports multi-currency and offers security at both model and dimension levels to restrict access to specific values in the report to named individuals. It also comes with auditing features for traceability. The users who have planning privileges can create their own versions of model data, use allocation features, add new data to the model, and copy and paste data into the model.

In this chapter, you will learn about the following:

- Creating a planning model
- Visualizing the data of a planning model
- Viewing the model's text data in a table
- Spreading, distributing, and assigning values
- Creating private versions of a planning model

Creating a planning model

Execute the following steps to create a planning model:

1. Click on the main menu icon, and go to **Create | Model**:

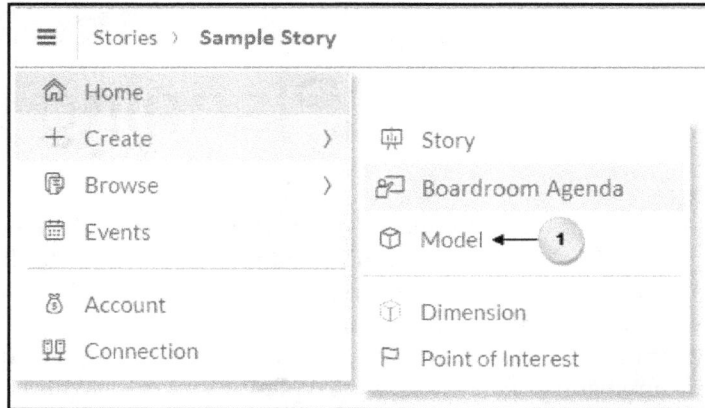

You can create a planning model from scratch in which you enter values manually in the cells or copy and paste data from a spreadsheet. You can also create this model type by importing data from a variety of sources. To keep things simple, you will fetch data from an Excel file named `StoresData.xlsx` in this exercise.

2. On the **New Model** page, click on **Import a file from your computer**:

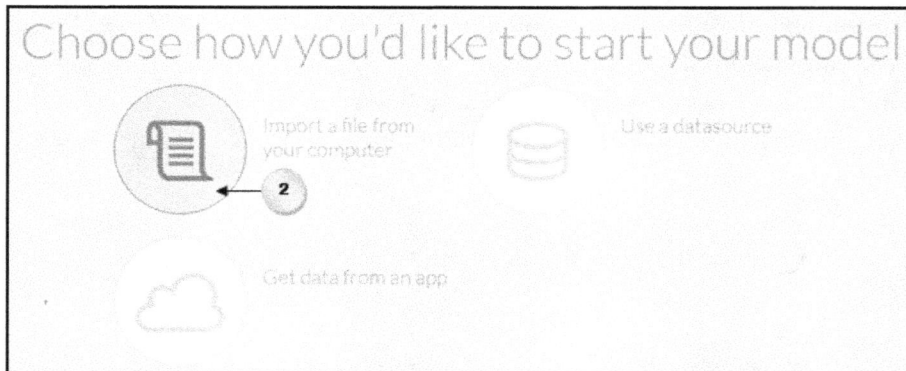

3. On the **Import Model From File** dialog, click on the **Select Source File** button (**A**), and in the **Windows Open** dialog, browse for the `StoresData.xlsx` file (**B**) that comes with the book's source. Note that this file has three sheets carrying data for the **Actuals**, **Budget**, and **Forecast** categories. Start the proceeding and import data by selecting the **Actuals** option (**C**) from the **Sheet** list. Data for the other two categories will be imported in the subsequent steps. Click on **Import** to start the process:

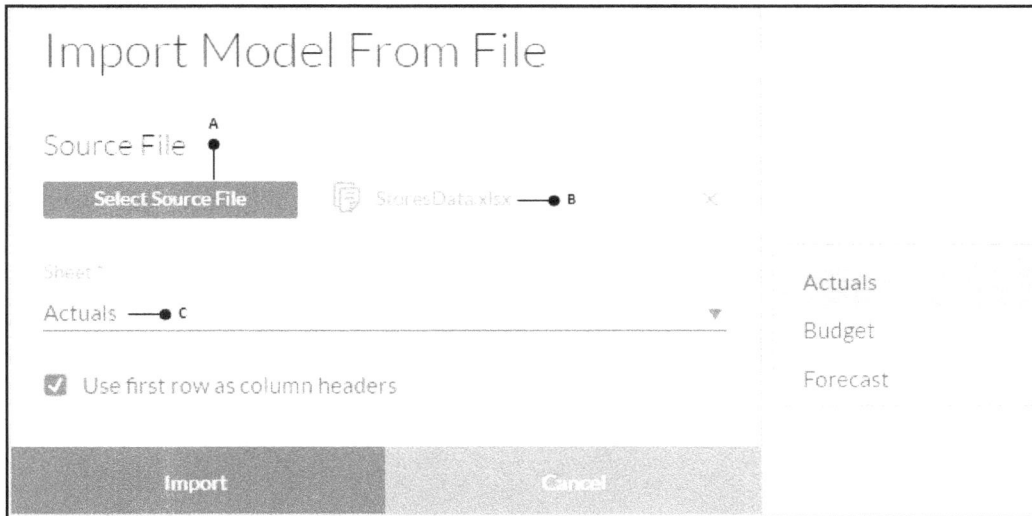

After a while, you will see the **Data Integration** screen, as illustrated in the following screenshot. The screen should be familiar to you as you worked with it in the previous chapter. Here, the only thing that needs your attention is the Planning Enabled option, which must be turned on for this model.

4. Type **StoresData** for the model name (**A**), and select the **Planning Enabled** option (**B**). Click on the **Create Model** button (**C**), and confirm the model creation in the subsequent dialog:

▼	🕐 Date	⟡ Store	🔍 Quantity so...
1	201701	Frills	1250
2	201701	Hudsons	350
3	201701	InterMart	50
4	201701	Farlos	600
5	201701	Kullens	1150
6	201702	Frills	8100
7	201702	Hudsons	600
8	201702	InterMart	32250
9	201702	Farlos	1300
10	201702	Kullens	250
11	201703	Frills	1200
12	201703	Hudsons	500
13	201703	InterMart	150
14	201703	Farlos	1400
15	201703	Kullens	600

StoresData

Rows	Columns	Dimensions	Measures
15	3	2	1

DATA
StoresData.xlsx

NAME
StoresData ———● A

DESCRIPTION
optional description here

MAPPING QUALITY
⊘ Mapping complete

DATA QUALITY
⊘ No data quality issues detected.

☑ Use First Row as Column Headers
☑ Planning Enabled ———● B
☑ Fill applicable empty ID cells with a default value?

DEFAULT CURRENCY FOR MODEL
USD

Create Model ———● C

The model will be created and its definitions will appear in the **Modeler** interface, as illustrated in the following screenshot. The **Store** dimension carries information about the five stores that you imported from the Excel file. For every planning model, a **Version** dimension is created automatically, which reveals what type of data the model holds.

Since you opted to import data for the **Actuals** category in step 3, the **Version** tab displays that the model currently holds data for the **Actual** category. Additional version categories (budget and forecast) will be added to this grid when you upload data into the model in subsequent steps:

The **Time & Categories** tab displays the **Lowest Granularity** section, which you went through in the previous chapter while creating the analytics model there. It now has a **Categories** section, which carries some categories that define what types of data you will be managing in your model. Note that analytics models contain only a single category to show the actual results. The drop-down lists beside the categories in a planning model let you define the planning horizon for each category separately. For example, you can set **Budget** to year, **Planning** to quarter, and **Forecast** to month. You can set a horizon by entering values in the **Look Back** and **Look Ahead** boxes. Do not forget to save your model whenever you make any type of change to it, whether it is the addition of a new dimension or the switching of categories.

Lowest Granularity			
Year	Quarter	Month	Day
2017 ▾	January ▾		
2017 ▾	December ▾		

Categories			
Name	Frequency		
Actual	Month		
Budget	Month ▾		
Planning	Month ▾		
Forecast	Month ▾	Range	Year ▾
Rolling Forecast	Month ▾	Look Back 3 Month	Look Ahead 3 Month

5. Click on the **Modeler** breadcrumb link to move back and access the main **Models** page, as illustrated in the next screenshot.

> In the first four wizard-led steps, we created a planning model and added data for the actual category from an Excel file. In the following steps, we will append the data for the remaining two categories.

6. On the **Models** page, select the **StoresData** model (**A**). Then click on the Import Data icon (**B**) on the toolbar. In addition to importing data from a file, you have several other options to populate your model with data. All these available options are displayed when you click on the Import Data icon. For this example, click on the **Import Data From File** option (**C**):

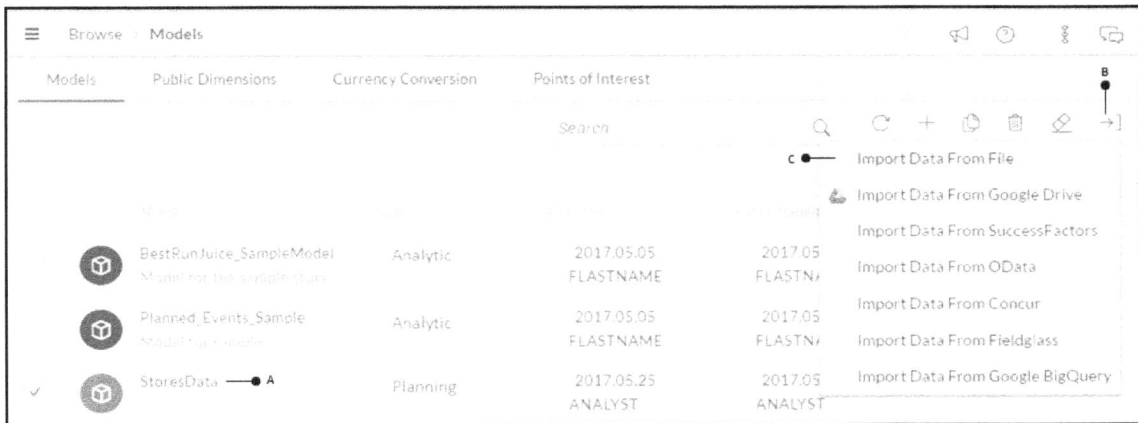

7. Once again, click on the **Select Source File** button (**A**) in the **Import Data From File** dialog. This time, select the **Budget** option (**B**) from the **Sheet** list to import data for the **Budget** category from the second sheet of the same Excel file:

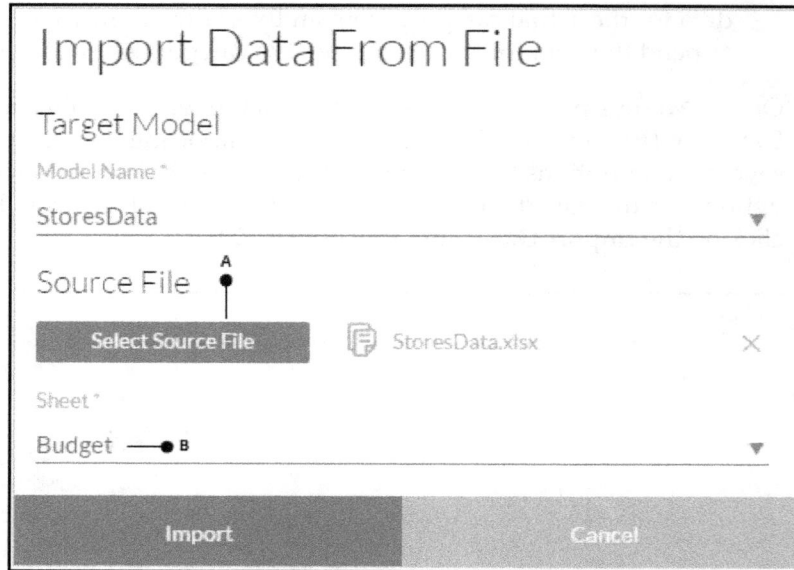

When you click on the **Import** button in the **Import Data From File** dialog, the **Budget** category data from the **Budget** sheet in the StoresData.xlsx file will be imported, and once again, you will see the **Data Integration** page, as illustrated in the following screenshot.

8. Click on the **Date** column header (**A**) to see its details on the **Column Info** tab (**B**). Right now, the column is not correctly mapped. In order to align the data in the file with the dimensions defined in the model, you need to map the column correctly, and this can be done by selecting **Date** (**C**) from the **Map To** list:

9. Click on the **Model Info** tab (**D**). Here, you have to specify the category to which you want to import the data. To incorporate the budget data, set **Category** to **Budget**, and enter **Budget** for the **Version Name**.

10. In the **Import Method** section, you have to select one of the three options. The **Update** option (**A**) updates the existing data and adds new entries to the target model. **Clean and Replace** (**B**) deletes the existing data and adds new entries to the target model. **Append** (**C**) keeps the existing data as is and adds new entries to the target model. For this exercise, choose the **Append** option to append the budget category data to the **Actuals** category data you already have in the model. Click on **Finish Mapping** to complete the mapping process and import the data:

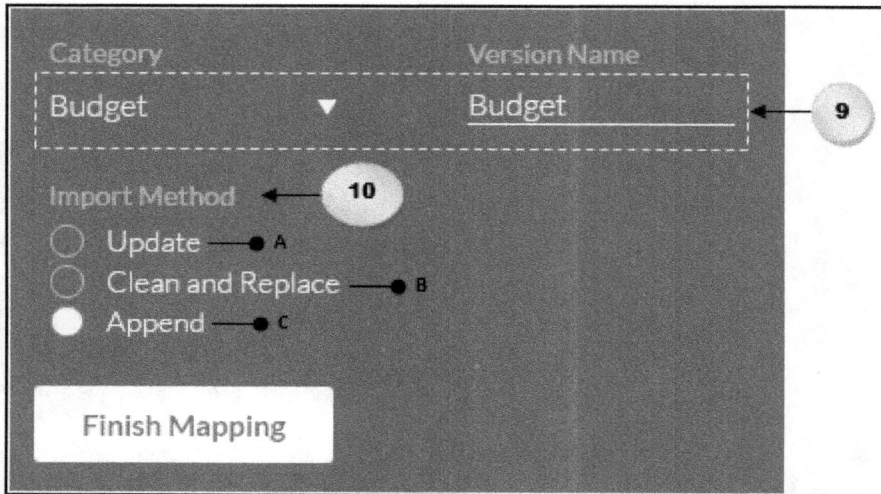

11. Import the forecast data from the same Excel file using the instructions provided in the previous steps and shown in the following screenshot. In the **Import Data From File** dialog, select the **Forecast** sheet (**A**) from the Excel file. On the **Model Info** tab, select **Forecast** (**B**) for **Category**, and type **Forecast** (**C**) for the **Version Name**. Finally, select the **Append** option (**D**) to avoid overwriting. Click on **Finish Mapping** to complete the process.

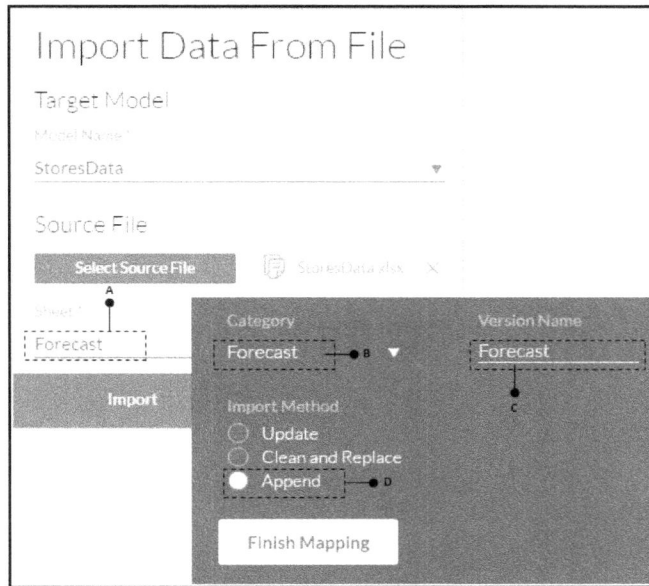

If you look at the **Version** tab after importing data for the three categories, you see that this tab is now showing all three versions (**A**), as illustrated in the following screenshot:

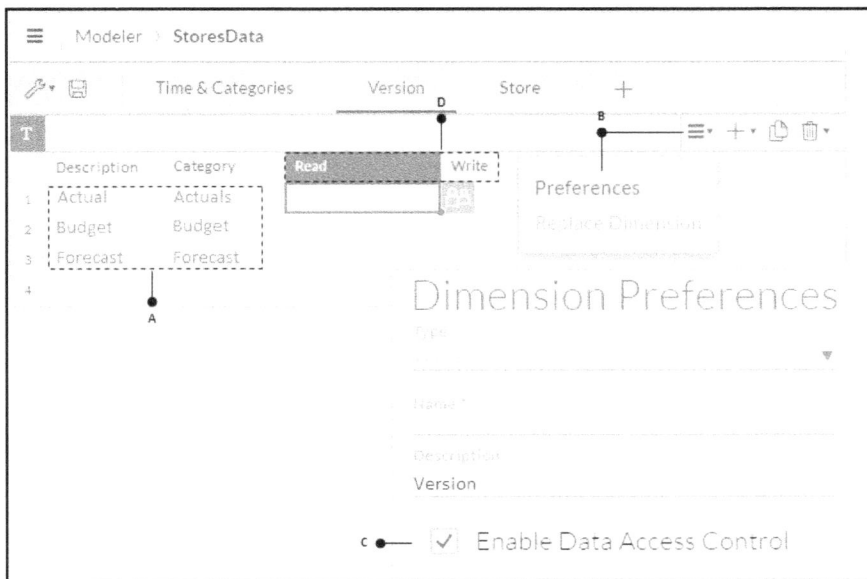

These are the public versions for each category that are currently being used in the model. You can also set restrictions on these versions. To add user restrictions, open the dimension preferences (**B**) and enable the **Data Access Control** option (**C**). Once we enable this option, the **Read and Write** columns (**D**) are added to the dimension, enabling you to specify the users you want to give read and write access to in each of the available versions. For further details on access privileges, refer to the *Setting security for models* section in Chapter 10, *System Administration*.

Visualizing planning model data

The model is ready for analysis. As with the analytics model, we once again need to create a temporary story to view the data of this model. Execute the following set of steps for this purpose:

12. From the main menu, go to **Create | Story**.
13. On the first wizard page that asks how you want to start the story, select the **Add a Canvas page** option. The story page will appear with a default name for the new story.
14. Click on the arrow in the **Data View** section on the toolbar. You will be prompted to add data.
15. On this screen, select **Use existing data**.
16. In the **Select Your Data** dialog, select StoresData. This is the planning model data you uploaded in the previous section. Click on **OK** to dismiss the dialog:

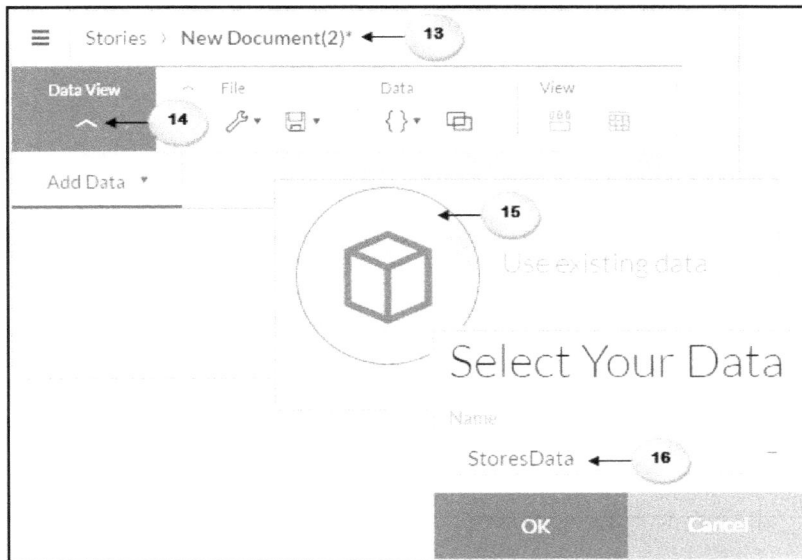

The data view panels that you worked with in the previous chapter will be presented again. Click on **Quantity sold** (**A**) in the **Measures** pane to see its actual figures. By default, the **Version** is set to **Actual** (**B**). Click on the Show Dimensions icon (**C**), and select **Show All** (**D**) from the list to view the **Date** (**E**) and **Store** (**F**) dimensions as well. Expand the **Date** node, and select the month of **January** (**G**). In the **Stores** pane, select **Farlos** (**H**). The actual sold quantity 600 for **Farlos** in January will appear in the lower pane. You can verify this figure from the source Excel file (**I**):

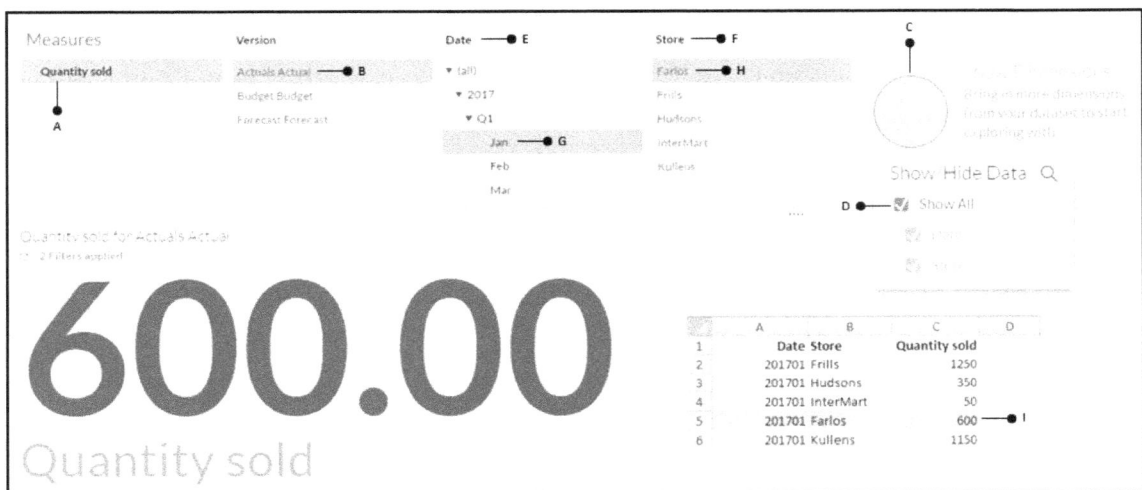

Let's see how the planning data can be visualized from a different perspective. In these steps, we will add a bar chart to a story page that will allow us to compare actual, budget, and forecast figures, all at the same time.

17. On the toolbar, click on the Chart icon to add a blank chart to **Page 1** of the story.

18. Click on the **Designer** link to see the **designer** panel:

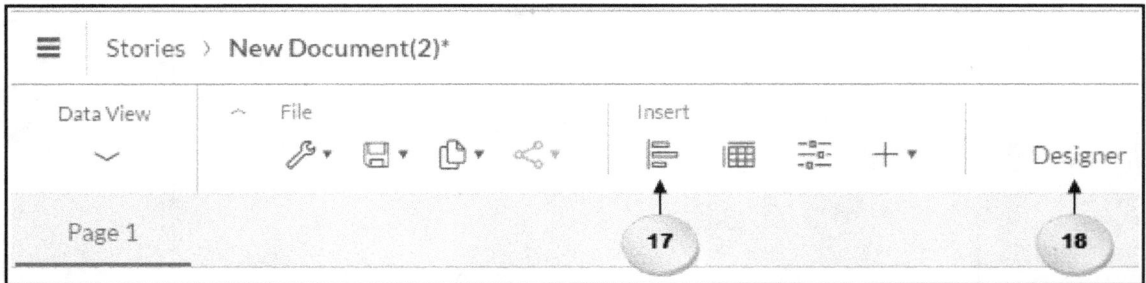

Click on the **Builder** tab in the designer panel to set the properties for the chart. Because you have already selected the model in step 16, the **StoresData** model will automatically appear under **Data Source** (**A**). Execute the following steps to populate the chart.

19. In the **Measures** section, click on the **Add Measure** link, and select **Quantity Sold** from the list.

20. In the **Dimensions** section, click on the **Add Dimension** link, and select the **Date** dimension.

21. In the **Color** section, click on the **Add Dimension** link, and select **Version**. A **Version** section will be added with the **Actual** version. Click on the **Add Version** link (**B**), and select **Budget** to add the **Budget** version under **Actual**. Repeat the process to add the **Forecast** version too. You can optionally set different patterns (**C**) and colors (**D**) to distinguish the three versions in the chart:

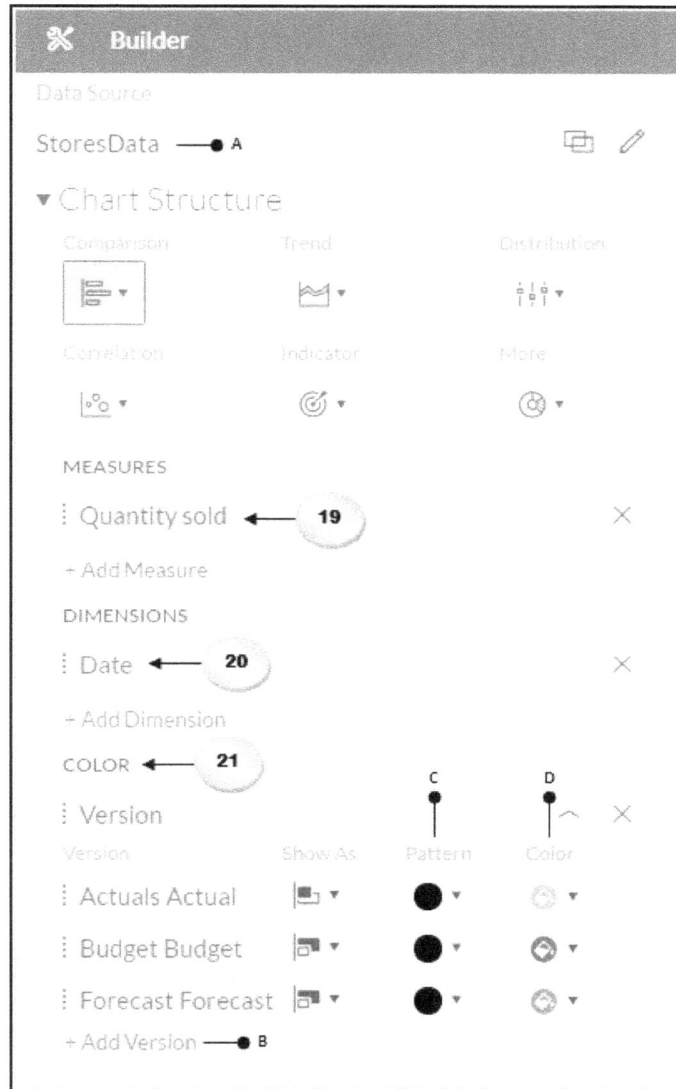

The chart will be transformed according to your selections and will display three bars that represent the three versions. Click on the **all** link (**A**) under the chart, and from the toolbar that appears, select the Drill Down on Date (**B**) icon. Click on this option three more times until you see months, which is the lowest granularity; you cannot drill down beyond this level.

22. Click on the More Actions icon on the chart's vertical toolbar.
23. Select **Add Variance** from the ensuing menu:

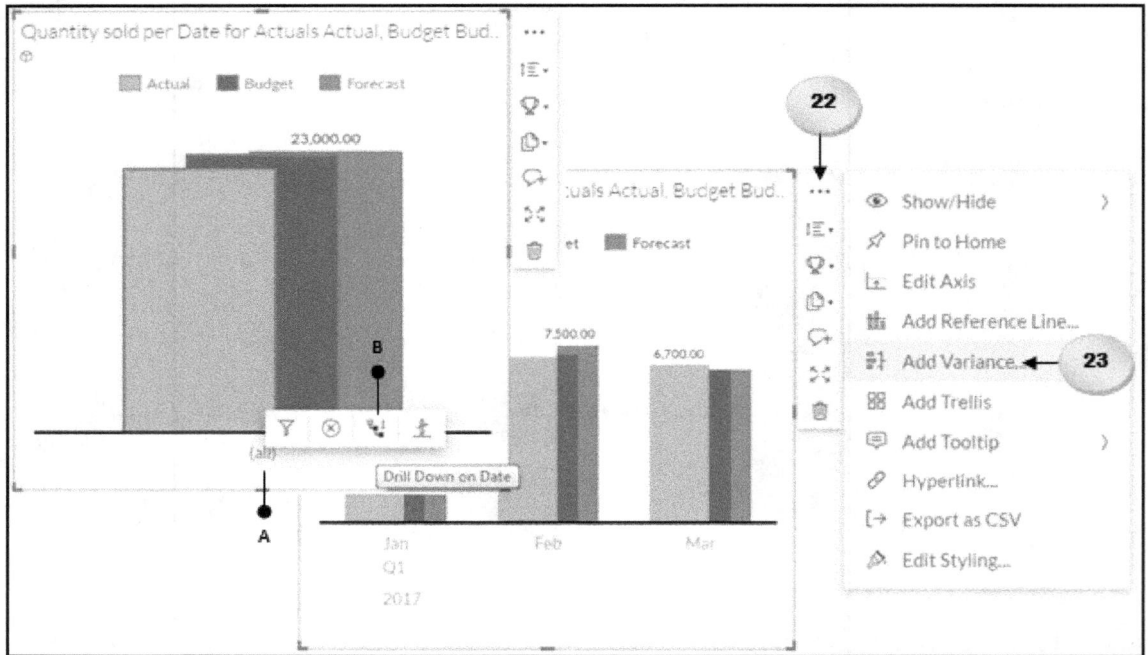

The **Create Variance** panel appears to your right. By adding variance to your chart, you can compare two values. For example, in the current scenario, you will create a variance that shows the difference between actual and budget values for the sold quantity.

24. In the **Compare (A)** section, select **Quantity sold** as measure.
25. Select **Actual** as the version in the **Compare (A)** section.

26. In the **To** (**B**) section, select the same **Quantity sold** column as the measure.
27. Select **Budget** as the version in the **To** (**B**) section.
28. Click on **OK** to save your variance settings.

The output of your setting will appear something like the following screenshot. The first variance data point shows a negative value of -1,200 (**A**). This figure is calculated by subtracting the actual value (8,000) and the budget value (9,200) in the month of January. The remaining points are calculated in the same manner. For your convenience, the values are made visible in the figure. If you want to also see the result in percentages, then turn on the **Percentage** option under the **Display options** section in the **Create Variance** panel:

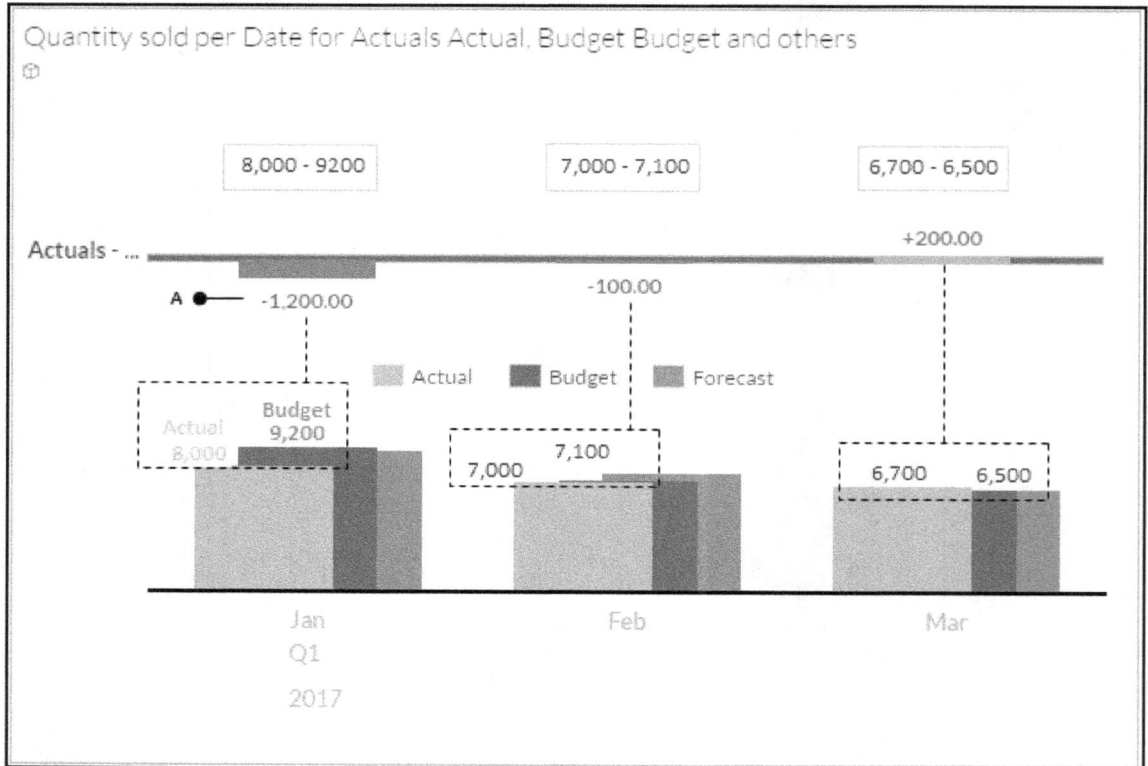

Viewing the text data

In SAP Analytics Cloud, you can use the table object to view your model data. A table is a spreadsheet-like object that can be used to view and analyze text data in a model. For further details on this object, see Chapter 7, *Working With Tables and Grids*. Execute the following steps to view the data of the three versions in a table object:

29. On your story page, click on the plus icon on the page toolbar, and select **Grid** to add a grid page to the story.

30. On the new grid page, click on the **Add** icon on the toolbar to add a table object.

31. In the **Select Model** dialog, select the first **Existing Model** option (**A**), and then select **StoresData** (**B**) from the **Name** list. Click on **OK**.

   In the **Builder** panel, set the following properties for the table object:

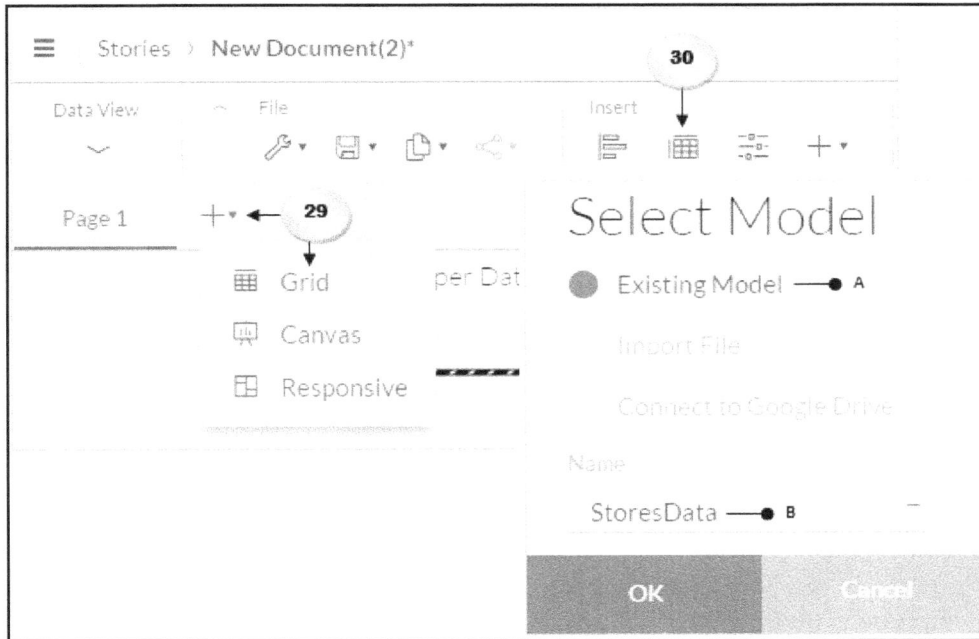

32. Click on the **Add Measures/Dimensions** link (**A**) in the **Rows** section, and select the **Store** dimension.

33. Again, click on the same link, and select the **Date** dimension.

34. In the **Columns** section, click on the **Add Measures/Dimensions** link, and select **Version**.

35. Hover your mouse pointer over the **Version** dimension, and click on the Manage Filter icon.

36. In the **Selected filters for Version** dialog, select all the three versions, as illustrated in the following screenshot:

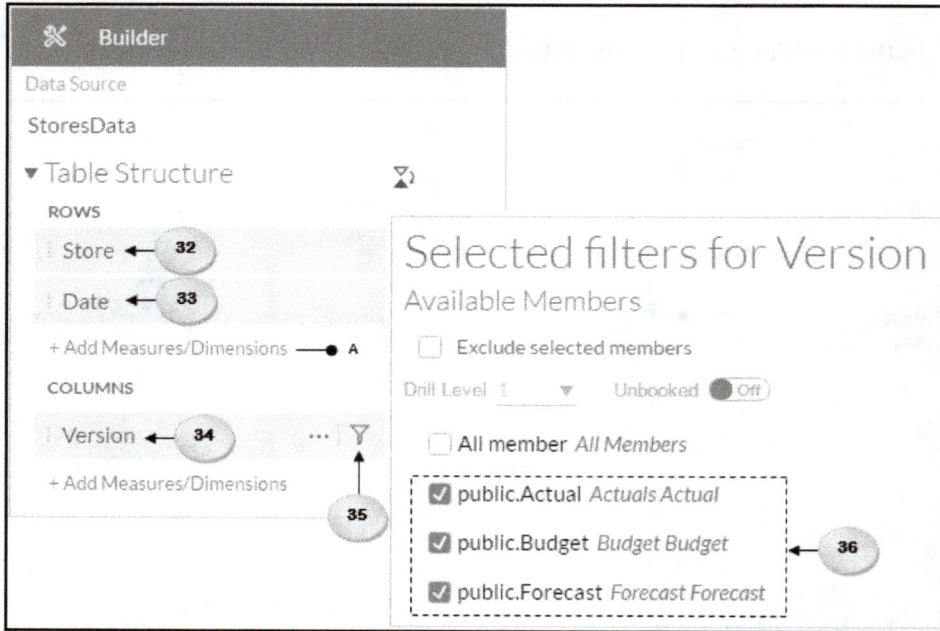

The output of your selections is depicted in the following screenshot. The **Store** and **Date** dimensions occupy the row position, while the three data versions appear in separate columns. The **Date** dimension is presented as a hierarchy, with year, quarter, and month nodes. Monthly figures are rolled up into quarter and then into year:

	A	B	C	D	E
	Page 1	Page 2			
1	StoresData				
2		VERSION	Actuals	Budget	Forecast
3		VERSION	Actual	Budget	Forecast
4	STORE	DATE			
5	InterMart	► (all)	5,200.00	6,500.00	6,600.00
6	Frills	► (all)	3,300.00	3,300.00	3,400.00
7	Kullens	► (all)	5,700.00	5,000.00	5,000.00
8	Farlos	▼ (all)	3,300.00	3,700.00	3,700.00
9		▼ 2017	3,300.00	3,700.00	3,700.00
10		▼ Q1 (2017)	3,300.00	3,700.00	3,700.00
11		Jan (2017)	600.00	900.00	800.00
12		Feb (2017)	1,300.00	1,000.00	1,400.00
13		Mar (2017)	1,400.00	1,800.00	1,500.00
14	Hudsons	► (all)	4,200.00	4,300.00	4,300.00

Spreading, distributing, and assigning values

In addition to fetching values from the model data, you can add your own values in the table. For this, you use the allocations feature of SAP Analytics Cloud, which includes spreading, distributing, and assigning values. Allocation is the process of splitting values derived from source data into multiple values and storing the values in target data. The allocation feature is used in planning and data analysis to gain insights.

The spreading, distribution, and assigning operations are ways of allocating values in a table to one or more target cells. These features can help you quickly book new values and adjust existing values in a plan:

- **Spreading**: In spreading operations, the value of a source cell is spread across leaf members. Values are taken from a higher level of a hierarchy and spread at a lower level. You can perform spreading automatically or manually.
- **Distribution**: In distribution, values are changed within a hierarchy by distributing amounts from a source member to leaf members of its siblings. You can move some or all of the values from one cell to other cells at the same hierarchical level or to members of a different branch of the same hierarchy. Unlike spreading, distribution subtracts value from the source cell to add it to the target cells. Leaf members that aggregate up to the source cell are decreased proportionally, and leaf members of the target cells are increased proportionally.
- **Assigning**: Using the assign feature, you can append or overwrite values to target cells without specifying a source cell. Here, you choose the amount to assign. The values you assign are not deducted from any other cell that occurs when you use spreading or distribution.

Let's see how the values are spread automatically when we specify a new value in a cell that already has some value. Change the first quarter forecast value of the Farlos store from 3,700 to 4,000. The whole hierarchy of this store will be affected by the change. As you can see in the following screenshot, the new value has been spread among the three months based on the values each month was previously assigned. When you specify a value in this manner, the existing weights among items at lower levels in the hierarchy are preserved. For example, the forecast value for the month of January before the amendment was 800, and the contribution of this figure to the total amount was 21.62% (800*100/3700). After the amendment, the same percentage is applied to calculate the new value for this month, that is, (4000 * 21.62% = 864.80).

StoresData				
	VERSION	Actuals	Budget	Forecast
	VERSION	Actual	Budget	Forecast
STORE	DATE			
InterMart	▸ (all)	5,200.00	6,500.00	6,600.00
Frills	▸ (all)	3,300.00	3,300.00	3,400.00
Kullens	▸ (all)	5,700.00	5,000.00	5,000.00
Farlos	▾ (all)	3,300.00	3,700.00	4,000.00
	▾ 2017	3,300.00	3,700.00	4,000.00
	▾ Q1 (2017)	3,300.00	3,700.00	4,000.00
	Jan (2017)	600.00	900.00	864.80
	Feb (2017)	1,300.00	1,000.00	1,513.60
	Mar (2017)	1,400.00	1,800.00	1,621.60
Hudsons	▸ (all)	4,200.00	4,300.00	4,300.00

In addition to spreading values automatically, you can also manually specify weights for members of a specific dimension and level by selecting the source cell and then going to **Allocate values** (⇕) | **Spreading** from the toolbar.

In the **Spreading** dialog, you need to specify **Target Dimension** to spread the chosen value on. In the current scenario, the **Date** dimension will be set as **Target Dimension**. Using the icons to the right of this dialog, you can choose the hierarchical level at which you want to spread the chosen value. The **Unbooked** option allows you to spread to members that do not have values.

> Note that if you do not choose the bottom level of the hierarchy as your target, the values will automatically be spread to leaf cells using the existing weights if these cells are already populated. If you have turned on the **Unbooked** option and the cells are empty, equal values will be spread to all leaf cells.

There are a couple of methods using which you can spread the values. You can enter numeric weight values, such as simple ratios between the members, or click on the eyedropper icon to copy values from other cells in the story sequentially into the available fields. When you enter values manually, it is the relative weights of the values that are spread, not the values themselves.

This feature is useful when we want to apply the same weighting between members. The **Preview** column shows the values that will appear in the table after spreading. Once you are satisfied with the statistics in this dialog, click on the **Apply Spreading** button to spread the values:

Spread 4000.00 $ X

Target Dimension

Date ▼

Choose Level & Weights

Unbooked ● Off

Level	Weight		Preview
Jan	864.80	21.62%	864.80 $
Feb	1513.60	37.84%	1513.60 $
Mar	1621.60	40.54%	1621.60 $

Apply Spreading   Cancel

Creating private versions

The three versions (actual, budget, and forecast) of data you added to your planning model in the previous section are known as public versions. Public versions are stored in the raw model data in the database. As mentioned earlier in this chapter, access to the model data is controlled by data privileges that you establish by enabling data access control for a dimension and assigning appropriate privileges to a user in the Modeler.

In SAP Analytics Cloud, you can create your own private versions of the data from these public version categories. Private versions are only visible to the creator or owner of the model. You use these versions to change or simulate plan values without making this visible to anyone else. When you publish a private version, it gets promoted to a public version, and the private version is dropped. You can create private versions within the given categories using the **Version Management** feature of SAP Analytics Cloud. By creating private versions, you can modify values without disturbing the public version data. Another advantage to this approach is that the public data is in your view when you make your changes.

Here are the steps to create a private version. In this exercise, you will create a private version of the **Forecast** category:

37. Select the table, and then on the toolbar, click on the Version Management icon (

). The **Version Management** panel, as illustrated in the following screenshot, is displayed on the right side of the screen.

38. In the **Version Management** panel, select the version you want to use as a private version, and click on the **copy** icon.

39. In the **Copy to a Private Version** dialog, enter a name for the version, for example, **Private Forecast**.

40. Click on the **OK** button.

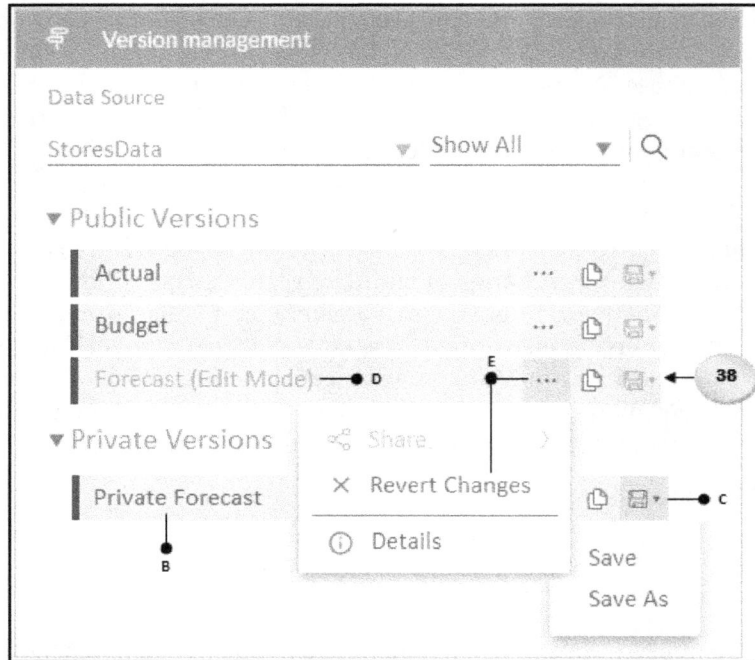

The new version (**A**) will be added to the table (see the next screenshot), and a corresponding entry (**B**) will also appear in the **Private Versions** section in the **Version Management** panel. You are free to make any changes to the new private version.

After changing the values in the private version, save it by clicking the Save icon (**C**). You will be provided with two options: **Save** and **Save As**. The **Save** option saves your work as an update to a public version, while **Save As** creates a new public version. In the latter case, you have to select a category, for example, planning, enter a name for the new version, and then choose **OK**. Choose the **Save As** option to publish the private version to a category that is not being used in the model yet, for example, planning or rolling forecast.

The **Save** option is used when you want to replace an existing public version in any category. For example, if you want to replace the existing public forecast, choose Save. Once you select the **Save** option, the existing public forecast values will be replaced by your private forecast, and the private forecast will be removed from the version management panel.

	StoresData						A
1	⊙						
2			VERSION	Actuals	Budget	Forecast	Forecast
3			VERSION	Actual	Budget	Forecast	Private Forecast
4	STORE	DATE					
5	InterMart	▸ (all)		5,200.00	6,500.00	6,600.00	6,600.00
6	Frills	▸ (all)		3,300.00	3,300.00	3,400.00	3,400.00
7	Kullens	▸ (all)		5,700.00	5,000.00	5,000.00	5,000.00
8	Farlos	▾ (all)		3,300.00	3,700.00	4,000.00	4,000.00
9	Hudsons	▸ (all)		4,200.00	4,300.00	4,300.00	4,300.00

You can, of course, make your changes directly in the public version without first creating a private version. The public version switches to the edit mode (**D**) in the version management panel when you are making the changes. While editing data in a public version, other users cannot see your changes and you cannot see their changes.

When you finish your edits, you must choose whether to discard your changes or publish them to the original public version. When you make such changes and try to leave the page, a dialog appears, prompting you to publish your edits or discard them. You can also discard your changes by selecting **Revert Changes** (**E**), which is available next to each version in the version management panel.

Summary

Fail to plan is a plan to fail. Because planning helps you decide short-term and long-term goals, its significance cannot be overlooked for an organization. Planning is a process that involves the determination of a future course of action. Why, how, and when you should take an action are main subjects of planning. Increasing an organization's ability to adapt to future eventualities, making the company more competitive in its industry, reducing mistakes and oversights, making effective use of an organization's resources, and exercising better control are some of the peculiarities of planning.

Keeping in view the importance of planning, SAP Analytics Cloud helps you create full-featured planning models. Creating and working with a planning model is a huge subject, and a complete book can be dedicated to this subject. In this brief chapter, you were given an overview of this vital area that is enough to give you a jump start. Once you get comfortable with these basics, you can explore other areas on your own. You learned how to enable a model for planning and use different versions of data in the same model.

You also experienced the methods to visualize and view the model data and created variance to compare the data from two different versions. Spreading, distributing, and assigning values were also discussed in this context. Finally, you went through the process of creating your own private version using an existing public version.

After creating a model, you visualize its data in different types of objects, such as charts, tables, and geomaps; the chapter provided you with a glimpse of this too. These objects are created on one or more story pages, which we will discuss in detail in upcoming chapters.

4

Creating Stories Using Charts

Stories are used in SAP Analytics Cloud to present data graphically using charts, tables, geo maps, text, images, and shapes. In this chapter as well as in the next few chapters, you will learn the use of different types of charts and other objects to create a story page, as illustrated in the following figure:

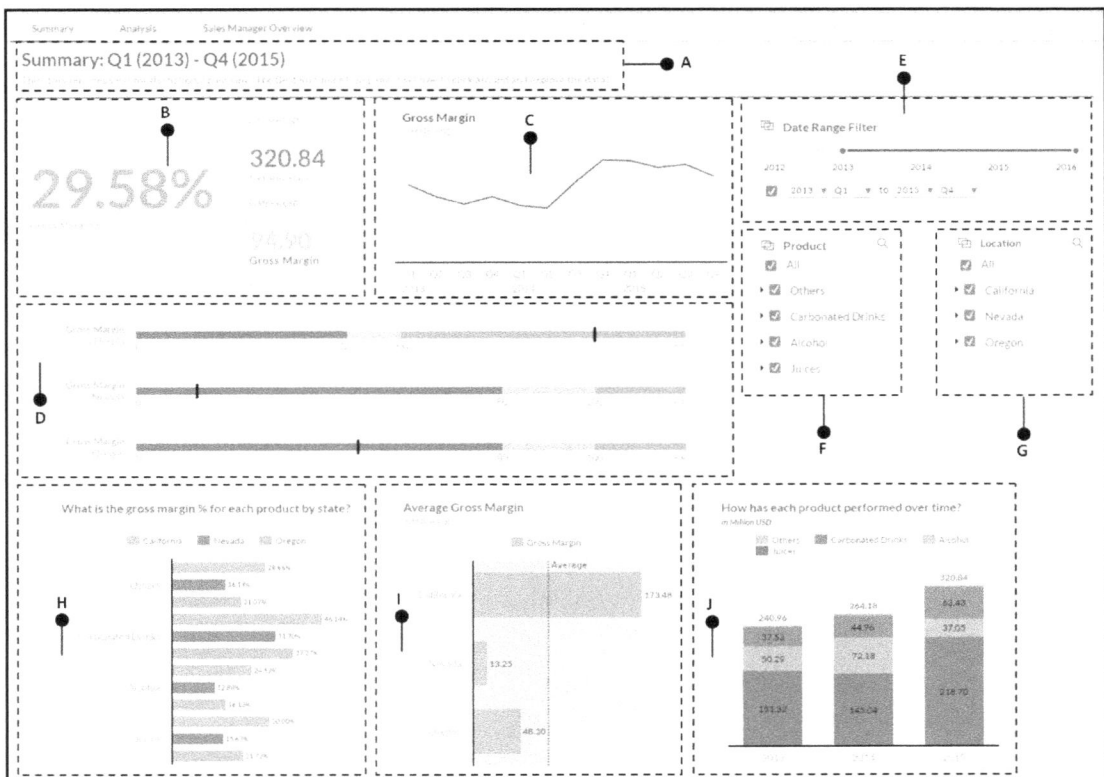

Here are the briefs of the illustrated story page:

- **A**: This is the title of the story page that describes its purpose.
- **B**: These are three separate tiles added to demonstrate how to create Numeric Point charts to dynamically render numeric data in different colors using custom-defined thresholds.
- **C**: The gross margin chart will be created using a line chart.
- **D**: The **key performance indicator** (**KPI**) is a type of success metric. Based on user-defined thresholds, KPI indicates the status of a measure.
- **E**, **F**, and **G**: These data filters will be created in the next chapter for date, product, and location dimensions.
- **H**, **I**, and **J**: These tiles will demonstrate the use of bar charts with different functions, such as drill up and down in the chart and draw a reference line to show important values on your chart.

Demo models

This chapter and some subsequent chapters will use a couple of demo analytic models (**Best Run** and **Planned Events**) that come with the trial version. The **Best Run** model is used because it is a comprehensive model and contains more data than the Bocage analytical model (created in Chapter 2, *Models in SAP Analytics Cloud*) to evaluate different scenarios. The **Planned Events** model, on the other hand, is an associate model, which demonstrates how to create linked dimensions using the two models that you will learn in Chapter 6, *Analyzing Data Using Geo Maps and Other Objects*. For now, let's go through these two models to get an overview. To access these models, click on the main menu, and then go to **Browse | Models**.

The Best Run demo model

On the **Models** tab (on the **Models** page), click on the **Best Run** link (**A**) under the **Name** column to open this model in the modeler interface:

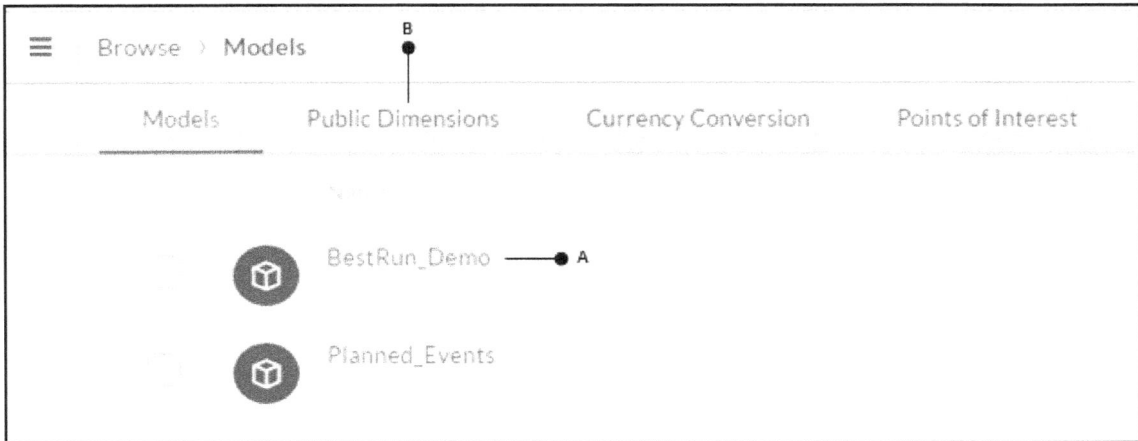

Click on the **Time** dimension tab, and see that the **time granularity** (**C**) is the same as you set for the Bocage model:

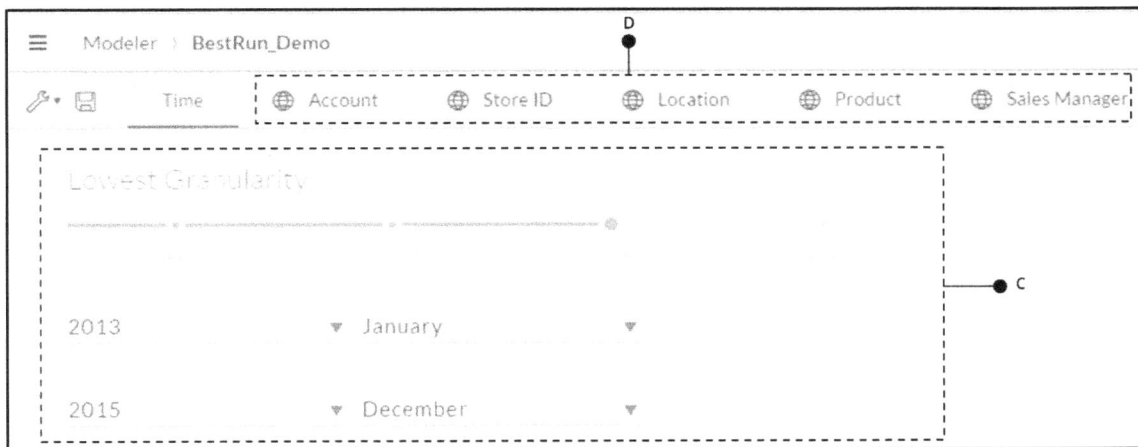

Note that the **Account, Store ID, Location, Product**, and **Sales Manger** dimensions (**D**) are marked as **Public Dimensions** in this model. A public dimension is identified by a globe icon. If you switch back to the **Models** page and click on the **Public Dimensions** tab (**B**), you will see all these dimensions under that tab.

The **Account** dimension carries the same set of measures you went through in `Chapter 2`, *Models in SAP Analytics Cloud,* having auto-generated IDs and column names as **Descriptions**:

	ID	Description
1	Quantity_sold_2081dc5195832029	Quantity sold
2	Gross_Margin_2081dc5195832029	Gross Margin
3	Discount_2081dc5195832029	Discount
4	Original_2081dc5195832029	Original Sales Price
5	Price_fixed_2081dc5195832029	Price (fixed)

(Tabs: Time, Account, Store ID)

In this model, the latitude and longitude coordinates are merged into stores to form the location dimension that you will use in a geomap in `Chapter 6`, *Analyzing Data Using Geo Maps and Other Objects*:

(Tabs: Time, Account, Store ID, Location, Product)

	ID	Descripti...	Latitude	Longitude	Store Name	Stores_DisplayName	Stores_GEOID
1	ST1			-121.7354	Second Hand	38.6362,-121.7354	0
2	ST2			-114.62	Meadow Depot	36.157,-114.62	1
3	ST3			-121.5713	Value Clothing	38.4359,-121.5713	2

Click on the **Location** dimension. The data appearing under this tab is entered manually. As you can see in the following screenshot, this dimension has a hierarchical relationship between states and cities. The three state IDs (**A**) are entered under the city IDs (**B**), then these state IDs are entered in a separate **State** column for each city to create the relationship. For example, in the following screenshot, you can see that the **California** state code (**SA1**) is assigned to **Los Angeles** and **San Francisco**, the **Nevada** state code (**SA2**) is assigned to **Reno** and **Henderson**, and the **Oregon** state code (**SA3**) is assigned to **Portland** and **Salem**. After manually creating such a relationship, you can view it in the **Hierarchy** tab on the right side:

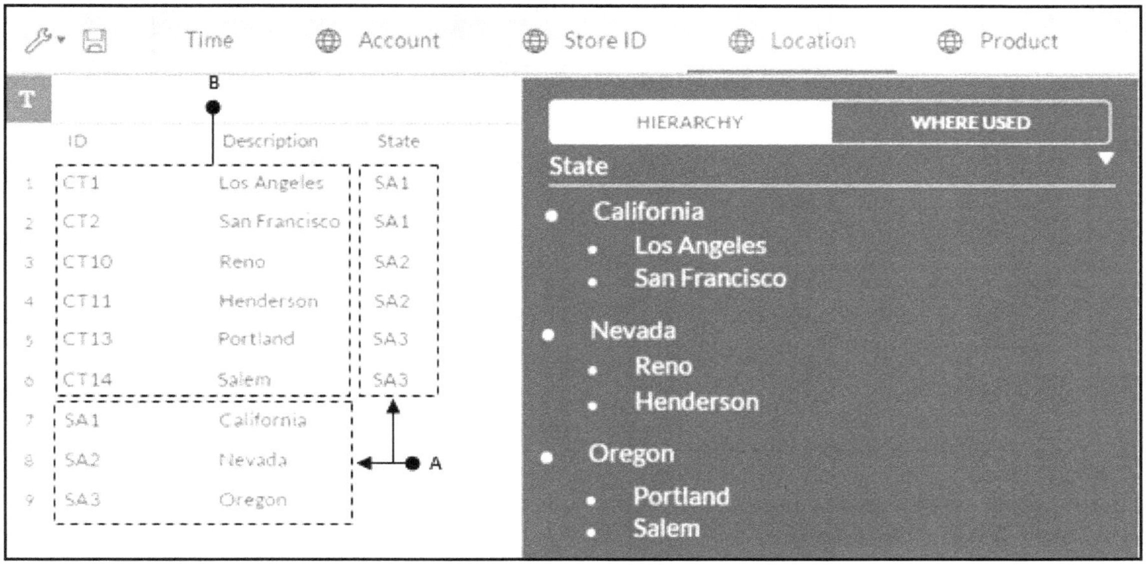

Just like the **State** and **City** hierarchy, the **Product** dimension also has a hierarchical relationship between **Category** and **Product**. The four product category IDs (**C**) are listed at the bottom, and each product (**D**) is assigned one of these categories in the **Product Category** column:

Finally, there is a **Sales Manager** dimension, which is the simplest of all. It has just two attributes: **ID** and **Description**:

The Planned Events model

The Planned Events model consists of two measures (*Number of Events for 2015* and *Planned Events for 2016*): the date-time dimension, and three public dimensions (**state**, **city**, and **event**). You will use this model in Chapter 6, *Analyzing Data Using Geo Maps and Other Objects*, to create a linked dimension that will show the amount of revenue earned with the number of events by city.

Creating a new story

1. To create a new story, you can either navigate through the main menu or launch the process directly from the home screen:

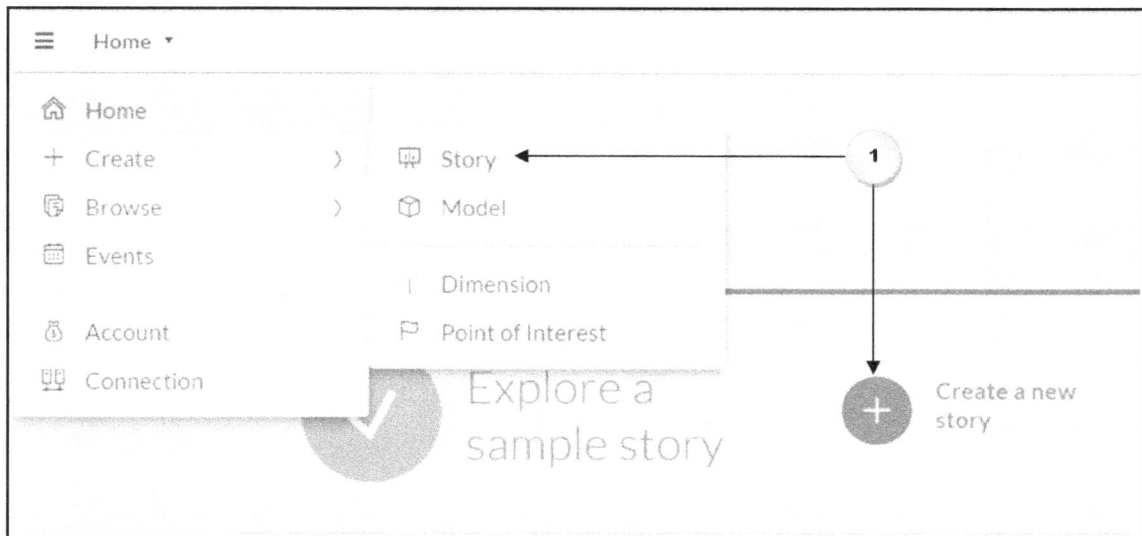

New Document (A): When you click on either of the two options illustrated in the preceding screenshot, a new document is created, and you are prompted to choose a predefined layout for the first page of your story, import data, add a blank canvas page, or add a grid page, which functions like a spreadsheet.

Templates (B): The four options provided in the **Templates** section let you apply formatting to your story. These templates come with predefined layouts and placeholders for objects, which help you build professional looking stories.

Import & Explore Data (**C**): Using this option, you can import data from an Excel or CSV (comma-separated-values) file, from Google Drive, or from an existing model.

Add a Canvas Page (**D**): By selecting this option, you can explore and present your data through charts, tables, geomaps, images, and other objects on one or more canvas pages. You can add multiple pages to your story to segregate your analyses. The pages you add through this option appear as horizontal tabs on top of the story page.

Add a Grid Page (**E**): As just mentioned, a grid functions like a spreadsheet, where you can add data either by typing or by pasting from another source or by adding a table based on another model. On a grid page, you can work with formulas that include values from multiple models.

2. For this example, select the **Import & Explore Data** option, as shown in the following screenshot:

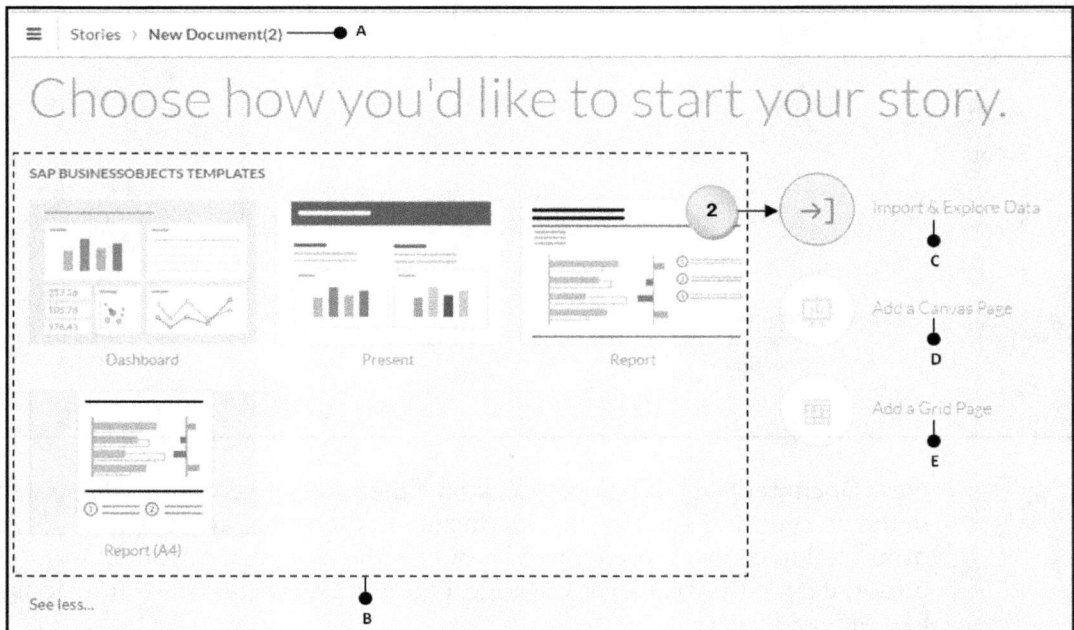

After selecting the **Import & Explore Data** option, you are prompted to select an option that determines how you want to add data to your story. The **Import a file** option allows you to import data from an external file, such as an Excel spreadsheet or a **comma-separated-values** (CSV) file into a new story.

When you create a new story by importing data from a file, the import process analyzes the source data and creates an initial data view with proposed measures and dimensions. After the data import process completes, you can refine the proposal by changing the types of columns and fixing any data-quality issues, as you did in Chapter 2, *Models in SAP Analytics Cloud*, where you created a new analytical model from scratch. The data you import either from a file or from Google Drive is displayed in the **Data Manipulation** view, where you can modify the data, define dimensions, and perform operations such as sorting and filtering. You can also switch to **Data View**, where you can begin analyzing data and creating visualizations. The first option (**Use existing data**, which you are going to select for this example) imports data from an existing model and opens it directly in **Data View**.

3. For this example, select **Use existing data**:

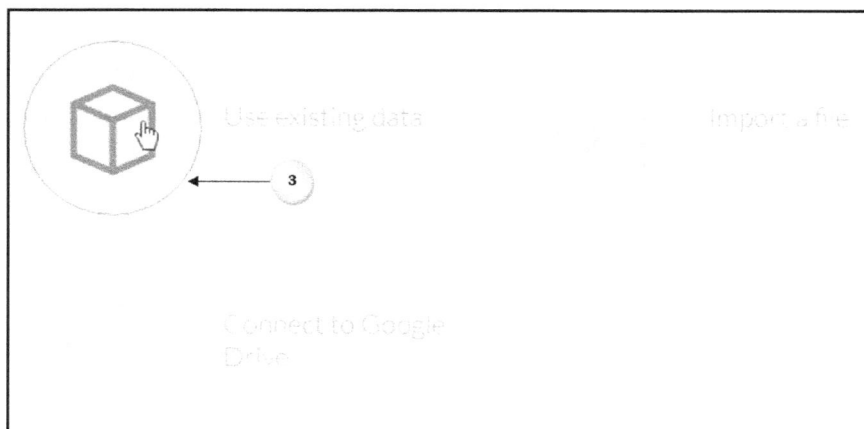

Selecting a model for the story

4. Select the **Best Run** model from the drop-down list. This model will be used in the next few chapters as well to create different stories:

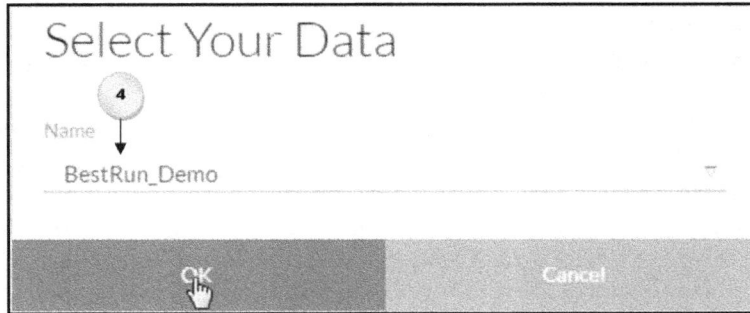

5. When you click on the **OK** button on the previous screen, you see the **Data View** interface, which you already went through in detail in Chapter 2, *Models in SAP Analytics Cloud*.

   For now, click on the arrow to hide the **Data View** panel, as shown in the following screenshot:

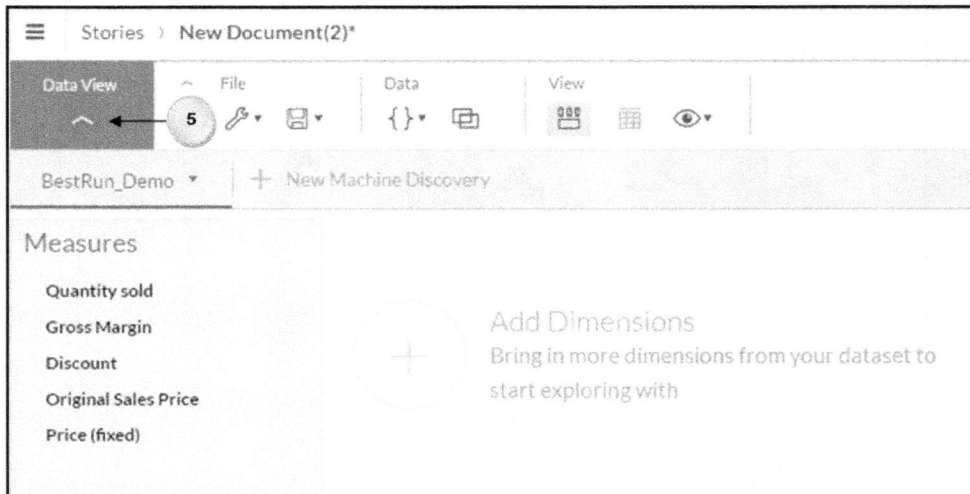

Creating a numeric point chart to show net revenue

6. When you hide the **Data View** panel, you see six options (chart, geomap, table, image, shape, and text) that you can add to the canvas. Also, note that a blank canvas labeled **Page 1** (**A**) is automatically created where you can place these objects.
Click on the chart option in the **Add an object to the canvas** section, or click on the Chart icon (**6**) on the Insert toolbar. Either way, a blank chart is added to **Page 1**:

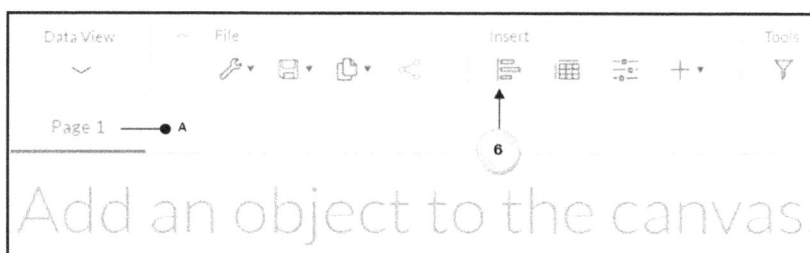

7. On the **Builder** tab in the **Designer** panel to your right, select the **Numeric Point** chart from **Chart Structure | Indicator**. As the name suggests, a numeric point chart displays bold-faced numeric data. In this example, you will display the value of a calculated measure named **Net Revenue** in this chart. The **Designer** panel is used to format and manipulate the data in your canvas elements:

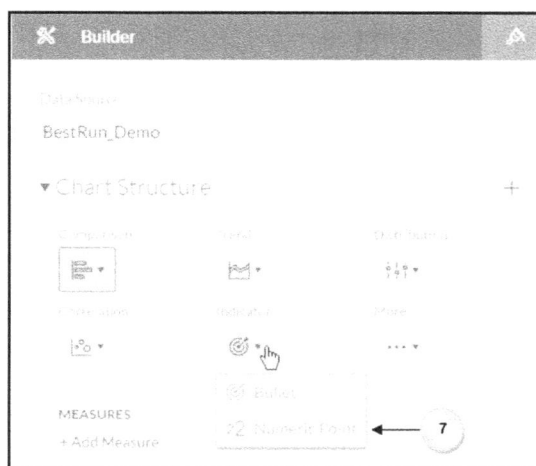

8. In the same **Builder** panel, click on the **Add Measure** link under the **MEASURES** section. Then select **Click to Create a New Calculation**. This will take you to the **Calculation Editor** interface, where you will create a new calculated measure for the **Numeric Point** chart:

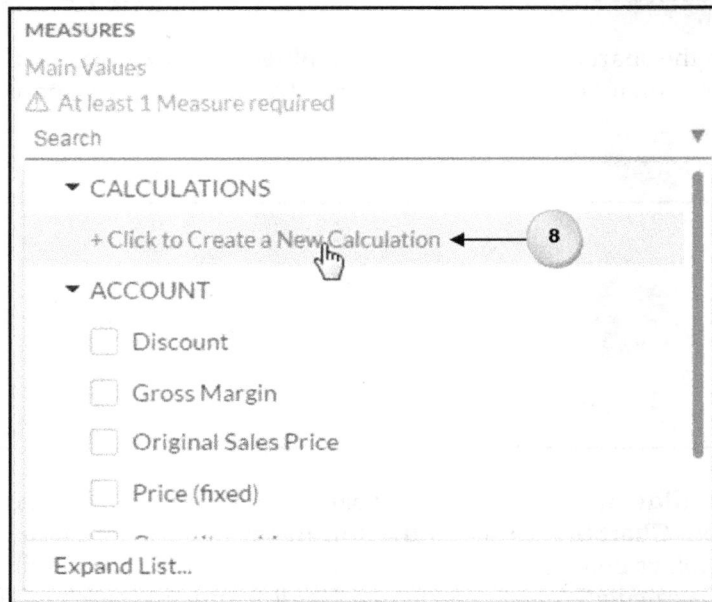

The calculation editor

In stories, you usually select measures (for example, gross margin or original sales price from the **Account** dimensions as depicted in the previous screenshot) from your model to display on your charts. In addition to selecting measures from your model, you also have the option of creating new measures based on some sort of calculation to visualize the result. In SAP Analytics Cloud, you can create custom calculations for use in a chart or table via the **Calculation Editor** interface. You can then use these calculations in your charts or tables.

You can create the following types of calculation in the **Calculation Editor** interface:

- **Calculated Measures**: In this type, you perform a calculation on one or more members of either the **Account** dimension or the **Calculations** dimension. A new calculated member of the selected dimension is created as a result. Calculated measures enable us to create formulas using a combination of functions, conditions, and mathematical operators (see **A** in the following screenshot).

- **Restricted Measures**: This it restricts the data from a member of either the **Account** dimension or the **Calculations** dimension to exclude certain members of one or more dimensions. A new restricted member of the selected dimension is created as a result.

- **Difference From**: This one finds the difference in an account's value between two dates. A new calculated account member is created as a result.

- **Aggregation**: As the name implies, you can use this type for aggregations, such as sum, count, average, max, and min to perform these operations on measures using aggregation dimensions.

You can use **Input Controls** (see **B** in the following figure) as the variable in your **Calculated Measures**. By adding **Input Controls**, you can further augment the functionality of your calculations. With input controls in place, end users can influence the result of a calculation without modifying the underlying data or formula. For example, when you add a list of predefined values for an input control, the users can select different values from this list to see the impact on their canvases. You will see the use of **Input Controls** at the end of this chapter.

In this example, we are creating a **Calculated Measure** option named **Net Revenue**, which is calculated by deducting the discount value from the original sale price. Here is how we proceed with it:

9. On the **Calculation Editor** screen, select **Calculated Measure** from the **Type** drop-down list.
10. Type **Net Revenue** for the **Name** of this new measure.
11. In the **Edit Formula** area, enter the left square bracket [, which returns all measures from the connected model, that is **BestRun_Demo**. From the list that pops up, select **Original Sales Price**.
12. In the **Formula Functions** list, click on **OPERATORS** to see a list of mathematical operators. Click on the minus (-) sign to add this operator just after the **Original Sales Price** measure in the **Edit Formula** section.
13. Once again, enter the left square bracket [in the **Edit Formula** area, and this time, select the **Discount** measure to complete the calculation.

Here is the image for a better understanding:

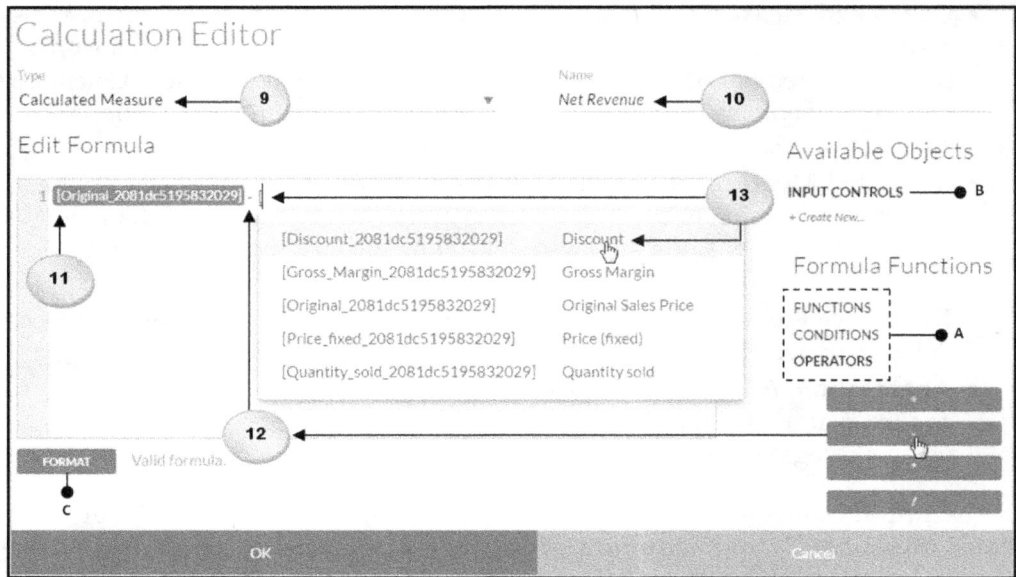

Next, click the **FORMAT** button (**C**) available at the bottom of the screen to validate the formula. Once the formula in validated, click on the **OK** button to close the **Calculation Editor** dialog box.

You can use the following shortcuts in the **Edit Formula** section to view a list of values:

- `[`: This returns all measures of the **Account** dimension
- `#`: This returns all calculations (measures created using the **Calculation Editor** interface)
- `@`: This returns input controls (only single-value numeric input controls are returned)

After you dismiss the **Calculation Editor** screen, you see the following **Numeric Point** chart on your story page. The border in which the chart is enclosed is called a tile. You also see a sidebar menu to the right of each selected tile. Here are some tips and important stuff about charts and the sidebar menu:

- **A**: Place your mouse in the title area, hold down the left mouse button, and drag to position the chart.
- **B**: The more actions icon displays several options that let you hide some chart elements; for example, the title or legend.

- **C**: Copy allows you to copy the chart to your clipboard, an existing story page, or to a new canvas. You can also duplicate the chart on the same canvas. Using the commands *Ctrl+C* (copy) and *Ctrl+V* (paste), you can copy an existing chart to the same story page or to a different story page.
- **D**: The comments icons allows you to place comments on your charts.
- **E**: Fullscreen expands the tile to fill the canvas.
- **F**: Remove allows you to delete the chart from the canvas.
- **G**: The new calculated measure **Net Revenue** will appear under the **MEASURES** section on the **Builder** tab, and the corresponding value will be displayed in the chart.
- **H**: Use these handles to resize your chart.

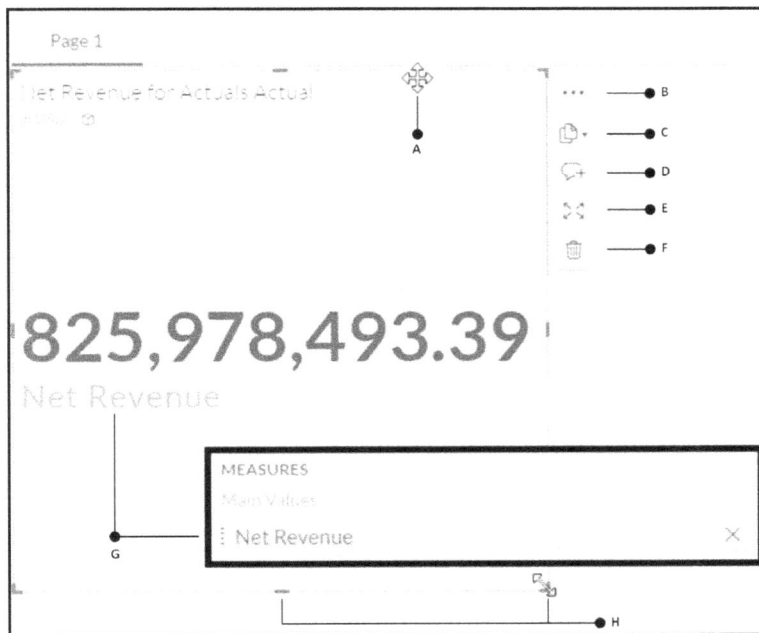

14. Click on the ellipsis icon representing the **Net Revenue** measure to display the available options in a small menu.
15. Select **Format** from the menu.

16. In the **Formatting** dialog box, set **Scale** to **Million**. This action will scale the value to **Million** to improve the presentation of numbers in the output:

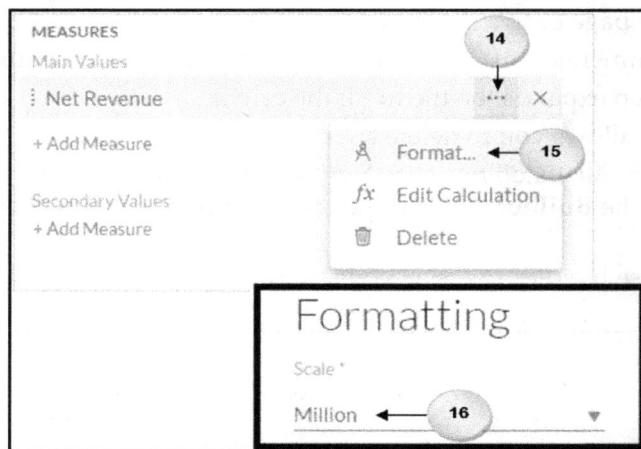

The value in the chart will appear in millions. Click on the chart, this will enclose the chart in a blue-colored border, and you will see a small sidebar menu (**A**). Clicking on the more actions icon (**B**), symbolized with an ellipsis icon, displays a menu. Clicking on the first **Show/Hide** menu option in this menu displays some chart options in a sub-menu. A check mark in front of an option in the sub-menu indicates that the option is turned on and is being displayed in the chart. To turn off an option, click on it. For example, click on **Chart Title**, **Subtitle**, and **Chart Details** to turn off these options from the **Net Revenue Numeric Point** chart:

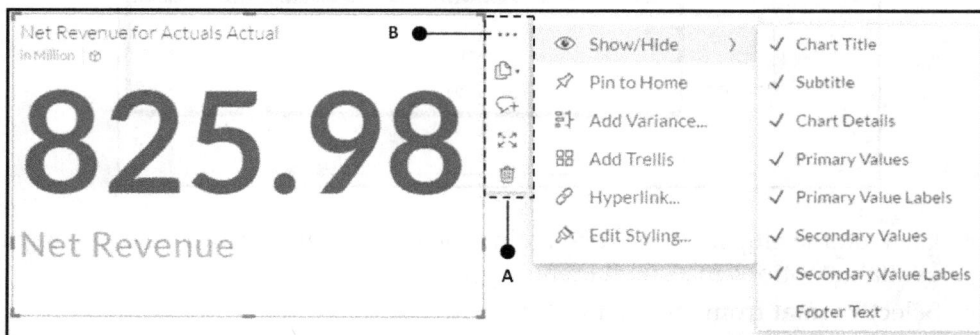

Apply conditional formatting using thresholds

In this exercise, you will add thresholds to the **Numeric Point** chart. Thresholds are used to provide visual cues for your information. By defining thresholds on your objects you can see at a glance what areas are performing well, and what areas need improvements. By default, you get three default ranges with the following labels and colors. However, you can use as many or as few ranges as you like, and you can change the label names and colors, too:

Label	Color
OK	Green
Warning	Yellow
Critical	Red

17. From the **Tools** section in the toolbar, click the Conditional Formatting icon. Then, click the **Add Threshold** link in the **Conditional Formatting** panel to your right. Using the **Conditional Formatting** feature, you can add thresholds and assign colors to highlight information, such as low sales in an area:

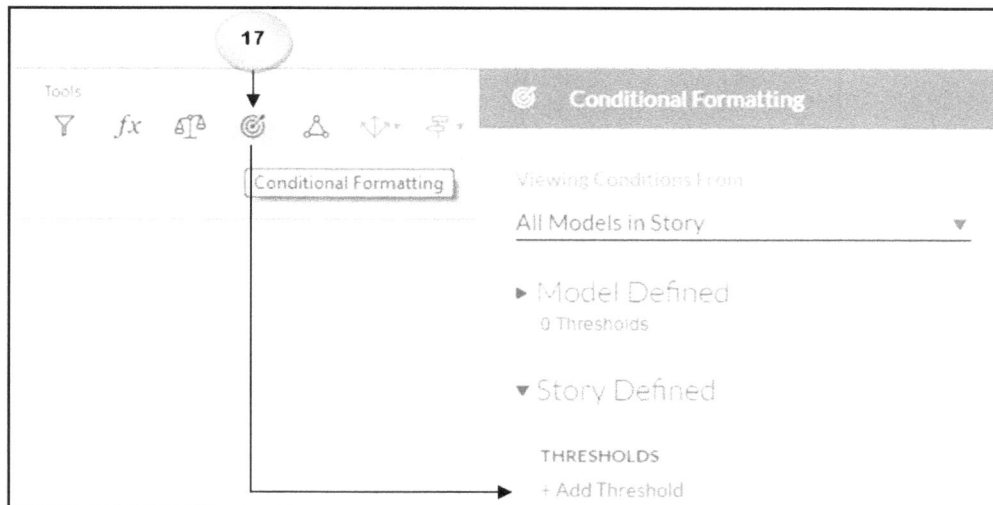

18. Ensure that the **BestRun** model is selected in the **Model** section. If not, select the model from the drop-down list. Next, select the calculated measure **Net Revenue** from the **Measure** list.

The initial view of this panel displays the **OK** range only. Use the + icon (**A**) to add more ranges:

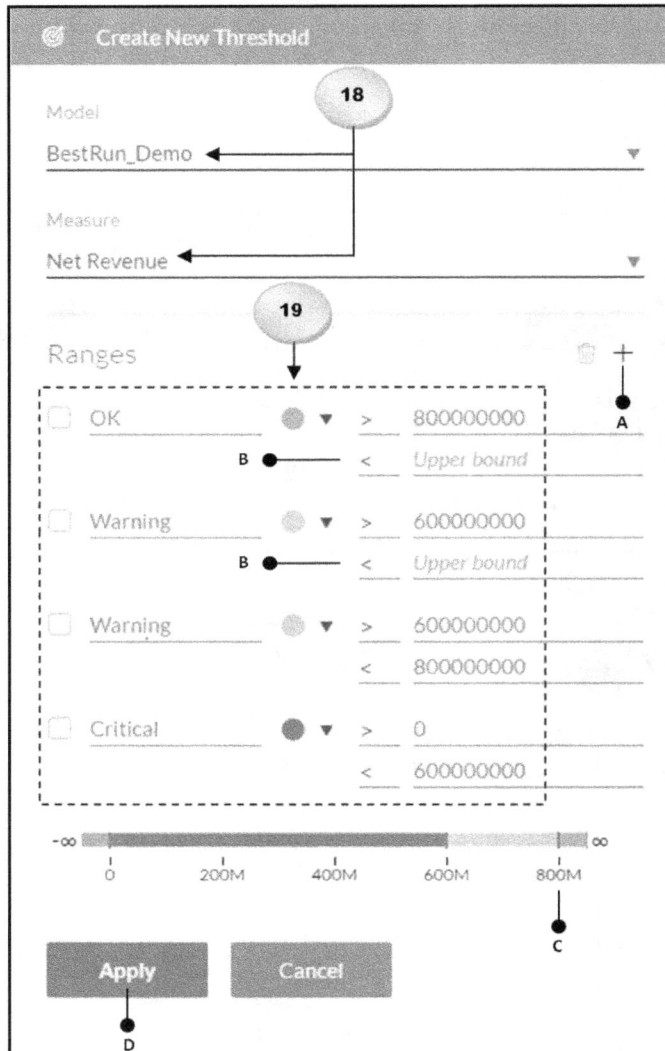

19. In **Ranges**, set a lower bound and an upper bound for your range. As you type your values for the upper and lower bounds, you will see a warning appear if the value does not fall within the range. For example, a lower bound cannot be larger than the upper bound. You do not need to set both an upper and a lower bound if you have only one range. When you add more ranges, you can leave either the upper or lower bound empty (**B**).

    When you enter the value for your range, you will see the value appear on the line at the bottom of the panel (**C**). The value will include a letter to designate, be it thousands, millions, and so on. After providing the threshold ranges, click on the **Apply** button (**D**) followed by **Done** in the **Conditional Formatting** panel.

20. When you get back, click on the chart to select it, and then on the **Builder tab**, click on the **Add Threshold** link in the **COLOR** section.

21. Select **Net Revenue** from the **THRESHOLDS** list. This action will set the chart's color scheme to the threshold you set up in the previous step for the **Net Revenue** measure. Once you set the threshold, the value in the chart will be presented in green, which points to the OK range because the value of **Net Revenue** is greater than 800 million. When you apply a threshold in the **Color** section, the chart changes to reflect the desired ranges.

The **Net Revenue** threshold will be displayed in the **Color** section (A). Note that you can modify the threshold ranges by clicking on the Threshold Options icon (**B**) and then selecting the **Edit Ranges** option (**C**) from the menu. This action will render the **Edit Story Threshold** panel, where you can redefine the thresholds:

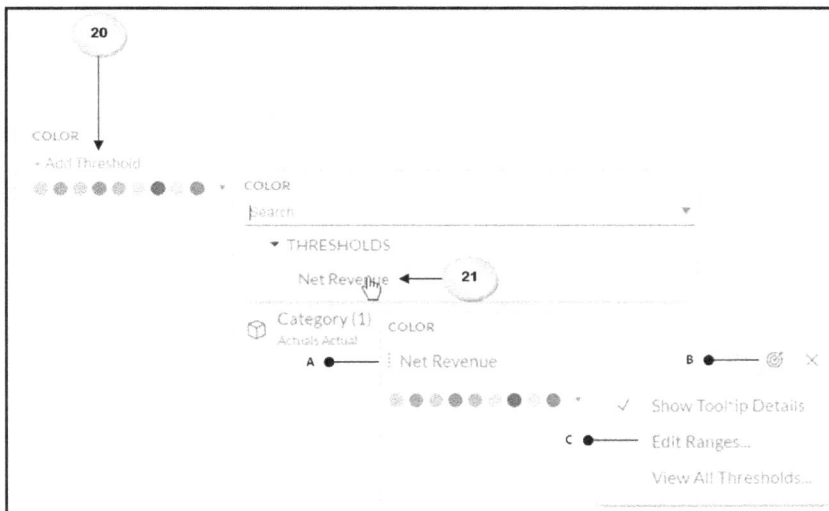

Gross margin numeric point chart

In the previous exercise, you created a **Numeric Point** chart to display the value of the **Net Revenue** calculated measure. Here, you will create a similar type of chart to display the value of **Gross Margin**.

22. Once again, click on the Chart icon on the **Insert** toolbar.
23. On the **Builder tab**, select the **Numeric Point** option.
24. Click on the **Add Measure** link under the **MEASURES** section, and select the **Gross Margin** measure by placing a check mark in its box. Note that this time, you have selected a measure from the model. The list displays all the measures from the **Account** dimension. Clicking on the **Expand List** link (**A**) exposes all these measures in a separate panel:

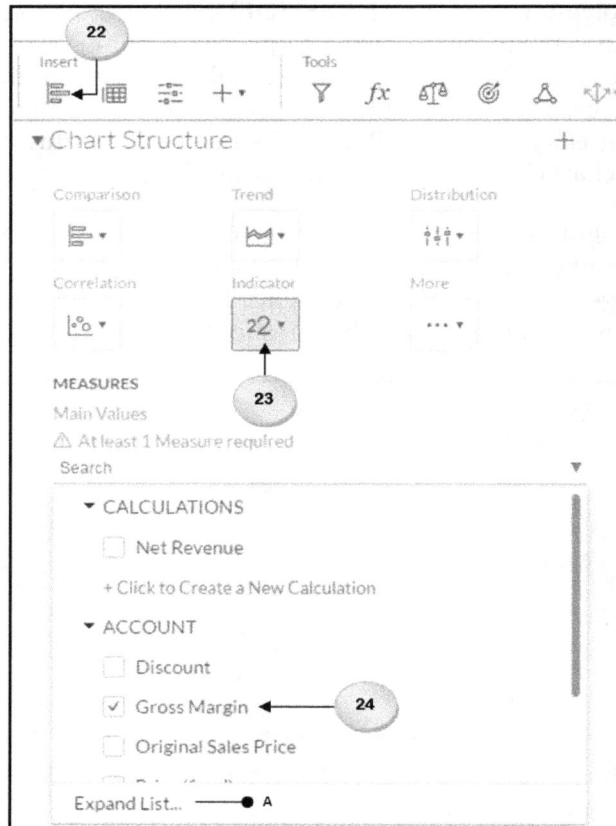

Using the instructions provided in steps 17 to 21, add another threshold for the **Gross Margin** chart, as illustrated here. This time, select the **Gross Margin** measure (**27**) in the **Create New Threshold** dialog box, and select the **Gross Margin** threshold (**29**) in the **Color** section. Once again, the color of this chart will change to reflect the status of the selected measure:

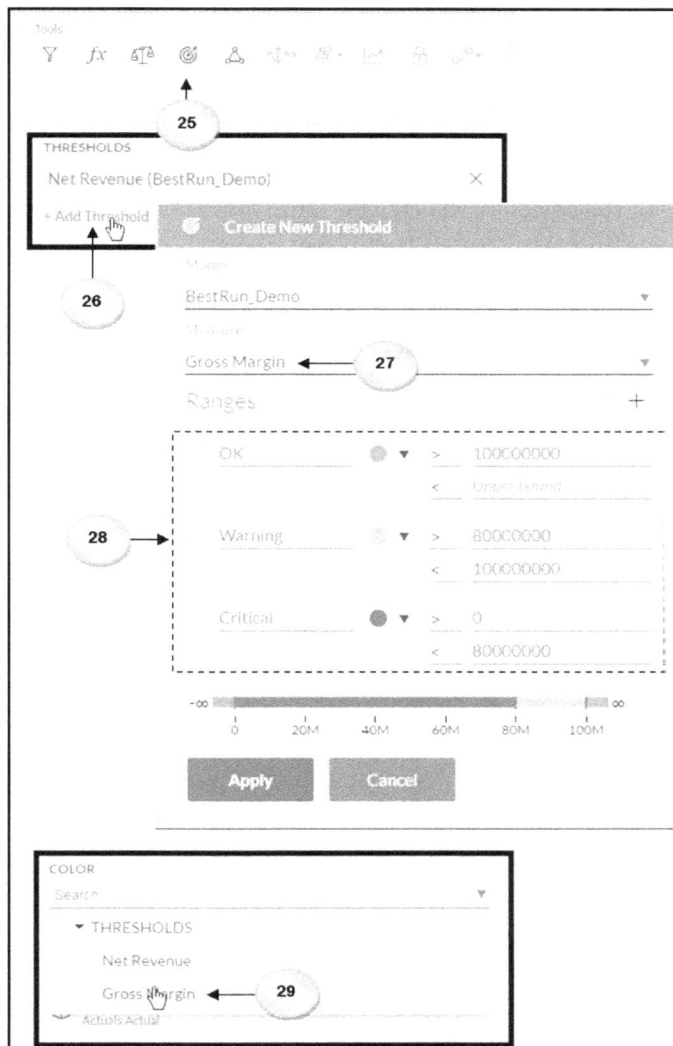

Styling tiles

You can style the appearance of a story page tile by changing fonts, colors, axis scaling on charts, and so on. Input controls, charts, tables, and other tile types have their own **Styling** options. You can change background colors or fonts, create hyperlinks, set alignments, and so on. Although the different tile types have their own styling options, the process to access the styling options is the same for all tiles. In this step, you will change the background and font color of the **Gross Margin** tile.

30. Select the **Gross Margin** tile on the page. To see the properties of an object, you must first select it by clicking on its tile on the page. If it is not visible, click on the **Designer** link (**30**) to open the **Designer** panel, where you can view the properties of the selected object. The same link is used to hide the panel.
31. Select the **Styling** tab. The **Styling** panel displays options available for the selected tile type.
32. Click on the down arrow, and select **background color** for the tile.
33. Select **font color**, and also set font style to **bold** (A).

The output of the **Gross Margin** tile should look like **B** as shown in the following screenshot:

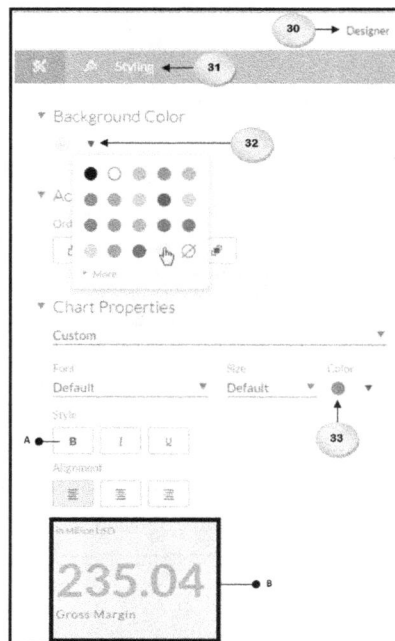

Gross margin percentage numeric point chart

This is the third **Numeric Point** chart that will show the **Gross Margin** percentage. The chart will be based on a calculated measure that will be assessed using an **Account** measure from the model and the **Net Revenue** calculated measure, which was created in a previous exercise. To render the derived value in an appropriate format, you will scale this calculated measure as percentage.

34. Click on the Chart icon to add a new chart to the page.
35. Once again, select the **Numeric Point** option.
36. Click on the **Add Measure** link, and then select **Click to Create a New Calculation** link:

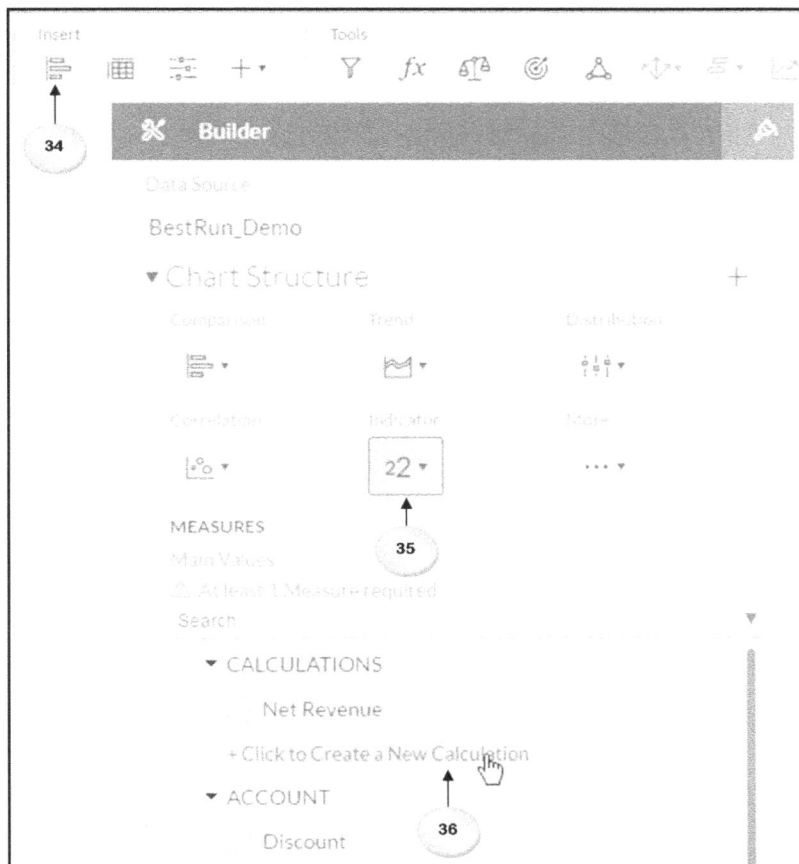

Create a calculated measure - Gross Margin %

In this example, you will create another **Calculated Measure** named Gross Margin %, which is derived using the **Gross Margin** measure divided by the **Net Revenue** calculated measure. Here are the steps:

37. Select **Calculated Measure** from the **Type** drop-down list.
38. Type Gross Margin % for the measure **Name**.
39. In the **Edit Formula** area, enter the left square bracket [, and select **Gross Margin** from the list of measures.
40. In the **Formula Functions** list, expand the **OPERATORS** list, and select the **division** (/) operator. The division operator will be placed just after the **Gross Margin** measure.
41. Press *Shift+3* keys to enter the # symbol. This will present a list of calculated measures. Select the **Net Revenue** measure, which is the only calculated measure available.

Click on the **FORMAT** button to validate the formula, and click on **OK** to close the **Calculation Editor** dialog box:

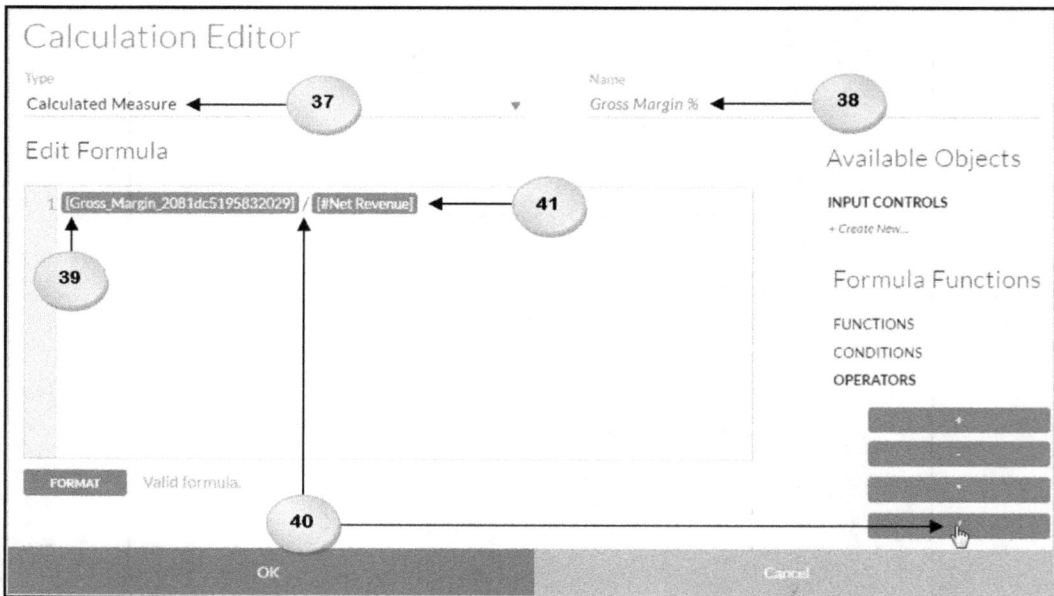

Formatting a measure

After creating the `Gross Margin %` calculated measure, you will format the result of this calculation:

42. Open the **Formatting** window for the calculation by clicking on the ellipsis icon in the **Builder** tab and selecting **Format** from the menu.

43. In the **Formatting** window, you can set the scale, decimal places, and unit. For this example, set **Scale** to **Percentage**, **Decimal Places** to 2, and **Unit** to %. Click on **OK** after setting these parameters:

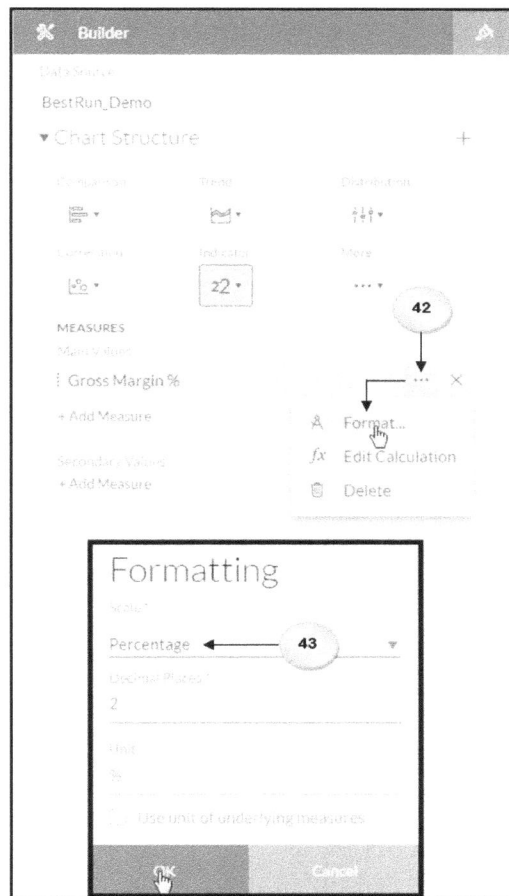

44. Click on the Conditional Formatting icon to add a threshold for the `Gross Margin %` measure.

45. Click on the **Add Threshold** link. As you can see, the two thresholds you created earlier are also visible in the **Conditional Formatting** panel.

46. Set the three ranges according to this illustration.

47. Select the `Gross Margin %` threshold in the **Color** section, and observe the change in the chart:

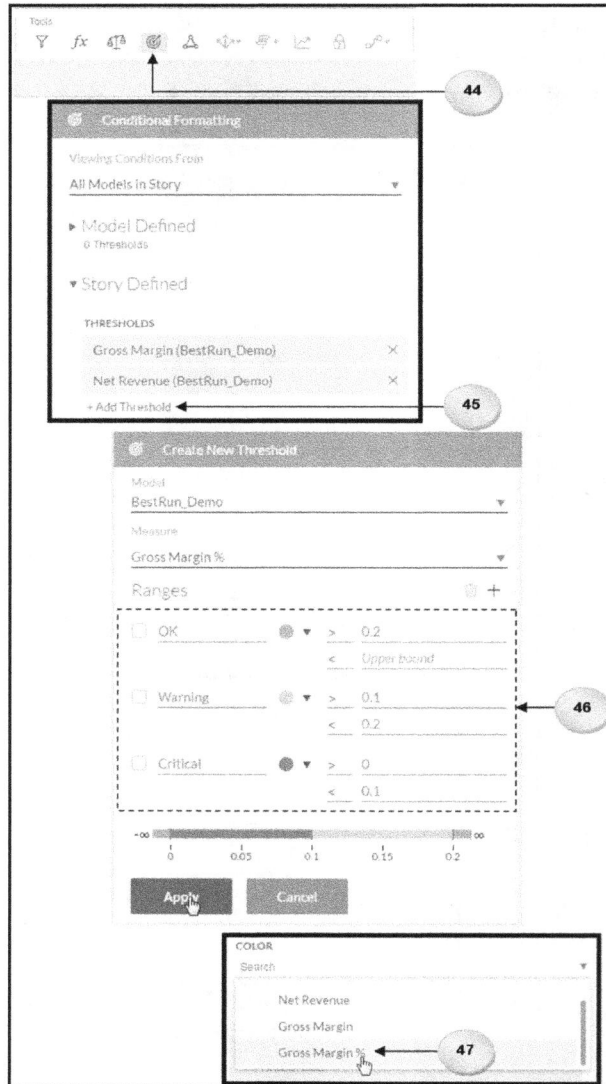

Viewing calculated measures in data view

At any time, when you're working on a story, you can select the arrow under **Data View** (**A**) to switch between the explorer and your story pages. For now, click on this arrow to hide the story page and show the data view panel.

> Note that the two measures **Net Revenue** and `Gross Margin %` (**B**) you created in the previous exercises have been added to the measures list.

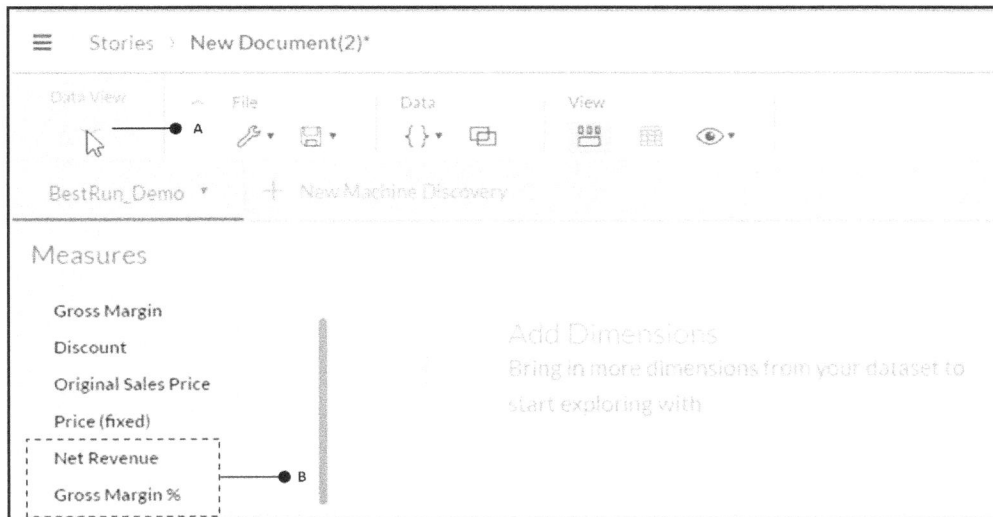

Presenting data with a line chart in a story

In this example, you will learn how to use a line chart that shows a trend in the data values, especially for dimensions that are time-based, such as year or the progression of your data and possible patterns.

48. Click on the Chart icon to insert a blank chart.
49. Select the **line chart** option from the trend list.
50. Select **Gross Margin** as the measure for this chart.
51. Add the **Date** dimension from the **Dimensions** section.

52. After adding the **Date** dimension, click on the filter icon, and then select **Filter by Member** from its menu:

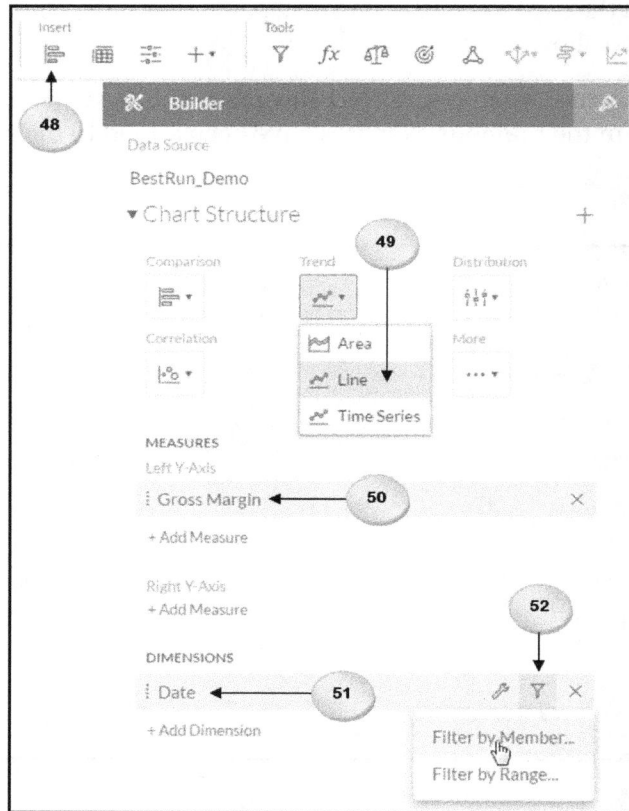

Applying filters to the time dimension

In SAP Analytics cloud, you can apply filters to your story and page to narrow down the scope of your analysis. In addition to these filters, you can add filters to individual dimensions that appear on your charts. For this example, you are going to add a filter to the date-time dimension that you added to your chart in the previous step. You are provided with a couple of options for applying filters on the time dimension:

- **Filter by Member**: This option is essentially the same as the standard filter with checkboxes to select or exclude individual members of the hierarchy.

- **Filter by Range**: Using this option, you can define time periods based on years, half years, quarters, months, weeks, or days (depending on the time granularity defined in the underlying model) and apply the date range as a filter so that only the details in the selected time period are visible. It is also possible to define multiple-range time filters and apply these together. You could use this, for example, to compare the first two months of the year over a three-year period by defining three separate ranges for months Jan-Feb for each of the three years. When these ranges are applied as a single filter, everything else except the selected periods is filtered out.

53. Expand the root node (**all**), and then expand **2013**. Select all four quarters for this year. As your place check marks in these boxes, your selections appear in the **Selected Members** pane on the right side. Expand **2014**, select all four quarters for this year, and repeat this process for **2015** too:

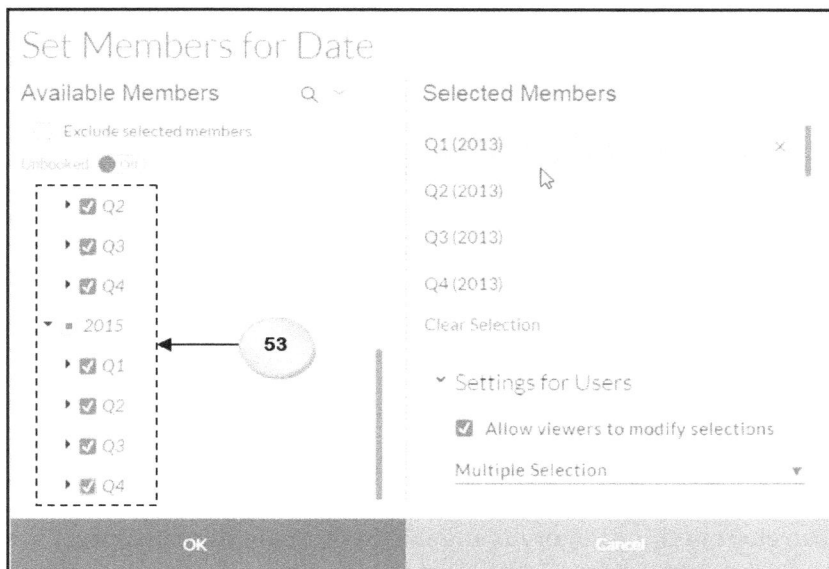

The output of your selections appear on the chart with all the quarters from the selected three years (**A**). You can further refine your data by deselecting years and quarters using the **Set Members** window, illustrated on the previous page. For now, retain these selections and execute the next two steps to style the chart's line and hide some attributes. Note that you will add some **Page Filters** to this story in the next chapter, which will dynamically apply the selected filters on all page objects simultaneously.

54. Click on the chart line. In **Designer,** click on the **Styling** tab, and pick a color for the chart's line from the **Fill Color** palette.

55. Uncheck **Subtitle, Chart Details, Legend, Data Labels,** and **Y-Axis Labels** to remove these chart attributes:

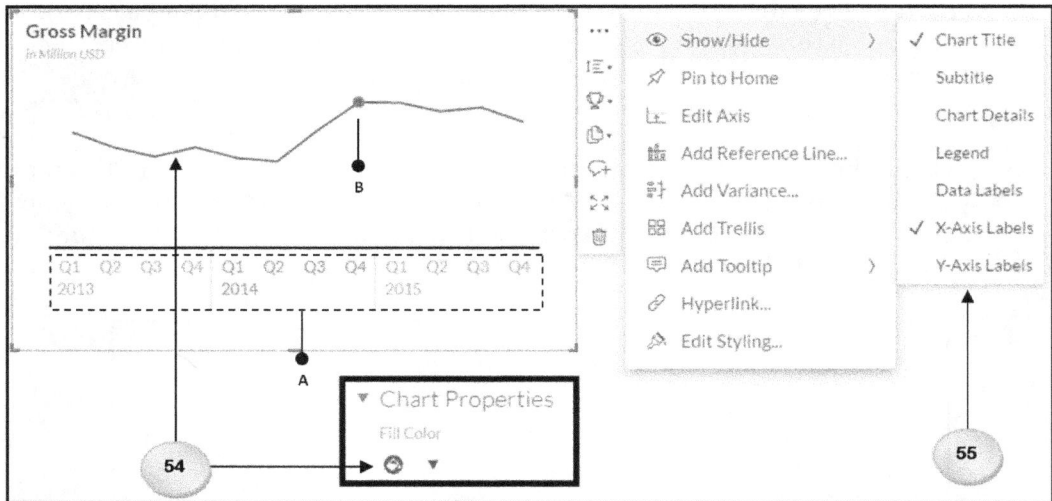

The line chart, as illustrated in the preceding screenshot, exhibits the gross margin trends in the quarters of three different years. According to this chart, the fourth quarter in 2014 (**B**) has the highest gross margin.

Creating a bar chart

The charts listed under the **Comparison** category let you compare the differences between values and are also used to show a simple comparison of categorical divisions of measures. The **Bar/Column** chart in this category is suitable to compare the differences in sales revenue by product, region, or for short time periods, such as a year or quarters. The bar chart you are creating in this exercise will show the gross margin percentage for each product by state.

56. Create a new chart using the Insert | Chart icon on the toolbar. Then, select the **Bar/Column** option from the **Comparison** category.

57. Select the calculated measure Gross Margin % as the measure for this chart.

58. Select **Product** as **Dimensions**.
59. Select the **Location** dimension in the **Color** section, which will enable analysis by state as well as by city:

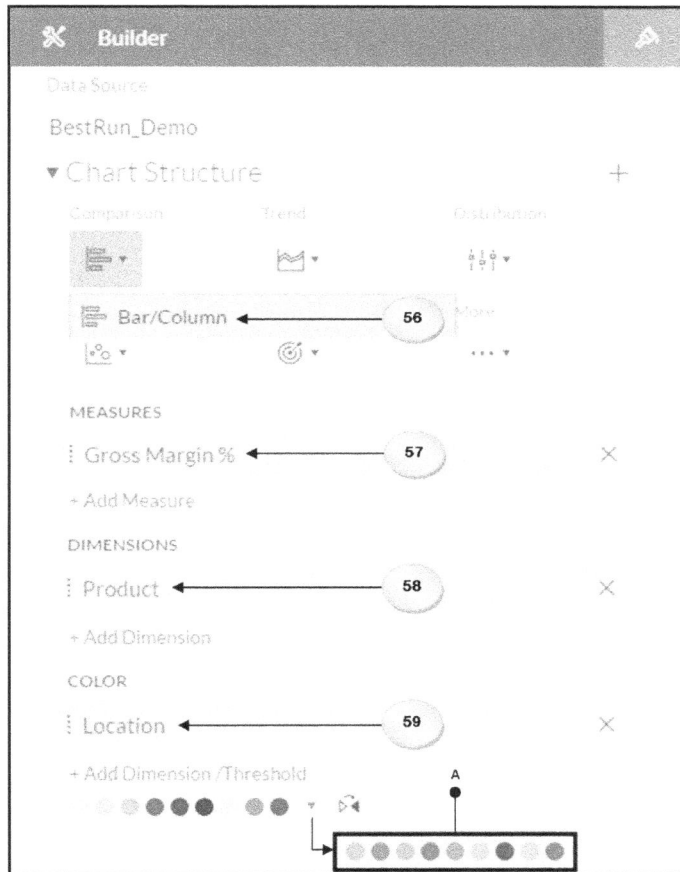

By selecting a dimension in the **Color** section, you break the data down further by color for the selected dimension. If desired, click on the small down arrow to select a different color scheme (**A**). The selected scheme will show each state's data in a different color. To replicate this, please proceed as per the following steps:

60. Click on the existing chart title, and replace it with the one illustrated here to describe the purpose of this chart. In this chart, the data is segregated by product categories, and each category shows the gross margin percentage for each state in a different color. Note that there are four product categories and three state's data in the **BestRun** model.

61. Click on an empty area in the chart (**A**) to see the chart's styling properties in the **Styling** tab. Change the chart's title color, and make it bold-faced by selecting **Chart Title** from the **Text Selection** list, choose a color, and make it bold:

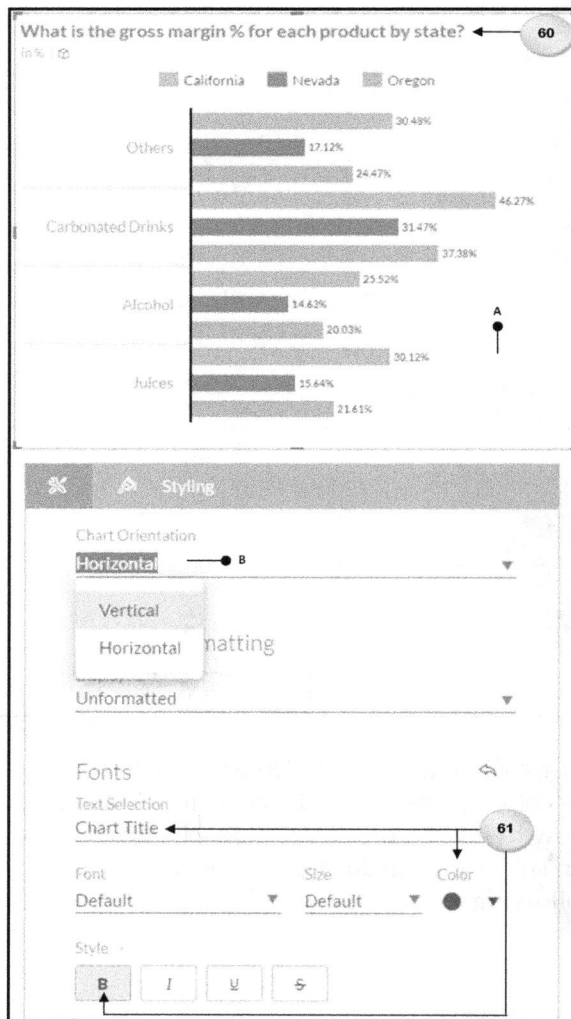

You can also change the orientation of a chart by selecting the **Vertical** option from the **Chart Orientation** list (**B**). For this example, keep the **Horizontal** orientation.

Drilling up and down in a chart

The initial view of this chart provides a high-level overview of the gross margin percentage for each product category by state:

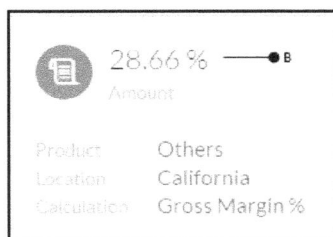

For example, if you mouse over the bar representing **California** in the **Others** product category (**A**), the tooltip (**B**) shows that the gross margin percentage is **28.66%** for this category in **California**. For **Nevada**, it is **16.19%**, and for Oregon, it is **21.07%**:

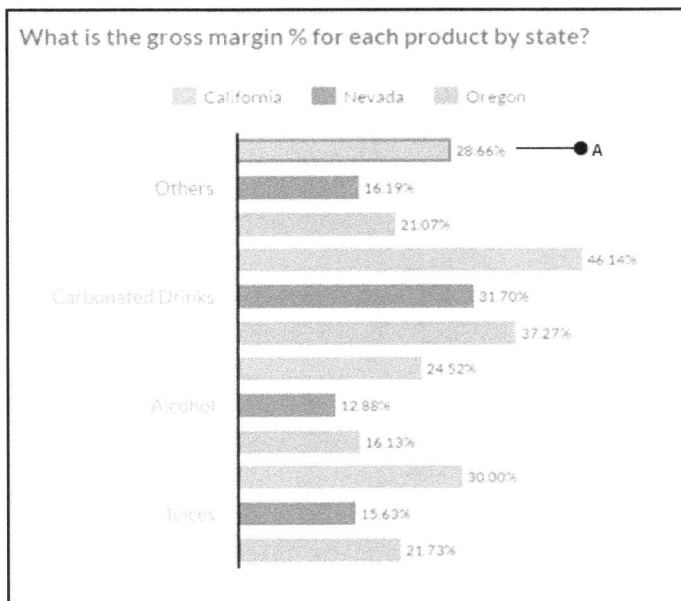

Click on the **Others** link(**C**). A small toolbar will appear. Click on the drill-down link (**D**) in the toolbar. You will drill into details of the **Others** product category, where you can analyze contribution of each product in this category in all three states, as depicted in the lower chart (**E**):

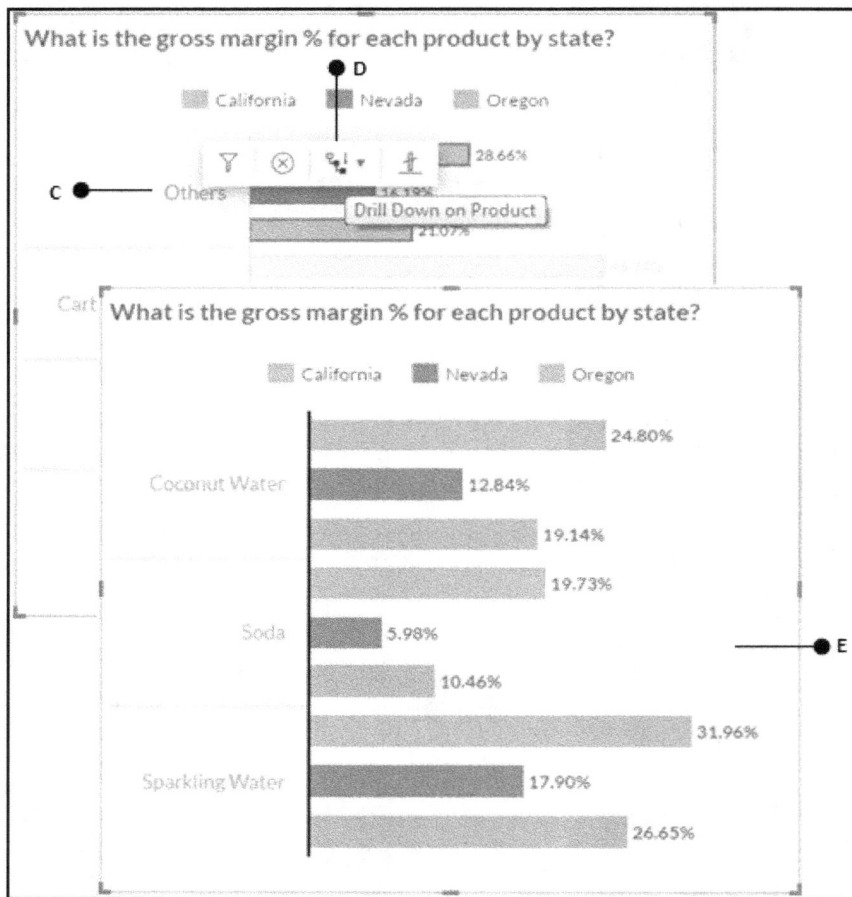

If hierarchical dimensions are included in a chart, you can drill up or down through dimensions to explore the data at different levels. In the current scenaric, you selected the product dimension, which is a hierarchical dimension comprising categories and products. So, you can drill up and down in this chart to analyze data at different levels. Note that if the chart contains more than one hierarchical dimension, you can select which dimension to drill into.

Click on any product link (**F**), bar in the chart (**G**), or state legend (**H**) to see the small toolbar. In the toolbar, click the drill down icon (**I**). You will drill down further on the location level, where you can analyze the gross margin percentage of individual products by cities, as illustrated in the following screenshot:

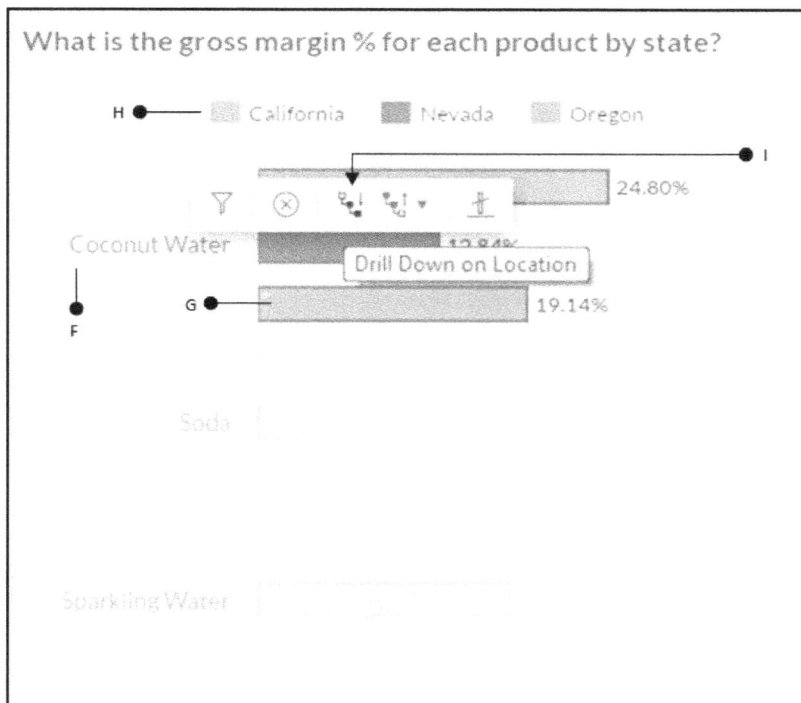

Click on any product link, chart bar, or city legend to see the small toolbar again. Click on the drill up icon (**J**) to move back to the high-level view:

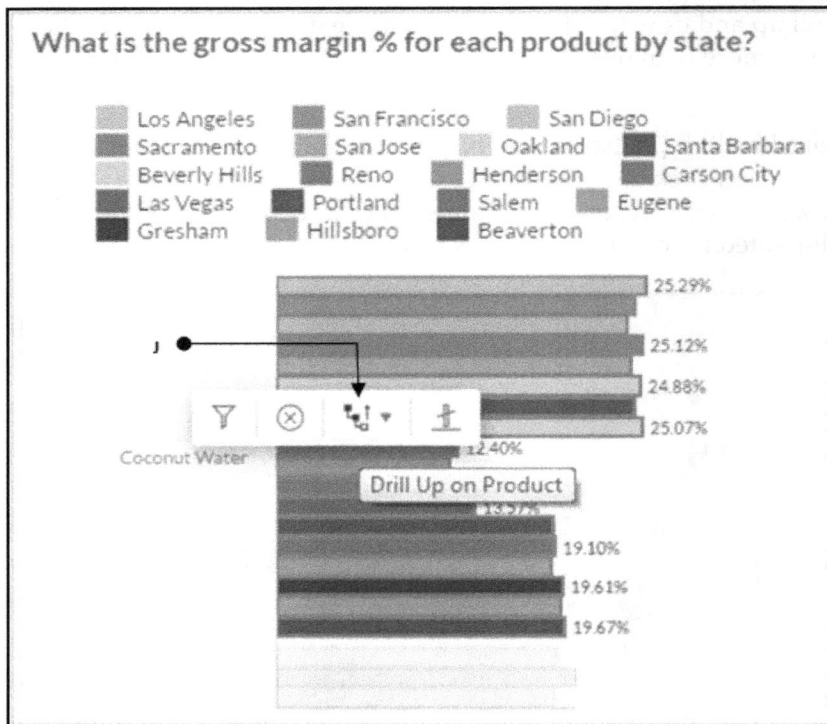

Creating a stacked Bar/Column chart

The stacked column chart is located under the **Comparison** category. You use this chart to show different category values on top of each other. It also enables you to compare the totals. In the following stacked chart, we have the product categories revenue as the column values on top of each other and the date as the dimension, which enables us to compare each year's net revenue. The **Stacked Bar/Column** chart is normally used to represent at least three series of data, where each series is represented by a color stacked in a single bar (for example, sales for 2013, 2014, and 2015).

62. Insert a new chart, and this time, select the **Stacked Bar/Column** option from the **Comparison** category.
63. Select the calculated measure **Net Revenue** as the measure for this chart.

64. Select **Date** as **Dimension**.

65. Select the **Product** dimension in the **Color** section, which will enable product sales analysis by date:

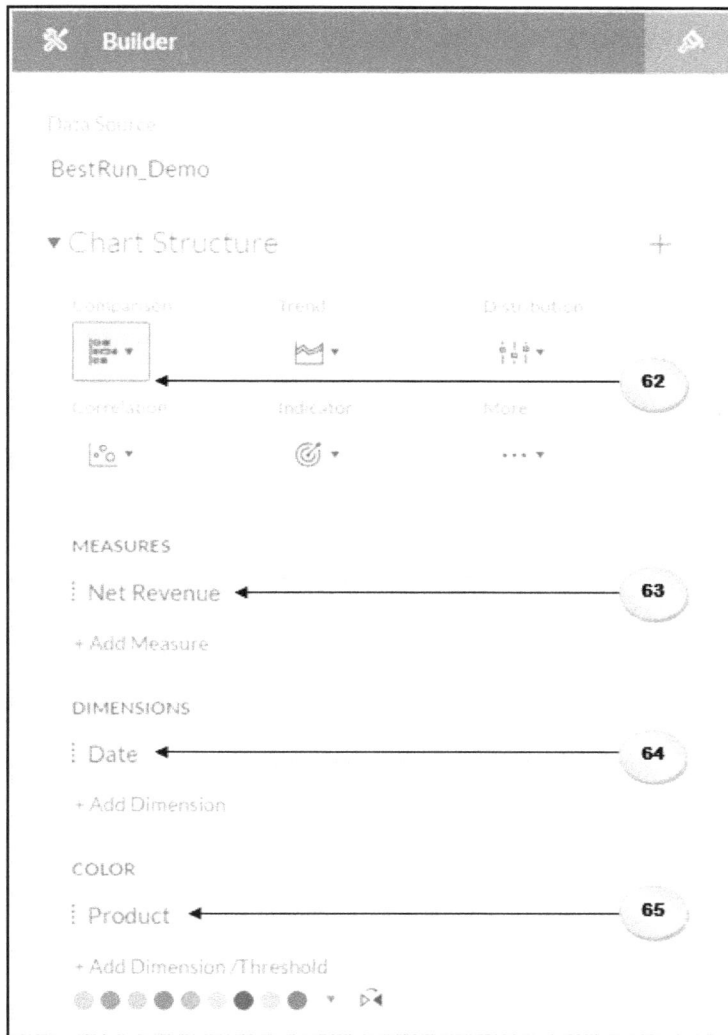

This is the initial output of the chart, where each product category is stacked on top of each other. This is a high-level overview of products sales for all three years. Click on the **all** link (**A**), and then on click the drill-down icon to see the output illustrated on subsequent pages:

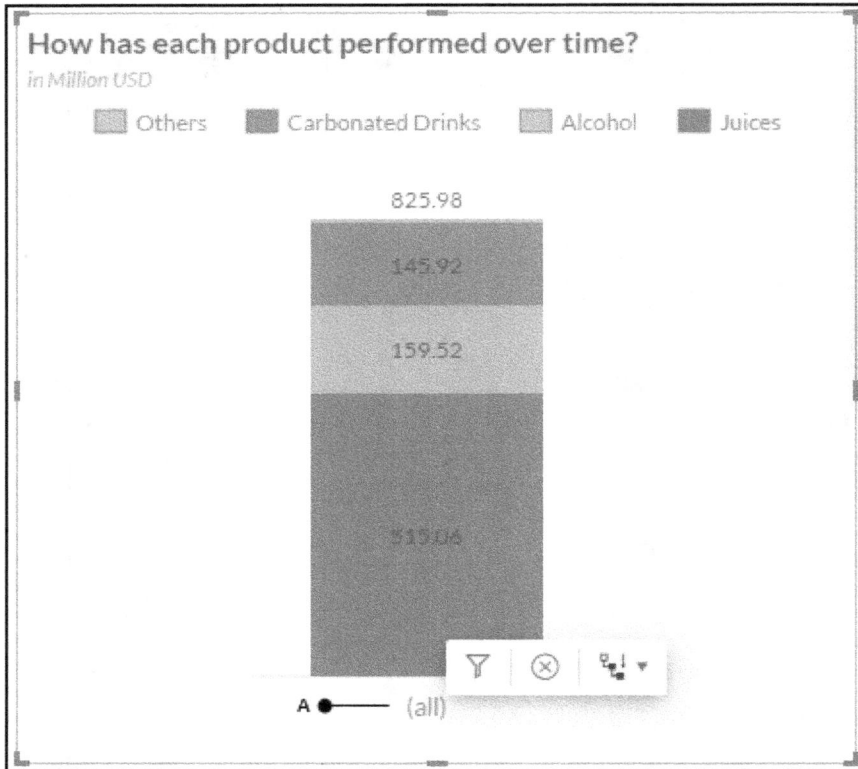

The second view of this chart displays product sales by year. The revenue figure for **Carbonated Drinks** in the previous view was 145.92M. The breakup (**B**) of that figure is presented in this view. Click on the 2013 link (**C**) in this view to drill down further:

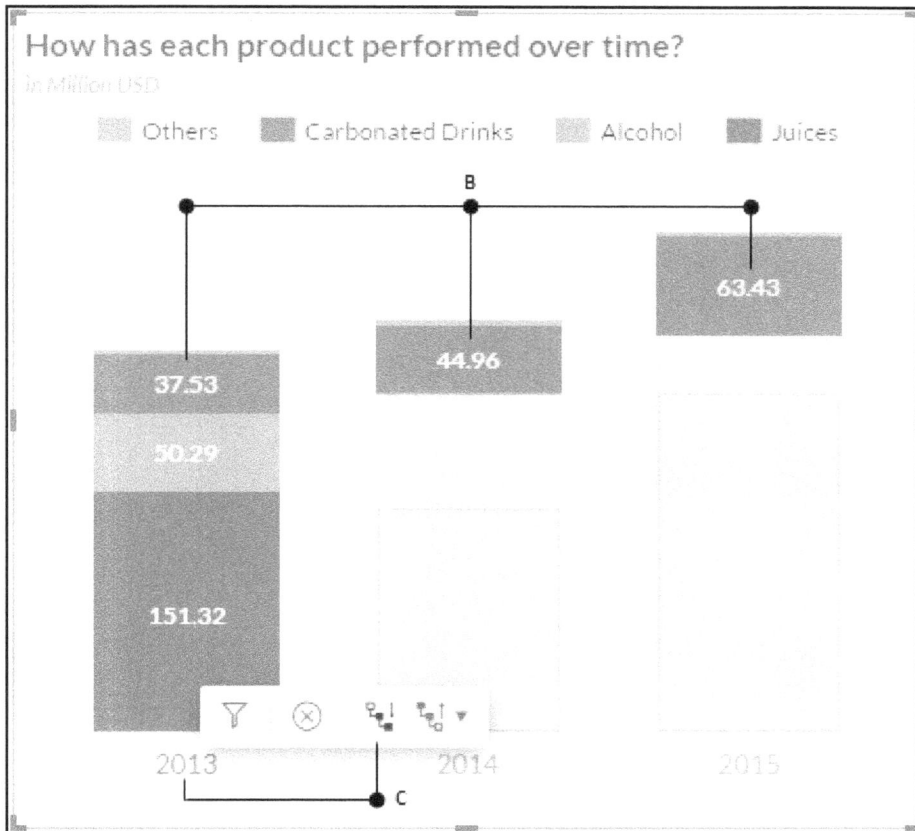

Now you will get the four-quarter view for the year 2013. The breakup of the revenue amount (37.53M) shown in the previous view is displayed here for **Carbonated Drinks**. Click on the **Q4** link (**D**) to drill down even further:

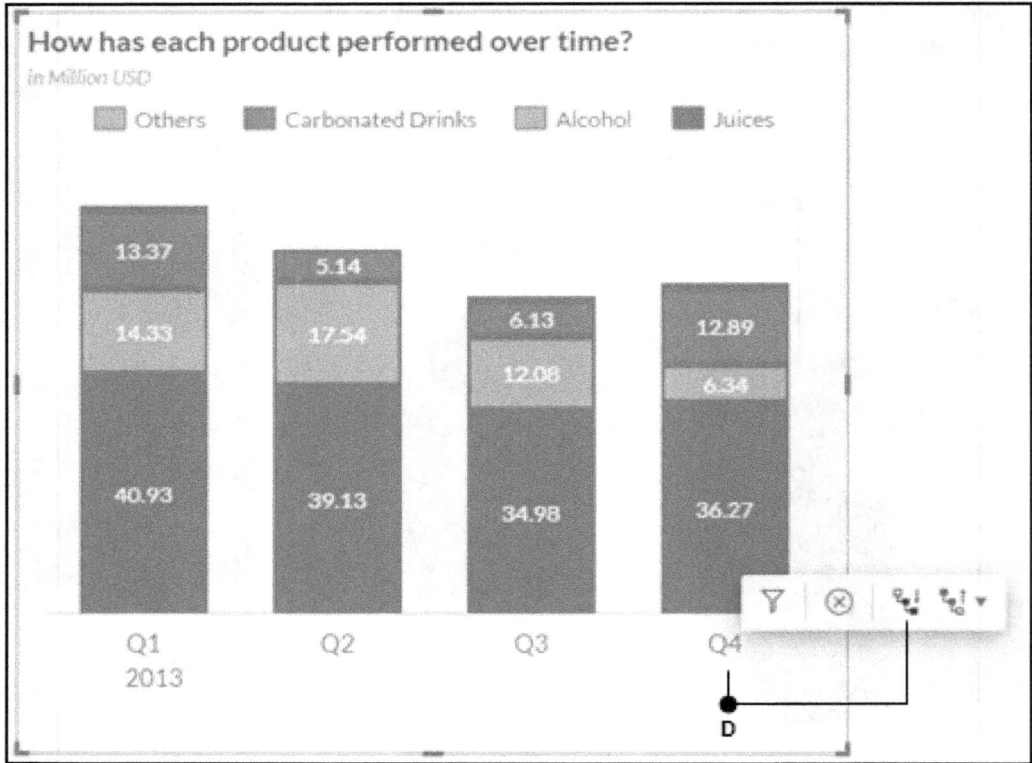

In the following view, the four-quarter revenue data for 2013 is further bifurcated into months, and the same 37.53M figure is fragmented under each month:

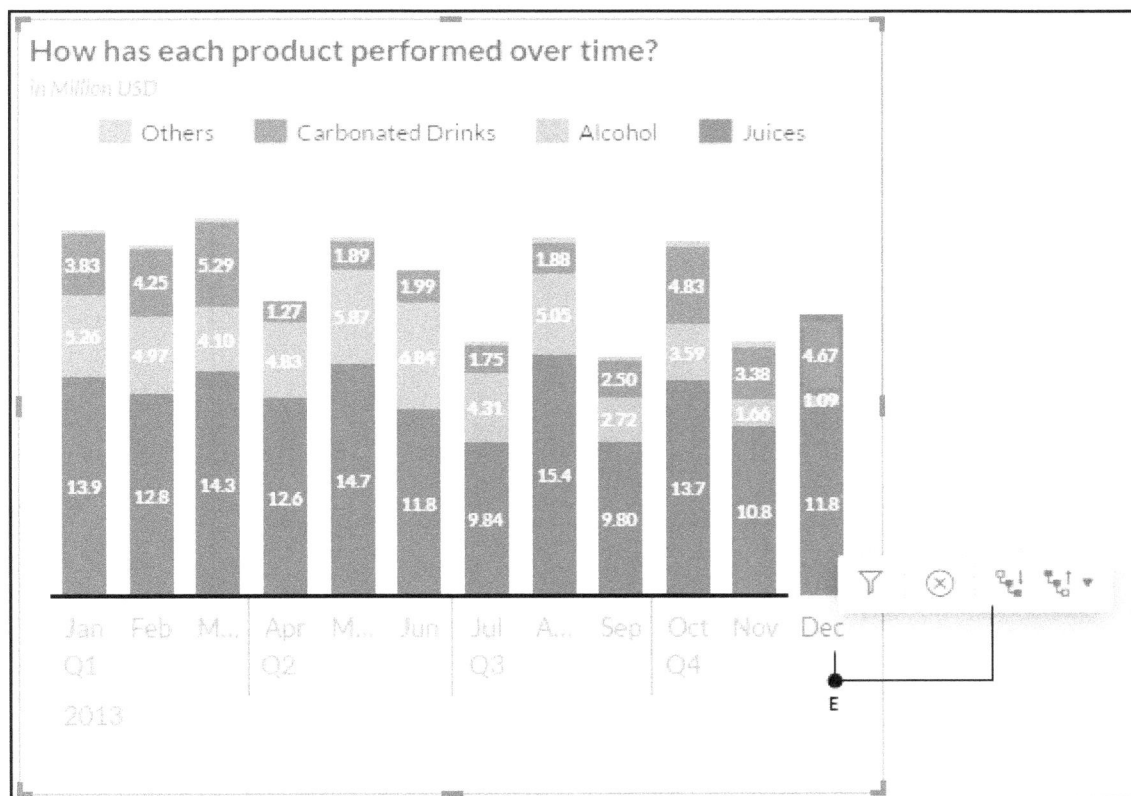

Click on the December link (**E**) and drill down to get the bottom level view of this chart, as illustrated in the lower view, which is the final view, where you can see revenue figures for all the products irrespective of categories:

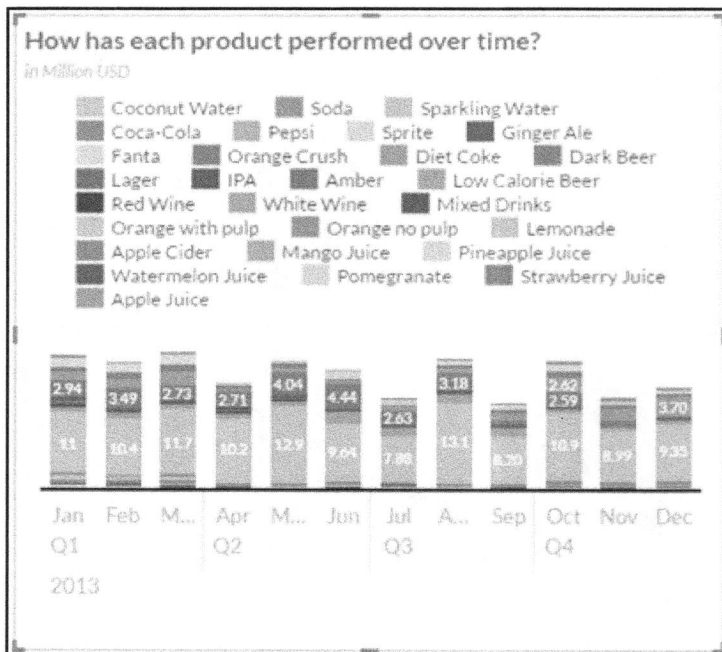

Creating calculated and restricted measures with input control

You went through the process of creating some calculated measures in the previous exercises through the **Calculation Editor** interface. In this exercise, you will create both the **Calculated** and **Restricted Measures** with **Input Control**. By adding the **Restricted Measures** to your chart or table, you can use only selected values in a measure that helps you compare one value to a set of others. Using the input controls, you define some values that act as variables in your **Calculated Measures**. By selecting these values in an input control, a user can influence the result of a calculation without modifying the underlying data or formula. For example, when you add a list of predefined values for an input control, the users can select different values from this list to see the impact on their canvases.

Let's create a chart to get some hands-on exposure. In this example, you will create a chart that will display sales for the four product categories you have been using so far. First, you will add a calculated measure with an input control to the chart to visualize the result of incremented sales using different values. Then, a **Restricted** Measure will be added to restrict the result to the **California** state only.

66. Create a new chart using the Insert | Chart icon on the toolbar. Then, select the **Bar/Column** option from the **Comparison** category.
67. Select **Original Sales Price** from the **Account** dimension list as the measure for this chart.
68. Select **Product** as its **Dimension**:

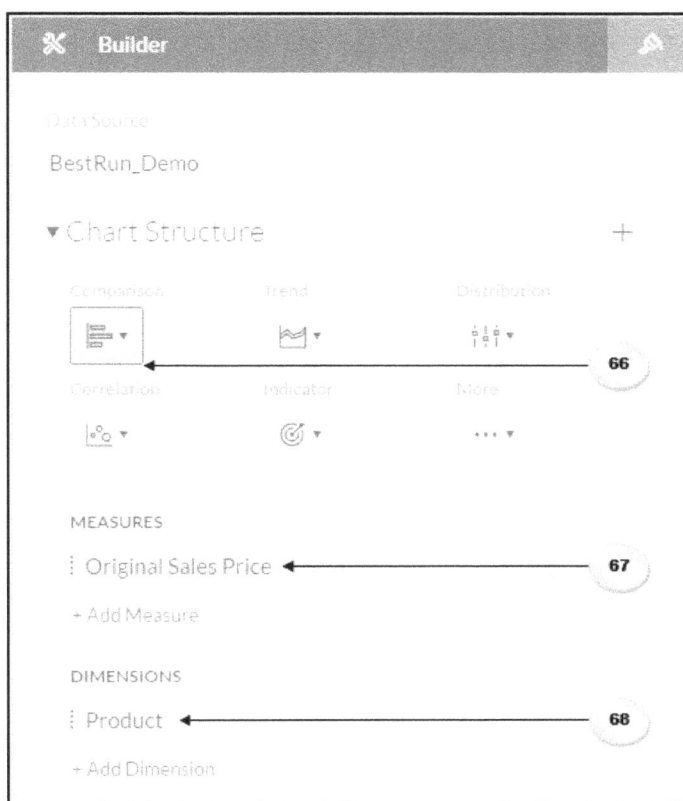

Creating Calculated Measure and input control

69. In the **Builder** panel, click on the **Add Measure** link under the **Measures** section, and select **Click to Create a New Calculation**. In the **Calculation Editor** interface, set **Type** to **Calculated Measure (A)** option, and enter **Incremented Sales (B)** for **Name** of this new calculation. Then click on the **Create New** link **(C)** under **INPUT CONTROLS**:

Calculation Editor

Type

Calculated Measure ——● A   ▼

Name

Incremented Sales ——● B

Available Objects

INPUT CONTROLS

+ *Create New...* ——● C

70. On the **Calculation Input Control** screen, enter **Incremental Factor (D)** for the name of this input control. Select the **Static List** option **(E)**. The **Existing Dimension** option allows users to pick from members of a dimension, whereas in the **Static List**, you can add custom values as options for the input control. Since you will define some static values for this input control, you should opt for the second option. In the **Values** section, click on the **Click to Add Values (F)** link.

You will see another dialog box (illustrated in the next screenshot) to enter values for the input control. The values you input in that dialog box will appear in the **Values** section (**G**):

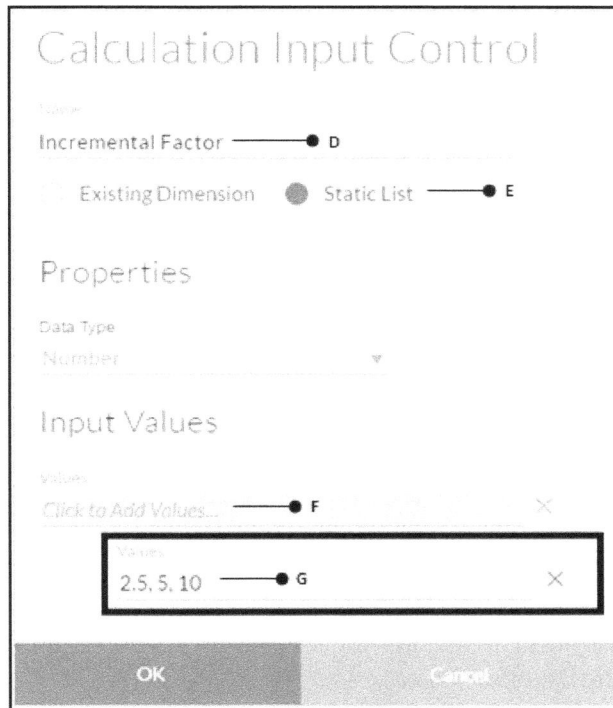

Adding values to input control

71. In the **Custom Members** area, enter comma-separated numeric values, such as 2.5, 5, 10.
72. After providing the values, click on the **Update Selected Members** button to move these values to the **Selected Members** pane on the right side.
73. In the **Settings for Users** section, choose **Single Selection**. Selecting this option will present the three values in a radio group from which you can select a single value to see its impact on the chart.

74. Finally, click on the **Set** button to dismiss this dialog box:

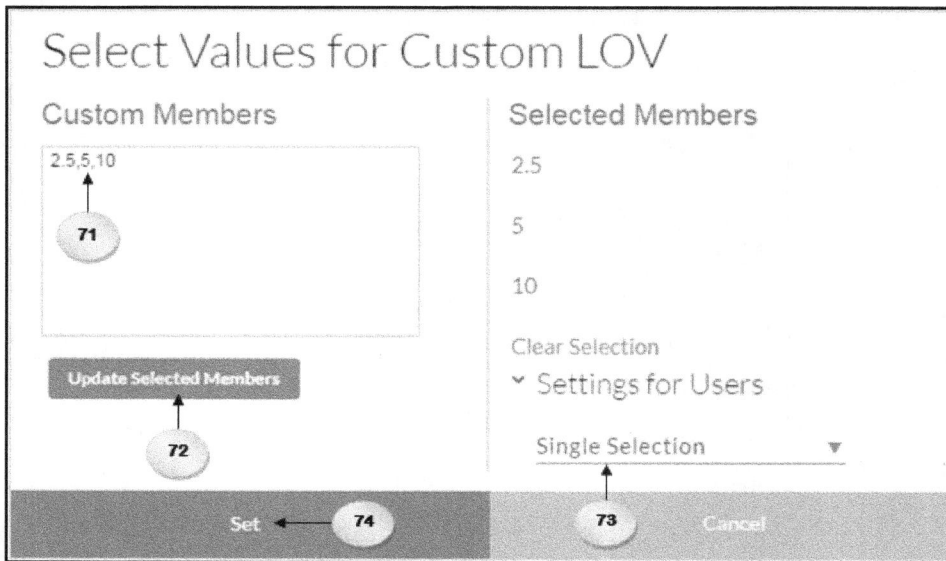

When you get back to the **Calculation Editor** interface, select **Input Control** using the following instructions:

75. In the **Edit Formula** area, enter the left square bracket [, and select **Original Sales Price** from the list of measures.

76. In the **Formula Functions** list, expand the **OPERATORS** list, and select the multiplication (*) operator, which will be placed just after the **Original Sales Price** measure.

77. Click on the **Incremental Factor** link under **Input Controls** to add this input control just after the multiplication operator to complete the calculated measure formula:

The chart will be updated with two measures: **Original Sales Price** (**A**) and **Incremented Sales** (**B**). Click on **Incremental Factor Input Control** (**C**) to expand the list. Select a value in the list, and see its impact on the **Incremental Sales** bars (**D**). As you can see from the first view, the sale value for **Carbonated Drinks** (172.82) displays an incremented figure of 432.04 (**D**) when the incremental factor is set to 2.5:

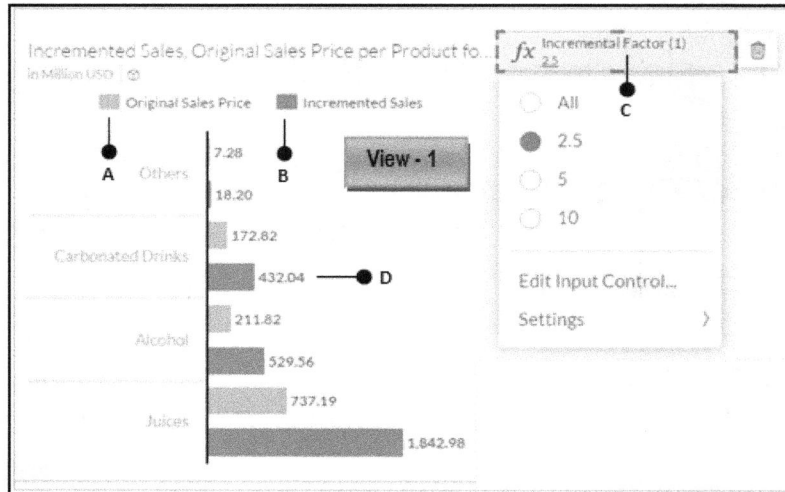

In the second view, the same sales figure is incremented five times and shows 864.08 (**E**):

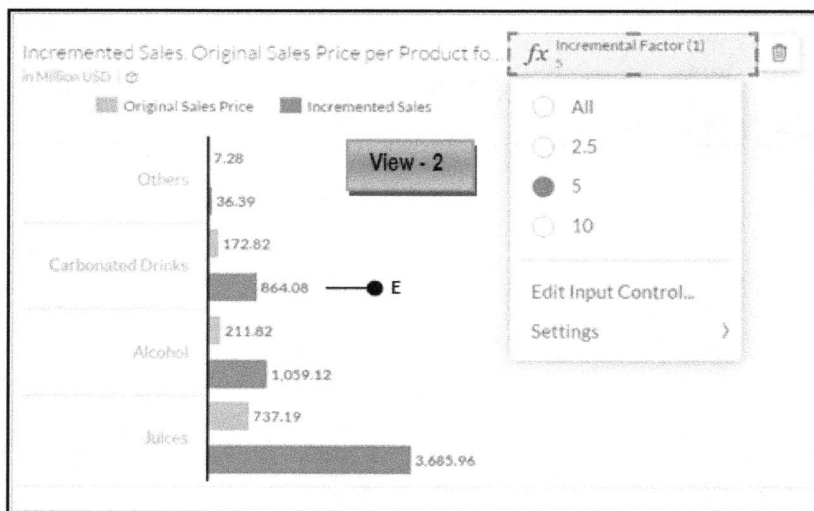

The third view shows the incremented effect when the volume of sales is increased by 10. If you wish to modify the list of values, click on the **Edit Input Control** link (**F**):

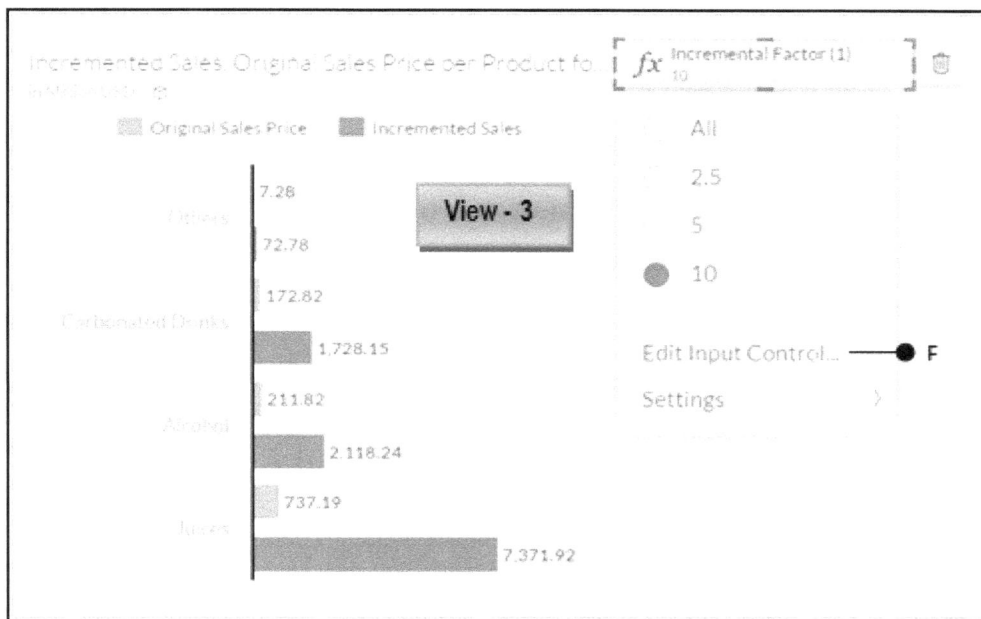

Creating a Restricted Measure

The **Restricted Measure** option acts like a filter. When you create this measure, you restrict your results to some specific measures. In this exercise, you will create a **Restricted Measure** to confine your analysis to a specific state:

78. Click on the **Add Measure** link in the **Builder** tab, and select **Create a New Calculation**. This time, select **Restricted Measure** for the calculation type.
79. Type California for the **Name** measure.
80. Select **Original Sales Price** for **Measure**.
81. Select **Location** for **Dimensions**. Members of the **Location** dimension will appear in the next screen, where you will select a member to restrict your results.

82. From the **Values** or **Input Controls** drop-down list, choose the first option, **Select by Member**. The value(s) you select on the subsequent screen will appear on this list (**A**):

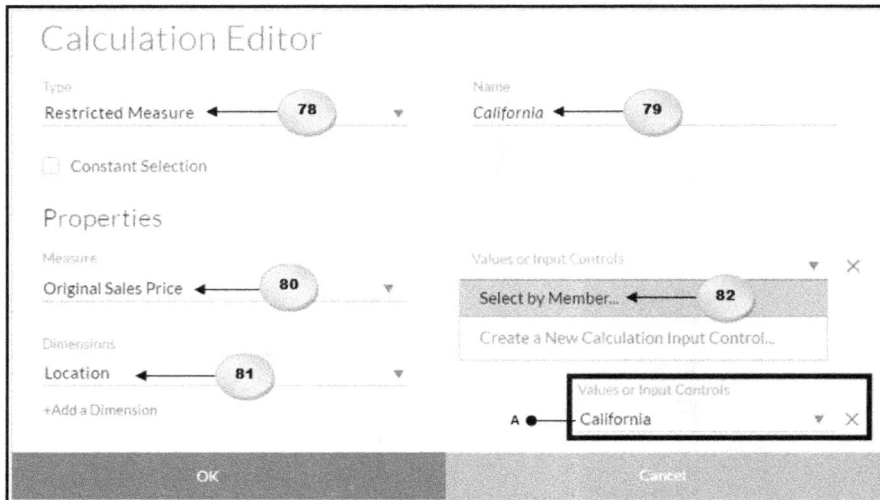

83. When you click on the **Select by Member** option in the previous dialog box, you see this one. Place a check mark in front of **California** to select this member from the **Location** dimension, and click on **OK**. The selected member from the **Location** dimension will appear in the **Values** or **Input Controls** List in the **Calculation Editor** interface, and the same member will be added to the chart as a **Restricted Measure** (**B**) option:

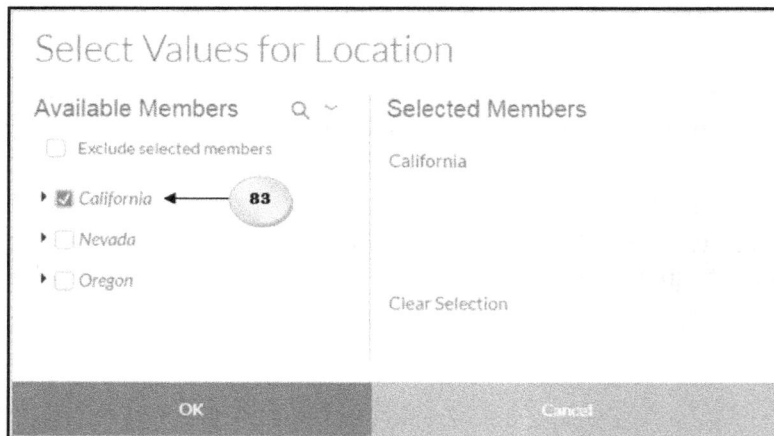

Now you can see three values for each product category--original sales, incremented sales, and actual sales reported in **California**:

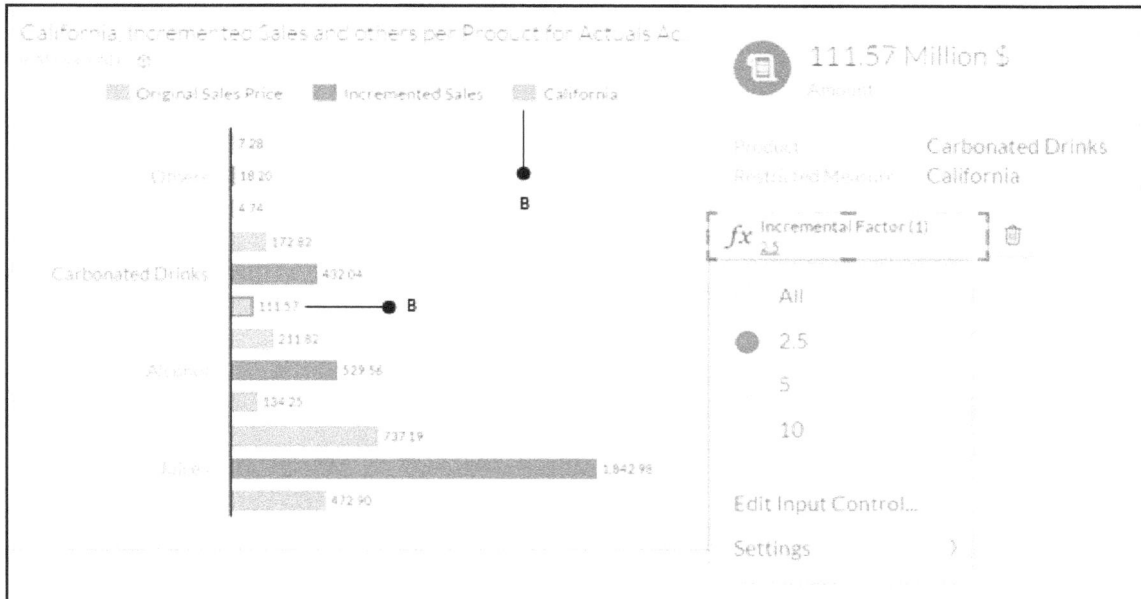

Creating the Difference From measure

The third type of calculation you can create in the **Calculation Editor** interface is **Difference From**. You create this type of calculation to compare values between time periods. In a previous exercise, you created a **Bar** chart to show the gross margin percentage for each product by state. Here, you will use the same chart to create a **Difference From** calculation in the **Calculation Editor** interface to evaluate the difference in gross margin percentage between 2014 and 2015.

To create a new chart from an existing one, you have three options: **Copy, Copy To**, and **Duplicate**. If you select an existing chart and select the **Copy** option (**A**), or press *Ctrl+C*, the chart is placed on the clipboard. Click on the **Paste** option (**B**) or press *Ctrl+V* to recover the clone from the clipboard on your current page. The **Copy To** option (**C**) has some sub-options that let you copy the selected object to a new canvas or to another page in the story. In the current scenario, you will use the **Duplicate** option to create a clone of the selected chart.

84. Click on the chart (as shown in the following screenshot), and select **Duplicate** from the Copy and Paste menu in the toolbar. This action will create a duplicate of the selected chart on the same page:

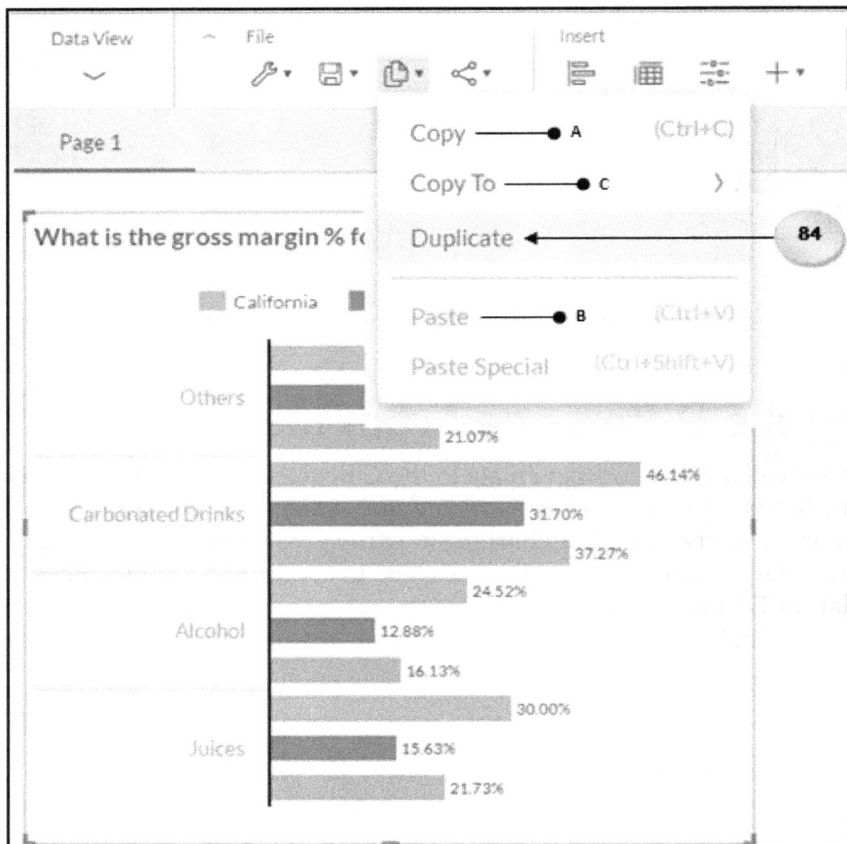

Select the duplicate chart, and open the **Designer** panel.

85. On the **Builder** tab, click on the remove icon under the **Measures** section to remove the `Gross Margin %` measure.

86. After removing the existing measure, click on the **Add Measure** link, and select **Click to Create a New Calculation** to create the new **Difference From** type calculation measure in the **Calculation Editor** interface:

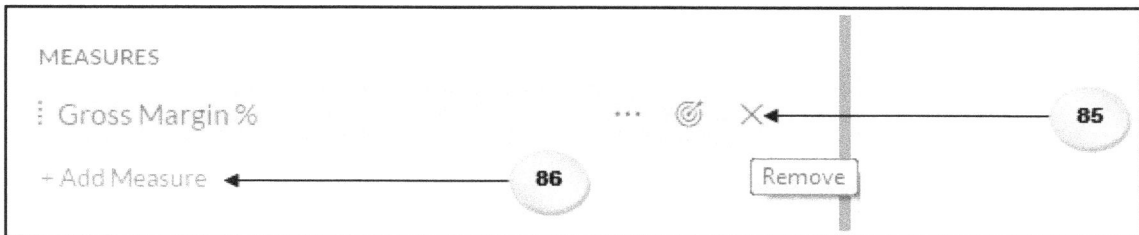

87. In the **Calculation Editor** interface, select **Difference From** for the **Type** of calculation.

88. Type **GM% Change Between 2014-2015** in the **Name** box.

89. In the **Measure** section, choose **Gross Margin**. This is the measure on which the calculation will be based. The **Time Dimension** is already set to the date dimension.

90. For **Current Value** or **Input Control**, choose **Select by Member**, and on the ensuing screen, expand the all node to select 2015. Click on **OK** to close the **Select Values** for the **Date** dialog box. The selected year (2015) will appear in the **Current Value** or **Input Control** box.

91. Select previous from the **Difference From** drop-down list; the other option is **Next**. Here, you can specify a previous period or a later period to compare the time period you selected in **Current Value**.

92. In the **Nth Period** section, you provide a number other than the current or baseline time period that you want to include in the calculation. The value you provide here uses the level of time granularity you chose in the **Current Value** section. So, in the current scenario, one period is a year. Enter 1 in the **Nth Period** section to compare the results from 2015 to those from 2014.

93. Check the **Calculate as Percentage** checkbox to see the results as a percentage.

94. When you check the **Calculate as Percentage** option, you also need to specify whether to divide by the **Current Value** or the **Nth Period Value**. In this case, select **Nth Period Value** to divide the results from 2015 by those for 2014. After providing all these parameters, click on **OK** to close the **Calculation Editor** interface:

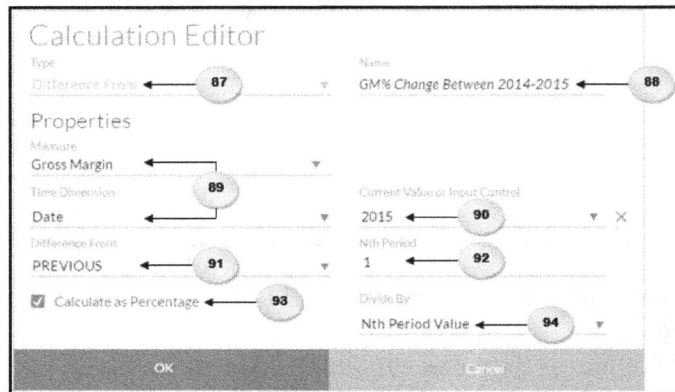

As you can see, the chart now displays the percentage change in the gross margin for each product category, for each state:

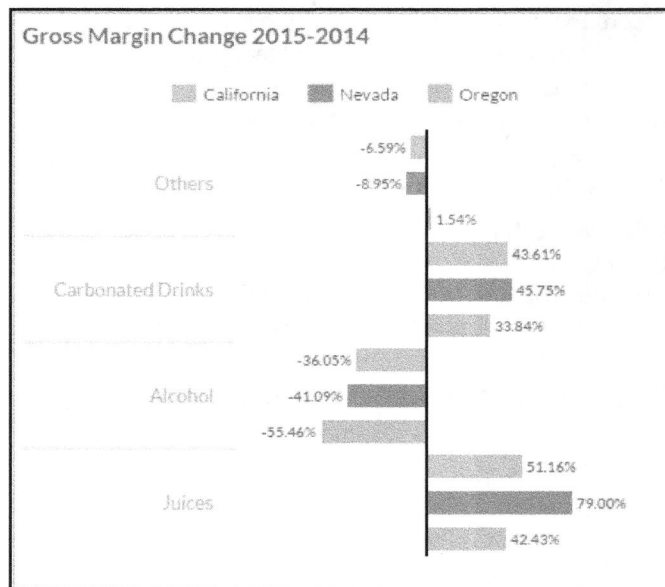

Summary

A story is the most significant component of SAP Analytics Cloud, where you visually analyze your data using different types of objects. In this chapter, you got hands-on exposure to this imperative subject and learned how to populate your story canvases by adding and configuring different types of charts. Here's a brief summary of the topics you went through in this chapter:

- An introduction to and creation of a story
- A brief about the two demo models that you will also utilize in subsequent chapters
- Using Numeric Point charts to display summarized information in bold-faced dynamic numbers
- Learning how to use the Calculation Editor interface to create your own formulas
- Adding thresholds to your charts to present the status of values in different colors
- Styling your charts with the help of options provided in the styling tab
- Using Numeric Point, Line, Bar, and Stacked Bar/Column charts to present data visually
- Applying filters to time dimension to present data for specific years
- Drilling up and down in charts to observe the data at different levels
- Creating a Calculated Measure with Input Controls and seeing how to confine your analysis by adding Restricted Measures.
- Finally, you learned how to create a measure using the Difference From calculation type to compare values between time periods.

In the next chapter, you will learn some more important techniques to present the data using key performance indicators (KPIs) in your story page and adding filters to your page to see specific data. You will also learn how to add a reference line to a chart, add static and dynamic text, shapes, images, hyperlink, and you will be guided to save a story.

5
Extending Stories with KPI, Filters, and Other Handy Objects

In the previous chapter, you created different types of chart to present data graphically. You will continue your efforts on the same story page in this chapter as well. Here, you will create a bullet chart, which is usually added to a story page to monitor an organization's performance via **key performance indicators** (**KPI**). You will also learn how to add page filters to narrow down the scope of your analysis. The two segments are illustrated in the following screenshot.

The bullet chart (**A**) will show the status of the gross margin for each state. **Date Range Filter** (**B**) is a page filter that is added to limit the results of all page charts to the selected period(s).

Similarly, the **Product** (**C**) and **Location** (**D**) page filters will allow you to see the data for specific products and locations.

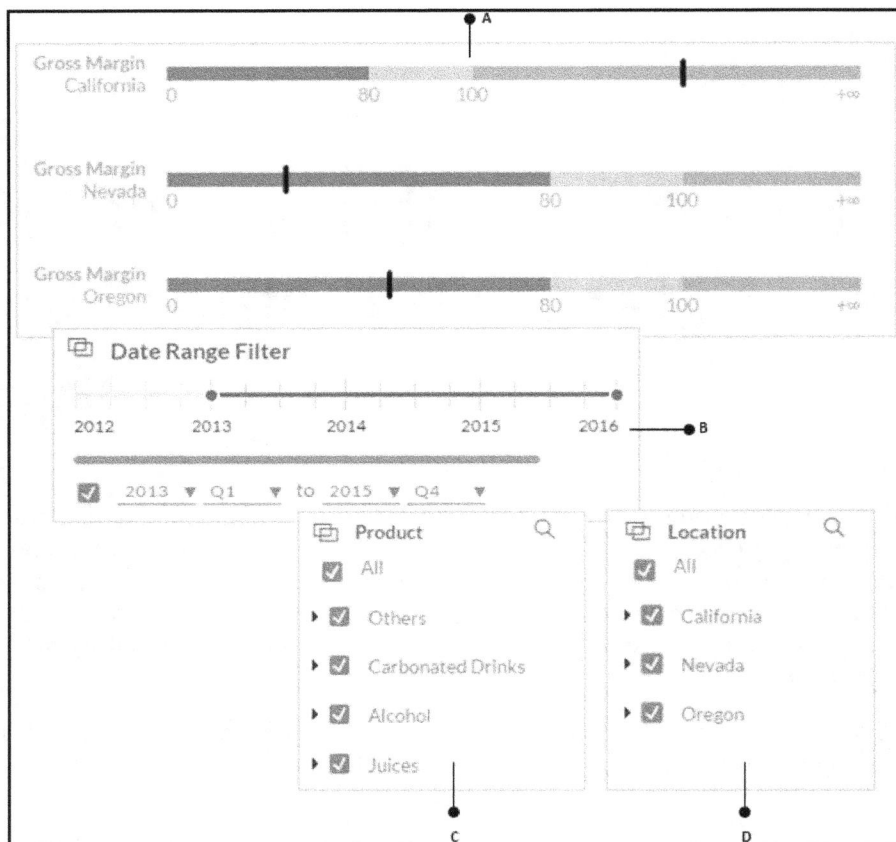

In addition to the aforementioned two story features, you will learn the following:

- Adding a reference line to a chart
- Creating a linked analysis
- Adding story headings via static and dynamic text
- Adding shapes and logos
- Creating hyperlinks
- Examining the data behind a visualization
- Setting story preferences, and more

Key performance indicators (KPIs)

The success of an organization depends on how the organization pursues its objectives. A business objective is an executive statement of direction in support of a corporate strategy. The business objective is a high-level goal, which is quantifiable, measurable, and result-oriented. Larger organizational strategies are evolved through business objectives. To monitor and improve these objectives, organizations use special measurements called **key performance indicators** (**KPIs**). Key performance indicators are the detailed specifications used to track business objectives.

The business objective is translated into a KPI, which enables the organization to measure some aspect of the process against a target that they define. When these targets fail, the concerned authority receives an alert in the notifications center. You create a KPI to evaluate and monitor the performance of objectives. When you create a KPI, you define thresholds to indicate the status of the value. The status is determined by comparing the actual value against the thresholds defined for the KPI and then placing the result in a corresponding range that defines levels of performance status (for example,).

> Each range in a KPI threshold is assigned a different color, which represents its performance status. You can define KPIs by selecting values from members of the **Accounts** dimension, such as **Net Revenue** or **Gross Margin**.

Story and page filters

As mentioned earlier, you add filters to your stories and pages to restrict the scope of your analysis result. In SAP Analytics Cloud, you can create two types of filters: story filters and page filters.

> If you want to apply filters to all charts in a story, use the story filter. The page filter, as the name implies, can be applied to just one page in a story. These filters can be created after adding at least one chart to a story.

If you have related page filters in the same story or page, they have a cascading effect. For example, if you have states and cities filters on a page and you switch the states filter from All to Oregon, the cities filter refreshes to show only cities in the state of Oregon. All other cities are hidden.

In addition to these filters, you can add filters to individual dimensions that appear on your charts. You added such a filter for the date-time dimension in the previous chapter for the gross margin line chart. A separate section is dedicated in this chapter to showcasing this type of filter.

Creating a chart to display key performance indicators

Recall that you created some thresholds in the previous chapter and utilized them in three **Numeric Point** charts. In this exercise, you will use one of the thresholds you defined for the **Gross Margin** measure to present the **Gross Margin** status for the three states using a **Bullet** chart.

As usual, click on the Chart icon on the **Insert** toolbar to create a new chart. On the **Builder** tab, make sure that the **Data Source** field is set to the **BestRun_Demo** model (**A**).

1. Select the **Bullet** option from the **Indicator** section.

2. Set **Measures** to **Gross Margin**.

3. Set **Dimensions** to **Location**.

4. Set **Color** to **Gross Margin**.

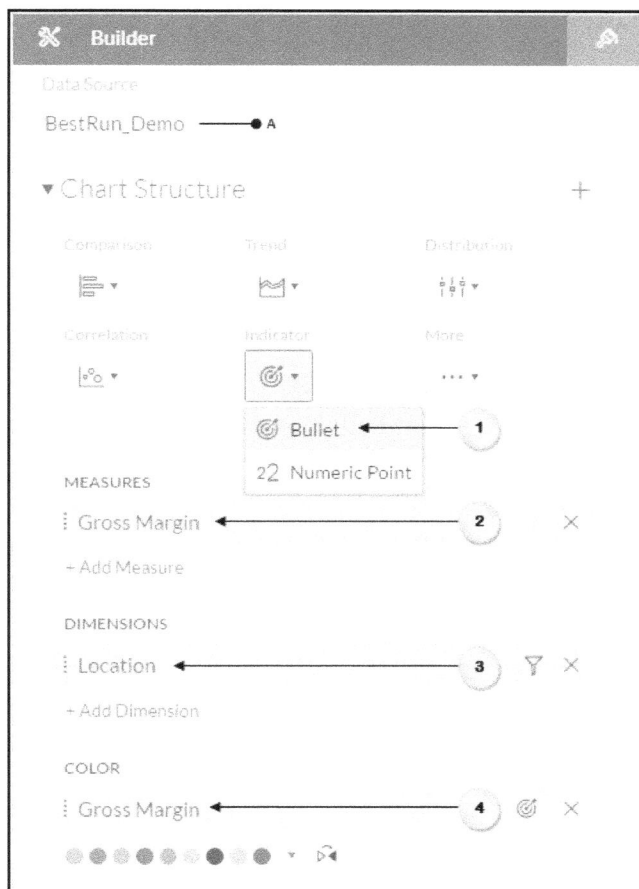

Setting a chart's attributes

The bullet chart, as illustrated in the following screenshot, will appear on the page.

5. Click on the chart to see its toolbar. Click on the More Actions icon (**A**) and select the first option, **Show/Hide** (**B**). In the **Show/Hide** menu, deselect the **Chart Title**, **Subtitle**, and **Chart Details** options (**C**):

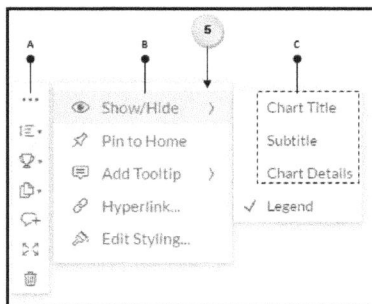

6. On the **Styling** tab, select **All Text** (**A**) from the **Text Selection** list, select a color (**B**) from the **Color** palette, and click on the letter **B** (**C**) to make all the chart text bold. The output of your selections is illustrated in the following screenshot (**D**):

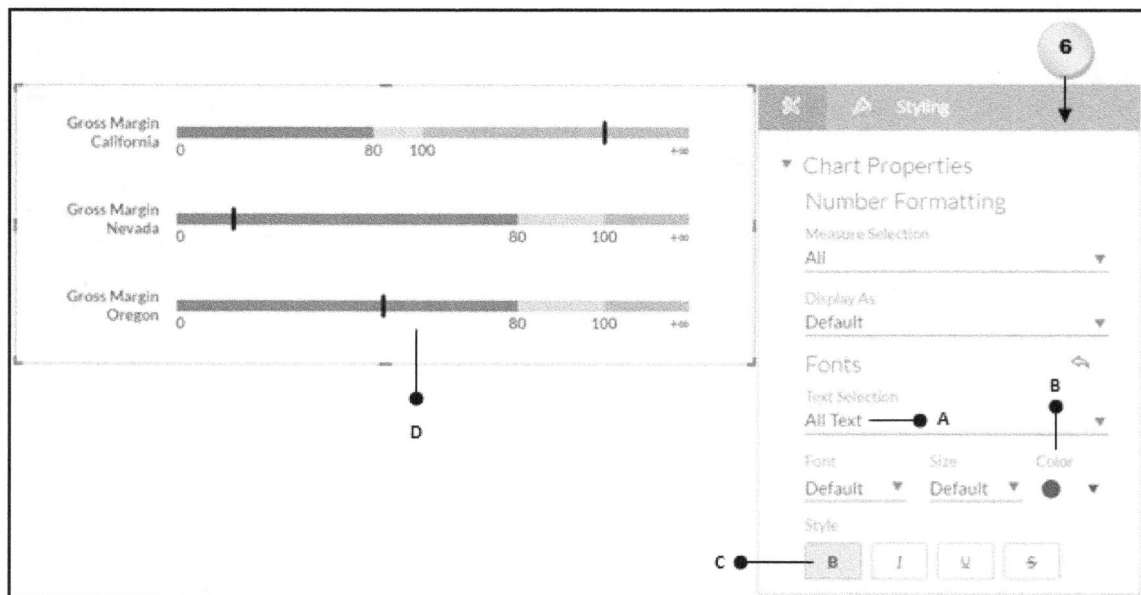

Match the result of these indicators with the thresholds specified for **Gross Margin** (**A**):

A value beyond 100 million is an indication of a good gross margin, and this is what you specified for the **OK** range. As you can see, the gross margin screenshot for **California** is 173.48 million, which is far ahead of the threshold set for the **OK** range. Hence, the performance indicator for this state appears in the green area (**B**), and the tooltip box also displays the **OK** status (**C**):

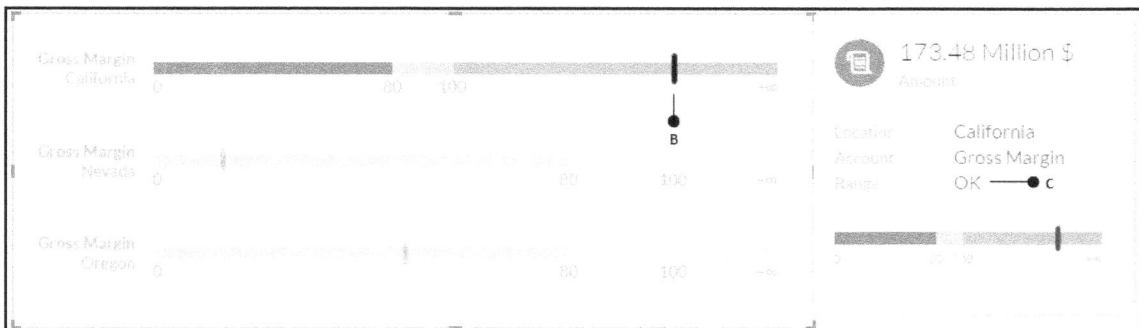

Next, the gross margin values for **Nevada** and **Oregon** are 13.25 million and 48.30 million, which are lower than the 80 million threshold set for the **Critical** state:

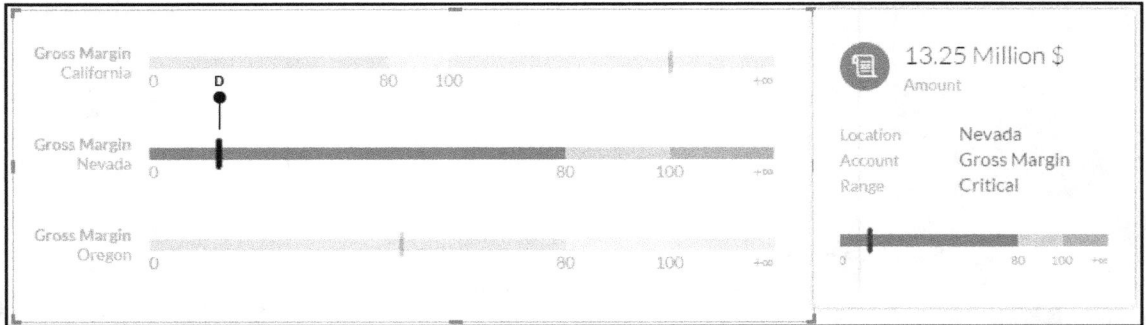

Consequently, the performance indicators for these states appear in the red zone (**D** and **E**):

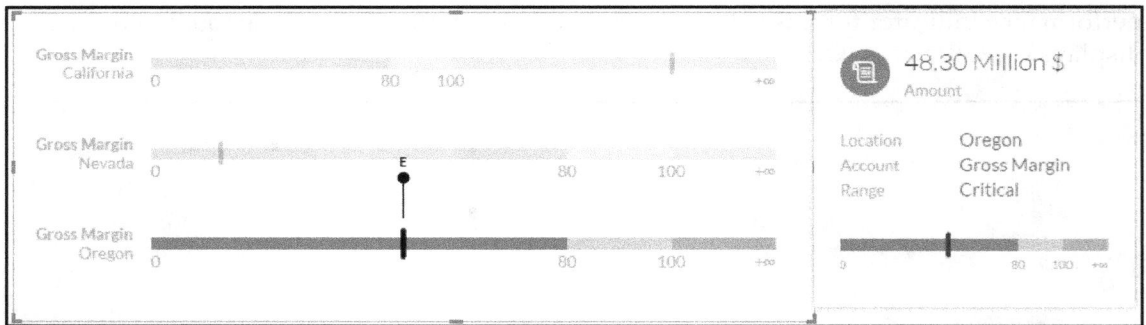

Adding a reference line to a chart

You can define reference lines to show important values on your chart, for example, the average and maximum prices of your products. You can add two types of reference line to some of your charts: **Fixed** and **Dynamic**. Fixed-value reference lines are created with a specific reference value and don't change when you change the data in your chart. For example, when you filter your data, the reference line remains static at the data point where it was before applying the filter.

Dynamic-value reference lines, on the other hand, are updated when filters, ranking, and sorting are applied to the chart. Dynamic-value reference lines can be used with any measure, including story calculation measures. When you add a reference line, you can choose to fill the background area above and below the line with color. Reference lines are maintained when you change the chart type. The chart being created in this example carries a reference line, showing average gross margin by location.

Create a new chart using the **Insert | Chart** option on the toolbar.

7. On the **Builder** tab, select the **Bar/Column** option from the **Comparison** category.

8. Select **Gross Margin** from the **Account** dimension list as the measure for this chart.

9. Select **Location** as the chart's **Dimension**.

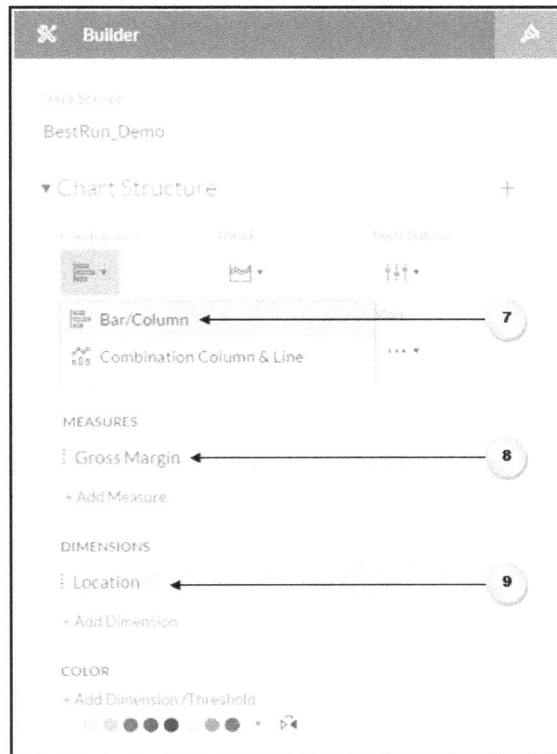

After selecting the **Location** dimension, the chart appears on the page.

10. Click on the More Actions icon.

11. Select **Add Reference Line** in the resulting menu.

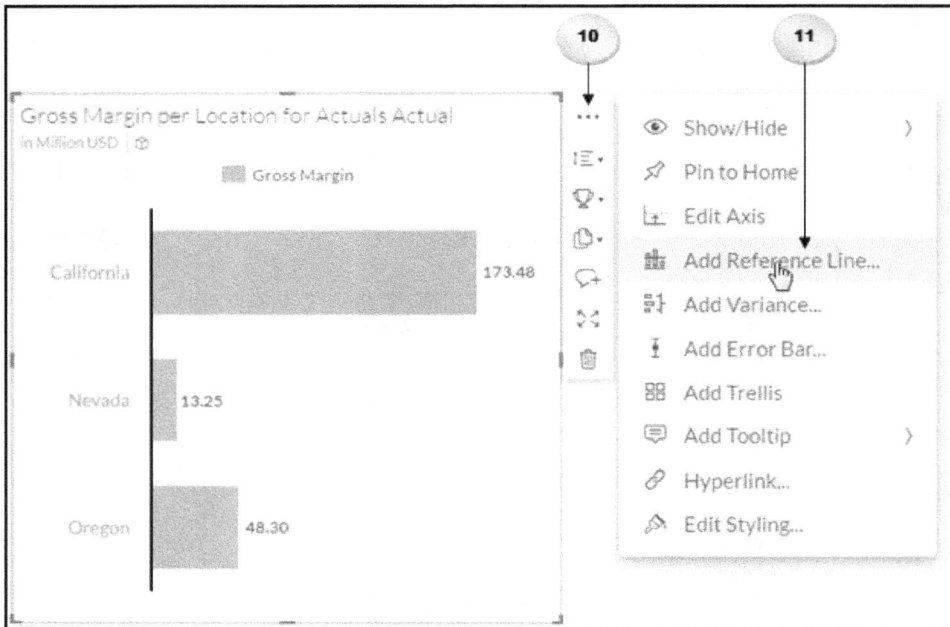

12. On the **Create Reference Line** panel, select the **Fixed** option (**A**), enter **100000000** (100 million) as the target value in the **Value** box (**B**), type **Average** in the **Label** box (**C**), and click on **OK**. The reference line and its label (**D**) appear on the chart. If you rest your mouse pointer over this line, you see the 100 million value in the tooltip (**E**). Now, try to interact with the chart to see whether the reference line takes effect following the changes you make.

You will notice that the fixed reference line remains set to a specific value and doesn't change when you modify the chart (for example, by drilling and applying filters and rankings). Let's evaluate this concept. Click on the **Gross Margin** legend (**F**), and then click on the Drill Down icon (**G**). You are taken down to the **City** level. Note that the fixed reference line didn't change to reflect the new context and has remained static at the 100 million average point (**H**), as shown in the following screenshot:

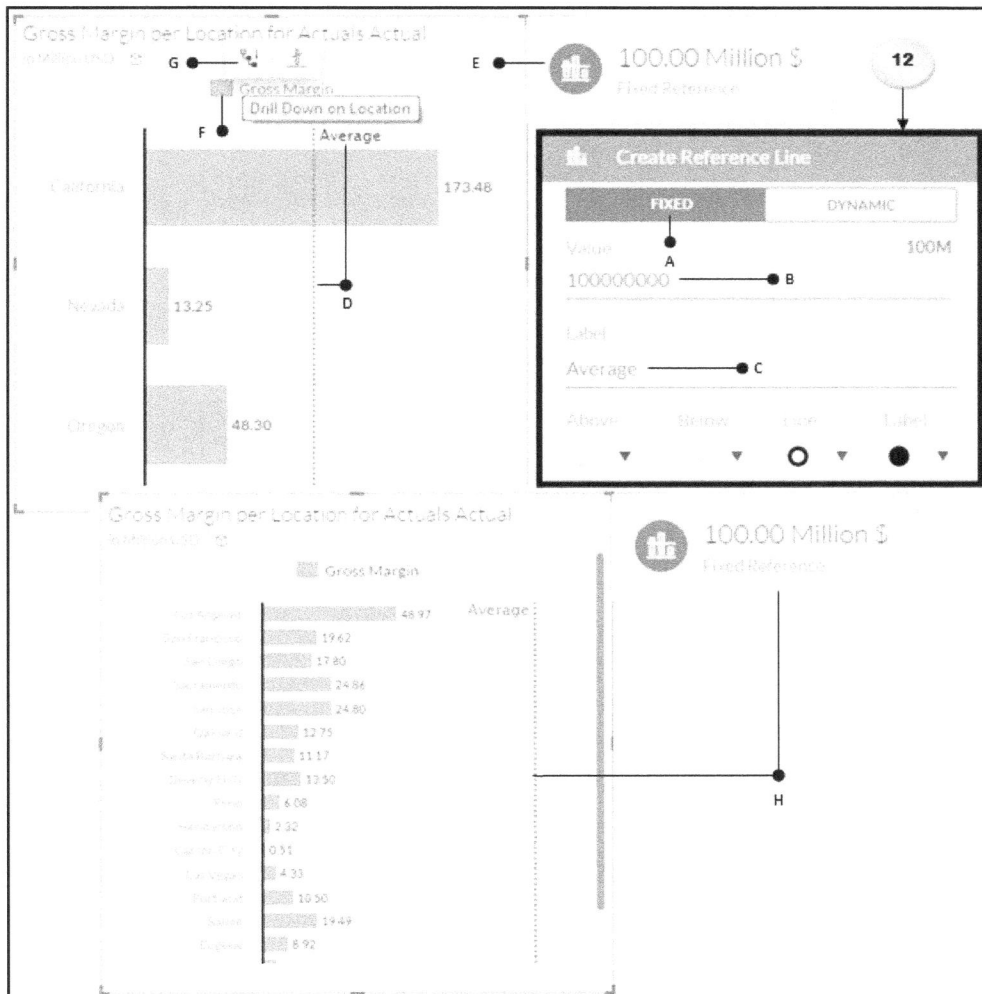

13. If you want the reference line to change when you interact with the chart, you need to change it from **Fixed** to **Dynamic**. Scroll down to the bottom of the **Builder** tab, and click on the Edit icon for **Fixed (Average)** in the **Reference Line** dialog box:

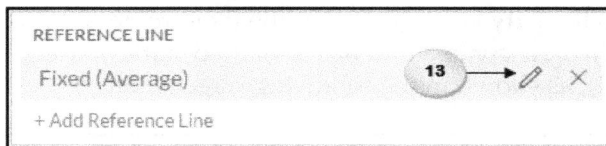

14. Click on the **DYNAMIC** tab to add a dynamic-value reference line.

15. Select **Gross Margin** from the **Measure** list.

16. Keep the default **Average** aggregation, which will display the average gross margin.

17. For **Version**, select **Actual**.

18. Type **Average** for the reference line **Label**.

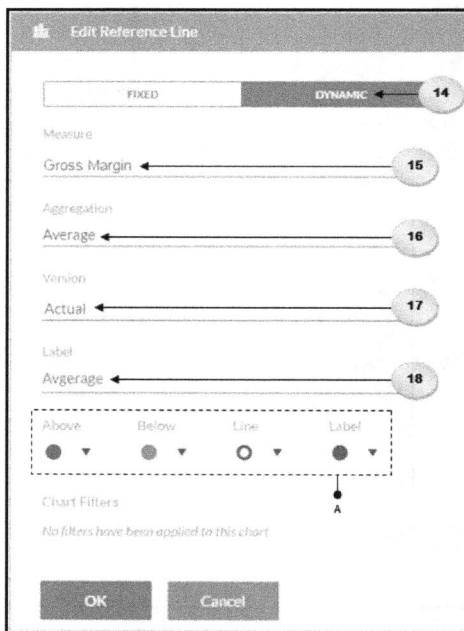

Optionally, you can color the background areas to the left and right of the reference line by choosing colors (**A**) in the **Above** and **Below** color-pickers. Additionally, you can set different **Line** and **Label** colors to make the reference line more visible.

After setting the parameters for the **Reference Line** section, click on **OK** to dismiss this screen.

The **Version** list in the **Edit Reference Line** panel displays the data versions available in the model. The five data versions you can use in SAP Analytics Cloud are: **Actual**, **Budget**, **Planning**, **Forecast**, and **Rolling Forecast**. When you are dealing with an analytical model (as in the current scenario), you see the **Actual** option only. The remaining four versions relate to the planning model.

Here is the outcome of your work. Using the instructions provided in the previous exercises, change the chart title, change its color, and make it bold (**A**). If you rest your mouse pointer over the **Reference Line** section, you will see the average gross margin screenshot of 78.35 million (**B**), which is calculated like this: (173.48+13.25+48.3)/3. Click on the **California** link (**C**) in the previous screenshot, and then click on the Drill Down icon to see the output illustrated in the following screenshot. Now, the **Average** value will show 21.69 million (**D**), and the **Reference Line** section will adjust accordingly.

To modify an existing **Reference Line** section or to add more, use the **REFERENCE LINE** section available at the bottom of the **Builder** tab (**E**).

Setting individual chart filters

The simplest type of filter is the one that you apply directly to a chart. This includes selecting a single value (**A**) in a chart, selecting multiple values (**B**) using *Shift+click*, or selecting a member in the legend (**C**) to apply the filter on an entire set of values. After making your selections, click on the Filter Selected Data Points icon (**D**). The filter you apply to a chart appears under the chart title (**E**). To remove the filter, click on the Remove icon (**F**).

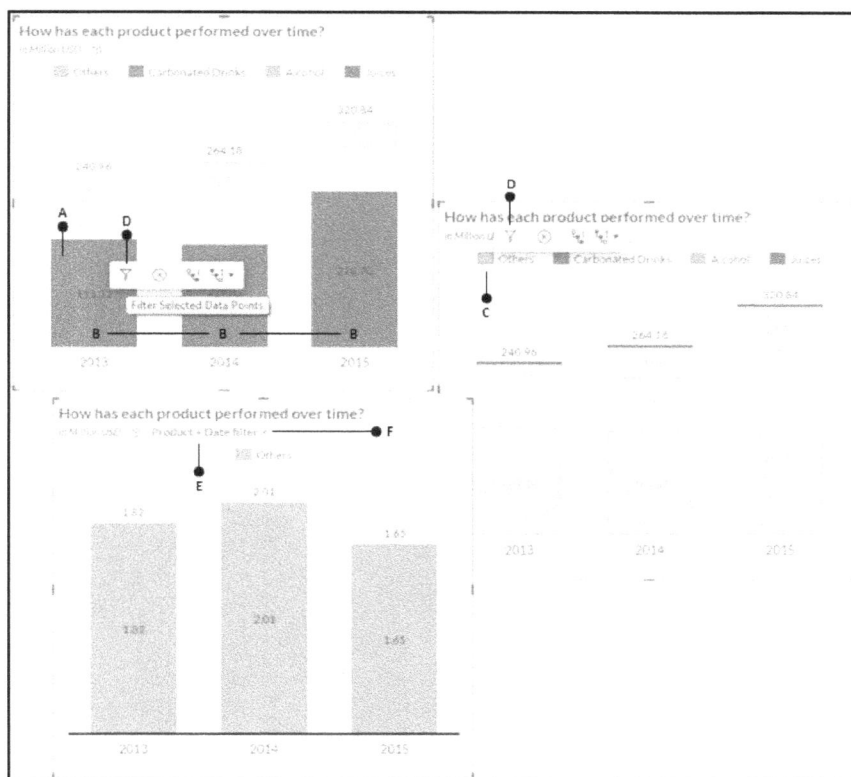

In addition to applying these visual filters, you can also add filters in the **Builder** tab. To add such filters, move your mouse over a selected dimension in the **Builder** panel, and select **Filter by Member** or **Filter by Range**. Recall that you applied this filter for the **Gross Margin** line chart in Chapter 4, *Creating Stories Using Charts*.

Adding a page filter

A page filter can be applied to just one page in a story. In this exercise, you will create a page filter that will allow you to filter data simultaneously by date on all the charts you have created so far. Recall that the time granularity defined for the underlying model was set to **Year**, **Quarter**, and **Month**. Therefore, the date range filter you are setting up here will show the same time granularity and will display the data only for the selected time period.

19. On the **Insert** toolbar section, click on the Input Control icon. This action will place a **Page Filter** (**A**) option on the current page. To delete this control, use the Remove icon (**B**).

20. From the list of dimensions provided with the **Page Filter** option, select the **Date** dimension.

21. When you click on the **Date** dimension, you see a sub-menu. Select **Filter by Range** from this sub-menu. If you're filtering certain types of dimension, for example, a date dimension, you can use **Filter by Range**. Recall that you used the **Filter by Member** option in `Chapter 4`, *Creating Stories Using Charts*, step 52.

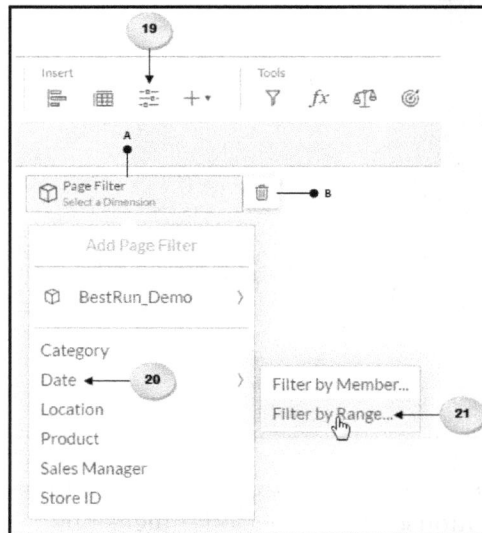

22. In the **Set Date Range for Date** dialog box, set **Hierarchy** to **YQM** to display **Year**, **Quarter**, and **Month** values in the **Granularity** drop-down list. If you select **YHQM**, the **Granularity** list will show **Year**, **Half Year**, **Quarter**, and **Month**.

23. From the **Granularity** list, select **Quarter** to display years and quarters in the filter. If you select **Year** from this list, the range spans from 2013 to 2015. If you select **Month**, the range will also show months in addition to years.

> Note that you can add more than one filter by clicking on the **Add a New Range** link (**A**). For now, keep just one filter, as illustrated in the following screenshot. Also keep the **Allow viewers to modify selections** box (**B**) checked, and click on **OK** to dismiss this dialog box. If you uncheck this option, the filter will become static. Keeping this option checked allows users to select multiple filter values.

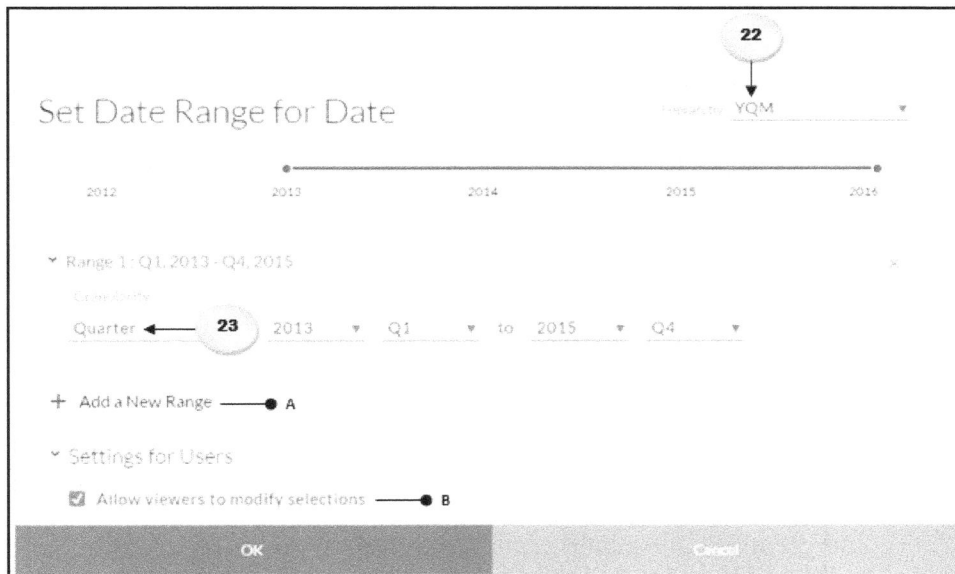

24. When you get back to the page, you can enlarge the filter object (**A**) on the page so that the filter values appear in respective lists (**B**). You can then view and change filter values from these lists, as shown in the following screenshot:

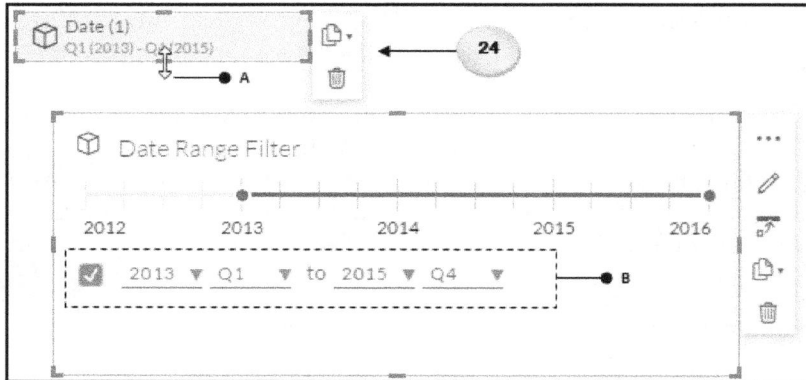

25. Click on the More Actions icon (**C**), and select **Edit Styling** (**D**) from the menu. On the **Styling** tab, expand the **Header** list (**E**), and choose a color for the filter heading. Also make the heading bold. If desired, you can also set **Background** and the **Content** color from their respective color pellets:

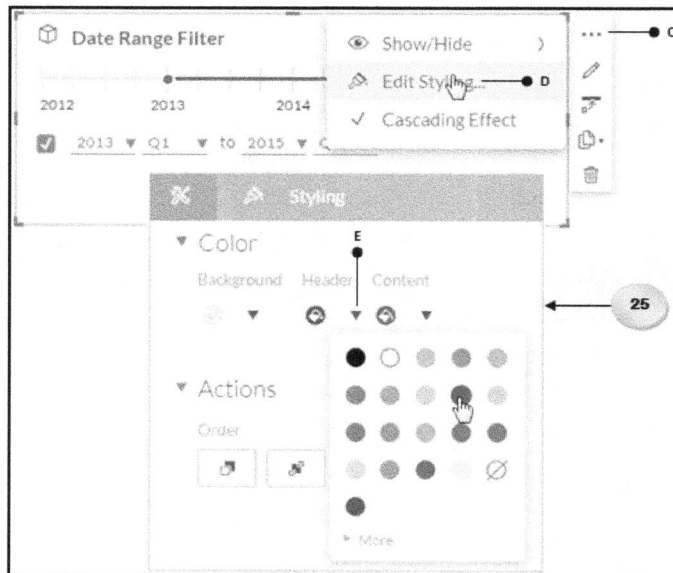

Select **2015** from the first drop-down list (**A**) in the following screenshot. This will set 2015 as a filter (**B**) for the whole page. All the charts on the current page will be refreshed to display the data for 2015 only. Refer to the following screenshot:

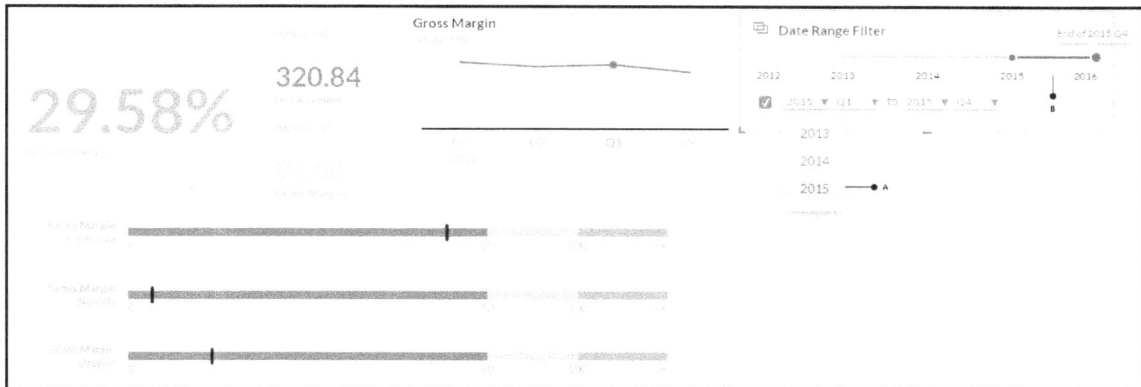

Now, select **2014** from the first list (**C**) in the following screenshot. Once again, the page will be refreshed to display the data for 2014 and 2015 (**D**). If you want to see the data for 2014 only, select this year in the third list carrying years information. Also, select different quarters from the two quarters list to see the effect.

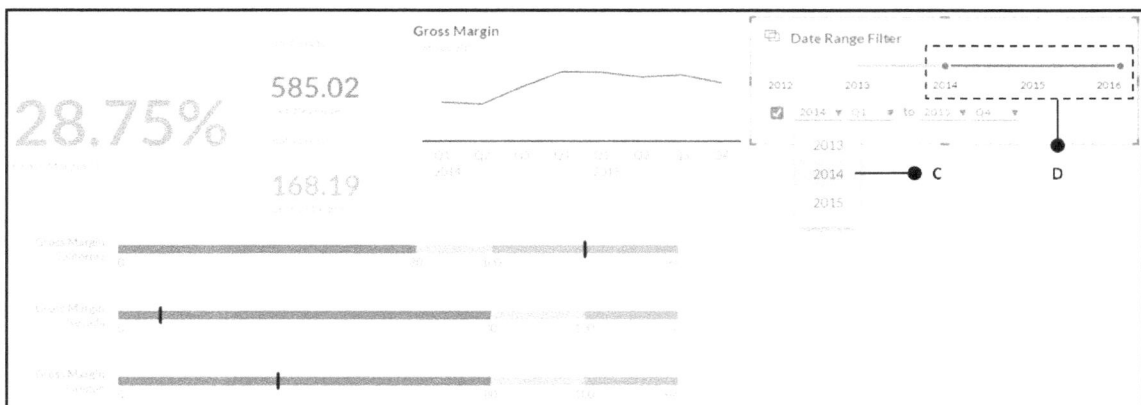

Finally, reinstate the filter to its previous state (**E**), as illustrated in the following screenshot:

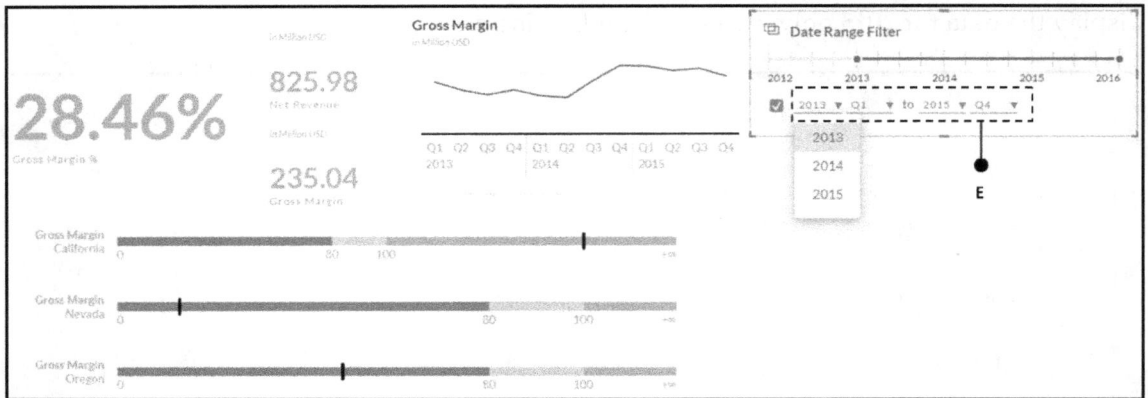

Adding a page filter for products

The filter being added in this exercise will be created for products to see the data for specific product(s) on all the charts created on the current page.

26. On the **Insert** toolbar section, click on the Input Control icon again to add another page filter. This time, select the **Product** dimension. Note the **Date** dimension, which is grayed out because you have already set a filter for this dimension:

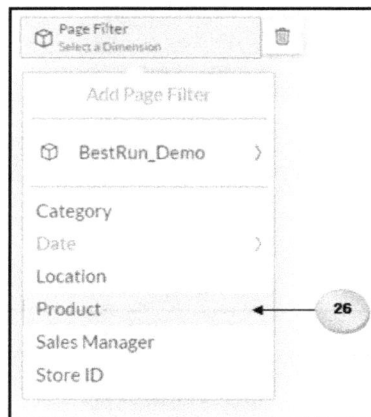

27. On the **Set filters for Product** screen, select **All Members** to add all products in the filter, and click on **OK:**

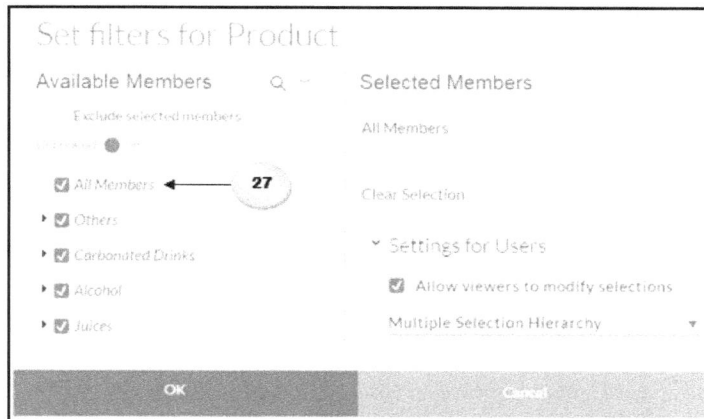

The filter will appear on the page. Drag the handles to resize it, and place it under the **Date Range Filter** screen, as illustrated in the following screenshot (**A**). Using the instructions provided for the **Data Range Filter**, style the heading of this filter. In the **Products** page filter, remove check mark from the All box (**B**), and select individual products, as illustrated in the following screenshot. As you check or uncheck a product, you see real-time reflections of your selections on all the charts.

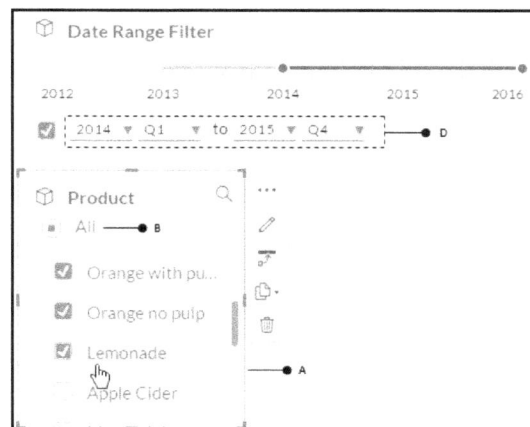

Note that the data shown in the screenshot (**C**) relates from **2014 Q1** to **2015 Q4** (refer to the applied filters in the **Date Range Filter** (**D**) screen).

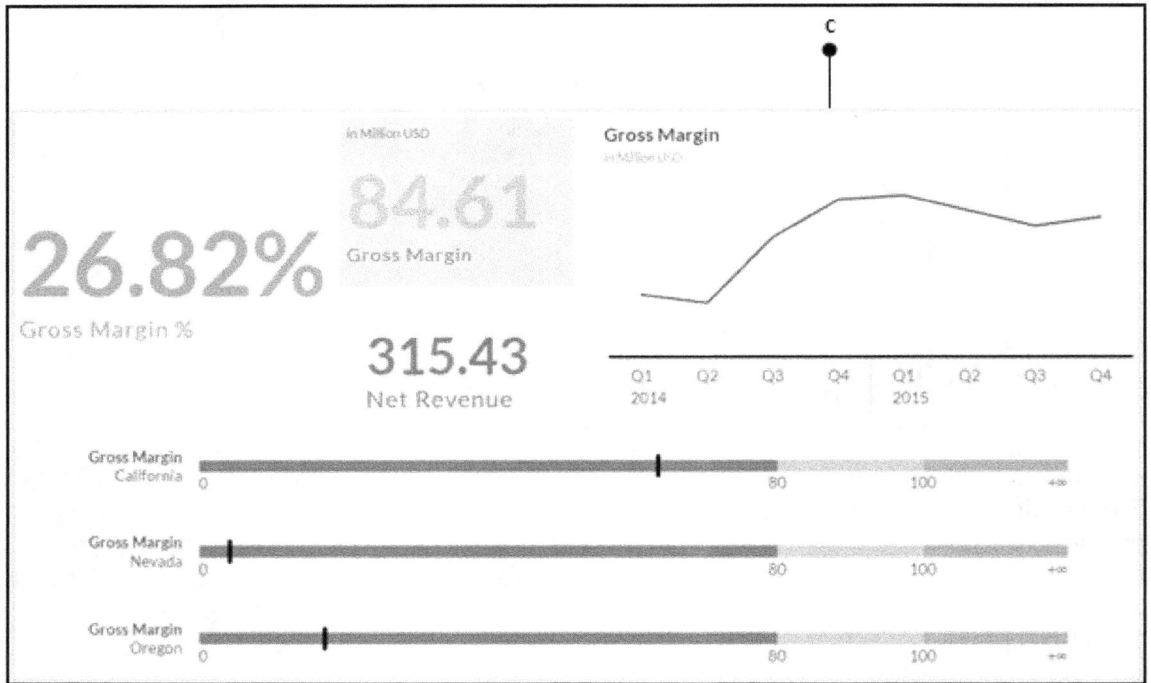

Adding a location page filter

This is the last page filter being added to the current page. This filter will allow you to confine your analysis to specific states or cities.

28. Once again, click on the Input Control icon on the **Insert** toolbar, and select the **Location** dimension:

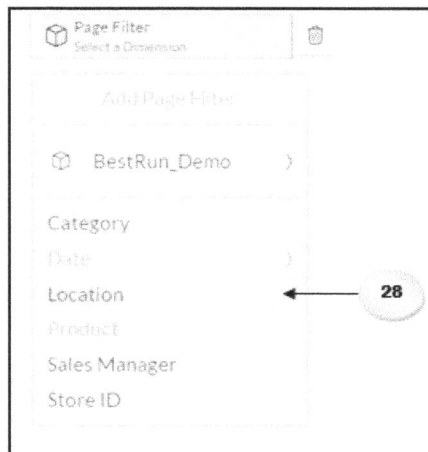

29. On the next screen, select **All Members** to include all states and cities to the filter:

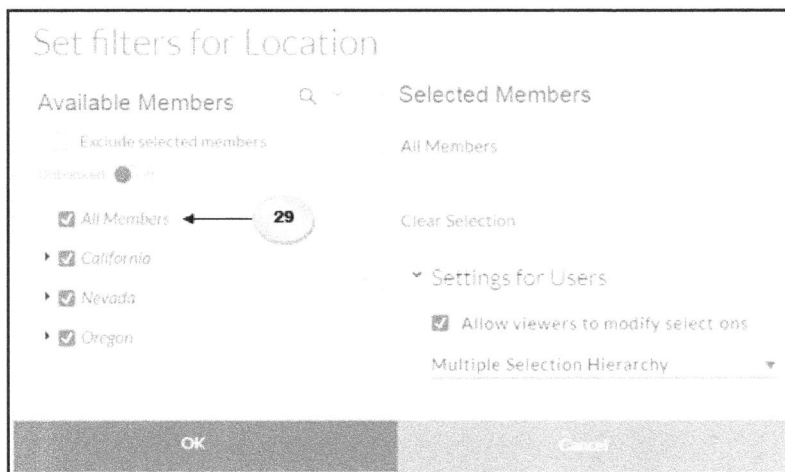

Adjust the filter, and drag to place it next to the **Product** filter (**A**). Deselect the **All** option, and click on **California** (**B**) to see this state's data on all the charts:

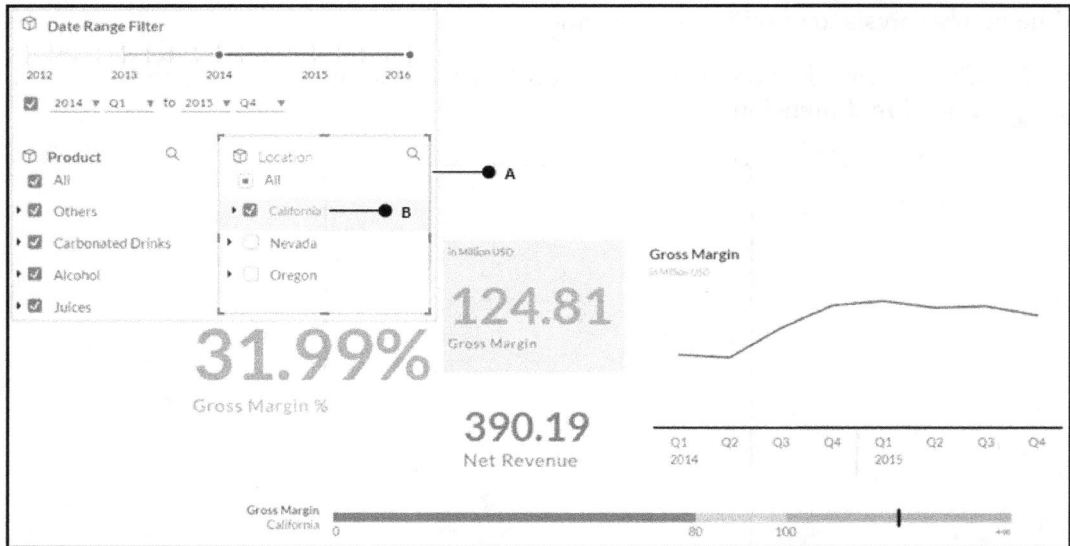

Deselect **California**, and expand its node to see the list of cities in this state. Select **Los Angeles** (**C**) in the following screenshot, to analyze the data of this city:

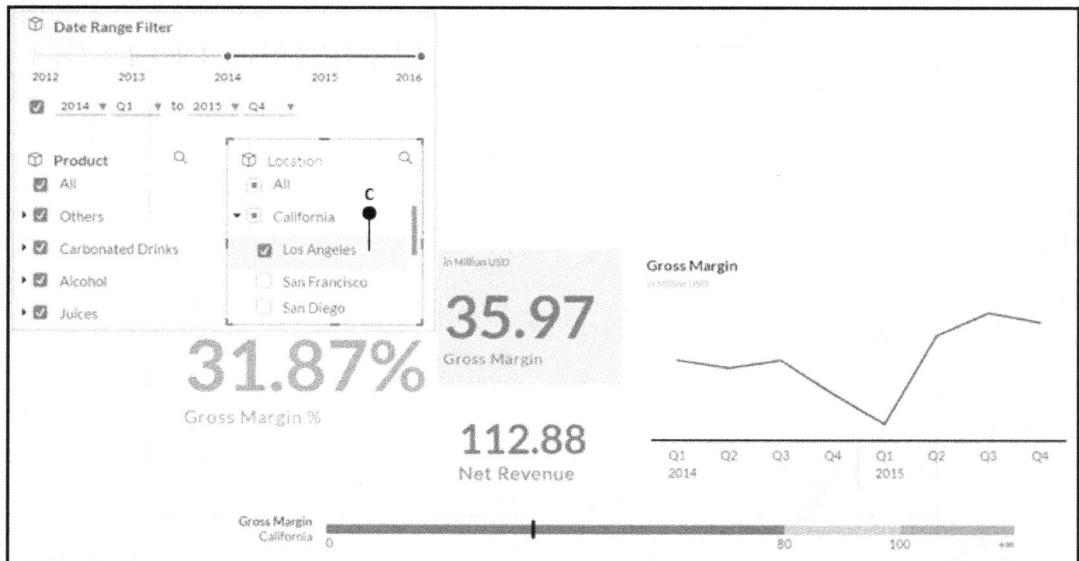

Adding a story filter

By adding a story filter, you apply filters that affect every object on every page of your story. In this example, you will create a story filter to display data only for the **California** state. Since you have just one page in your story at the moment, you can revisit this exercise after completing all story pages in `Chapter 7`, *Working with Tables and Grids*.

30. On the toolbar, click on the Story Filter icon (**A**). An icon labeled **Add Story Filter** (**B**) will emerge just under the toolbar. Click on this icon, and select **Location** (**C**) from its menu. In the **Set filters for Location** dialog box, select the **California** state, (**D**) and click on **OK** to close the dialog box. The California state filter will be applied to the whole story. Later, if you wish to remove this filter, just click on the cross icon (**E**). All the story pages will be reinstated to their previous states, as shown in the following screenshot:

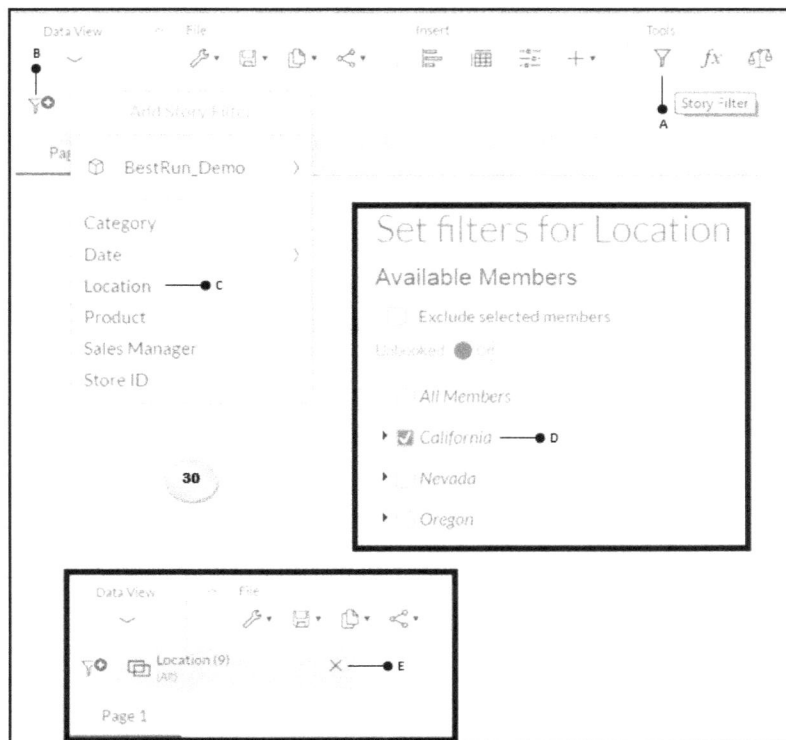

Creating a linked analysis

You saw how to restrict the scope of your analysis result by applying different types of filters on your story page objects. When you apply filters (for example, 2015 Q1 in the Date Range page filter), all other charts on the page are refreshed to display the data for the selected criteria. In addition to these filters, you can create linked analysis, using which you can create an interaction between charts within a story. When you create a linked analysis and drill through hierarchical data or create filters, multiple charts in your story are updated simultaneously.

> The main difference between filters and linked analysis is that, in linked analysis, the filters are applied only to the charts you include in the analysis, whereas page and story filters affect all the charts.

You can set up linked analysis for charts that belong to the same model. If the charts are based on different models, the models must contain linked dimensions. You will see an instance of a linked dimension in the next chapter. Now that we have a bunch of charts on our story page, we are in a position to create a linked analysis so that any actions performed on one chart (referred to as the main chart in this exercise) affect other linked charts in the story, but the actions performed on other charts have no effect on each other or on the main chart that stimulates the update. To apply the chart interaction, select the main chart. In this example, I selected the chart (illustrated next) that shows the gross margin percentage for each product by state.

31. On the **Tools** toolbar, click on **Linked Analysis** to open the **Linked Analysis** panel on the right side:

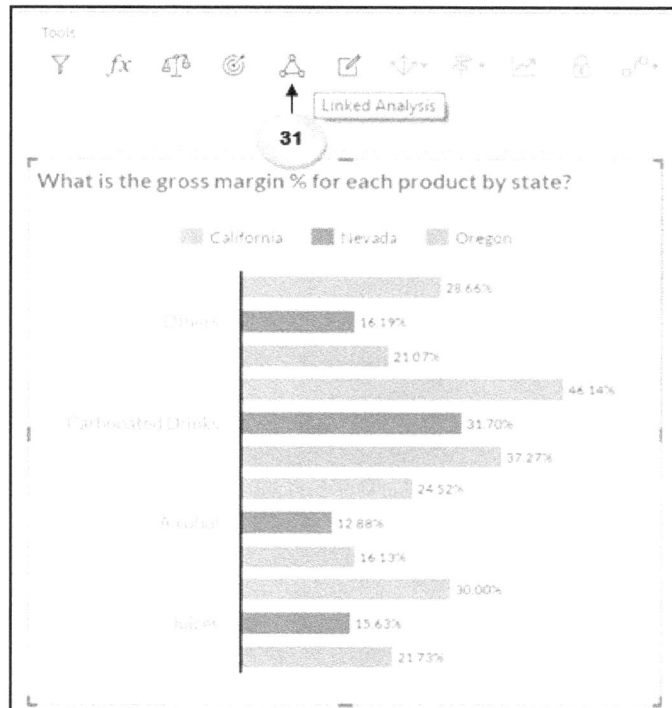

You see three chart interaction options on the **Linked Analysis** panel, which are as follows:

- **This chart** (default option)(**A**): When you select this option, filtering and drilling through hierarchical data will only update the selected chart.
- **Linked chart set** (**B**): Filtering and drilling through hierarchical data on the selected chart will update all the charts in the set based on the same model or with linked dimensions to this chart's model. Choosing the filter on the datapoint selection option allows you to refine the setting so that, when you click a specific member in the main chart, other charts will be updated as well. If this option is not selected, other charts are affected only by drill or filter actions.
- **Entire story** (**C**): Filtering and drilling through hierarchical data on this chart will update all the charts in the story based on the same model or with linked dimensions to this chart's model.

By default, all the charts in your story are included in the linked chart set. To exclude a chart, select it, and deselect the **Include this chart in set** (**D**) option. The excluded charts will be moved from the **Linked chart set** area to the excluded charts area.

32. For now, just set the Chart interactions option to **Linked chart set**, and check **Filter on datapoint selection**. Keep all other values to their defaults, and click on **Done**. This will set interactions on the main chart to affect the others. Note that the chart interaction option for all other charts is set to the default **This chart** option. You can verify this in the **Linked Analysis** panel by selecting any other chart on the page and clicking on the Linked Analysis icon.

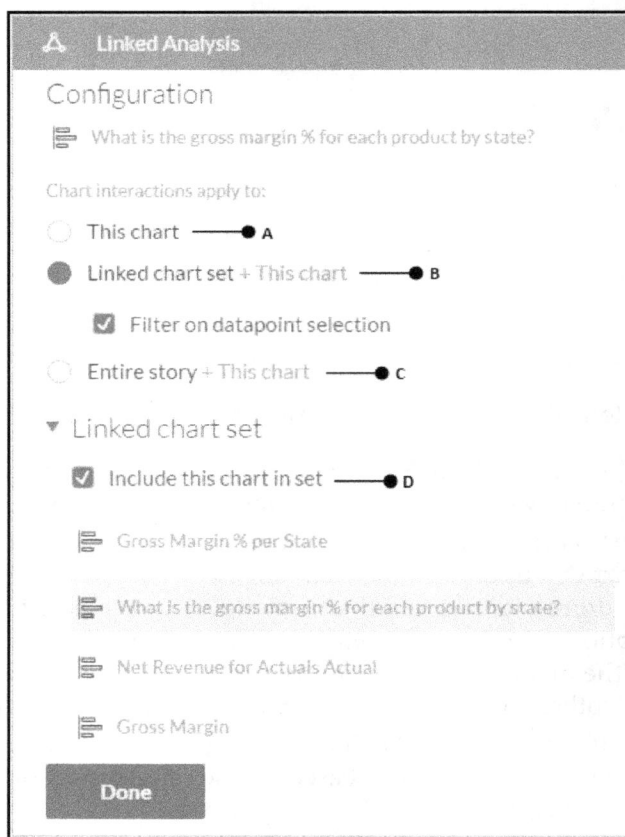

In the main chart, just click on the **Others** product link (**E**), and see the effect of this action on other charts, as illustrated in the following two charts, which are linked to the main chart. Click on the others link again to revert to the previous state. You can also try the drill-down and filter options on the main chart to observe the effect of these actions on other charts. Now, perform the drill down and filtering operations on some other chart that is not set up for linked analysis. You will notice that the actions you perform on such a chart affect that particular chart only, and nothing happens to other charts on the page.

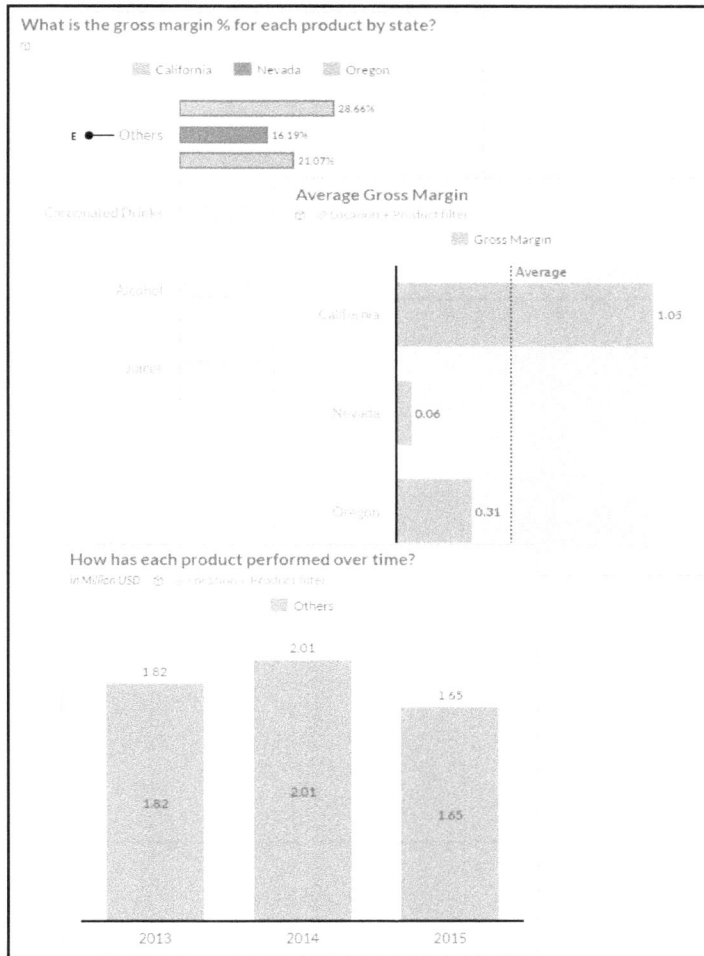

Adding dynamic text

You add headings and titles to your content to describes its purpose. In the same way, you add static and dynamic text to your story pages to explain the type of content these pages contain. In the current scenario, you will add dynamic text to your **Story** page to describe the type of content it renders.

33. Click on the Add icon on the **Insert** toolbar, which displays a menu. From this menu, select the **Text** option (**A**). A text box, as illustrated in the next screenshot, will be placed on your page with some default text. You can use the text box to display static heading and title information, such as **Summary Report From Q1-2013 To Q4-2015**. But what if you change the page data using date range filter by selecting some other duration? To cope with this situation, you can transform the static content of the same text box into a dynamic text. You will do this next! This transformation will change the page heading according to your selected filters.

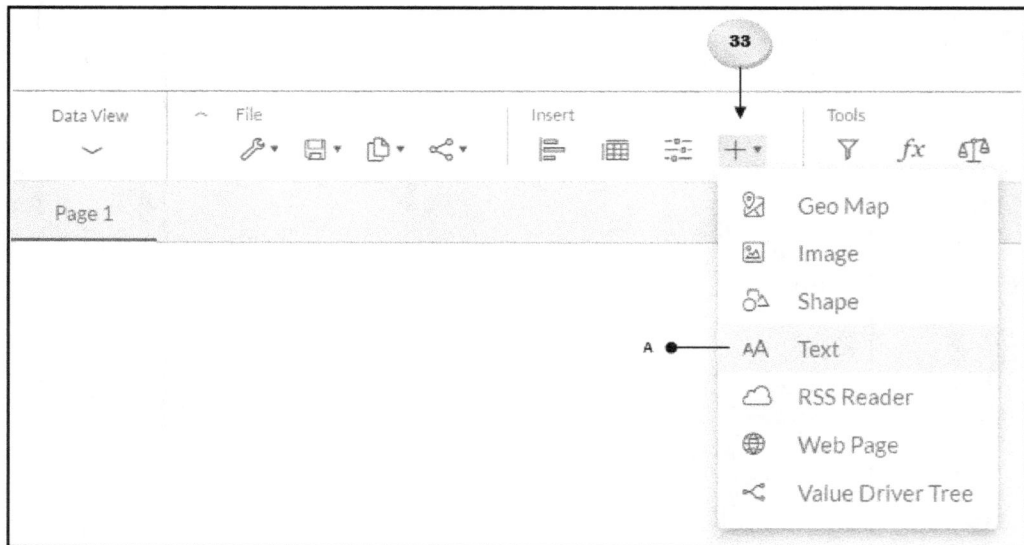

34. In the text box's toolbar, click on the More Action icon, and select **Dynamic Text** from the menu; see the following screenshot. Dynamic text is a text that is automatically updated based on the values from the source input control or filter.

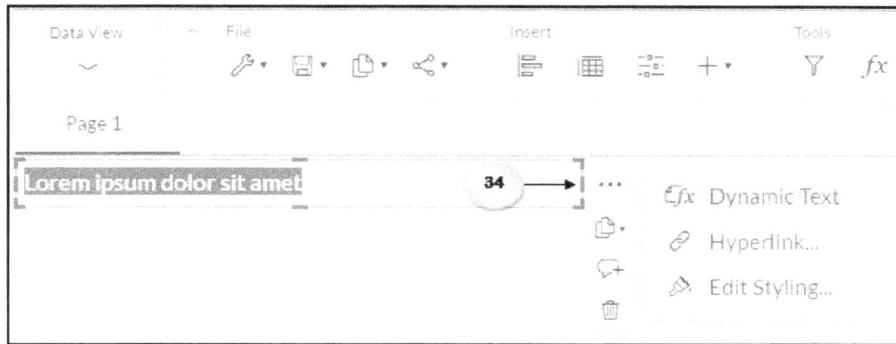

35. When you click on the **Dynamic Text** option in the menu, you see the **Insert Dynamic Text** dialog box. This dialog box displays five options in the left pane, and when you select an option in this pane, relevant options appear in the right pane. For this example, select the **Input Controls** option in the left pane to see the three filters you created in previous exercises. Select the checkbox for the **Date** filter to use this object as the source for your dynamic text:

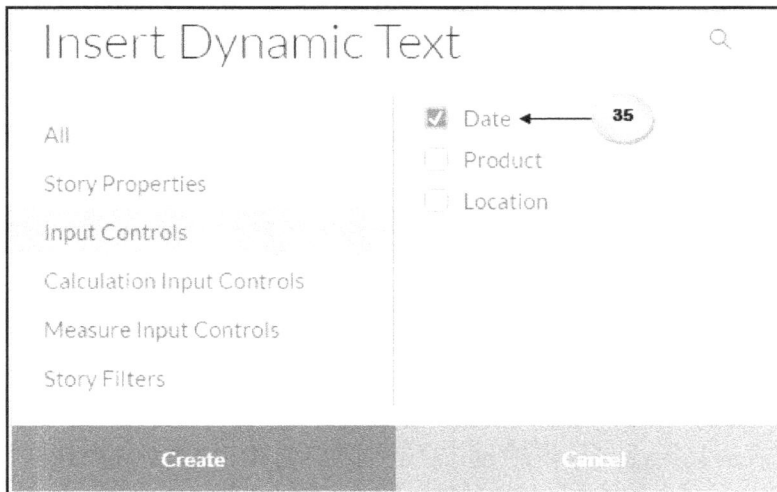

When you dismiss the **Insert Dynamic Text** box by clicking on the **Create** button, you see the text **Q1(2013) - Q4(2015)** in the text box. Yours might be different depending upon the date filters you have applied in the **Date Range Filter** screen.

36. Click on the text box, and type **Summary** in front of the dynamic date text. Click on the More Actions icon (**A**), and select **Edit Styling** (**B**) from the menu. Change the **Color** (**C**) and **Style** (**D**) of the text, as illustrated in the following screenshot:

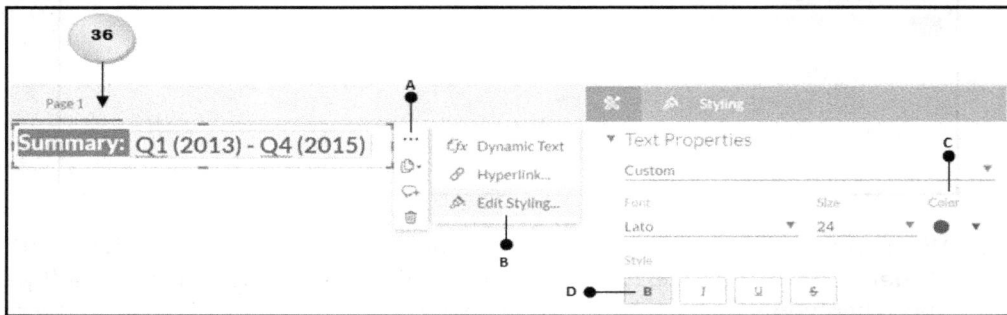

In the **Date Range Filter** screen, select **2015** in the first list, **Q2** in the second, again **2015** in the third, and **Q4** in the last one. The dynamic text will be updated accordingly to show the selected period, as shown in the following illustration:

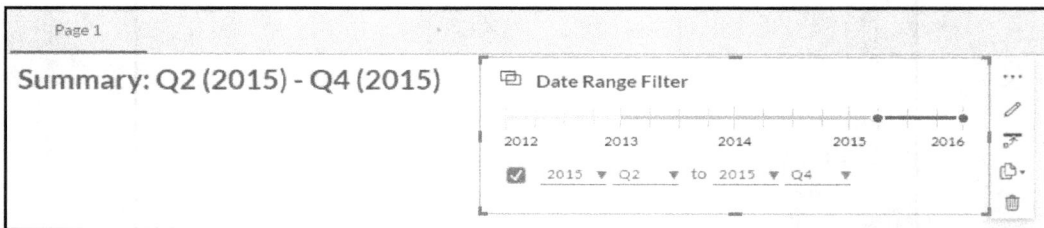

Adding static text

Adding a static text to a story page, as shown in the following screenshot, is a very simple deal. As the name implies, the text you add to your story page in this exercise will remain static.

37. Once again, click on the Add icon (**+**) on the **Insert** toolbar, and select the **Text** option from the resulting menu. Replace the default text with the text depicted as follows under the main summary text. You are provided with several options to format your text, such as changing **Font**, **Size**, and **Color** (**A**).

Make it bold and italicized, underline it, or strike it through (**B**). Align it using the four alignment options provided (**C**), or create bulleted or numbered lists (**D**).

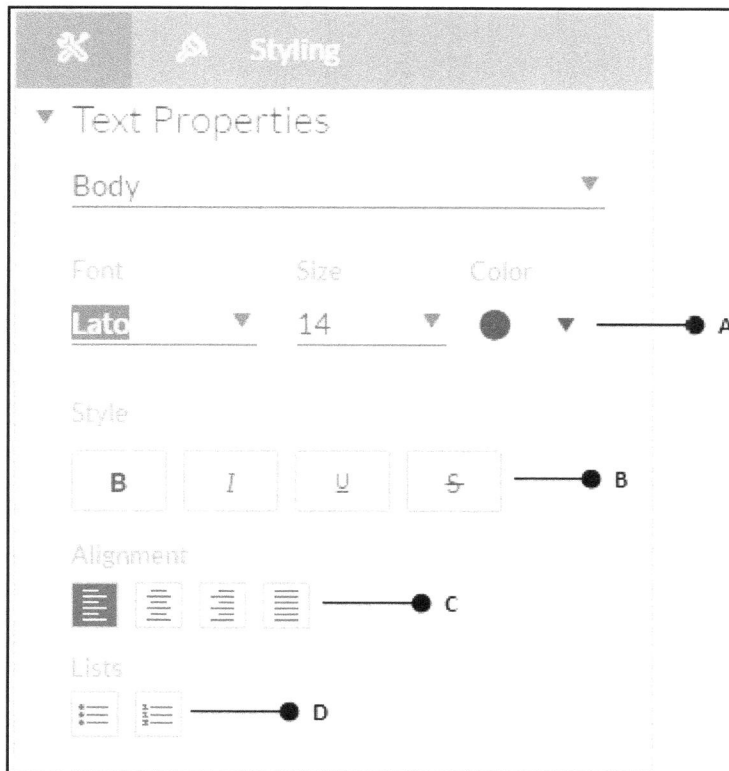

Adding shapes

In addition to dynamic and static text, you can also add shapes, such as line, square, or circle to your page. In this exercise, you will add a line just after the two text items you added to this page.

38. Click on the same Add icon on the **Insert** toolbar, and select **Shape** from the menu:

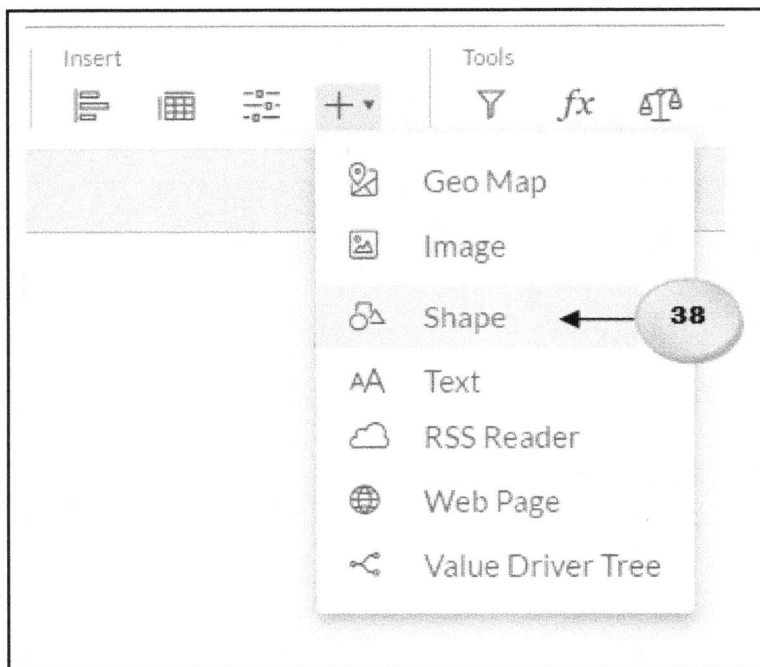

The **Insert Shape** dialog box comes up. As you can see, the **Insert Shape** dialog box contains many shapes for different categories.

39. Select the **line** shape (listed first in the **Basic** category), and click on **OK**. A line object will be added to the page. Place it under the two text boxes. Expand the line using its right handle to cover the page (**A**).

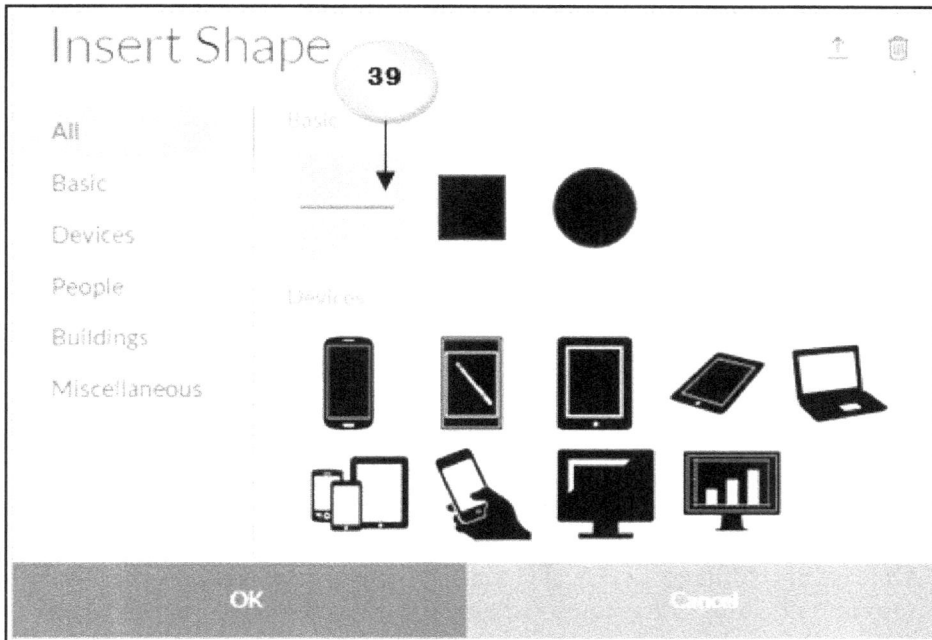

Drag the three objects and place them at the top of the page, as shown in the following screenshot:

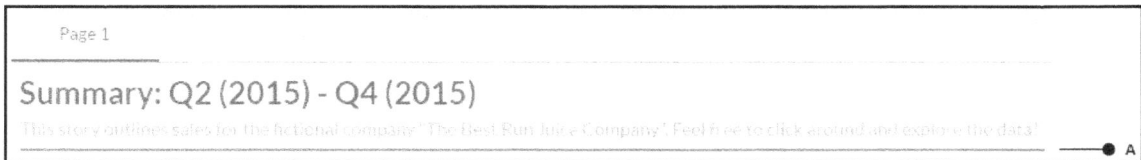

Adding images

You can add images (such as your company logo) to your story page by uploading them from your computer. The image you upload is saved as part of the story definition and can be added to other story page. In this exercise, you will add a logo to your page.

40. Click on the Add icon again, and select **Image** from the menu:

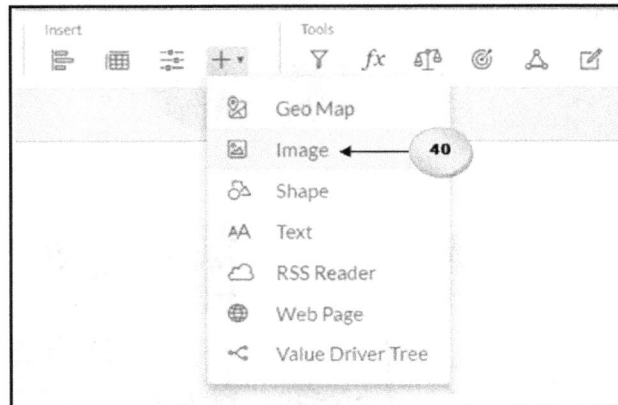

41. On the **Insert Image** screen, click on the Upload icon, and select an image in the **Open** dialog box. Once you see the selected image on this screen (**A**), click on the **OK** button to close the screen, as shown here:

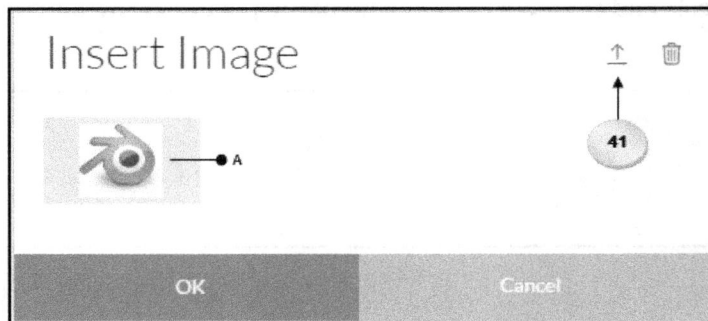

The image will be placed on your page. Drag and position it according to the following screenshot (**B**):

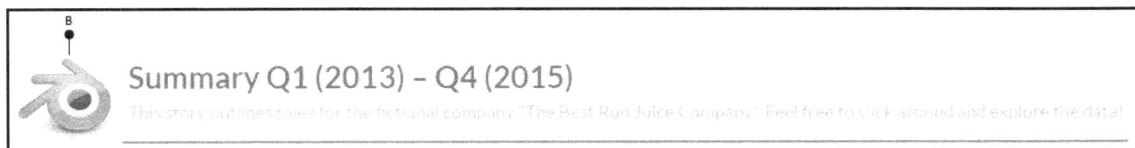

Summary Q1 (2013) – Q4 (2015)

Present mode

After completing the page, you can preview it by clicking on the **Present** option under the *More* toolbar section to check how it will appear to other users. In this mode, the story page is displayed full-screen, without toolbars.

42. In the toolbar, click on the ellipsis icon under the **More** toolbar section, and select **Present**:

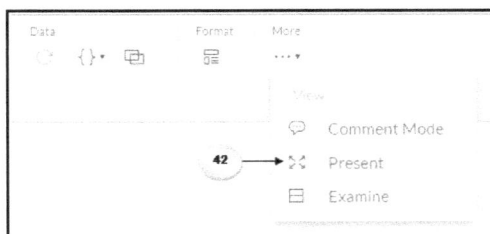

When you click on the **Present** option, the page should look like the following screenshot. To switch out of **Present** view, hover at the top of the page selector bar, and select the Present icon (**A**) again.

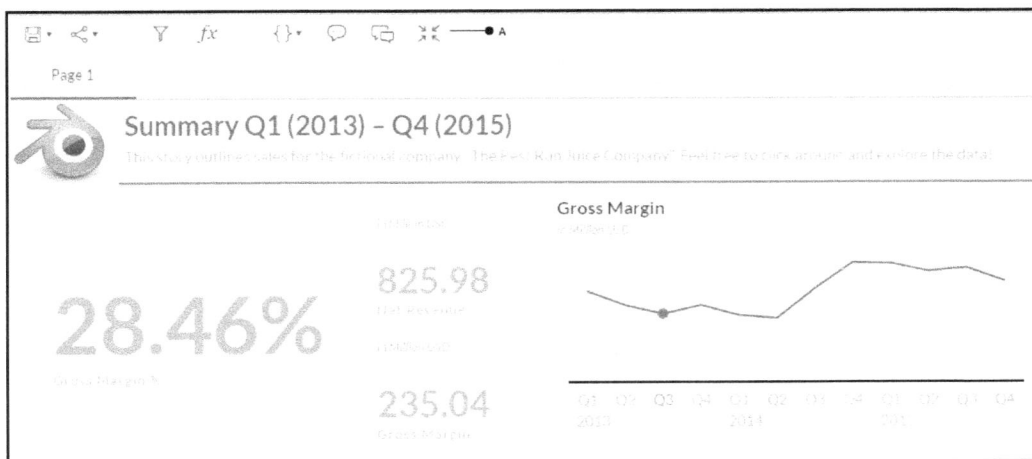

Creating hyperlinks

You can transform the various objects in your stories into hyperlinks that take you to other stories, other pages within the same story, or external websites. Static charts, pictures, and text objects are the best candidates for creating hyperlinks. In this example, you will set up the logo to act as a hyperlink.

43. Click on the **logo**, and select **Hyperlink** from the **More Actions** menu. Select **External URL** (**A**) from the **Link to** list, and enter the URL of an external website, for example, `http://www.sap.com` in the **External URL** text box (**B**). To open this website in a new tab, check **Open in New Tab** (**C**), and click on **Done**. View the page in **Present** mode, and click on the logo to open the external website:

Examining data behind a visualization

While working on charts in a story, you sometimes want to see the underlying data to evaluate the results being displayed on those charts. Here's how you can examine the data behind the charts.

44. Select the **KPI** chart, and select **Examine** (**A**) from the More menu. A grid will appear in the lower section of the page (**B**), with all the values that the chart is based on along with hierarchies:

If you make any changes to the chart's definition in the **Builder** panel or apply any filters on the chart, the data being displayed in the grid is also affected. To test this scenario, uncheck **California** and **Oregon** in the **Location** filter, and keep the **Nevada** state checked. As you can see in the following screenshot, the applied filter not only affects the chart (**A**), but the data in the grid is also filtered to only display the selected state (**B**).

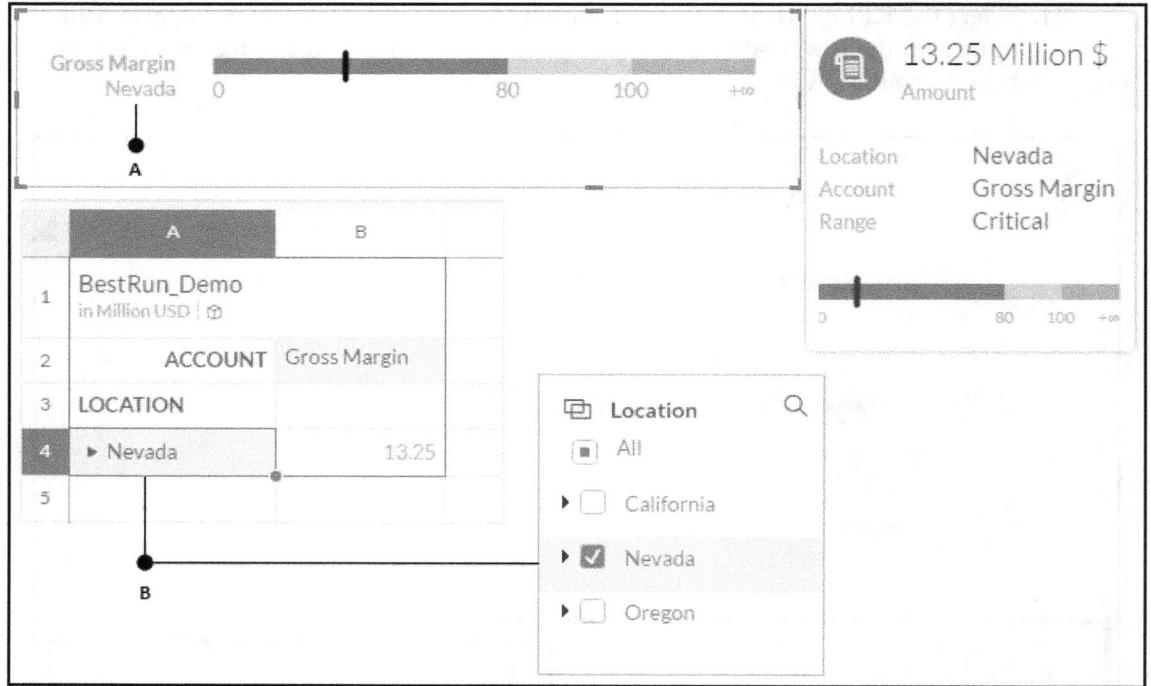

Setting styling preferences for your story

In some of the previous exercises, you went through the procedures to apply styles to different objects on your story page using the Styling tab in the **Designer** panel. In addition to these individual styling options, SAP Analytics Cloud allows you to set preferences that apply styles to all of your story pages. These formatting options set styling preferences at the story level to provide a consistent look and feel to all of your story pages.

45. To set story-level styling preferences, click on the Edit Story icon under **File** in the toolbar, and select **Preferences**:

After selecting the **Preferences** option, you see the **Story Preferences** dialog box. The left pane in this dialog box lets you style your story pages and tiles on those page. The **Tile Settings** option is further divided into five sections that provide relevant styling options: **Charts** and geomaps, **Text**, **Shapes**, **Input Controls**, and **Others**.

If you select **Page Settings** in the left pane, you see two styling options--**Default Page Background (A)** and **Default Page Size (B)**--in the right pane to define settings for your story pages. You can set a background color for all your story pages by picking a color from the **Default Page Background** palette (**C**). Switching the **Fix Page Size** slider (**D**) in the **Default Page Size** section to the **On** position launches some options to set the size, width, height, and orientation of the page. By checking the **Continuous Height** option (**E**), you ensure that your new tiles will always have room at the bottom of the page. You have the option to also specify whether new tiles should automatically snap to the grid.

Finally, in the **Apply to** section (**F**), you choose whether to apply these setting to all existing pages and tiles or to only new pages and tiles.

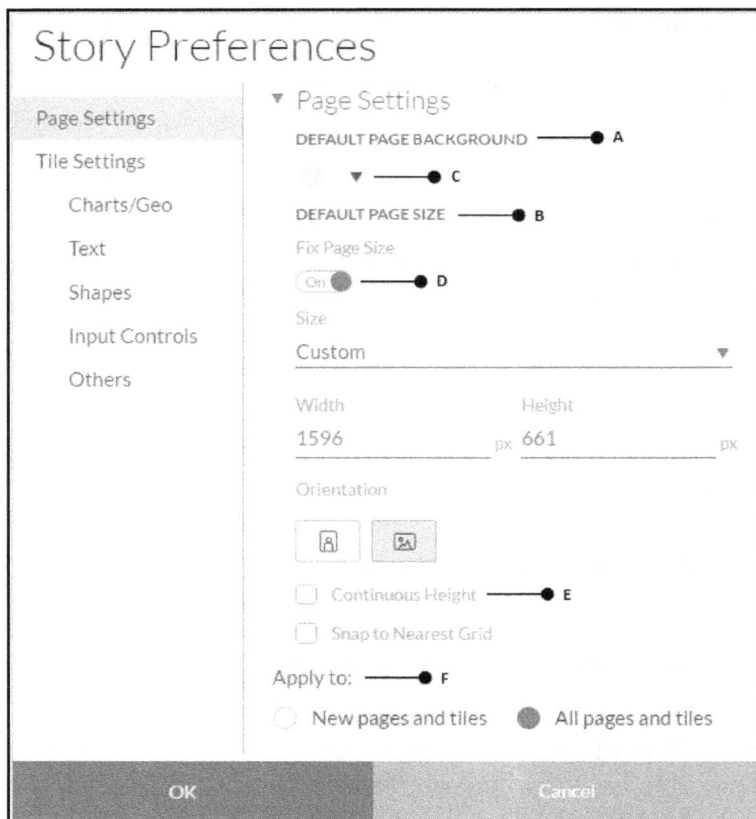

Story Preferences

▼ Page Settings

Page Settings	DEFAULT PAGE BACKGROUND ——● A
Tile Settings	▼ ——● C
Charts/Geo	DEFAULT PAGE SIZE ——● B
Text	Fix Page Size
Shapes	On ● ——● D
Input Controls	Size
Others	Custom ▼

Width   Height

1596   px 661   px

Orientation

[A]   [🖼]

☐ Continuous Height ——● E

☐ Snap to Nearest Grid

Apply to: ——● F

○ New pages and tiles   ● All pages and tiles

OK	Cancel

The **Tile Settings** section lists options for charts and other objects. Here, you can set different backgrounds and texts for your different page objects. In the **Chart/Geo** section, you have an additional option to set color palettes. In addition to a range of default color settings, you can also create your own palette (**G**). Even after specifying these default styling options, you can override these preferences for your page objects in the **Designer** panel.

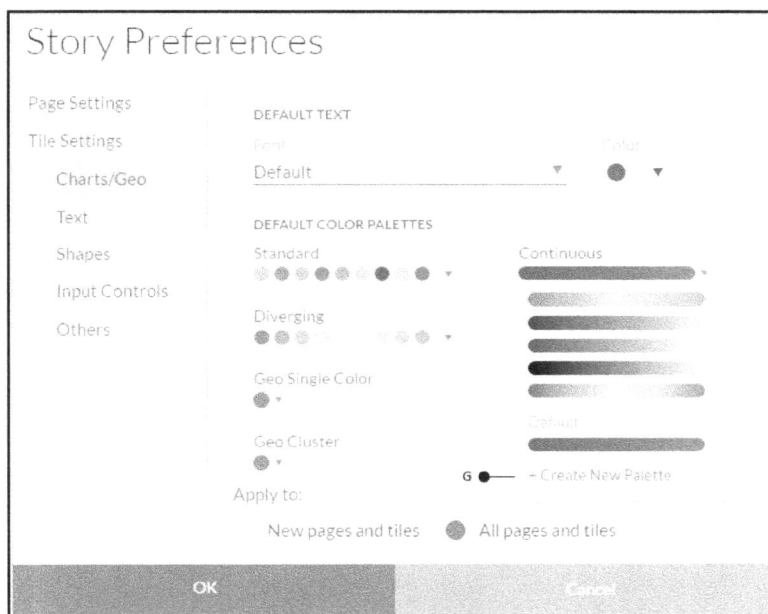

Creating an aggregation calculation

You went through three of the four calculation types in the previous chapter. In this exercise, you will see how the aggregation calculation type works. You can use this type in your chart and tables. You will learn about tables in Chapter 7, *Working with Tables and Grids*, so here you will create a new chart to experiment with this calculation type. The chart will display the average gross margin per store for each product type in each state.

46. Create a new chart using the **Chart** option on the **Insert** toolbar.

47. Set **Data Source** to **Best Run Demo**.

48. From the **Comparison** category, select the **Bar/Column** option.

49. Click the **Add Measure** link, and then select **Click to Create a New Calculation**. The instructions to create the aggregation calculation are provided on the next page.

50. After creating the aggregation calculation named **Store Average Gross Margin** on the next page, select **Product** as the chart's **Dimension**.

51. Click on the **Add Dimension/Threshold** link in the **Color** section, and select **Location:**

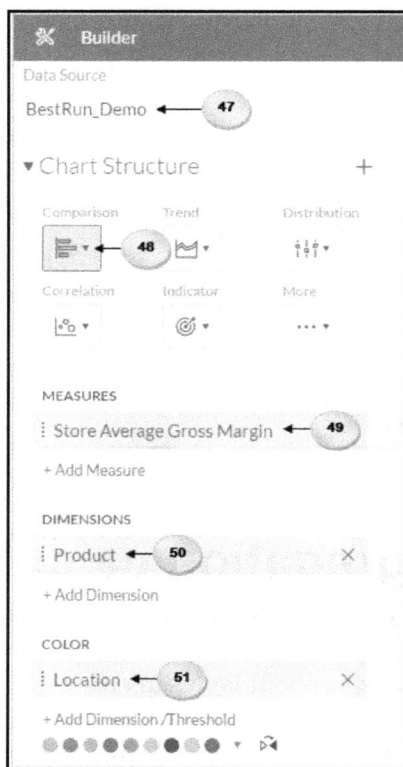

When you select the **Click to Create a New Calculation** option in step 49, you see the **Calculation Editor** screen.

52. In the **Calculation Editor** window, select **Aggregation** for the calculation **Type**.

53. Type **Store Average Gross Margin** for the calculation **Name**.

54. Select **Average** from the **Operation** drop-down list. This is the aggregation type you will use in the current scenario. The **Count** type in this list counts the number of dimension members with values for the measure, while **Count Dimensions** is used to count the number of dimension members, whether or not they have values for the measure. The remaining types are self explanatory.

55. Select **Gross Margin** as the **Measure**. This is the measure on which you will apply the aggregation.

56. Select **Store ID** for **Aggregation Dimensions**. By selecting **Store ID** as the **Aggregation Dimension**, you specify to use this dimension to perform the aggregation. The average gross margin will then be calculated at the store level. If needed, you can add more aggregation dimensions using the link provided in this section.

57. Check the box labeled **Use conditional aggregation**. This option is used when you want to add further restrictions to the aggregation calculation.

58. Select **Do not have Measure values for Conditions**. With conditional aggregation, you can choose to apply the aggregation when there are measure values under specified conditions, or when there are no measure values under these conditions. In this example, you chose the **Do not have Measure values for Conditions** option to exclude a closed store from the calculation.

59. In the **Conditions** section, select **Store ID** from the **Dimensions** list to select the store you want to exclude.

60. From the **Values or Input Controls** drop-down list, choose the first option **Select by Member**. The value(s) you select on the subsequent screen will appear in this list. Note that if desired, you could instead create an input control to allow users to specify the condition value when they view the story.

Calculation Editor

Type
Aggregation ← 52 ▼

Name
Store Average Gross Margin ← 53

Properties

Operation
AVERAGE ← 54 ▼

Measure
Gross Margin ← 55 ▼

Aggregation Dimensions
Store ID ← 56 ▼ ✕

+Add a Dimension

☑ Use conditional aggregation ← 57
Aggregate when aggregation dimensions

Do not have Measure values for Conditions ▼ ← 58

Conditions

Dimensions
Store ID ← 59 ▼

Values or Input Controls
ST101 ← 60 ▼ ✕

+Add a Condition

OK	Cancel

61. When you click on the **Select by Member** option in the **Calculation Editor** window, you see this dialog box. Place a check mark in front of the **ST101** store ID to select this member, and click on **OK**. The selected store will appear in the **Values or Input Controls** list (**60**) in the **Calculation Editor** window.

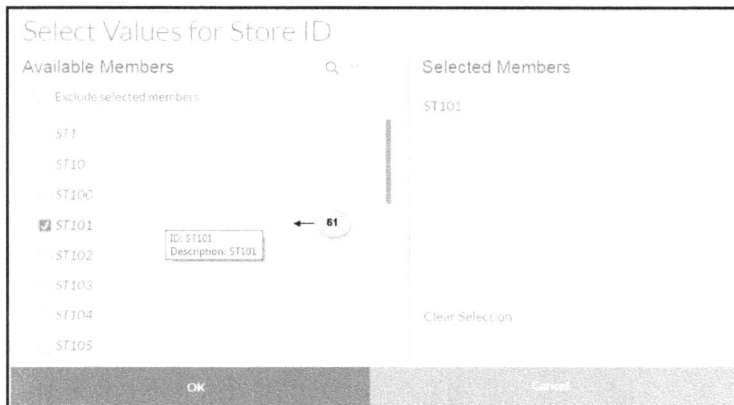

In the **Calculation Editor** window, click on the **OK** button and provide dimension information, as mentioned in steps 49 and 50. Here's the chart you will see after completing the aforementioned steps, which reveals the average gross margin for each store in the three states and for each product category, excluding store 101.

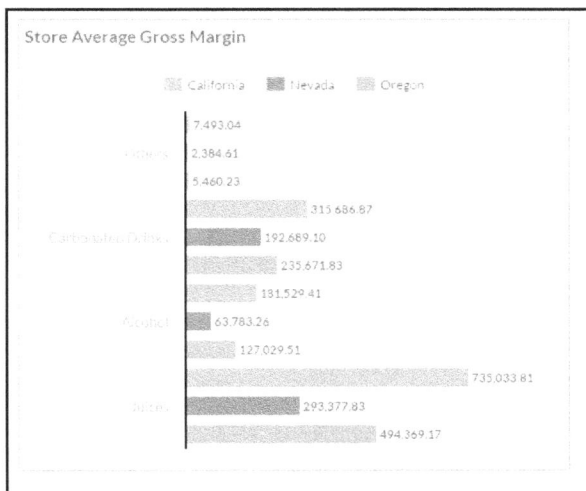

Pinning and commenting on a data point

In some of your story charts, you can pin individual data points to add annotations or additional information. The sole step in this exercise will show you how to do that:

62. Select the **Store Average Gross Margin** chart you just created. Select a bar in the chart (**A**), and click on the Pin icon (**B**) from the pop-up toolbar. A **Numeric Point** chart (**C**) is placed on the story page that represents the pinned data point, with a dotted line (**D**) connecting it to the source chart's data point.

   Replace **Enter footer text** (**E**) at the bottom of this chart with your annotation (**F**). You can drag and place the **Numeric Point** chart anywhere on the page. As you move this chart, the dotted line is adjusted automatically to maintain the link. However, if you drill down into the chart, the dotted line vanishes because the chart's scenario has changed. If you drill up again, the line comes back. You can remove this link by clicking on the **Break Link** option (**G**) from the **Numeric Point** chart's More Actions menu. After the breakup, the annotation turns into an ordinary **Numeric Point** chart:

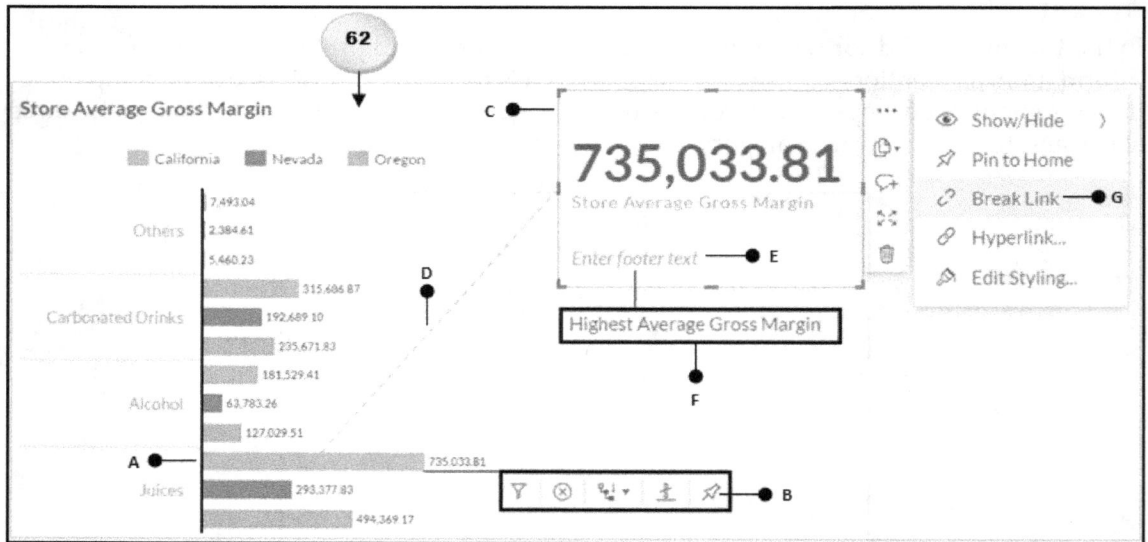

Saving your story

It is considered a good practice to save your story after short intervals. To follow this practice, execute the following steps:

63. Click on the Save icon in the toolbar, and select the **Save** option (**A**), which opens the **Save** dialog box. You can save a story in three ways: **Public**, **Teams**, and **Private**. Click on the menu icon (**B**) to see these options. If you choose the **Public** option, your story will be publicly available. The **Team** option grants the access to your story to a specified team. And if you opt for the **Private** option, then your story will be available to users with whom you share it with. After selecting one of these sharing options, enter a unique **Title** (**C**) and a **Description** (**D**) so that other users can easily recognize the story.

Once you provide all the information and click on the **OK** button, the story will be saved, and its name will appear in the breadcrumb (**E**) next to the **Stories** breadcrumb entry at the top of the page. If you navigate to the main **Stories** interface (either by clicking on the main Stories breadcrumb or via Main Menu | **Browse | Stories**), you will see your story in the list of available stories (**F**). The **All** option lists all stories; the stories listed under the **Public** tab are available to everyone; the **My Stories** tab carries stories that you created, whereas the **Shared with me** tab displays the stories shared with you. Using the stories toolbar, you can search for stories, edit the name and description of a story, and copy, delete, or share selected stories.

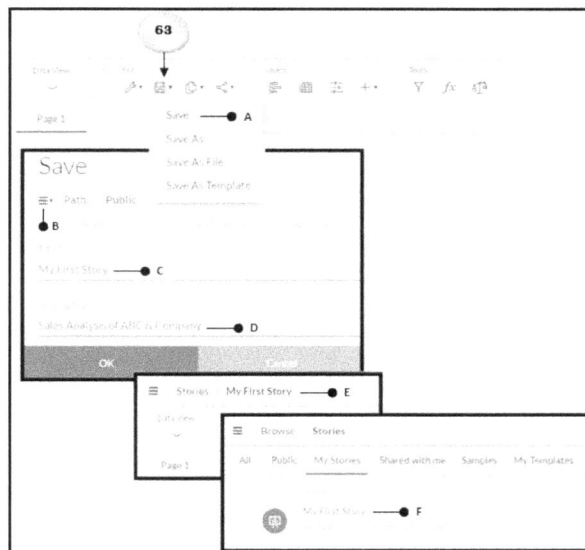

Summary

Congratulations! You have successfully created your first story page. Here's a brief summary of the topics you went through in this chapter:

- Learned how to display key performance indicators using a bullet chart
- Added a reference line to a chart
- Learned how to apply individual filters on charts
- Saw how a page filter works
- Created a story filter to apply a filter on all story pages
- Created a linked analysis to establish interaction among charts
- Went through the process of adding dynamic and static text
- Added shapes and logo to the story page
- Viewed the story page in the present mode
- Created a hyperlink, using which you can access both internal and external resources
- Examined the data behind a visualization
- Learned how to set styling preferences for a story
- Used the aggregation type calculation on a chart
- Added an annotation to a chart's data point
- Saved the story and went through different saving options

The next chapter will move you further ahead. In that chapter, you will create another page in your story to learn some more significant segments, such as geomaps, scatter plot charts, combination column and line charts, and linked dimensions, to name a few.

6
Analyzing Data Using Geomaps and Other Objects

You completed the first page of your story and saved it with its default name (Page 1) in the previous chapter. In this chapter, you will create another page entitled "Analysis". The page will comprise a geomap, a scatter plot chart, and a few more charts. As these objects will be created on a new page, you have to first learn how to add pages to your story and replace their default names with some meaningful names.

Here's a list of topics covered in this chapter:

- Adding new pages to a story and providing expressive names to your story pages. You will also learn about the other options available to manipulate pages, such as delete, copy, duplicate, and so on.
- Sharing your views about the page content with other users by adding comments.
- Visualizing data in geomaps using different types of layers.
- Using location clustering to better visualize the data in geomaps.
- Applying filters to geomaps.
- Linking multiple models via linked dimensions.
- Comparing different values using a combination of a column and line chart.
- Using predictive forecasting through a trend time series chart.
- Adding time calculation to a chart.

The story page you will create in this chapter is illustrated in the following screenshot along with its objects:

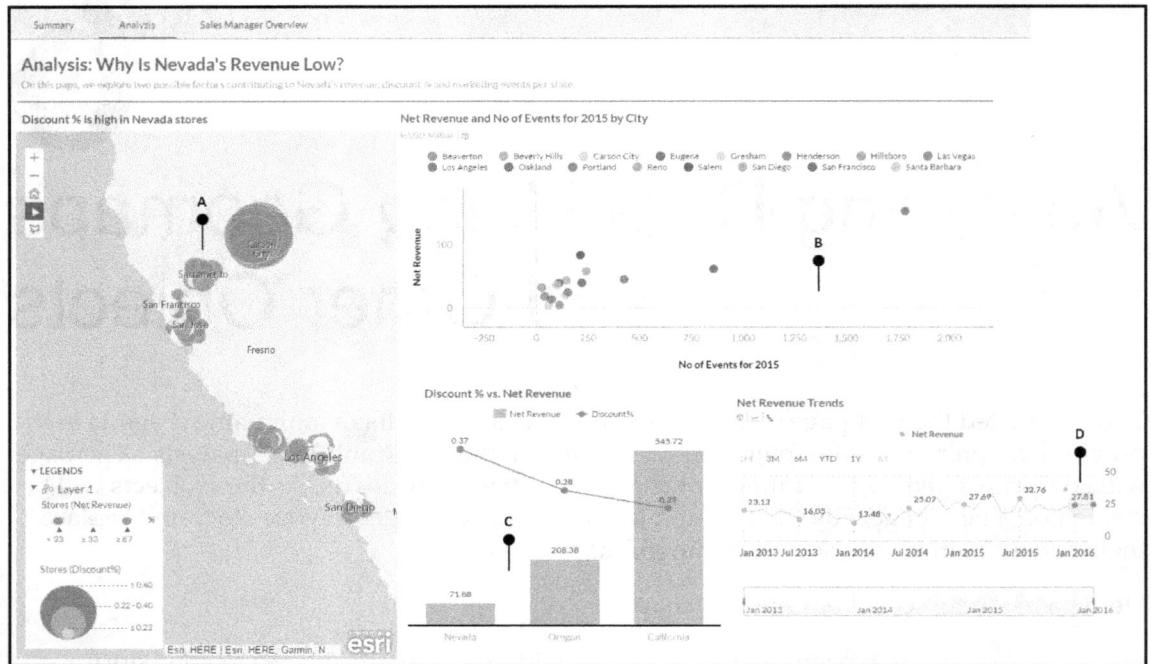

Here are some briefs about the page objects:

- **A**: This is a geomap that will the show net revenue and discount percentage for each store in the three states using a bubble layer
- **B**: The scatter plot chart showcases the use of linked dimensions, in which the data is displayed from two different models
- **C**: This is a combination of a column and line chart, which reveals discount percentage (using a line) provided against net revenue (displayed in columns) for each state
- **D**: This is a trend-time series chart that will demonstrate how to perform predictive forecasting
- **E**: You will also make use of the time calculations feature of SAP Analytics Cloud to compare yearly results in a bar chart (not visible in the screenshot)

Use the instructions provided in the previous chapter to add the heading, subheading, and line object (as depicted in the illustration) after completing this page.

Working with story pages

You can segregate your story on multiple pages according to the subject. In this exercise, you will learn how to add and rename pages and will be introduced to other topics related to story pages:

1. Hover your mouse pointer in the page name area to see the Add New Page icon (**A**). Clicking on this icon displays two options: **Grid** and **Canvas**. Choose the **Canvas** option. As you click on the **Canvas** option, a new page labeled **Page 2** will be added beside **Page 1**. Repeat this step to create one more page:

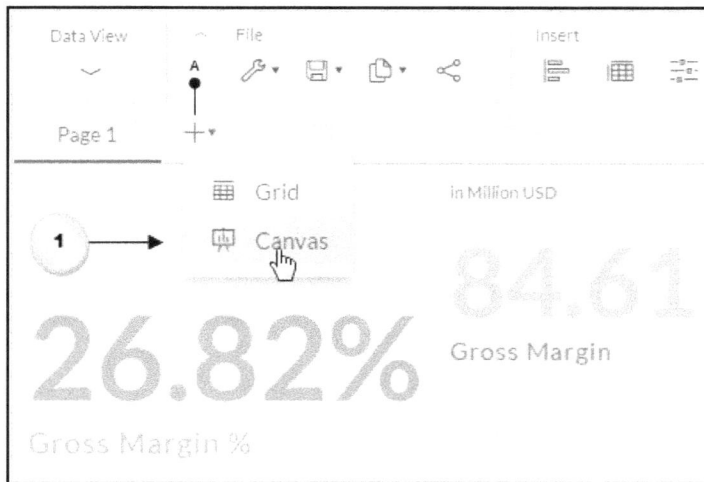

2. Move your mouse pointer over **Page 1**. A tiny arrow (**B**) will appear next to the page name. Click on this arrow to see a menu (**C**). From this menu, select the **Rename** option (**D**). In the **Rename Page** dialog box, enter **Summary** (**E**) for the page name, and click on **OK**. The page name will change. Repeat this step for **Page 2** and **Page 3**, and enter **Analysis** and **Sales Manager Overview** for their names, respectively:

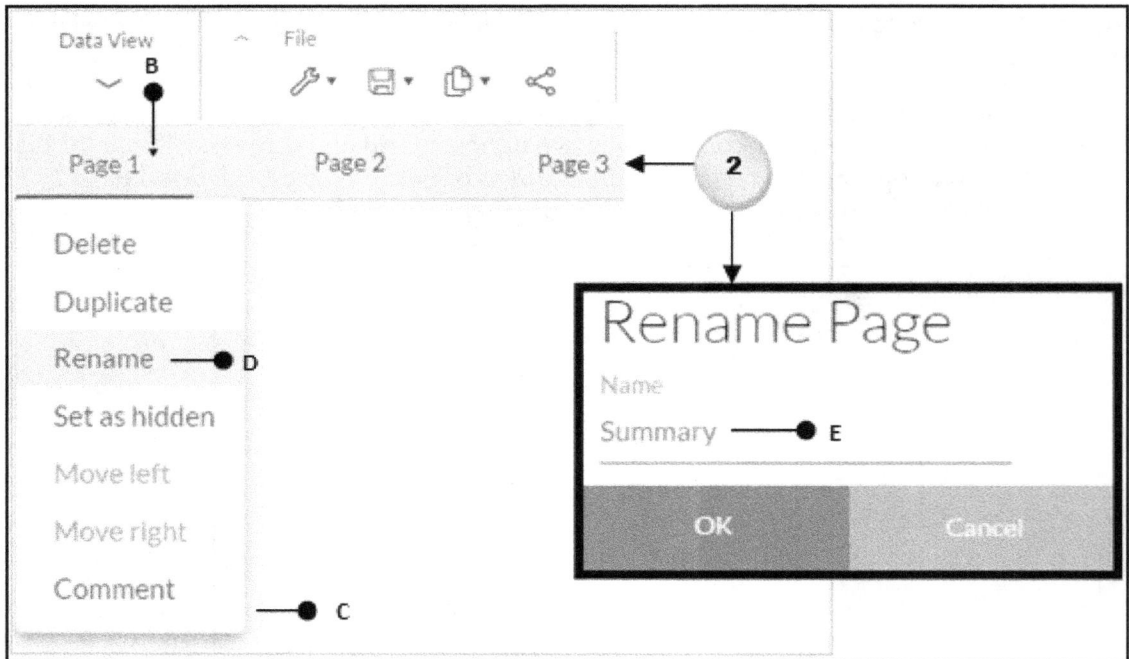

After creating multiple pages in your story, you can arrange them in some specific order to make the content easier for other users to understand. When you hover the mouse cursor over a page name in the page tab bar, you see a tiny down-arrow icon. Clicking on this icon displays a menu for that page. You have already used the **Rename** option from this menu. Here are the other menu utilities that allow you to perform some important tasks on your story pages:

- (**F**) **Delete**: This removes the page from where you invoked the delete operation.
- (**G**) **Duplicate**: This makes an exact copy of the page. The new page takes the name of the existing page with a post fixed number, which you can change using the **Rename** menu option.
- (**H**) **Set as hidden**: In situations where you do not want to share some specific story pages with other users, you can utilize this option to mark those pages as hidden. When you mark a page as hidden, the name of that page is stricken off (**I**) and the menu label changes to **Set as visible**, which, when clicked, reinstates the page.
- (**J**) **Move Left/Right**: Using these two options, you can arrange the position of a page. When you use either of these options, the page is moved to the left or right by one place. Alternatively, you can click and drag a page to a new location.

The page names, order, and visibility are saved when you save your story. These definitions are then rendered according to the saved settings to other users with whom you share your story. For example, the page names are shown in the order you defined them, and those marked as hidden do not display on their screens:

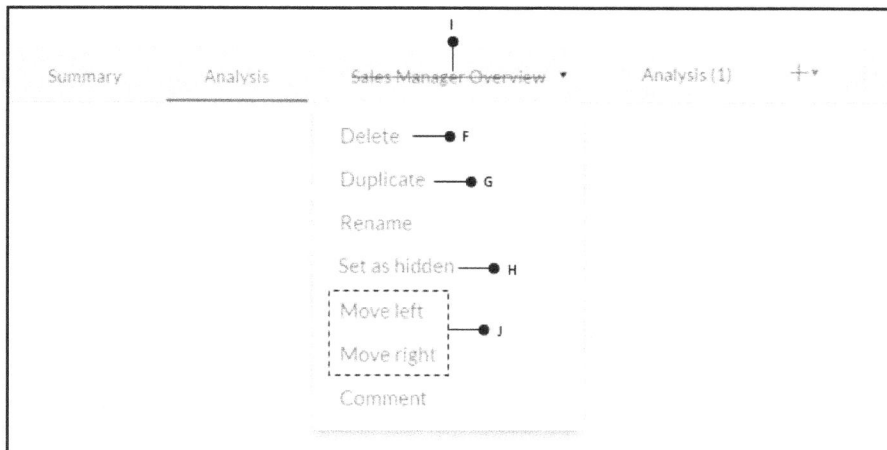

Adding comments to a page

In the previous section, you were briefed about the options available in a page menu. Among those options was **Comment**, which you will see in action here. As the name implies, you use this option to add comments on the selected page to provide some vital information to other users. When you add a comment, other users can see and reply to it.

Here are the steps to add comments for a story page:

3. Hover the mouse pointer over the **Analysis** page to see the tiny menu icon (**A**). Click on this icon, and select **Comment**.

4. You will see the **Comment** dialog box. Type some comments in this dialog box and click on the **Place Comment** button (**B**). Each comment you add to a story page is assigned a number, which appears at the top of the page name (**C**).

5. Click on the Save icon, and select the **Save** option from the menu to save the story and to publish the new comment to others. You will see a message story and comment saved successfully at the bottom of your screen:

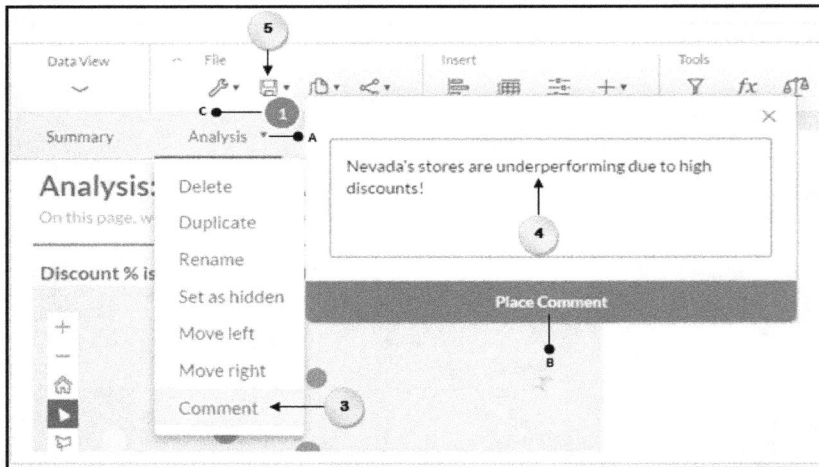

Hit your browser's reload button (**D**) to refresh the view. The Comment View icon (**E**) in the view toolbar will change to show that you have a comment to view. Hitting this icon will show the comment number (**F**) at the top of the **Analysis** page. Click on this number to see the comment (**G**). You can reply to this comment by entering some text in the **Reply here...** area (**H**) and clicking on the Send icon (**I**). When you add a reply, another comment is added to the thread. Reload the page and observe that the comment view is now showing **2** under its icon. Click on the Collaboration icon (**J**), and then click on the **Comments** tab (**K**) to see the thread. To delete the comment, click on the trash can icon (**L**). Note that you can delete only your own comments. When you are viewing a comment posted by someone else, the trash can icon doesn't display.

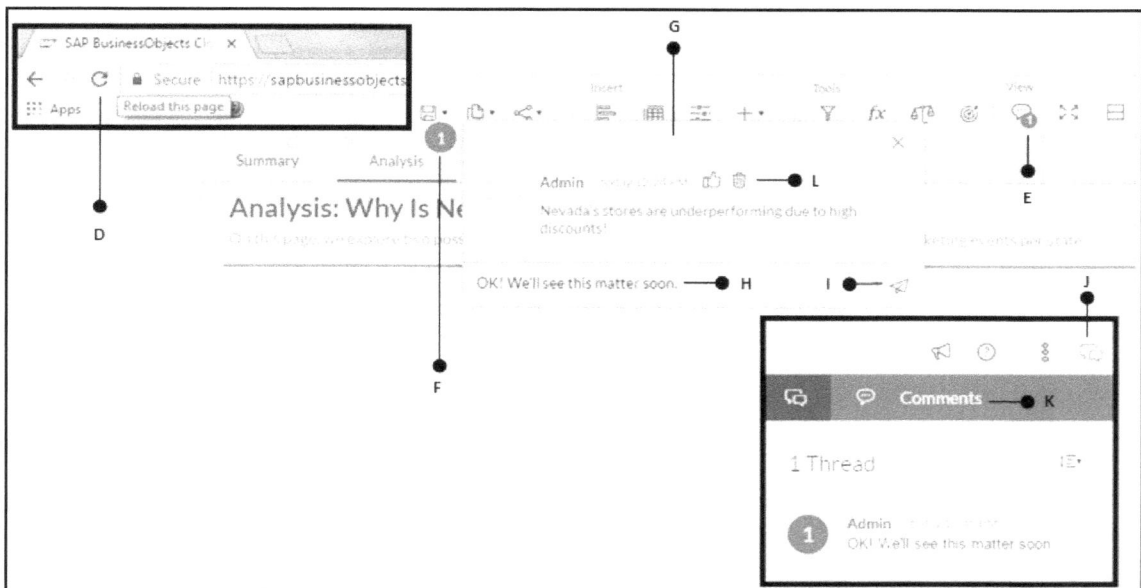

Creating a geomap with a bubble layer

Models that include latitude and longitude information can be used in stories to visualize data in geomaps. By adding multiple layers of different types of data, we can show different geographic features and points of interest, enabling us to perform sophisticated geographic analysis. In this exercise, we will create a geomap based on the **BestRun_Demo** model, which is already geo-enriched.

6. Select the **Analysis** page (**A**) to put the geomap on. Click on the Add icon (**B**) on the **Insert** toolbar section, and select **Geo Map**:

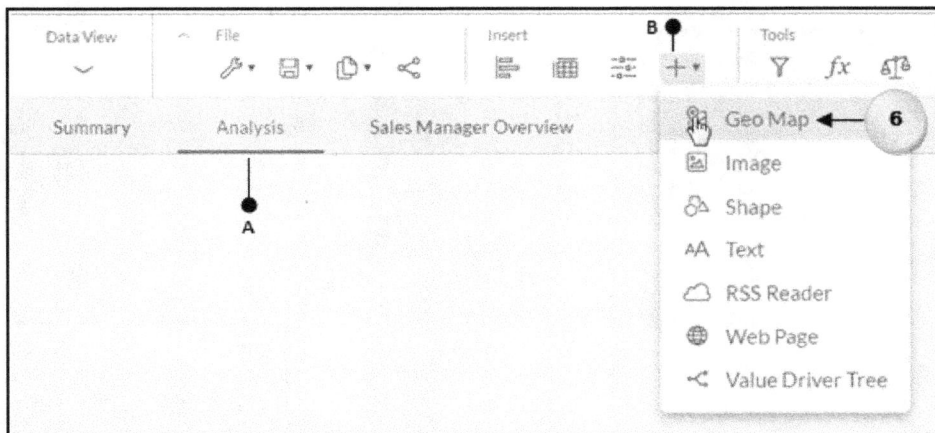

7. A blank map (**C**) will be added to the page, as illustrated in the following screenshot. The menu under the **Base Layer** section contains some built-in maps for you to choose from. For this exercise, keep the default **Light Gray** option (**D**) selected, and click on the **Add Layer** link:

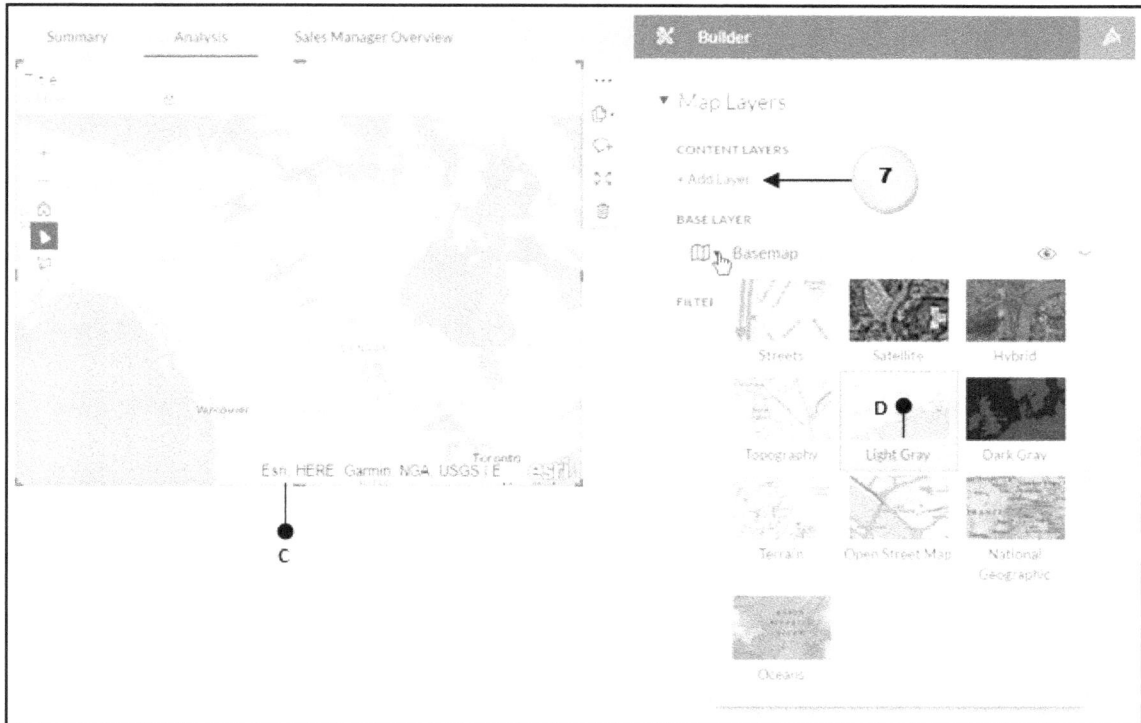

8. On the **Builder** tab, click on the Edit icon (**A**) in the **Data Source** section. On the **Select Datasource** screen, select the **Existing Model** option (**B**), and then select the **Best Run Demo** model (**C**) from the **Name** list. Click on **OK**. If you do not select a model as your data source for a given layer, no data points will display for that layer. Once you add a model to your geomap, it serves as the default model for any subsequent layers you create. You can always change the data source for any given bubble, choropleth, heat map, or flow layer by selecting the Edit icon in the **Data Source** section.

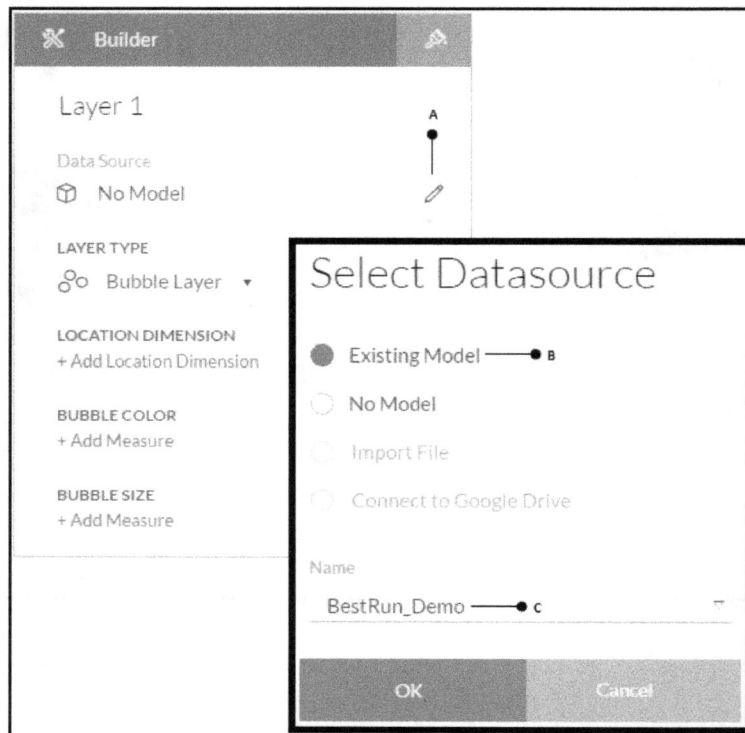

9. Click on the arrow in the **Layer Type** section. A list of layers appears with six different types of layers. From this list, select **Bubble Layer**. The **Bubble Layer** option in this example will display data points using bubbles to visualize net revenue by stores.

10. Click on the **Add Location Dimension** link, and select **Stores** from the list. The dimension was created as part of the geo enrichment for the model to capture the latitude and longitude of each store location. To add data from a model to a bubble, choropleth, or heat map layer, the model must contain at least one location dimension. The flow map layer requires at least two location dimensions. As you select the stores location dimension, the bubble layer appears on the map based on the store locations generated in the model.

11. Click on the **Add Measure** link under **BUBBLE COLOR**, and select **Net Revenue**. The colors you defined for this measure in `Chapter 4`, *Creating Stories Using Charts*, will be associated with the measure.

12. Click on the **Add Measure** link under **BUBBLE SIZE**, and select **Click to Create a New Calculation**. Here, you will specify the size of bubbles by the discounts offered in stores:

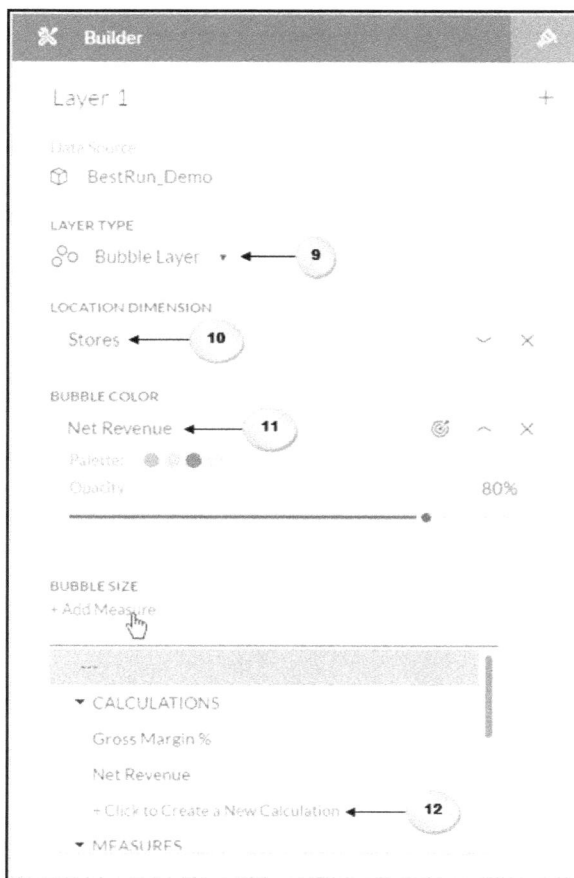

13. In the **Calculation Editor**, set **Type** to **Calculated Measure**.

14. Enter `Discount%` in the **Name** box.

15. In the **Edit Formula** area, enter the left square bracket [, and select **Discount** from the measures list.

16. In the **Formula Functions** list, click on **OPERATORS** to see a list of mathematical operators. Click on the division (/) operator to place this operator just after the **Discount** measure in the **Edit Formula** section.

17. Once again, enter the left square bracket [in the **Edit Formula** area, and this time, select the **Original Sales Price** measure to complete the calculation. Click on the **FORMAT** button available at the bottom of the screen to validate the formula. Once the formula in validated, click on **OK** to close the **Calculation Editor** dialog box. The `Discount%` calculated measure appears under the **Bubble Size** section, which determines the percentage of discount provided against sales:

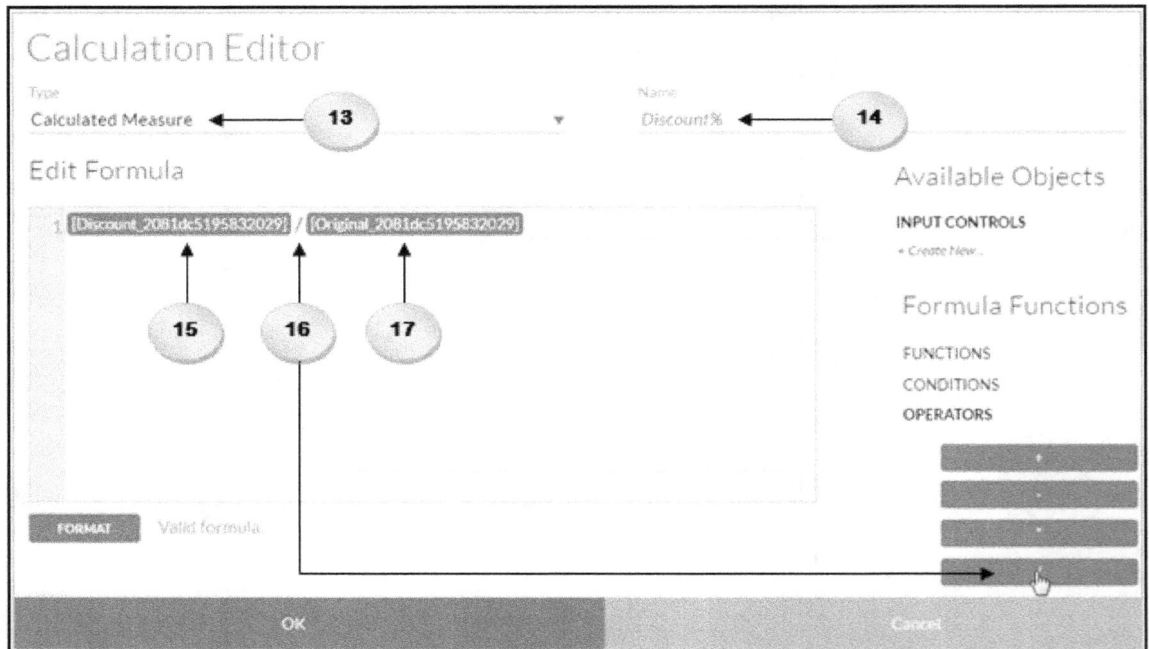

18. Click on the threshold icon representing **Net Revenue**.

19. Select **Show Threshold | None** from the menu. When you selected this measure in step 11, a story defined threshold (created in `Chapter 4`, *Creating Stories Using Charts*) was associated with it. We set it to **None** because in the current scenario, we will define a new threshold for this measure.

20. Expand the **Palette** list (**A**), and select the second scheme from the **Diverging** section:

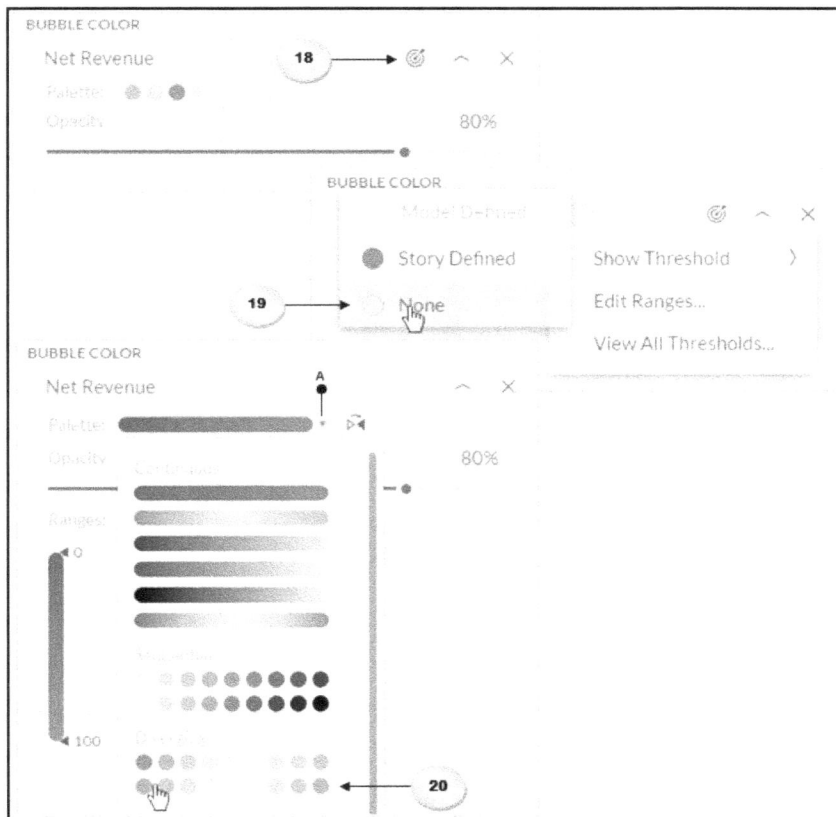

21. Set the **Opacity** value of the bubbles to **100%,** or adjust it so that the basemap or other layers are visible. The switch icon (**A**) can be used to reverse the **Palette** order, and the scale slider (**B**) is used to adjust the size of bubbles.

22. The switch beside the ranges list is used to show the KPI values as percentages or as absolute values. For this exercise, turn this switch from the default percentage (%) position to the absolute values (**22**) position.

23. Double click on the value representing the warning (yellow) range (**C**), and enter 4,000,000 (four million) replacing the existing warning value, as shown in the following screenshot. The same value will appear in the critical range but with a different comparison operator. Now, double-click on the value being displayed in the OK range (**D**), and replace it with 7,000,000 (seven million). If the **Net Revenue** value of a store is less than 4 million, the bubble for that store will appear in red. A value of more than or equal to 4 million will be shown in a yellow bubble. Anything equaling 7 million or beyond will be displayed in a green bubble. When you enter these values and click away from these ranges, the effect of these values is immediately reflected in the geomap. As you can see, the stores on the geomap are displayed in clusters with three different colors according to the KPI values. To support the rendering of large numbers of locations, the bubble layer is set, by default, to display clusters rather than all the individual points. Using this section, you can group the bubbles together by specifying the **Maximum Display Points** number (discussed in the next section) to display in the map. You can also adjust the opacity of the clusters and the cluster color in your map.

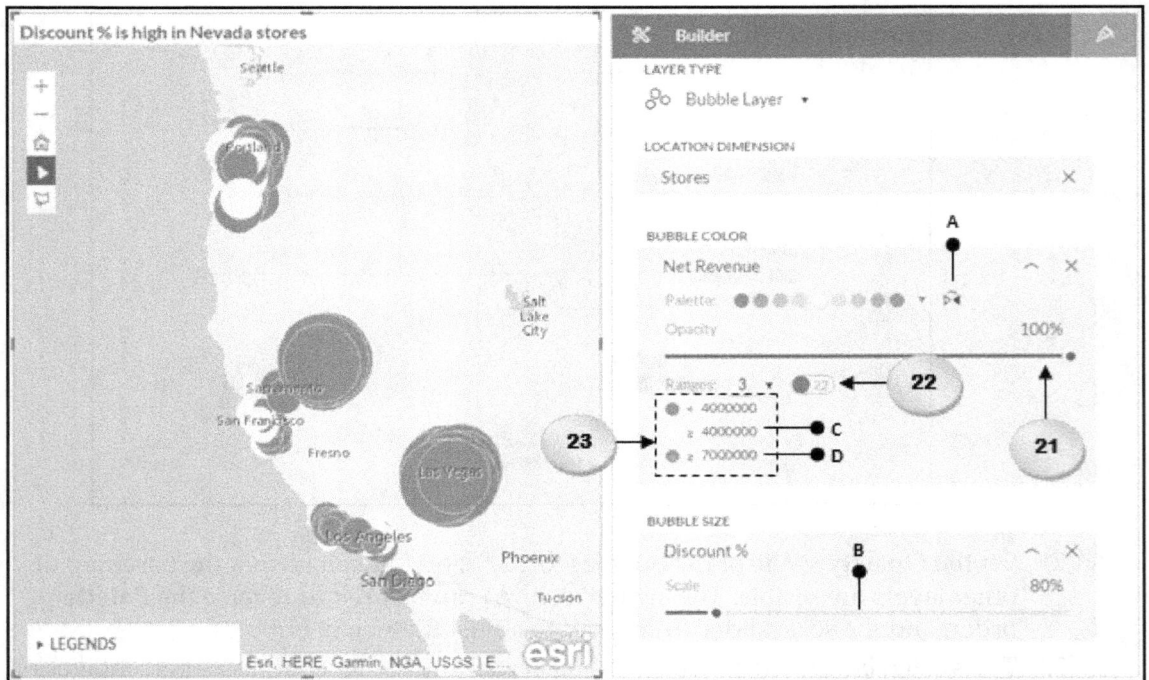

As you can see in the following screenshot, all the stores in the **Nevada** state (**E**) are shown in red bubbles because the net revenue of all these stores is less than 4 million. Click on the + icon (**F**) or use the mouse wheel to zoom in to see stores in **Los Angeles**, as illustrated in the following screenshot:

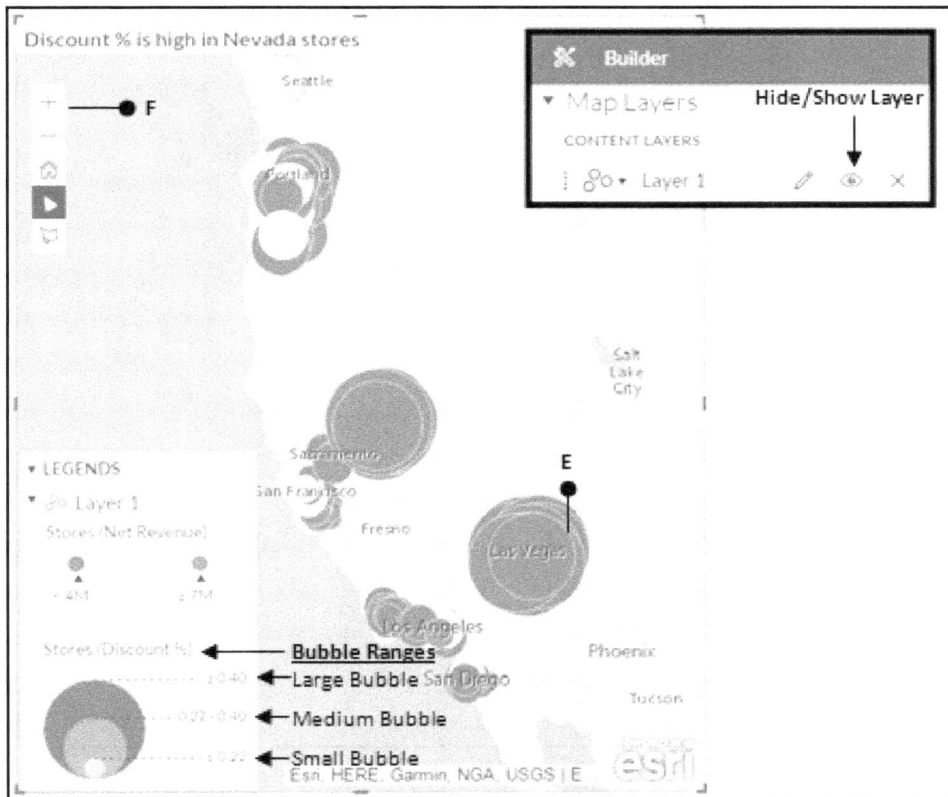

In this view, the **Conoco Food** Stop is shown in a green bubble because the net revenue of this store is 8.3 million, which is more than the OK threshold, which is 7 million.

The **McLeods** store's position is displayed as a warning because its net revenue is 6.26 million, which falls between 4 million and 7 million.

Finally, the **Park Market** store is shown in a red bubble as its revenue is 3.43 million, which is below the critical 4 million threshold.

The size of the bubble signifies the percentage of discount; the larger the bubble, the greater the percentage of discount in that store. For example, the **Aegis Market** store (**G**) in the following screenshot has given more discount than any other store, hence its bubble is the largest.

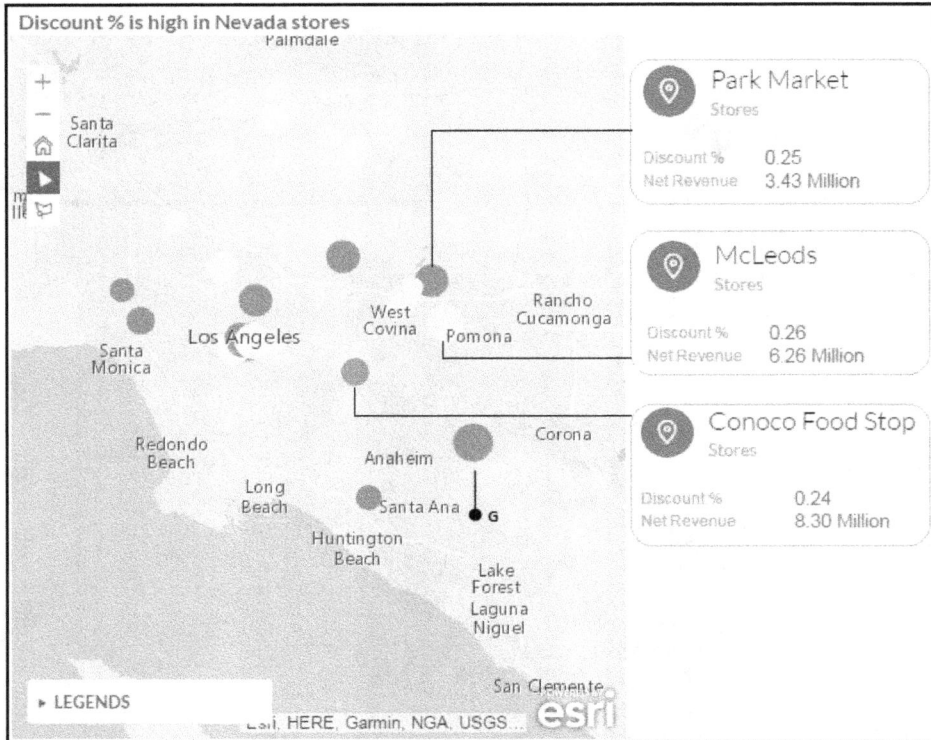

Location clustering in geomaps

The initial view of this map, as illustrated in the following screenshot, is crowded with bubbles, and you cannot interpret the results from this view. With the help of location clustering, you can make the map easier to work with.

Execute the following steps to see how location clustering works:

24. Select the map, and expand the **Cluster Properties** section located at the bottom of the **Builder** panel. Note that if you arrive from another story location to this page and click on the map, you see the map layers information on the **Builder** tab. In the content layers section, click on the Edit icon next to **Layer 1** to access the **Cluster Properties** section:

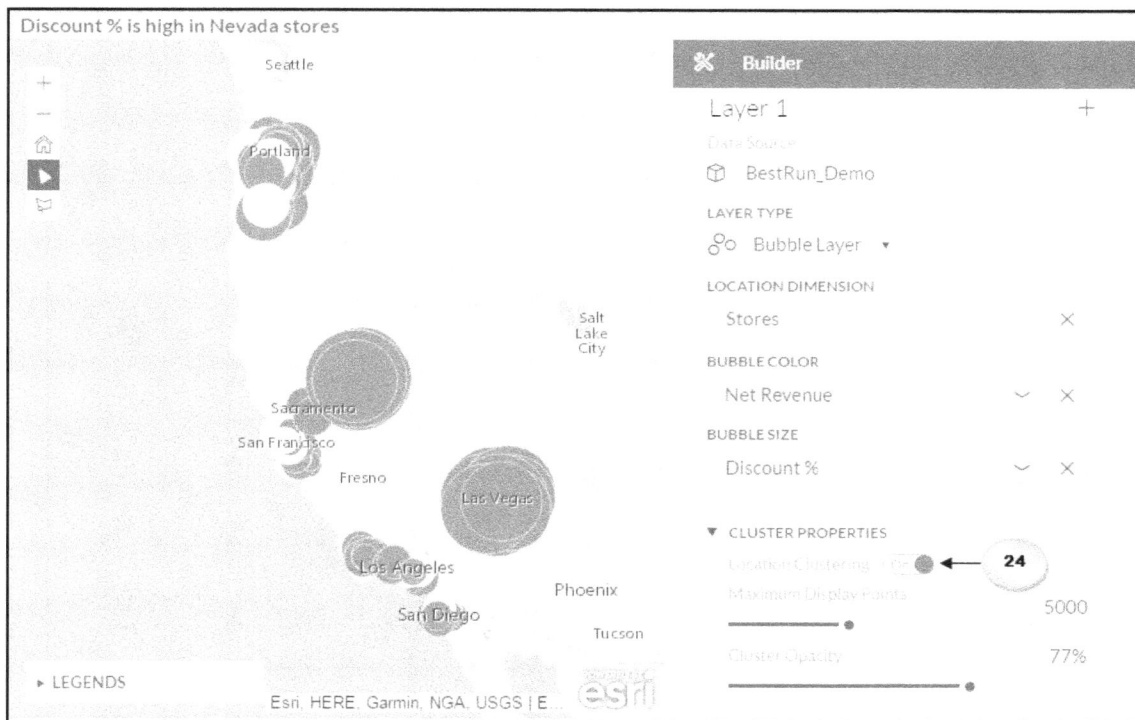

25. If not turned on, switch **Location Clustering** to the **On** position.

26. Double-click on the existing **Maximum Display Points** number (5,000), and replace it with 10.

27. Set **Cluster Opacity** to **100%**, and, if needed, change the default blue cluster color using the cluster color palette. Click on **OK** to close this panel.

The map view changes. Now the individual bubbles are clustered into one big bubble for each city. The cluster size indicates the number of bubbles. You can also see these numbers displayed on each cluster. For example, the following screenshot reveals that there are **70** stores in **San Francisco** and **54** in **Los Angeles**. Since there are more stores in **San Francisco**, its bubble is larger than the bubble of **Los Angeles**:

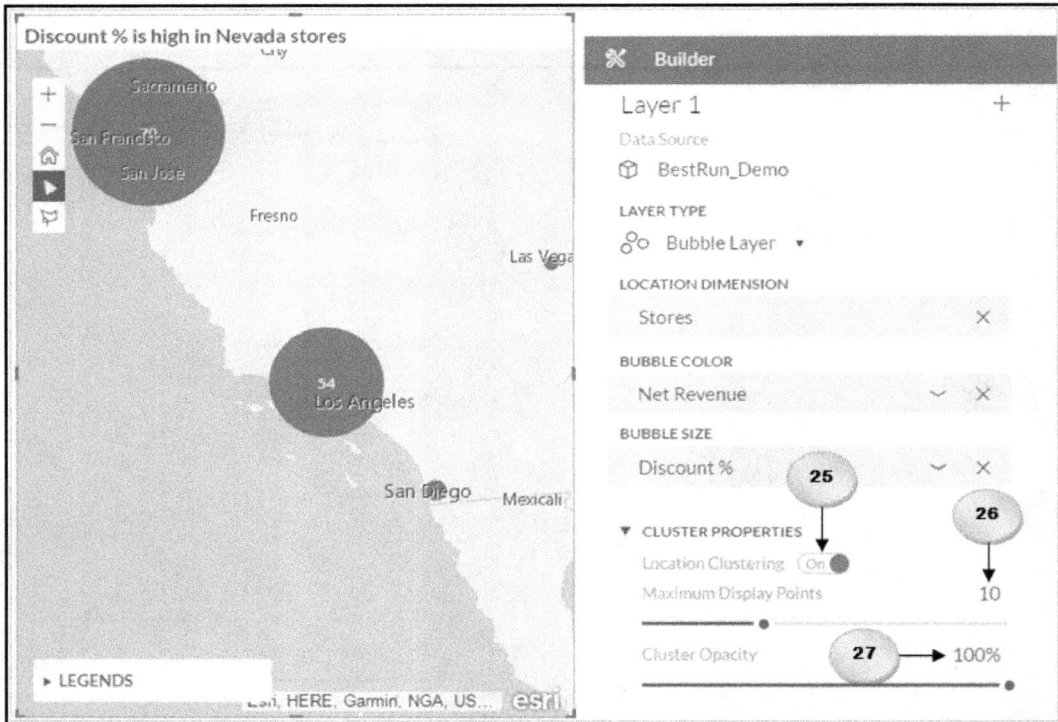

When you zoom in on the map, new clusters are generated based on the new number of display points on the map. When you zoom in enough that the number of display points is below the maximum you set, you once again see the individual bubbles. Let's see how it works:

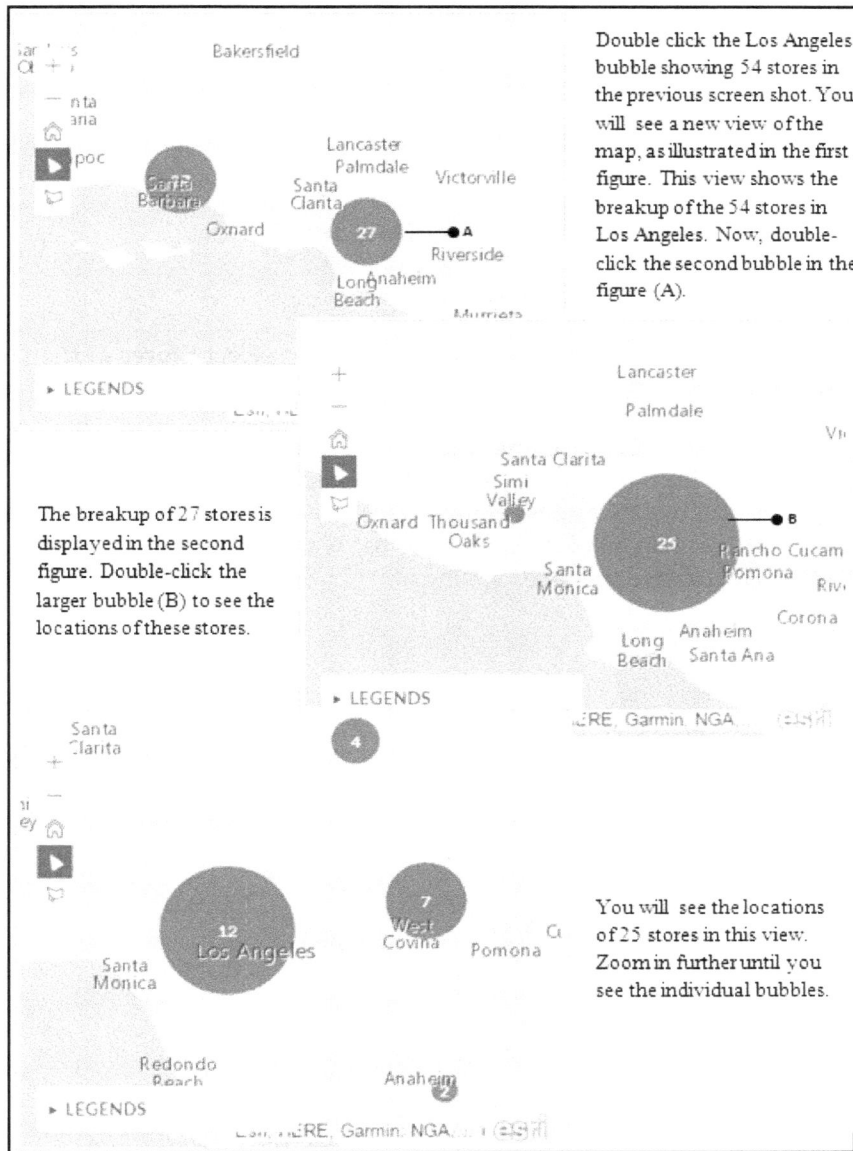

Double click the Los Angeles bubble showing 54 stores in the previous screen shot. You will see a new view of the map, as illustrated in the first figure. This view shows the breakup of the 54 stores in Los Angeles. Now, double-click the second bubble in the figure (A).

The breakup of 27 stores is displayed in the second figure. Double-click the larger bubble (B) to see the locations of these stores.

You will see the locations of 25 stores in this view. Zoom in further until you see the individual bubbles.

Creating a geomap with a choropleth layer

In this exercise, you will create a geomap based on a choropleth layer, which displays divided geographical areas in color. This provides a way to visualize values over a geographical area to show variation or patterns across the displayed location. Here are the steps to create this layer:

28. Click on the Add icon on the **Insert** toolbar, and select geomap.

29. In the **Builder** panel, select **Topography** from the **Basemap** list, and click on the **Add Layer** link.

30. Select the **BestRun_Demo** model for **Data Source**.

31. For layer **Type**, select **Choropleth Layer**.

32. Click on the **Add Location Dimension** link, and select **Stores** as the **Location Dimension**.

33. Click on the **Add Measure** link under the **Choropleth Color** section, and select **Net Revenue** from the list. Select a color scheme from the **Palette** list (**A**). Move the switch (**B**) in the **Ranges** section to use the actual values, and enter **200,000,000** (**C**) and **400,000,000** (**D**) for the warning and OK ranges respectively. Click on **OK** to save the layer settings.

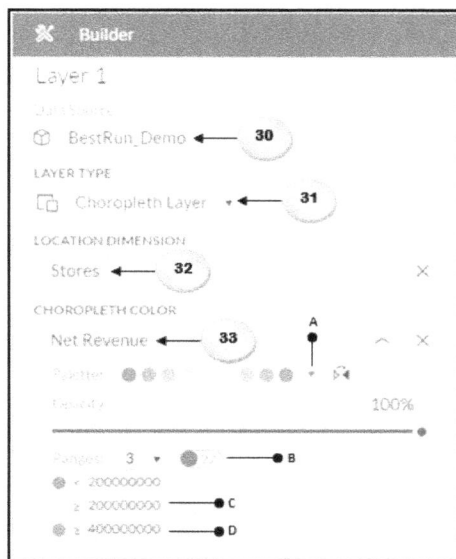

The map will refresh to show a country-level view. Since the value of net revenue for the country is 815.83 million, the **OK** status is applied to the whole country because this value is more than the 400 million range set for the **OK** status in the previous step. In the map's title area, you will see a hierarchical navigation icon (**E**) using which you can navigate up and down in the hierarchy. Click on this icon, and expand the list by clicking on **Layer 1** (**F**). As you can see, you have four navigation levels. The **Country** option (**G**) is selected by default to provide the top level view, as illustrated in the following screenshot:

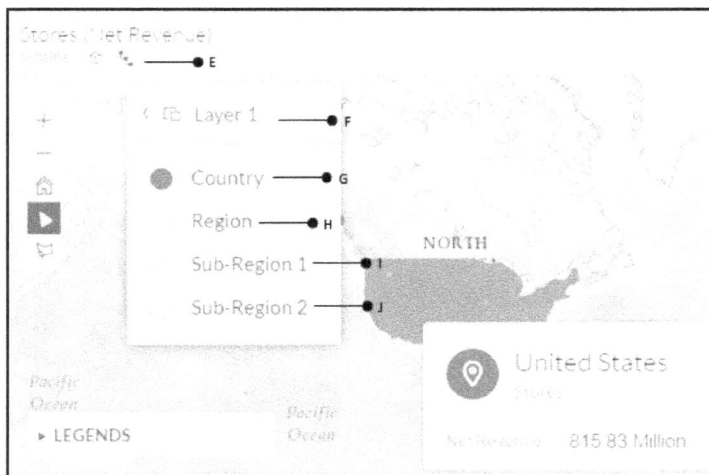

Click on the **Region** option (**H**) from the navigation list. The map is refreshed to show the state-level data. The three states' data is presented in different colors according to the specified ranges:

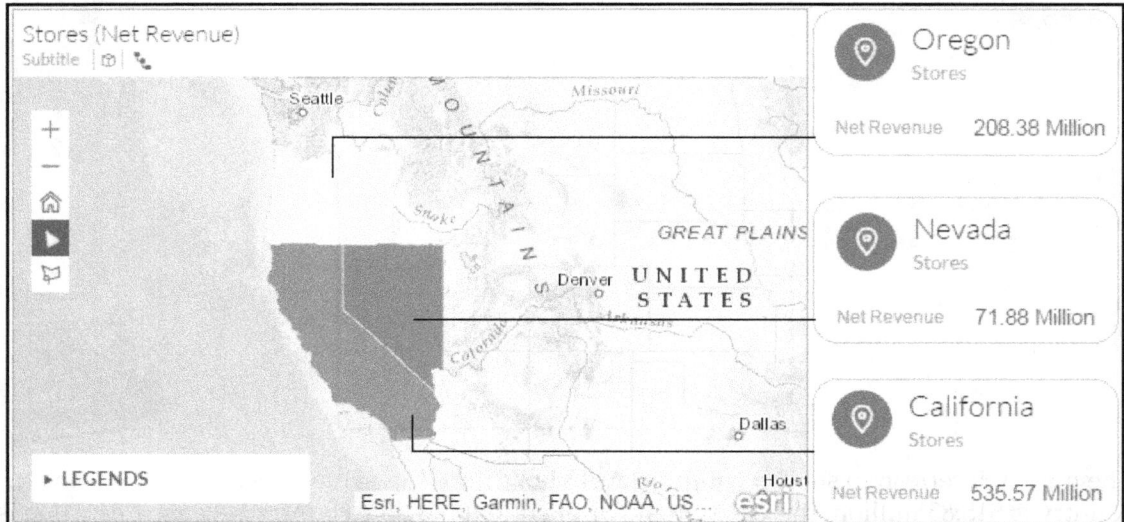

Click on the navigation icon, and select **Sub-Region 1** (**I**) to drill-down to the city level. All the cities in the map are shown as critical due to the high thresholds that are appropriate for the region level but are not suitable at this level. Modify these ranges by setting 20,000,000 and 40,000,000 for the warning and OK ranges respectively. After making these adjustments, you will see a reasonable view of the map:

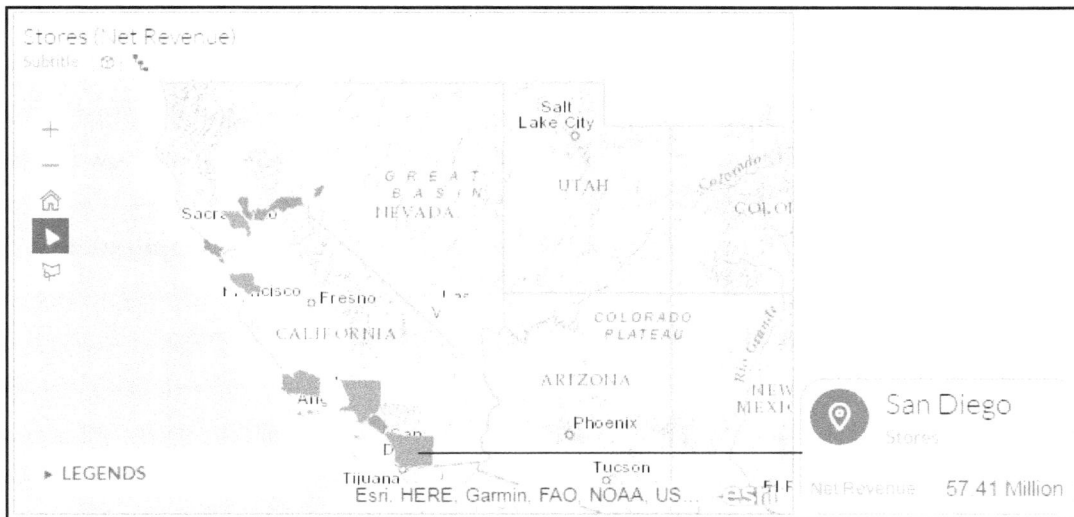

Click on the navigation icon again, and select the final level **Sub-Region 2 (J)**. At this final level, you are provided with store-level information for each city. Once again, you need to adjust the range figures. Set the warning to 2,000,000 and OK to 4,000,000. The **Net Revenue** for the **Los Angeles** stores is 40.21 million, so this area is shown in green. The **Garden Grove** stores have earned 3.68 million and are, therefore, shown in the warning range. Finally, the stores in Anaheim have earned just 1.87 million and hence are placed in the critical range:

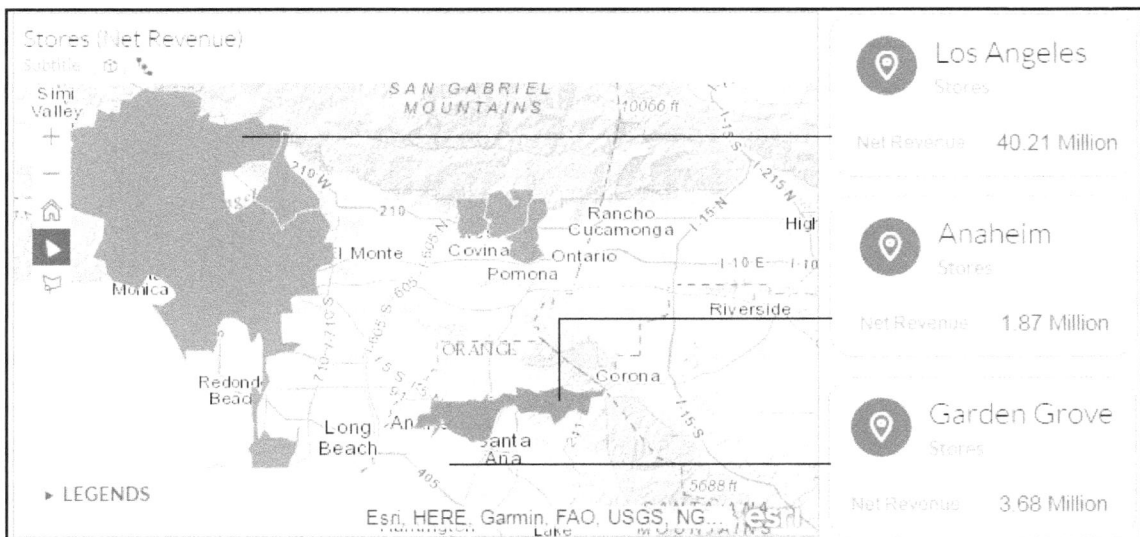

Applying a filter to a geomap

The vertical toolbar in a geomap is equipped with a filtering option using which you can filter your data directly on the map by drawing a shape, a polygon, circle, or square a around the data points you want to focus on. Execute the following step to see how filters can be applied to a geomap:

34. Select the polygon shape from the vertical toolbar, and draw a shape on the geomap, as illustrated in the following screenshot:

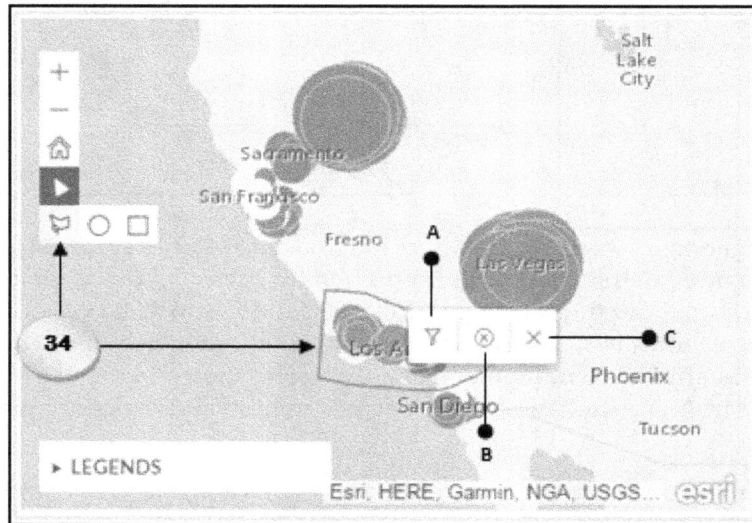

After drawing the shape, you are provided with a few options. The first option (**A**) lets you filter the selected data points, the second one (**B**) excludes the selected data points, and the third one (**C**) removes the filter. The outputs of the first two options are illustrated in the following screenshots. When you apply the filter to the selected data points, other data points on the map vanish (see **View-1**). If you opt for the second option, the selected data points disappear from the map, as shown in **View-2**:

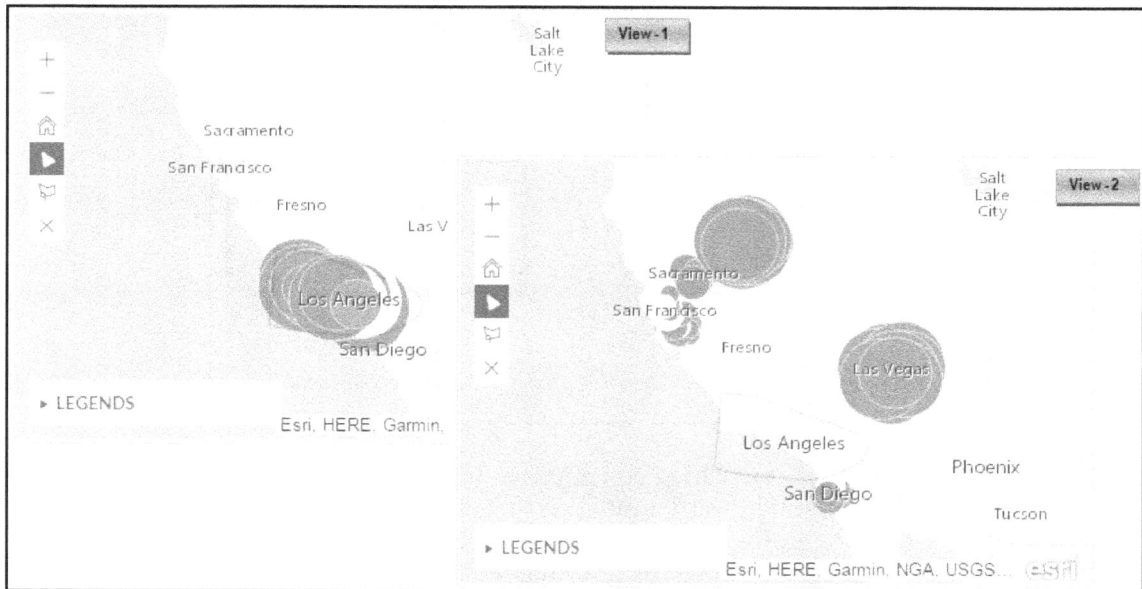

Linking different models

In your stories, you can display data from multiple models in a single chart by linking dimensions in those models. In this exercise, you will link the two models (**BestRun_Demo** and **Planned_Events**) to view the data from both models in a scatter plot chart.

Here are the steps to link dimensions:

35. Click on the **Link Dimensions** option in the **More** menu. On wider screens, this option is listed in the data toolbar section (**A**). Alternatively, you can find this option in the **Data Source** area of the **Builder** panel when you are creating or editing a chart:

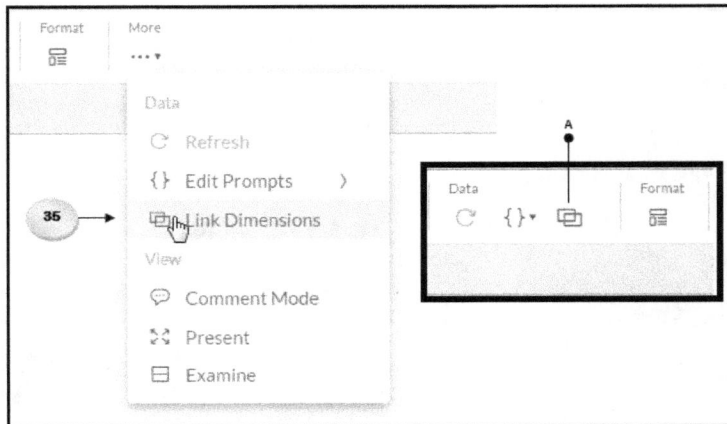

36. The **Link Dimensions** dialog box appears. In this dialog box, you have to link dimension from the primary model on the left with those from the secondary model on the right. Expand the drop-down list in the left pane, and click on the **Add model** option. In the **Select Models To Add** dialog box, select the existing **Planned_Events** model, and click on **OK** to close the dialog box. The dimensions from this model will appear under the left pane:

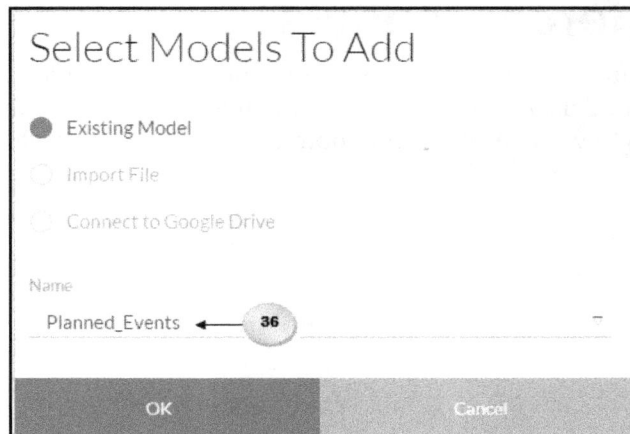

37. In the right pane, select the **BestRun_Demo** model from the corresponding drop-down list. The dimensions from this model will appear as well.

38. Once you select these models, you need to create a link between the two models by mapping at least one dimension that appears in both models. The dimensions you select from these models do not need to share the same name, but the data they contain must be of the same type. From the **Planned_Events** model, select **City**, and from the **BestRun_Demo** model, select **Location**. The link will be validated by the system (**A**). In this example, we need just one match. However, the **Linked Dimension** dialog box lets you match on more than one dimension. Establish the link by clicking on the **Set** button:

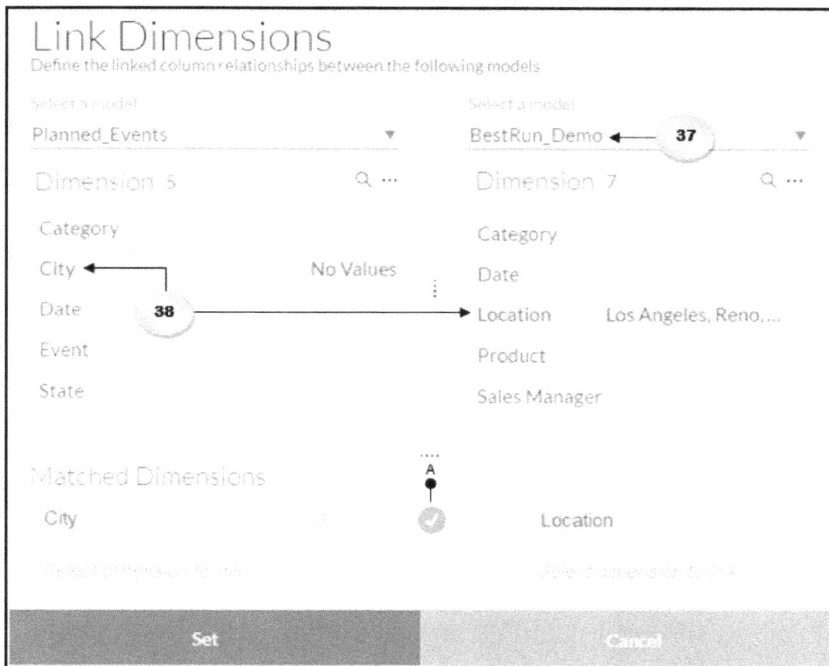

39. The **Link Dimension** dialog box, as illustrated in the following screenshot, comes up to review the link. It allows you to modify (**A**), delete (**B**), or add more links (**C**). For now, click on **Done**:

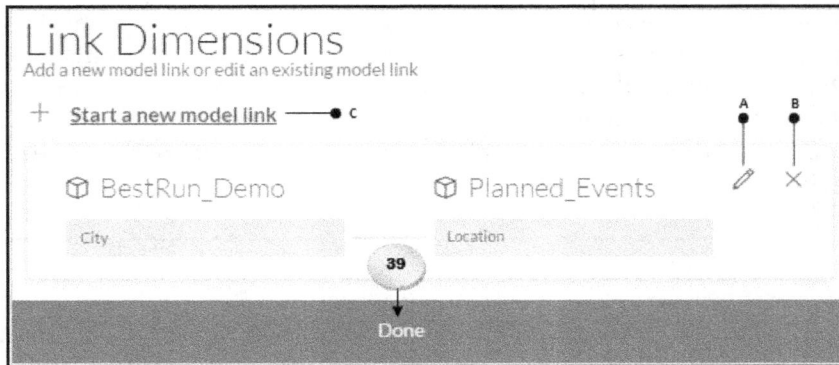

Create a chart based on linked dimensions.

Now that we have linked the two models, we can create a chart to display the data from both the models. In this example, we will create a scatter plot chart to obtain the result from the two models using the linked dimensions. Execute the following set of steps to create this chart:

40. As usual, add a blank chart by clicking on the chart icon on the Insert toolbar.
41. In the **Builder** panel, click on the **Edit** link under **Data Source**.
42. Select the **Planned_Events** model on the **Select Your Data** dialog box. This model will be treated as the primary model for the chart:

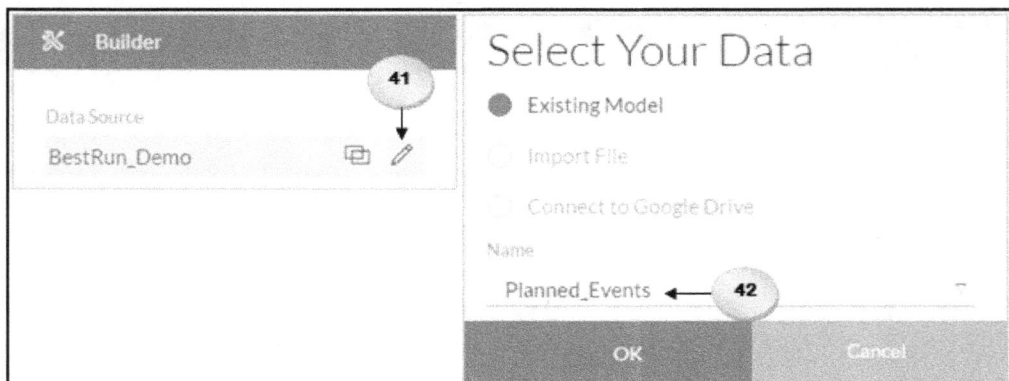

43. From the correlation category, select scatterplot chart.

44. Click on the **Add Measure** link in the **X-axis** section, and select **No of Events for 2015**. Note that this is a measure in the **Planned_Events** model.

45. Click on the **Add Dimension/Threshold** link in the **Color** section, and select **City**. This is the **Planned_Events** model dimension that was linked to the **Location** dimension in the **BestRun_Demo** model in the previous section. Note that linked dimensions have a link icon (**B**).

46. Now, click on the Link dimensions icon (**A**) in the **Data Source** section, and select the **BestRun_Demo** model. A blue dot (**C**) beside the model name, measure, and dimension is an indication that they are from the primary model.

47. In the **Y-axis** section, click on the **Add Measure** link, and select **Net Revenue** from the **BestRun_Demo** model. When you select the **Net Revenue** measure from the **BestRun_Demo** model, you see a new section named **Join Type** (discussed in the next section) under **Data Source** in the **Builder** panel:

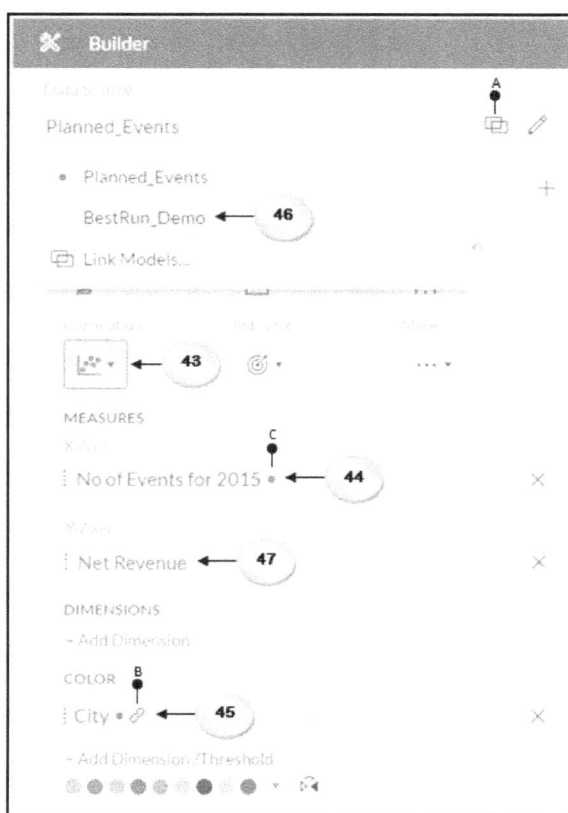

The chart is refreshed to display the data from the two models. The data on X-axis is fetched using the **No of Events for 2015** measure from the **Planned_Events** model, whereas the **Net Revenue** measure data on the Y-axis arrives from the **BestRun_Demo** model:

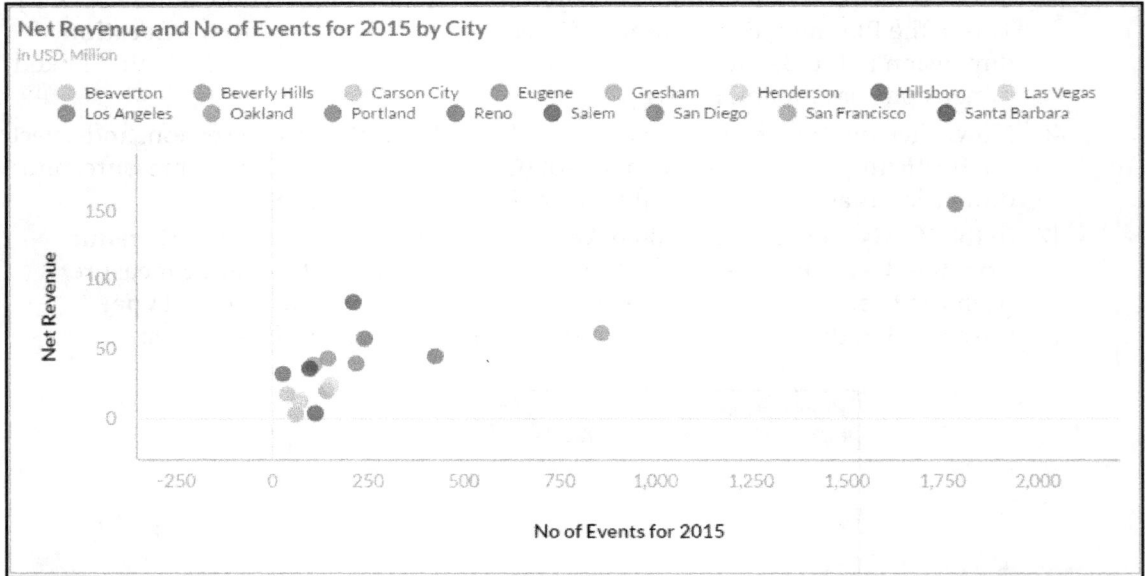

Join types

When you select a secondary model and add a measure from it to the chart, you see an additional section in the **Builder** panel. This section is labeled **JOIN TYPE**, as illustrated in the following screenshot. The options provided in this section allow you to select the type of data you want to display on the chart:

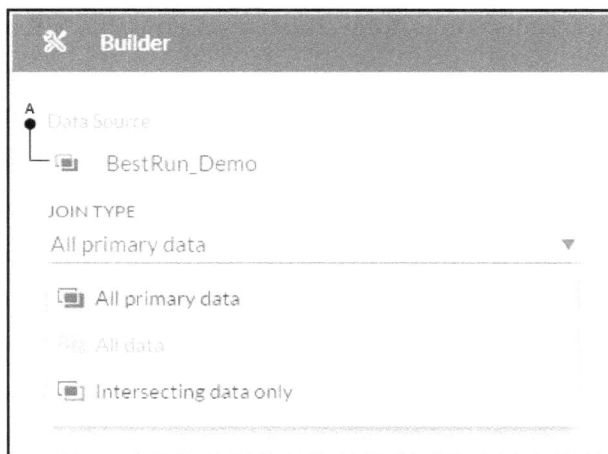

All primary data: This is the default option. It displays all of the data in the primary model and the corresponding data in the secondary model. This means that all the events data from the **Planned_Events** model are displayed, whether or not they have associated records in the **BestRun_Demo** model.

All data: As you can see, this option is grayed out because it is available only for the linked models whose data sources are SAP HANA. When this condition is met, the option becomes accessible and fetches all data from the primary and secondary models.

Intersecting data only: This option will allow only the linked data to appear in the chart. Refer to the next section, where this join type is demonstrated using an example.

When you select any of these options from the list, the icon beside the secondary model (**A**) changes to indicate the type of join that is currently in effect.

Intersecting data example

The scatter plot chart you created in the previous exercise displayed event data for 16 cities. However, the number of cities in the **BestRun_Demo** model is 18, as shown in the following screenshot, which is taken from the **Data View** panel. There is no event data in the **Planned_Events** model for the two highlighted cities: **Sacramento** and **San Jose**. This scenario will allow us to test the **Intersecting data only** join type.

Execute the following set of steps to test the effect of selecting the **Intersecting data only** join type:

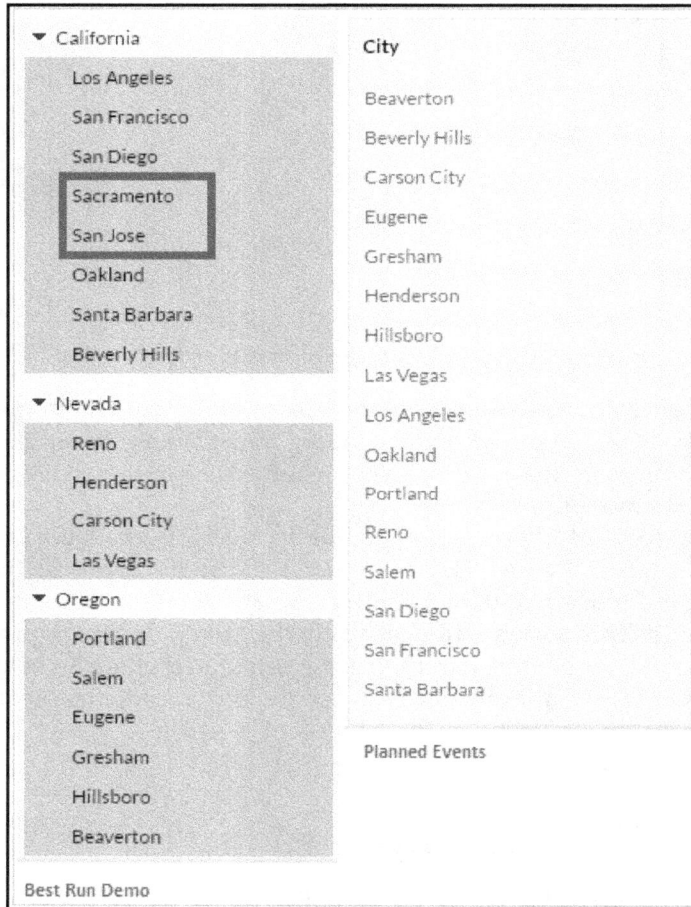

48. Add a blank chart by clicking on the chart icon on the Insert toolbar.
49. Select the **BestRun_Demo** model for **Data Source**.
50. Select the area chart from the **Trend** category.

51. Click on the **Add Measure** link, and select **Net Revenue**.
52. Click on the **Add Dimension** link in the **Dimensions** section, and select **Location**.
53. In **Data Source**, click on the Link dimensions icon, and select the **Planned_Events** model to select a second measure from this model.
54. In the **Measures** section, click on the **Add Measure** link, and select **No of Events for 2015**, as shown in the following screenshot:

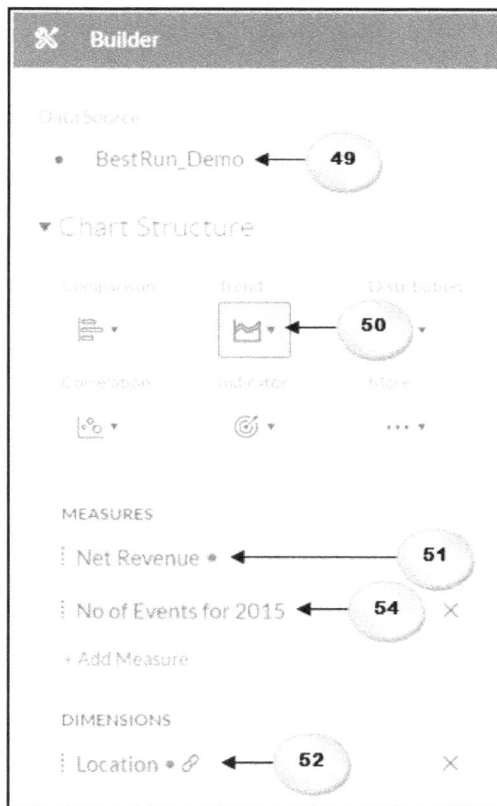

The trend chart appears on the page. Click on the **California** link (**A**) at the bottom of this chart, and then click on the drill-down icon (**B**) to drill-down on this state:

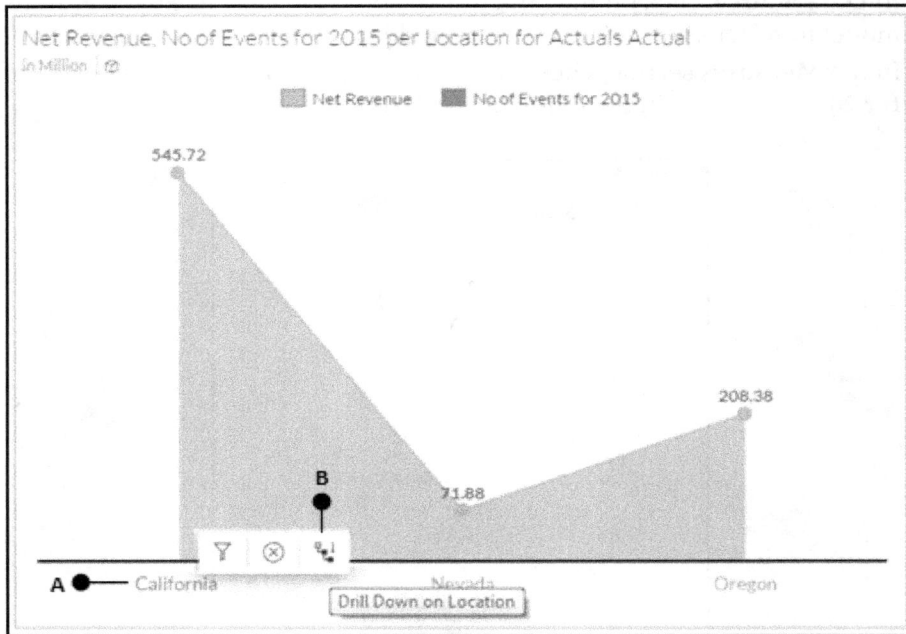

On the **Builder** panel, select the **Planned_Events** model in the **Data Source** section to view the **Join Type** section. With the default option set to **All primary data** for the Join Type, the chart will be presented as illustrated in **View-1** in the following screenshot. In this view, the two cities (**Sacramento** and **San Jose**) are visible with the respective net revenue figures from the **BestRun_Demo** model.

Now, switch the **Join Type** option to **Intersecting data only**. The chart refreshes, and you get **View-2**. Here you go! The two cities have vanished from the scene because their corresponding data doesn't exist in the Planned Event model:

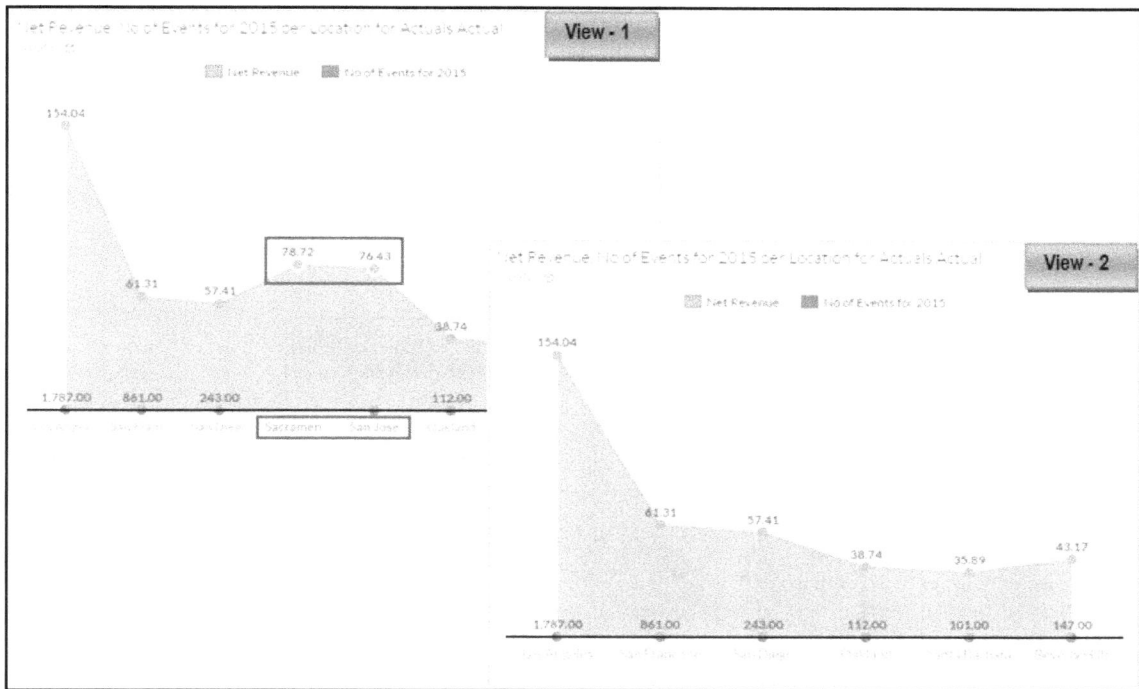

Creating a combination column and a line chart

A combination chart is used to compare two different types of data in the same chart. In this exercise, you will create a combination column and line chart to show the percentage of discount provided against net revenue. The initial chart view will provide this information for the three states. The chart will allow you to drill-down, either using the legend or via the state's links, to see relevant details. If you drill-down via legends, you see the data for all eighteen cities in the three states. On the other hand, if you drill-down on a state, you get city data for that state only. Here are the steps:

55. Add a blank chart from the Insert toolbar.
56. Set **Data Source** to the **BestRun_Demo** model.
57. Select combination column and line chart from the **Comparison** category.

58. In the **Measures** section, click on the **Add Measure** link, and select **Net Revenue** for **Column Axis**. The value of the measure you select for **Column Axis** is displayed using columns.

59. Click on the **Add Measure** link under **Line Axis**, and select **Discount %**. The values from the discount percentage measure will be presented using a line.

60. Finally, click on the **Add Dimension** link, and select **Location** to display the selected measures information for each state, as shown in the following screenshot:

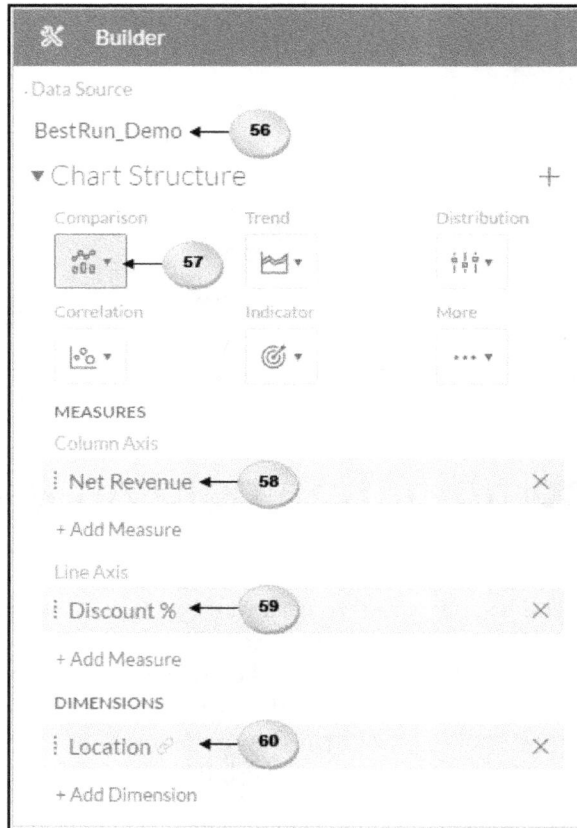

The chart appears on the page. The three columns in the chart represent net revenue for the three states, while the line represents the discount percentage given in each state. Execute the following steps to sort the chart columns from the lowest revenue to the highest:

61. Click on the Sort options icon. You will see a menu carrying the names of measures and dimensions used on the chart.

62. Select the **Net Revenue** measure from the menu.

63. As you select the measure, a submenu pops up with a couple of sorting options. Select **Lowest to Highest** from the submenu to sort the chart columns from the lowest net revenue to the highest:

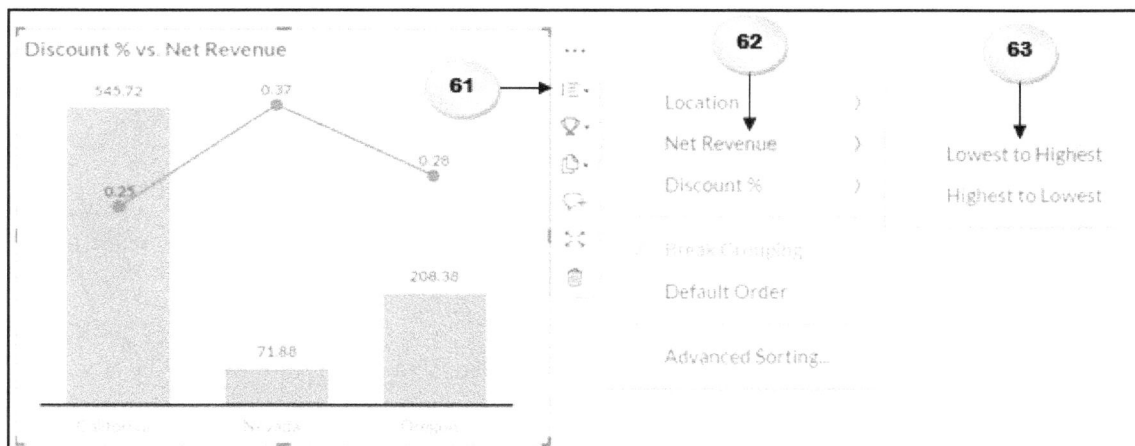

The chart is updated to take the sorting effect, as illustrated in the following screenshot:

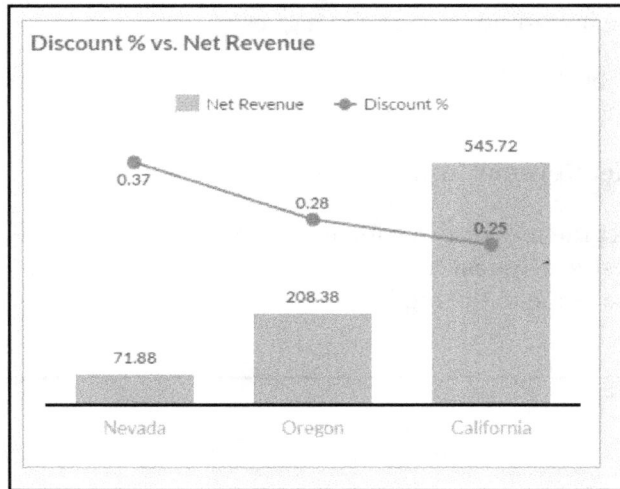

64. Click on the **Net Revenue** legend (**A**), and then click on the drill-down icon. You will see the chart, as illustrated in **View-1**. The view provides data for all cities in all states. Again, click on the **Net Revenue** legend, and select drill-up to see the top-level view of the chart.

Now, click on the **Nevada** state link (**B**) in the top-level view, and select drill-down. The output of this selection is illustrated in View-2, in which only **Nevada** state cities are fetched:

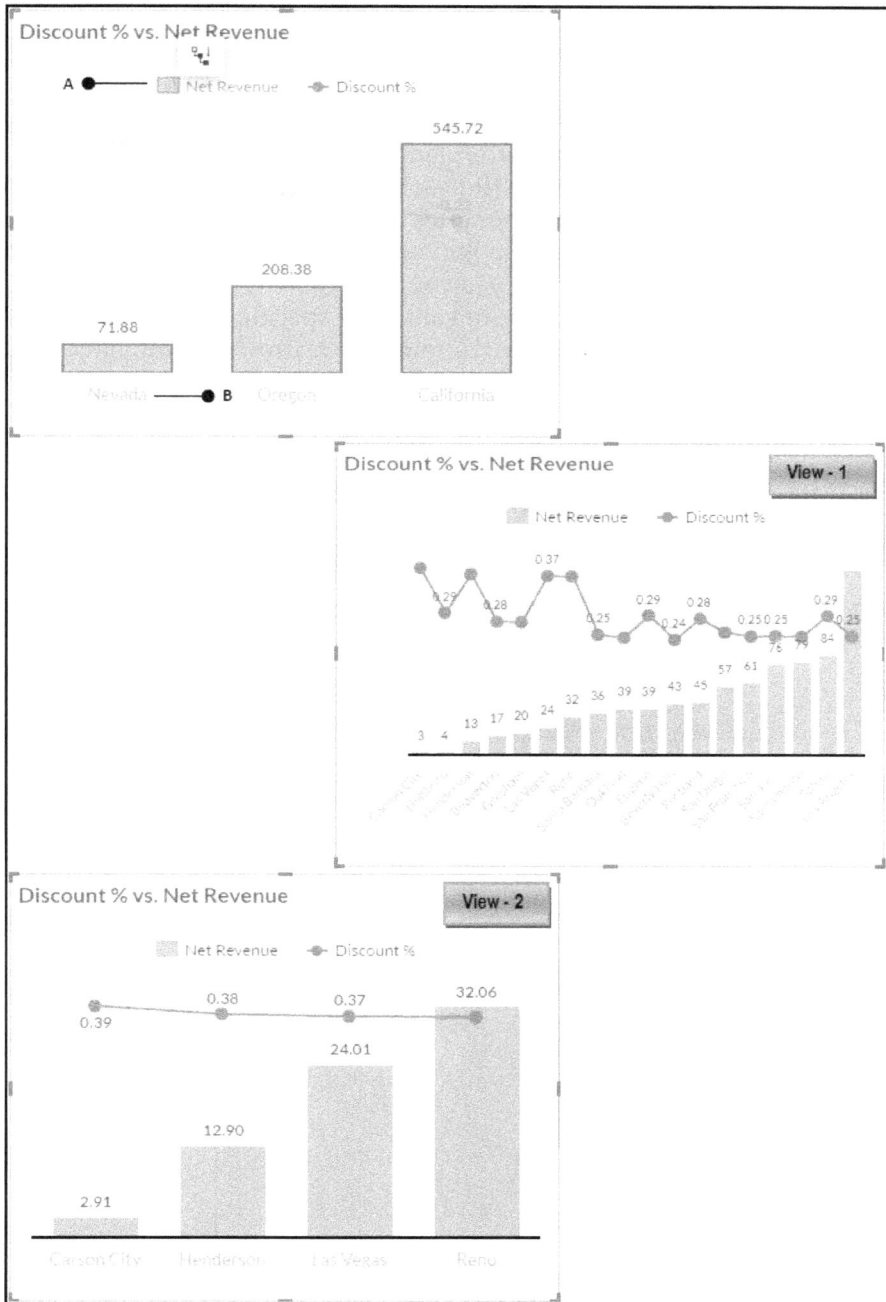

Using predictive forecasting through a trend time series chart

Time series forecasting is only supported for planning models. So, you need planning rights and a planning license to run a predictive time-series forecast. However, you can add predictive forecast by creating a trend time series chart based on an analytical model to estimate future values. In this exercise, you will use a trend time series chart to view net revenue trends throughout the range of a year. A predictive time-series forecast runs an algorithm on historical data to predict future values for specific measures. For this type of chart, you can forecast a maximum of three different measures, and you have to specify the time for the prediction and the past time periods to use as historical data.

Add a blank chart from the Insert toolbar.

65. Set **Data Source** to the **BestRun_Demo** model.
66. Select the **Time Series** chart from the **Trend** category.
67. In the **Measures** section, click on the **Add Measure** link, and select **Net Revenue**.
68. Finally, click on the **Add Dimension** link in the **Time** section, and select **Date** as the chart's dimension:

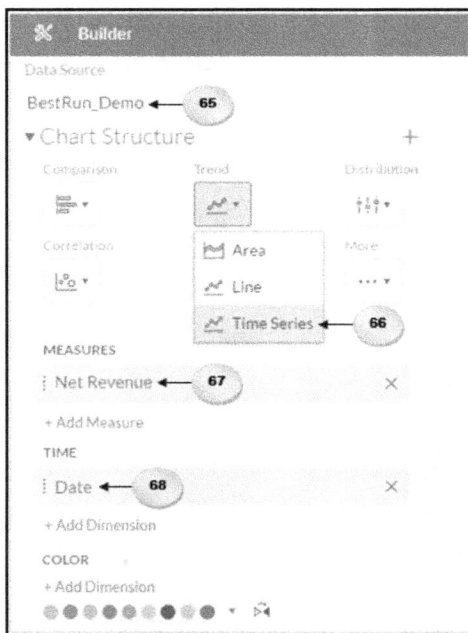

The output of your selections is depicted in the first view in the following screenshot. Every chart you create on your story page has its own unique elements that let you navigate and drill into details. The trend time series chart also allows you to zoom in to different time periods and scroll across the entire timeline. For example, the first figure in the following illustration provides a one-year view (**A**) of net revenue trends, that is from January to December 2015. Click on the six months link (**B**) to see the corresponding output, as illustrated in the second view. Drag the rectangle box (**C**) to the left or right to scroll across the entire timeline:

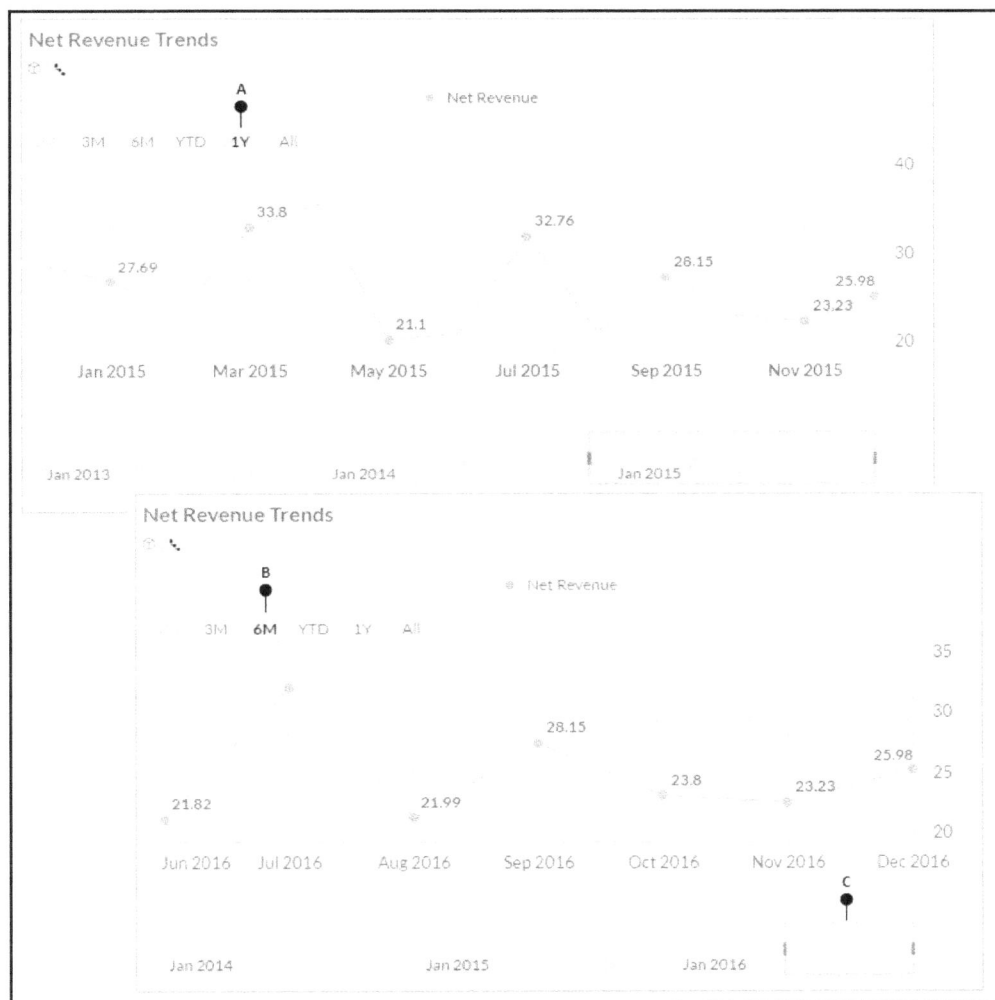

Adding a forecast

69. Click on the last data point representing December 2015, and select **Add Forecast** from the More Actions menu (**D**) to add a forecast:

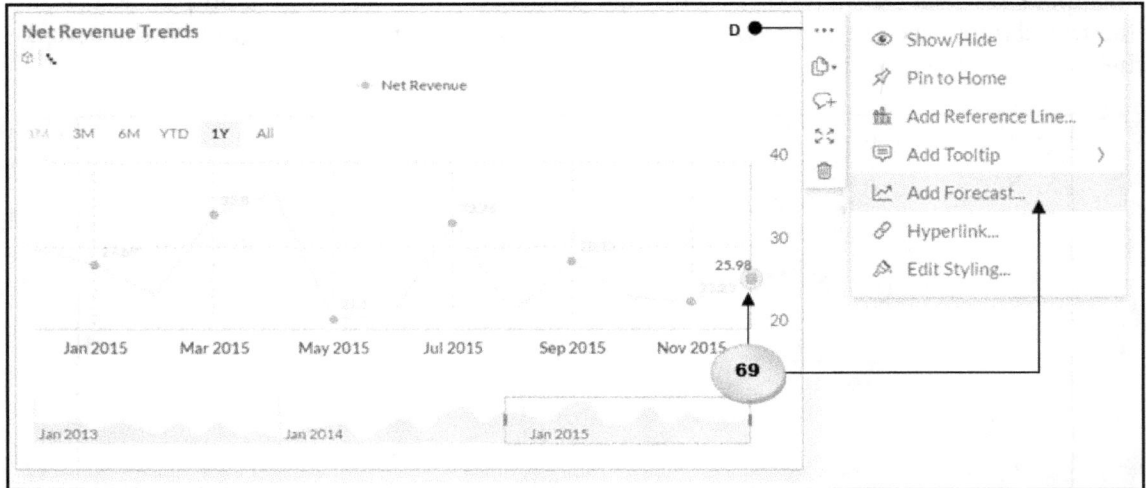

70. You see the **Predictive Forecast** panel on the right side, which displays the maximum number of forecast periods. Using the slider (**E**) in this section, you can reduce the number of forecast periods. By default, you see the maximum number (in the current scenario, it is seven) in the slider, which is determined by the amount of historical data you have. In the **Forecast On** section, you see the measure (**F**) you selected for the chart. If required, you can forecast a maximum of three different measures in this type of chart that you can add in the **Builder** panel. For the time being, click on **OK** to accept the default values for the forecast, as illustrated in the following screenshot:

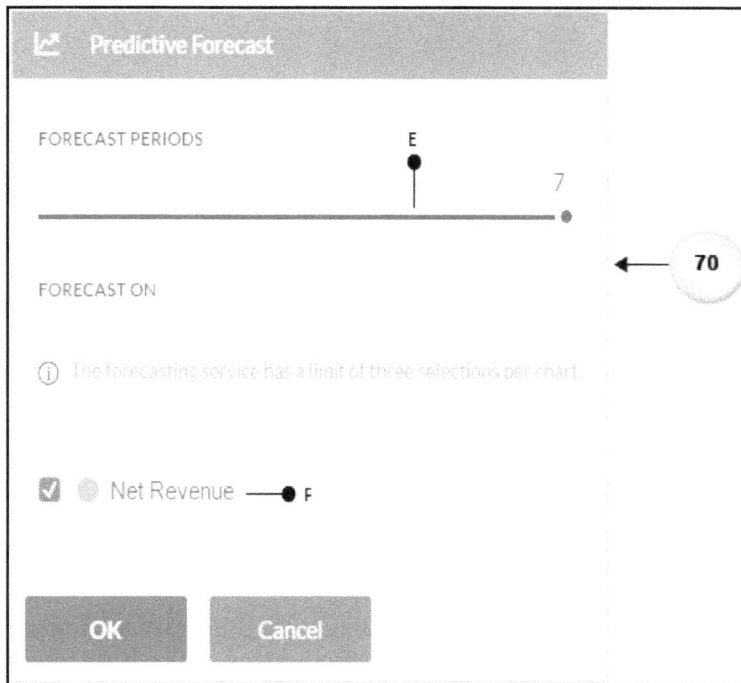

The forecast will be added to the chart. It is indicated by a highlighted area (**G**) and a dotted line (**H**). Click on the **1** year link (**I**) to see an output similar to the one illustrated in the following screenshot under the *Modifying forecast* section. As you can see, there are several data points that represent forecast. The top and bottom of the highlighted area indicate the upper and lower bounds of the prediction range, and the data points fall in the middle (on the dotted line) of the forecast range for each time period. Select a data point to see the **Upper Confidence Bound** (**J**) and **Lower Confidence Bound** (**K**) values:

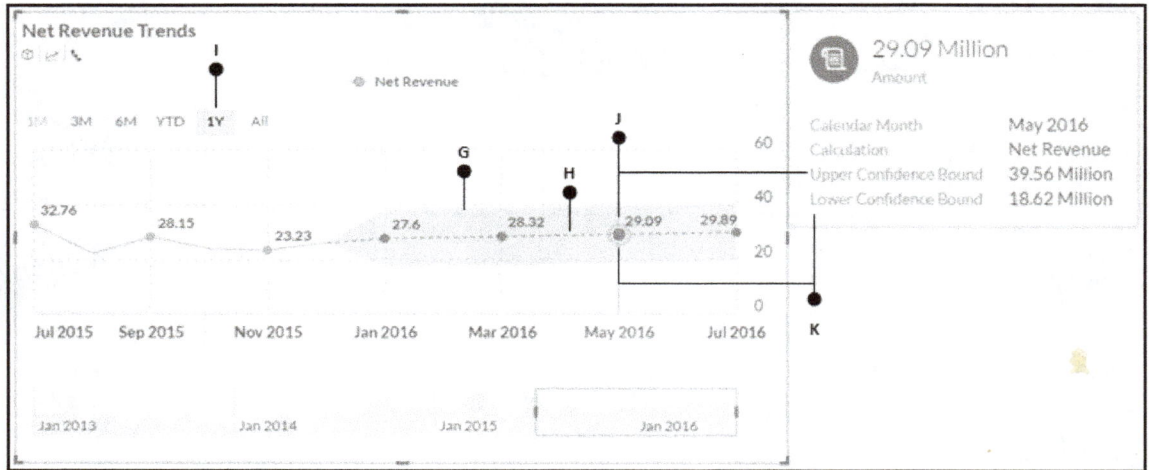

Modifying forecast

You can modify a forecast using the link provided in the **Forecast** section at the bottom of the **Builder** panel. Select the chart, and scroll to the bottom of the **Builder** panel. Click on the Edit icon (**L**) to see the **Predictive Forecast** panel again. Review your settings, and make the required changes in this panel. For example, drag the slider toward the left to set the **Forecast Periods** value to 3 (**M**). Click on **OK** to save your settings.

The chart should now display the forecast for three months--January, February, and March 2016 (**N**):

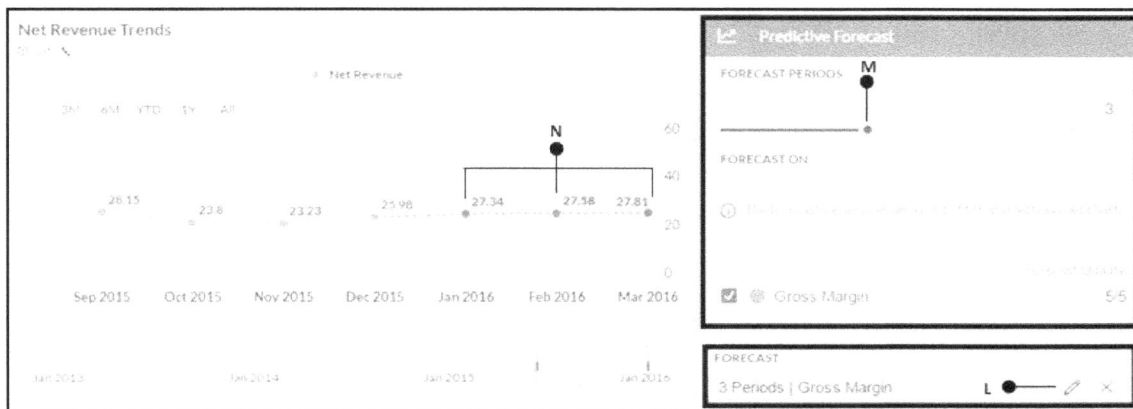

Adding a time calculation

If you want to display values such as year-over-year sales trends or year-to-date totals in your chart, then you can utilize the time calculation feature of SAP Analytics Cloud. The time calculation feature provides you with several calculation options. In order to use this feature, your chart must contain a time dimension with the appropriate level of granularity. For example, if you want to see quarter-over-quarter results, the time dimension must include quarterly or even monthly results. The space constraint prevent us from going through all these options. However, we will utilize the year-over-year option to compare yearly results in this exercise to get an idea about this feature. Execute the following instructions to first create a bar chart that shows the sold quantities of the four product categories. Then, add a time calculation to the chart to reveal the year-over-year changes in quantity sold for each category.

71. As usual, add a blank chart to the page using the chart option on the Insert toolbar.
72. Select the Best Run model as **Data Source** for the chart.
73. Select the **Bar/Column** chart from the **Comparison** category.

74. In the **Measures** section, click on the **Add Measure** link, and select **Quantity Sold**.

75. Click on the **Add Dimension** link in the **Dimensions** section, and select **Product** as the chart's dimension, as shown here:

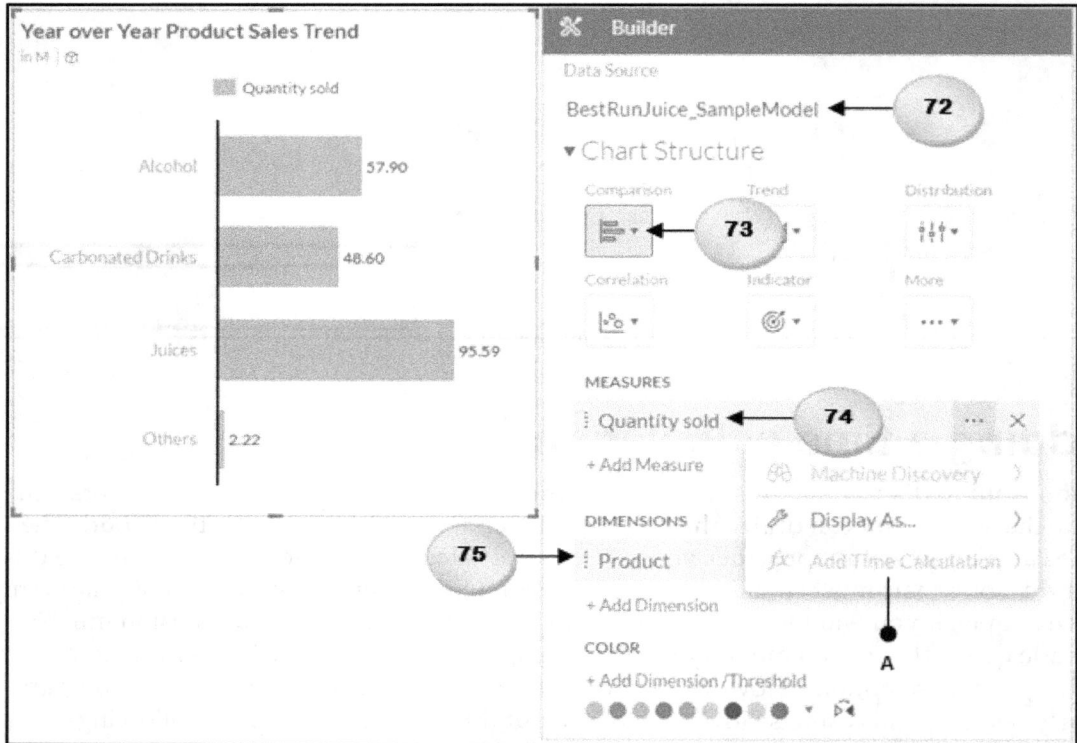

The chart appears on the page. At this stage, if you click on the More icon representing **Quantity sold**, you will see that the **Add Time Calculation** option (**A**) is grayed out. This is because time calculations require a time dimension to the chart, which we will add next.

76. Click on the **Add Dimension** link in the **Dimensions** section, and select **Date** to add this time dimension to the chart. The chart transforms, as illustrated in the following screenshot:

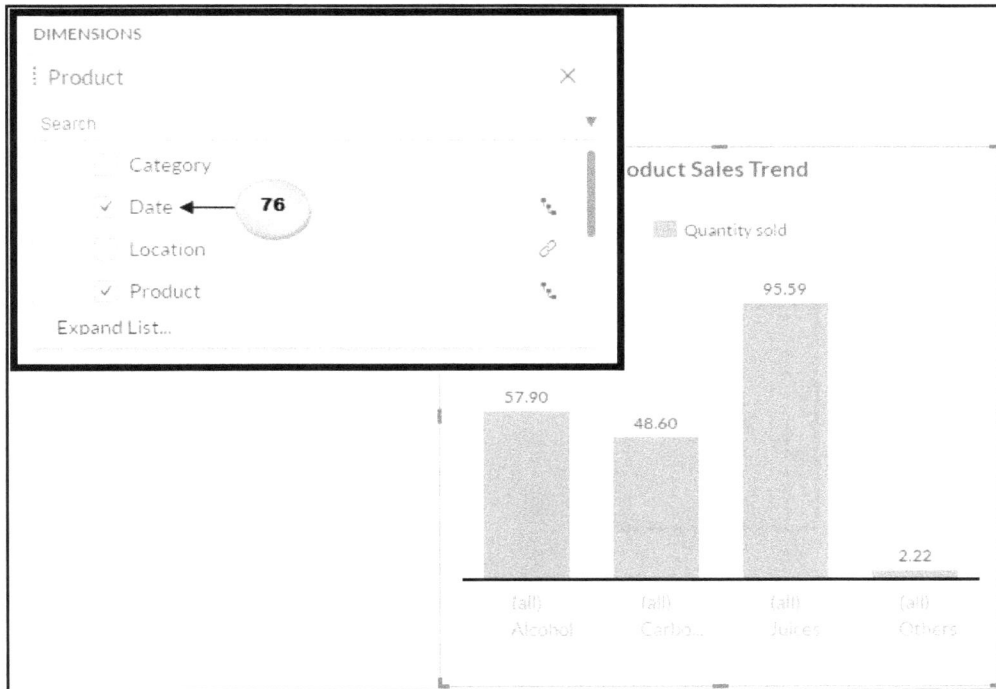

To display the results in the chart at the year level, you need to apply a filter as follows:

77. Click on the filter icon in the **Date** dimension, and select **Filter by Member**.
78. In the **Set Members for Date** dialog box, expand the **all** node, and select **2014**, **2015**, and **2016**, individually. Once again, the chart changes to reflect the application of filter, as illustrated in the following screenshot:

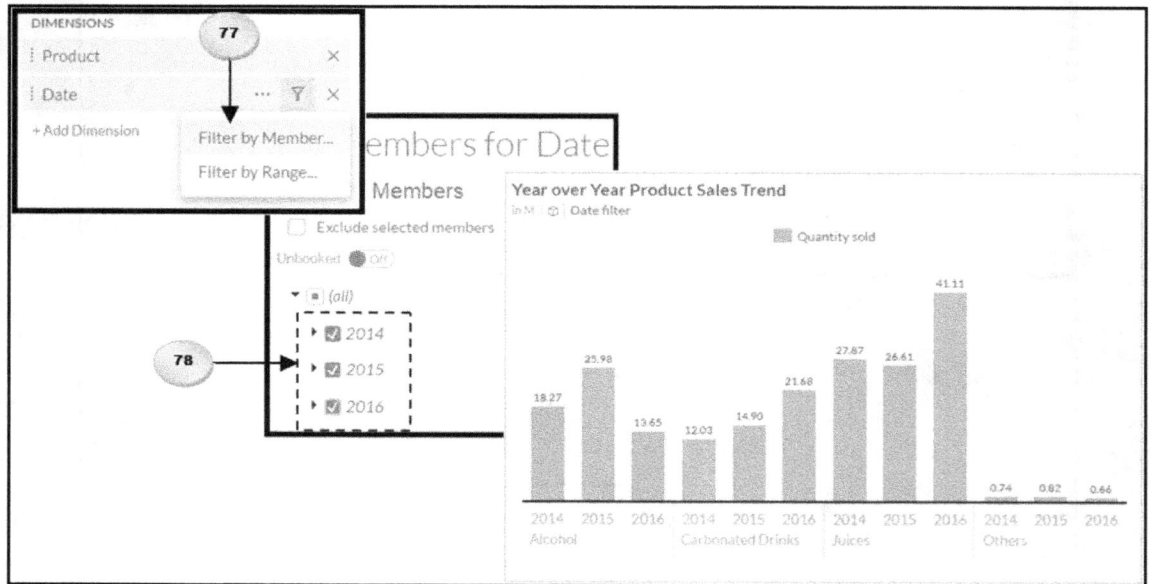

Now that a time dimension has been added to the chart, we can add a time calculation to it as follows:

79. Click on the More icon in the **Quantity sold** measure.
80. Select **Add Time Calculation** from the menu.
81. Choose **Year Over Year**.

New bars (**A**) and a corresponding legend (**B**) will be added to the chart, which help you compare yearly results, as shown in the following screenshot:

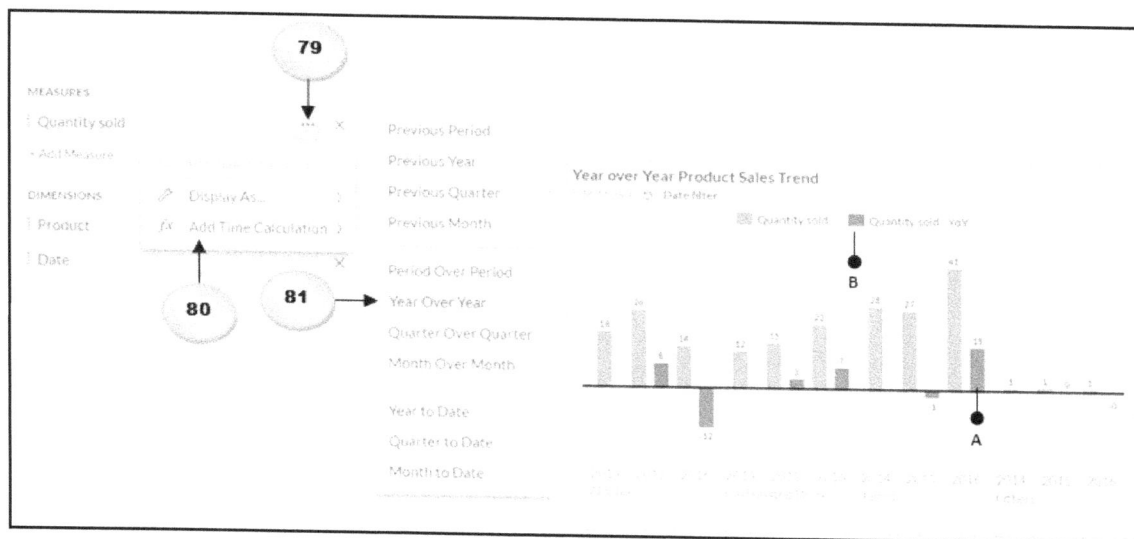

Summary

This chapter provided hands-on exposure to some of the very important topics of SAP Analytics Cloud. You created second page in your story and named it **Analysis** of your story. New pages are added to a story to segregate the analysis.

You also learned how to provide expressive names to your story pages and, at the same time, learned about some other page manipulation options that allow you to add, delete, rename, hide, and move a page. Then, you learned how to share your views about the analysis provided on a story page with other users by adding comments. You created bubble and choropleth layers to visualize data in geomaps and applied location clustering to better visualize the data in the map.

You also learned about the different types of filters you can apply to a geomap to restrict your analysis to specific regions. You connected two different models via linked dimensions and created a combination column and a line chart to compare different values. In the final sections, you learned the technique for predictive forecasting on an analytical model through a trend time series chart and went through the process of adding time calculation to a chart to compare year-over-year values.

The next chapter will teach you how to use tables in your analysis. A table is an object that presents data in a row/column matrix, such as an Excel spreadsheet.

7
Working with Tables and Grids

After completing the **Summary** and **Analysis** pages in which you added some useful objects to visualize data, here is the third one--**Sales Manager Overview**. As the name implies, this page will have objects to analyze the performance of the sales team. Some of the objects to be created on this page (filters and bar charts (**A**)) are already known to you. The table object (**B**) is the one that is new to this chapter. A table is a spreadsheet-like object that can be used to view and analyze text data. You can add this object to either canvas or grid pages in stories, as shown in the following screenshot:

Summary   Analysis   Sales Manager Overview

Sample: Sales Manager Overview
How did the sales team perform from 2014 to 2016?

Product
- ☑ Alcohol
- ☑ Carbonated Drinks
- ☑ Juices
- ☑ Others

Location
- ☑ California
- ☑ Nevada
- ☑ Oregon

Top 5 sales managers

Kiran Raj
David Carl
Janet Bury
Gabriel Walton
John Minker

● A

Bottom 5 sales managers

James Frank
Ed Young
Gary Dumin
Lois Wood
Lia Armand

● B

| ACCOUNT | Net Revenue | | | |
DATE	▼ (all)	▶ 2014	▶ 2015	▶ 2016
SALES MANAGER				
Kiran Raj	162.84	43.65	54.20	64.99
David Carl	136.54	38.66	44.28	53.60
Janet Bury	106.07	27.42	39.02	39.63
Gabriel Walton	72.18	20.94	23.40	27.84
John Minker	71.92	23.83	16.21	31.88
Nancy Miller	69.55	22.17	22.13	25.24
Lia Armand	67.12	17.43	23.55	26.14
Lois Wood	64.23	21.12	17.63	25.48
Gary Dumin	32.56	11.76	8.53	12.27
Ed Young	31.20	10.12	11.55	9.54
James Frank	11.76	3.89	3.67	4.20

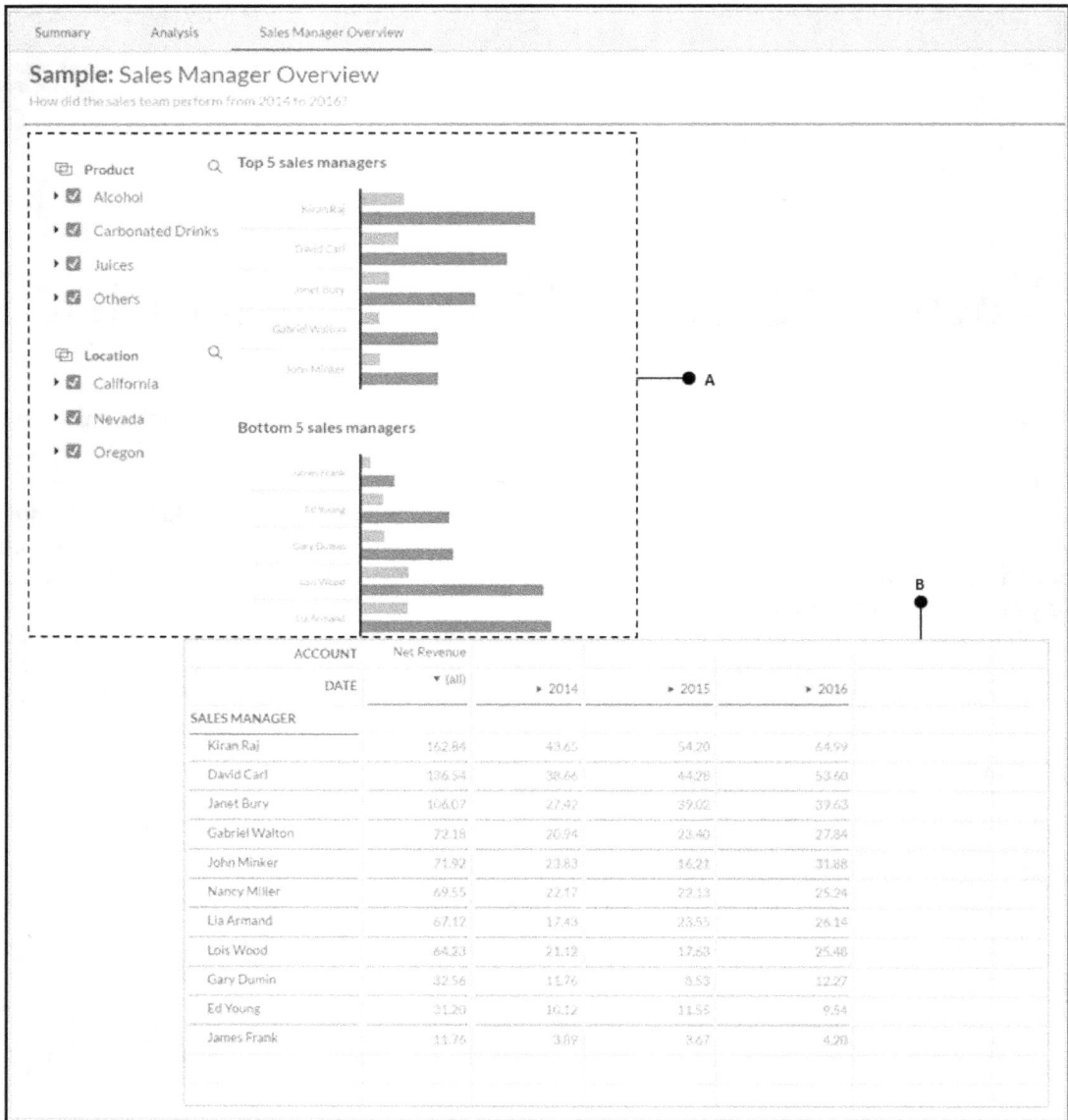

In addition to the table object, you will have hands-on experience with grid, which is a type of page used to create analysis comprising text and formulas. Here is a list of topics covered in this chapter:

- Copying objects between pages and a to the same page
- Applying ranking
- Creating a table
- Applying filters to tables
- Showing/hiding table elements
- Sorting data in tables
- Showing totals
- Styling tables
- Creating formatting rules to apply custom styles to a table
- Setting visibility filters
- Swapping the table axis
- Freezing rows and columns in a table
- Using KPIs in a table
- Working with grids
- Creating a blended table
- Making copies of objects, pages, and stories
- Saving a story as a PDF
- Creating a dashboard for your story
- Setting reminders using text notes

Copying objects between pages

As illustrated in the previous screenshot, there are a couple of filters placed to narrow down the scope of your analysis on this page. Recall that these two filters were created in Chapter 5, *Extending Filters with KPI, Filters and other Handy Objects*, for the **Summary** page. In this exercise, we will utilize the same filters by copying them to the **Sales Manager Overview** page. So, let's get started!

1. Click on the **Summary** page, and then select the **Product** filter, as illustrated in the following screenshot.
2. Click on the Copy icon in the menu.
3. Select **Copy To** from the sub-menu.

4. Finally, select the **Sales Manager Overview** page as the target for this filter. Recall that this page was created and renamed in `Chapter 6`, *Analyzing Data Using Geo Maps and Other Objects*. The filter will appear on the selected page.

5. Repeat steps 2 to 4 to also copy the location filter to the **Sales Manager Overview** page.

Here is the screenshot illustrating the preceding points:

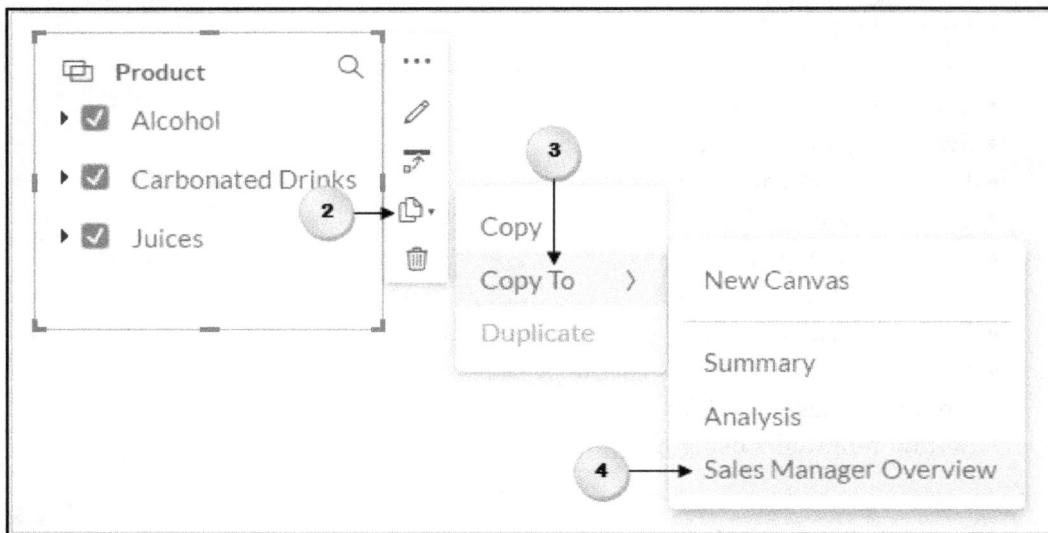

Applying ranking

Now, you will add two charts to the page. Both the charts will be created using the same measures and dimensions. The only difference between these charts is that the first chart will display the top five managers, while the second one will show the bottom five managers. This ranking will be applied by choosing **Top N Options** in the menu. Filtering data by rank focuses a chart on a specified number of data points with the highest or lowest values. Let's see how to apply ranking in a chart.

6. Add a blank chart from the Insert toolbar.
7. Select the **BestRun** model as the **Data Source** for the chart.

8. Select the **Bar/Column** chart from the **Comparison** category.

9. In the **Measures** section, click on the **Add Measure** link, and select **Quantity Sold**.

10. Once again, click on the **Add Measure** link in the **Measures** section, and select **Net Revenue** as the second measure for this chart. Both the charts on this page will reveal the values of the sold quantity and the amount earned from sale proceeds by sales managers.

11. Finally, click on the **Add Dimension** link in the **Dimensions** section, and select **Sales Manager** as the chart's dimension.

12. Optionally, click on the **Add Dimension/Threshold** link in the **Color** section, and select a color scheme, as illustrated in the following screenshot:

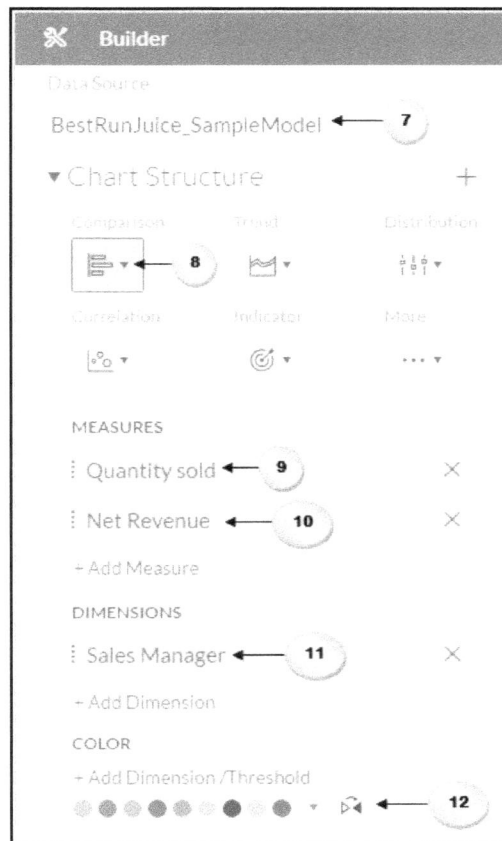

The chart, as illustrated in the following screenshot, will appear on the page.

13. Select the chart and replace its title with **Top 5 sales managers**.
14. Click on **Top N options** in the chart's menu.
15. Select **Top N Options** from the sub-menu.

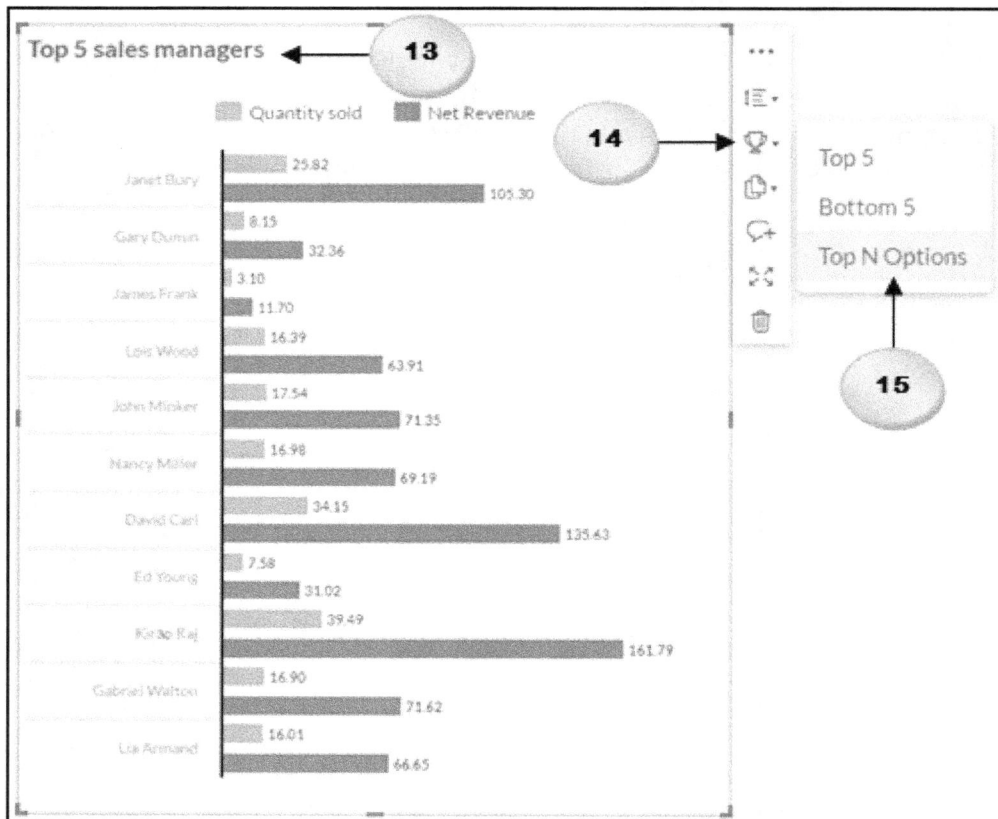

16. In the **Top N Options** dialog box, set **Mode** to **Top** (**A**) to show the top results. Set **Value** to 5 (**B**) to show the top five results in the chart. Select **Net Revenue** (**C**) for **Measure** to display the top five records with the highest net revenue. Click on **Apply** to close the dialog box:

Here's the output of the chart, which shows the five top-ranking sales managers, ranked according to the net revenue they have earned for the company. **Kiran Raj** has been ranked on top of the chart for his **161.79** million sales:

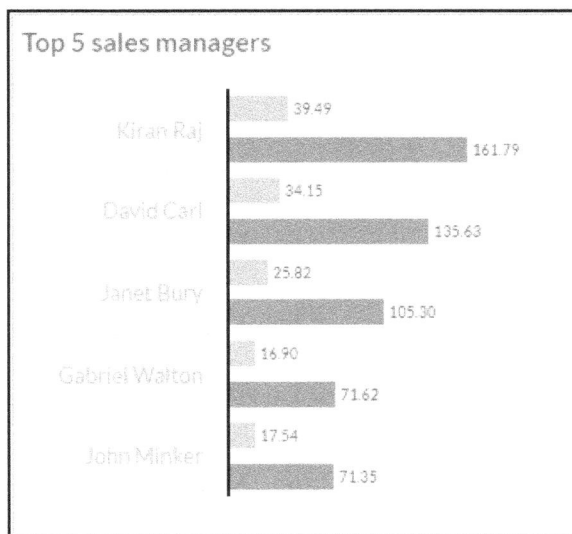

Copying objects to the same page

Now you will see the other side of the picture by creating another chart to display the bottom five sales managers.

17. Select the **Top 5 sales managers** chart, and click on the Copy icon.
18. In the sub-menu, click on **Copy**. The selected chart will be copied to clipboard, and a corresponding message (**A**) will appear on your screen:

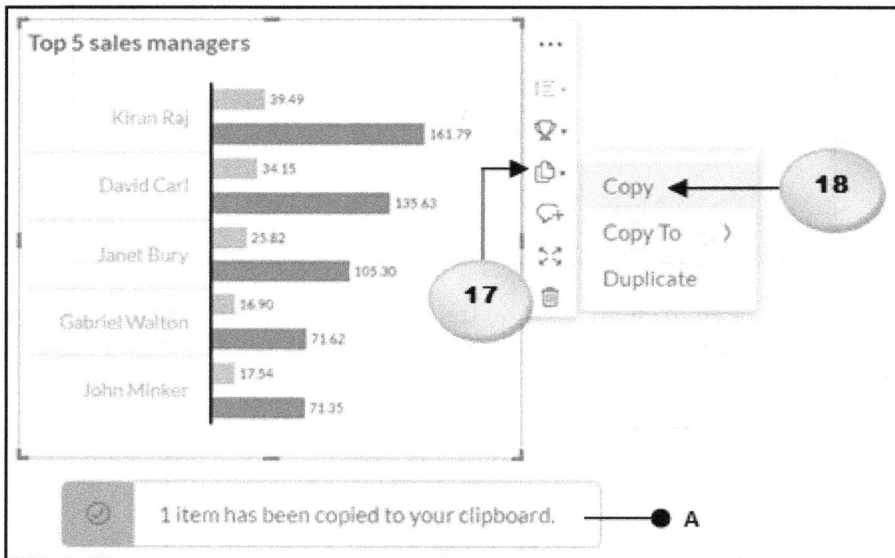

19. Click on an empty area in the page, and press *Ctrl+V* to paste the chart from the clipboard onto the page. Alternatively, you can use the **Paste** option from the **Copy and Paste** menu on the **File** toolbar. A copy of the **Top 5 sales managers** chart appears on the page.
20. Select the new chart, and replace its title with **Bottom 5 sales managers**.
21. Click on the **Top N options** on the chart's menu.
22. Select **Top N Options** from the sub-menu.

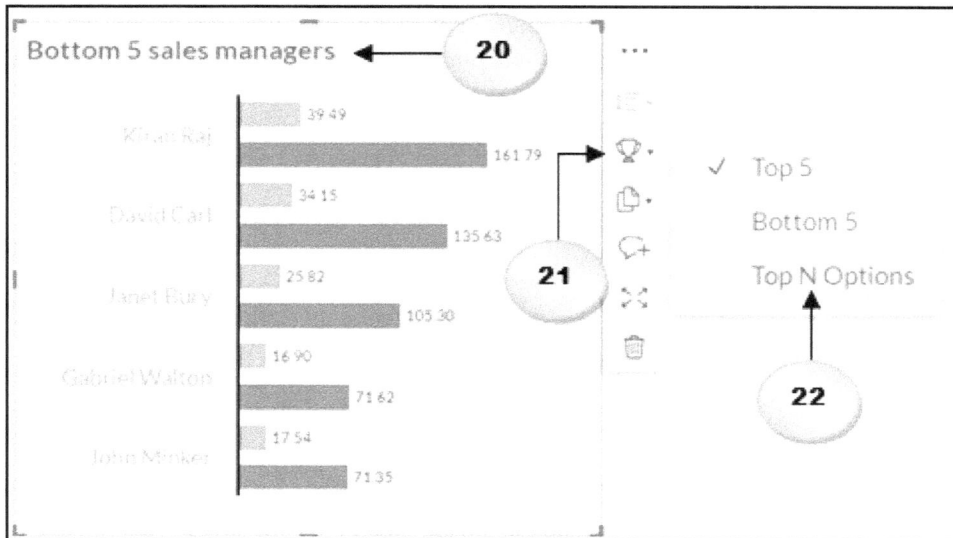

23. In the **Top N Options** dialog box, set **Mode** to **Bottom** (**A**) to show the bottom results. Set **Value** to 5 (**B**) to show five results from the bottom. Select **Net Revenue** (**C**) for **Measure** to display five records with lowest net revenue. Click on **Apply** to close the dialog box:

This is the result of the bottom ranking. As you can see, James Frank is the lowest revenue generating sales manager, who has generated just 11.70 million. Play around with the two charts by applying filters using the two page filters:

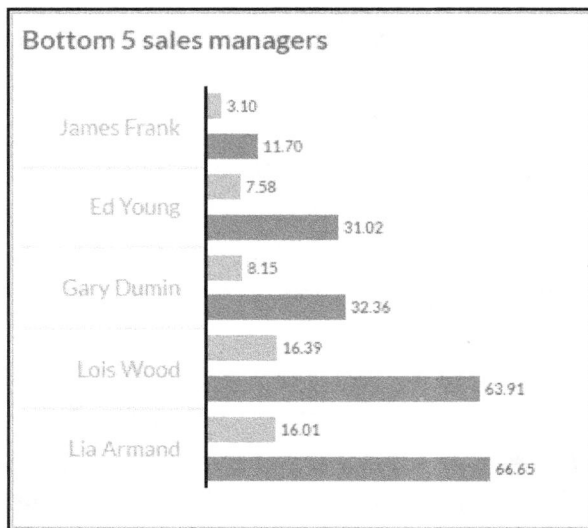

Grids and tables

A grid is a space where you can create and work with formulas, with or without a table that has been generated from existing data. Tables, on the other hand, can be used to view and analyze data. Both tables and grids provide the feel of a spreadsheet, and both can be used in stories to work with the data that has been loaded into a model or to work with data manually without a model.

You can add tables to either canvas or grid pages in stories. In the former case, tables are integrated with an underlying model, as you will see in the next exercise. On a grid page, tables may be bound to a model, but you can also create blank tables and type or paste the data in manually. On a canvas page, a table acts as a tile and can be moved around like any other object. On a grid page, you can change the position of the table by adding rows and columns above or to the left of the table.

Working with tables

In this exercise, you will work with the table object that you will create on a canvas page and will go through the grid later in this chapter. Execute the following steps to create a table on your story page to evaluate this object:

24. Click on the table icon on the **Insert** toolbar. A table object (**A**) will be added, populated with all the members from the **Account** dimension (**B**) in the **BestRun** model:

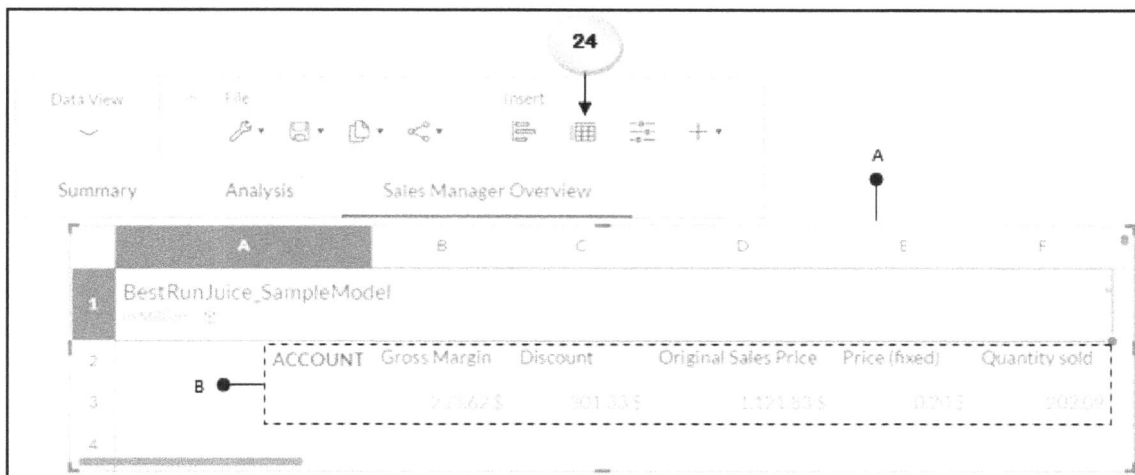

25. In the **Builder** panel, click on the **Add Measure/Dimensions** link in the **Rows** section, and select the **Sales Manager** dimension. The table will be refreshed to show values from the selected dimension in the first table column (**C**). Also note that all the five measures are updated as well to show the corresponding values for each sales manager:

26. Under the **Columns** section, click on the **Add Measures/Dimensions** link, and select the **Date** dimension. Once again, the table will be refreshed to show all the members of the selected dimension under every measure. For example, **Gross Margin** will show data for **2014**, **2015**, and **2016** (**D**). Similarly, all the other measures will also have these three columns in the **Date** row. Click on the **all** node under the **Gross Margin** column to see the top-level members (years) in the date dimension. Click on any year to expand its node and see second-level members (quarters). Finally, expand a quarter node to see the monthly statistics of the selected measure for sales managers:

Applying filters to a table

The table object allows you to apply filters to the measures and dimensions you select in the **Rows** and **Columns** sections to confine your analysis to some specific criteria. In this step, you will add a filter to the **Columns** section. The filter being applied here will only show values for the **Net Revenue** measure. Note that the table is created with all the measures from the **Account** dimension and doesn't show any of the three calculated measures. But when you intend to apply filters to a table, you are provided with a list comprising all measures, including the three calculated measures you created in the previous chapters.

Here are the steps:

27. In the **Builder** panel, click on the Manage Filters icon representing the **Account** dimension.

28. On the **Selected filters for Account** screen, select **Net Revenue**, and click on **OK**. The filter will remove all the default measures from the table and display the data for **Net Revenue** only (**A**):

29. Add another filter to show the data for 2016. Click on the manage filters icon (**A**) for the **Date** dimension. Select **By Member** (**B**), and select **2016** (**C**) in the **Selected filters for Date** window. The net revenue data for **2014** and **2015** will vanish from the table:

Showing/hiding table elements

You can apply some formatting options to change the look and feel of a table. These options are available in the **Show/Hide** (**B**) menu under more actions (**A**) to turn table elements on or off. All the sub-menu options are marked with corresponding alphabets and dotted lines in the table on the left side. The **Freeze Lines** option will be discussed in the *Freezing Table Rows and Columns* section later in this chapter.

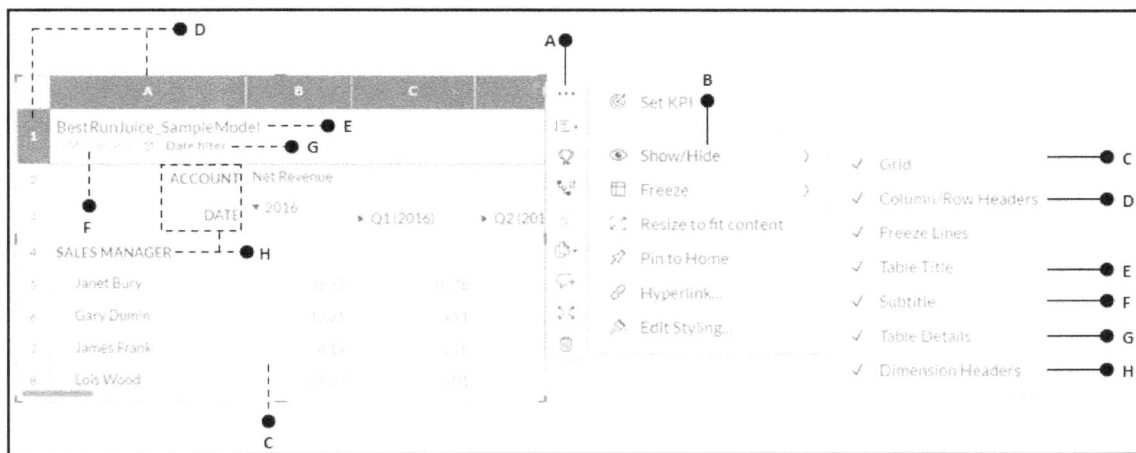

In addition to the aforementioned elements, you can change the appearance of the table using the options provided in the **Styling** tab under **Designer**. Besides the conventional styling options you have already applied in previous exercises, the **Styling** tab allows you to change the table pattern, merge cells, and add rows and columns. These options will be discussed later in this chapter.

Sorting table data

Execute the following steps to sort the dimension values in a table:

30. Click on the **Net Revenue** cell.
31. Select the **Sort** options, and then choose **Value Sorting** (**A**) from its menu. Not all values in a table can be sorted. The sort options icon is only enabled for dimensions that can be sorted.

32. In the **Create Value Sorting** dialog box, set **Type** to **Descending** (**B**) to sort the values in descending order. The **Direction** list carries two options: **Vertical** and **Horizontal**. This list is only enabled if more than one sort direction is possible in the table. If you choose **Vertical**, the column the dimension is included in will be sorted. If you choose **Horizontal**, the row the dimension is included in will be sorted. For this exercise, keep the default **Vertical** option (**C**) selected. Make sure that **Account** is set to **Net Revenue** (**D**). For **Date**, select **Q1** (**E**) using the Edit icon (**F**), and click on **OK**. The table will be sorted using the first quarter column in descending order (**G**). Clicking on the **Date** filter (**H**) shows a menu carrying the date filter you applied in step 29 and an option to modify the filter. To modify the sort parameters, click on the **Net Revenue** link (**I**), as shown in the following screenshot:

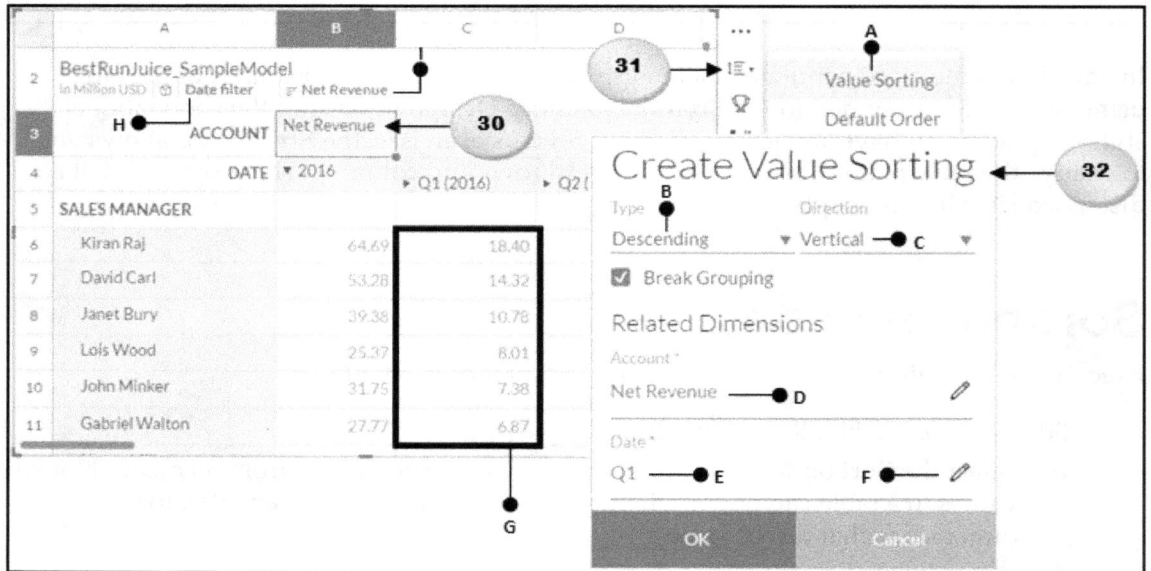

Showing totals

You can also show the sum of the dimension values. Here's how to show totals in a table:

33. Click on the More icon (**A**) representing the **Sales Manager** dimension, and select **Show Totals** (**B**). A new row (**C**) will be added just before the first sales manager record to show totals. Using *Shift+click*, select all the cells in this row, and on the **Styling** tab, change color (**D**) and style (**E**) of this row to make it appealing. To highlight the entire row, click on its heading (number), and set a different **Fill** color in the **Cell** section. If you want to show this row at the bottom, click on the **Totals** cell, and in the **Styling** tab, check the box labeled **Arrange totals / parent nodes below**.

Applying a date filter

The current status of the page is depicted in the following partial illustration. As you can see, the contribution of **Kiran Raj** towards net revenue in the chart is showing 161.79 million (**A**), whereas the table is showing 64.69 million (**B**) for the same sales manager. This is due to the filter applied on the table data in step 29 to restrict the table results to 2016. Execute the following steps to apply a similar filter to the chart to match the results:

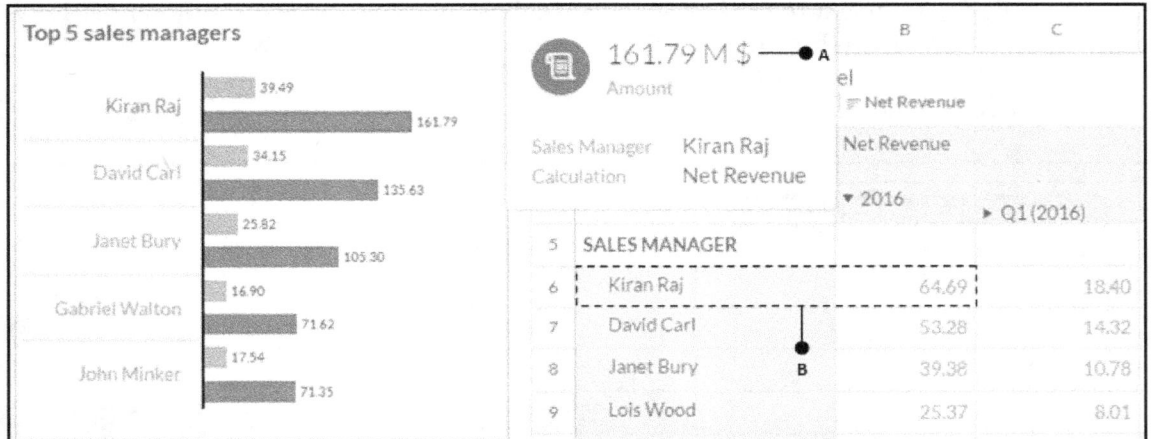

34. Select the chart, and then click on the **Add Filters** link (**C**) located at the bottom of the **Builder** panel. From the list that pops up carrying the list of dimensions, select **Date (Member)** (**D**).

    This will show a **Set Members for Date** window. In this window, select **2016** (**E**) and click on **OK**. The chart's figures (**F**) now match those shown in the table:

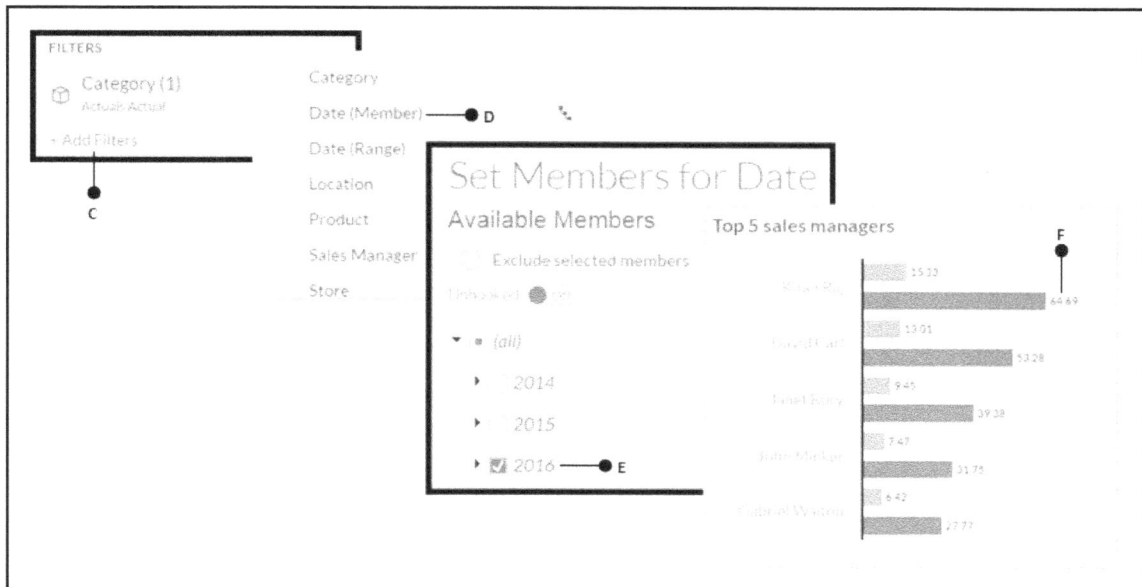

Testing the effects of page filters on a table

You used story and page filters in Chapter 5, *Extending Filters with KPI, Filters and other Handy Objects*, to narrow down the scope of your analysis. In that chapter, you applied these filters to charts. In this exercise, you will see how a page filter affects a table. In order to see accurate results, you have to modify the sorting order you set in step 32.

35. Click on the **Net Revenue** link displayed in the title area of the table to see the **Edit Value Sorting** window.

36. In the **Edit Value Sorting** window, click on the **edit** link to modify the sort value.

37. In the **Select member for Date** dialog box, switch the sort value from **Q1** to **2016** and click on **OK**. The selected value will appear in the *Edit Value Sorting* dialog box (A). Click on **OK** to dismiss this dialog box.

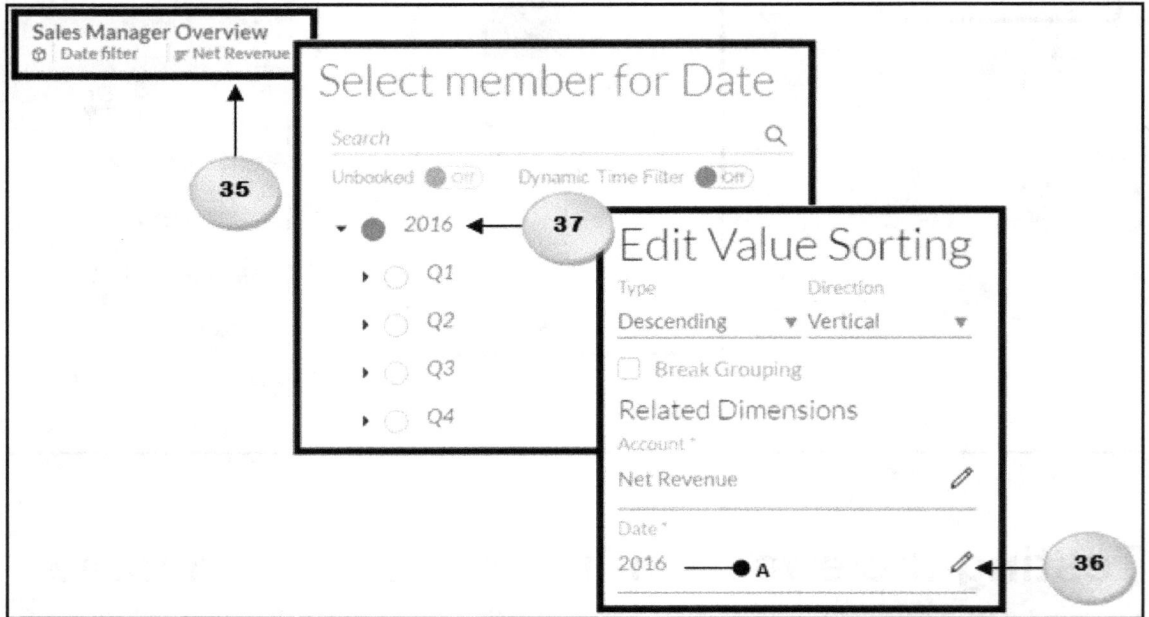

As you can see in the following screenshot, the result of the table now matches the first chart:

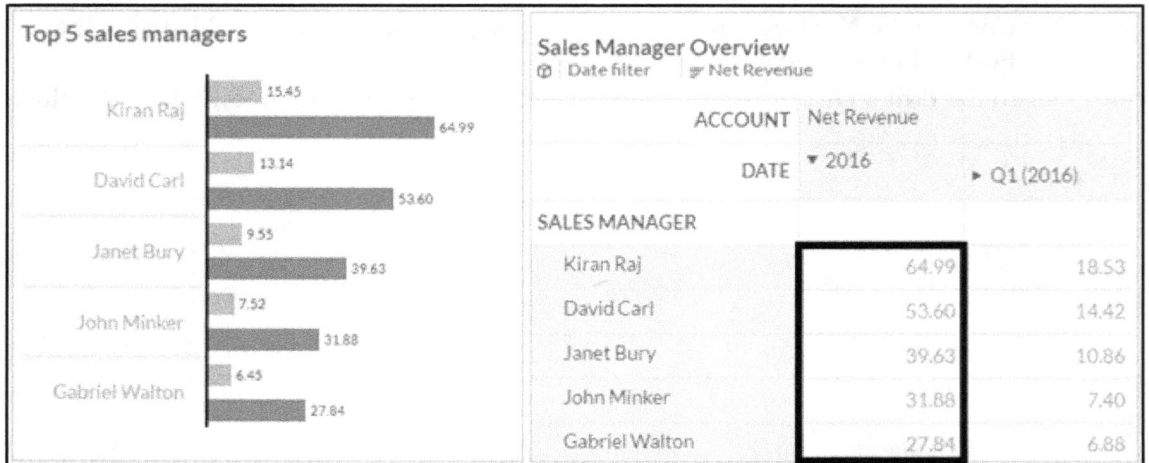

After reconciling the two objects, you can apply a filter to test the filter effect on the table. Deselect all the options in the **Product** filter, keeping the **Others** filter turned on (**B**). Both objects will be refreshed to display similar values, as illustrated in the following screenshot. If you compare this output with the previous one, you will notice the difference between the two outputs. Here, **David Carl** is ranked on top for the **Others** product category as compared to **Kiran Raj** who was on top for all categories in the previous output. The bottom line is that, by adding different types of objects to a page, you can produce analyses from different perspectives with a few clicks.

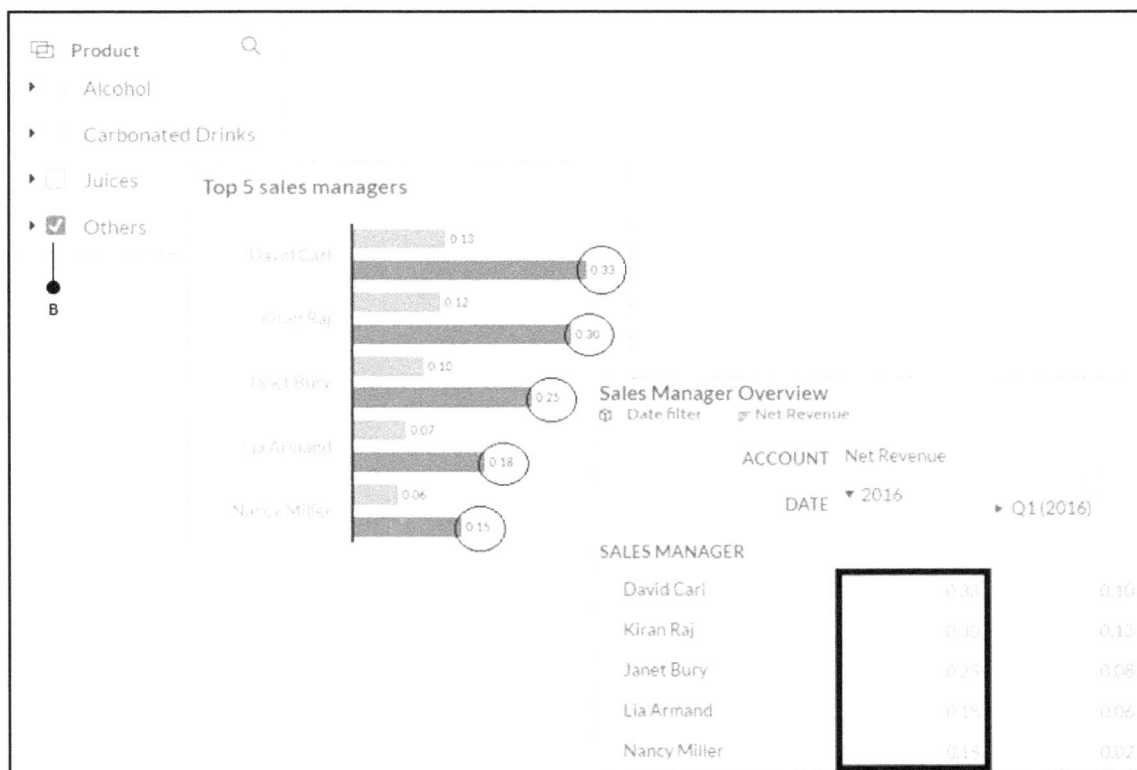

Styling tables

In addition to turning the table elements on or off via the **Show/Hide** menu, the **Styling** tab under **Designer** has some more formatting options which you can use to control the appearance of tables. For example, you can change the standard table pattern to **Report-Styling** in the **Templates** section. In this exercise, you will go through the options available in the **Templates** section. Before you change the table pattern, execute the following step to add one more dimension to it:

38. Select the table. Click on the **Add Measures/Dimensions** link in the **Builder** panel, and select the **Location** dimension. The hierarchical data of the new dimension will be placed on the table (**A**):

Table Structure					
ROWS					
Sales Manager	×				
Location ← 38	×		ACCOUNT	Net Revenue	
+ Add Measures/Dimensions			DATE ▾ 2016		▸ Q1 (2016)

SALES MANAGER	LOCATION	A		
Totals			320.84	85.60
Kiran Raj	▸ California		50.05	14.53
	▸ Nevada		10.20	2.71
	▸ Oregon		4.75	1.28
David Carl	▸ California		39.41	10.90
	▸ Oregon		14.19	3.52

39. Click and drag the **Location** dimension to place it above the **Sales Manager** dimension in the **Builder** panel. On the **Styling** tab, switch **Pattern** from **Standard** to **Report-Styling** (**B**). The appearance of the table will change and will now display the results grouped by the three locations (**C**):

The **Arrange totals / parent nodes below** option(D) displays the total and parent nodes at the bottom of the data set, as illustrated in the previous screenshot. If you turn this option off, the output will change to show the totals and parent nodes at the top (**E**):

		▼ 2016	▶ Q1 (2016)	
▶ California	Totals	216.75	57.44	● E
	Kiran Raj	50.05	14.53	
	David Carl	39.41	10.90	
	Janet Bury	31.26	8.33	
▶ Oregon	Totals	76.09	22.16	
	David Carl	14.19	3.52	
	Nancy Miller	10.21	3.13	
	John Minker	9.66	3.72	
▶ Nevada	Totals	28.00	6.01	
	Kiran Raj	10.20	2.71	
	Gary Dumin	5.83	1.43	
	Nancy Miller	4.45	0.83	

By setting a value for **Frequency of reading lines**, you can make reading easier for the users. For example, if you set the line frequency to **4** (**E**), the record-separating lines (**F**) will be placed after every four records. You can also remove these lines by turning off the option:

☑ Arrange totals / parent nodes below			
☑ Frequency of reading lines: 4 ▾	David Carl	14.19	3.53	3.57
☑ Show group lines	Nancy Miller	10.21	2.11	2.11
	John Minker	9.66	3.22	1.61
E	Lia Armand	8.65	2.79	2.10
	Janet Bury	8.37	2.53	2.30
	Ed Young	5.84	1.37	1.28
	Lois Wood	5.79	1.42	1.83
	Kiran Raj	4.73	1.28	1.76
	Gabriel Walton	4.37	1.31	0.60
	James Frank	4.20	1.57	0.79
▸ Oregon	Totals	76.09	22.16	18.73

To see the effect of the **Show group lines** option, revert the **Sales Manager** dimension to place it above the **Location** dimension (**G**). Then, turn off the **Show group lines** option. The group lines (**H**) will vanish, as illustrated in the following screenshot (**I**):

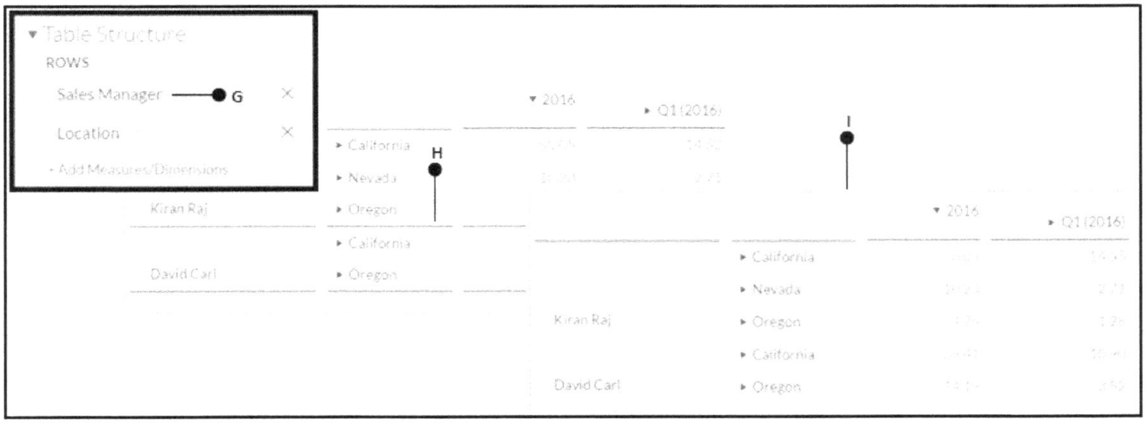

Creating formatting rules

The **Formatting Rules** section under the **Styling** tab lets you create rules, wherein you specify how to format dimension members and hierarchies. In this exercise, you will create a couple of rules to highlight the net revenue earned by the sales manager **Kiran Raj** in the three states. Execute the following steps to achieve this task:

40. Select the table, and open the **Styling** tab under **Designer**. Click on the **Add Formatting Rule** link in the **Formatting Rules** section. On the **Formatting Rule** panel, enter **State Rule** (A) for the rule name. Click and hold the first cell showing **50.05** (B) in the **Net Revenue** column and drag down to select all the three net revenue figures for **Kiran Raj**. As you select these three cells, relevant information (C) appears under the **Selected Content** area in the **Formatting Rule** panel. From the **Level** list representing location, select **Self & Children** (D), as shown in the following screenshot:

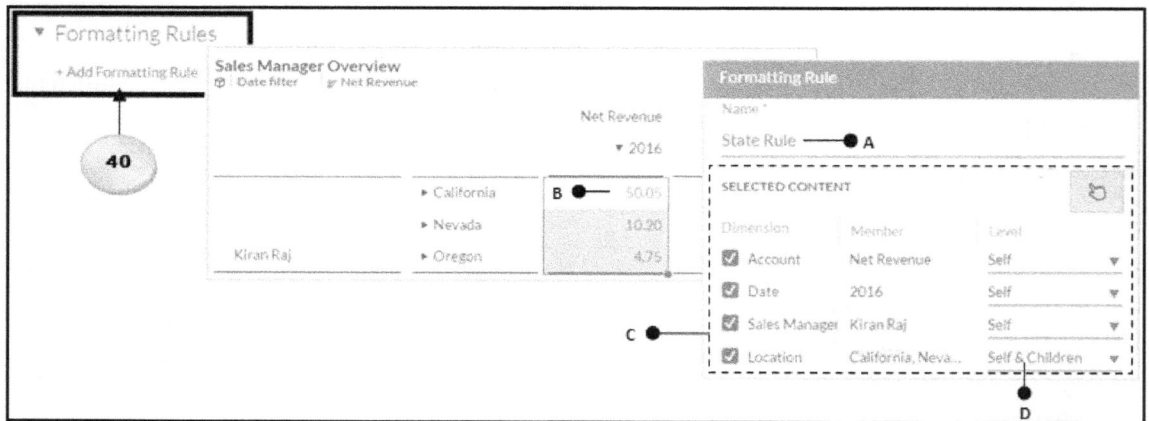

The checkboxes in the **Selected Content** section are provided to select which dimensions you want to apply the rule to and how the rule applies to different members of the dimension. For example, if you select **Self** from the **Level** list for the **Account** dimension, the formatting will be applied to the **Account** dimension only. The **Level** list provides a number of options (briefed hereunder) for hierarchical dimensions. For others, it has just two options: **Self** and **All**.

- **Self**: This applies the formatting only to the currently selected members of the hierarchy
- **Self & Children**: This applies to the currently selected members as well as those one level below them in the hierarchy
- **Self & Sibling**: This one applies to the selected members as well as to other members at the same hierarchy level
- **Self & Descendants**: This applies to the selected members and to all the lower levels of the hierarchy
- **Children**: This applies to one level below each of the currently selected members
- **Descendants**: This applies to all members below the top level currently selected

41. In the **Style** section, select **New Style** to set a new style for the state rule:

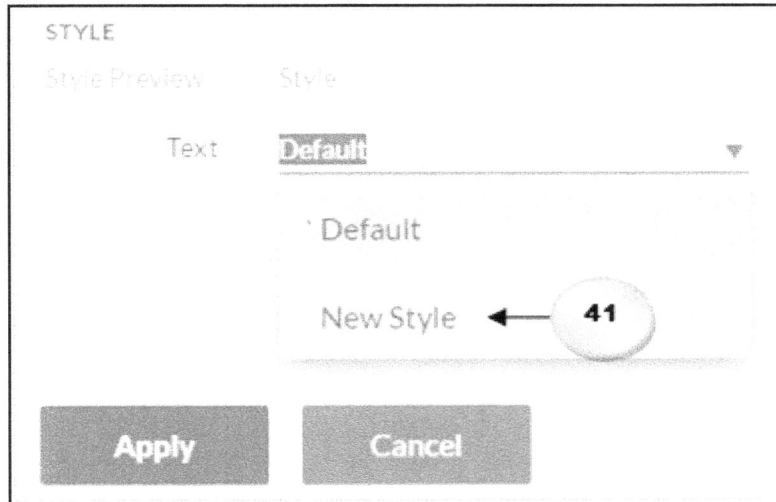

42. In the **Style** dialog box, enter **StateStyle** (**E**) for the name of the new style. In the **Font** section, select a font, size, and a different color (**F**). Click on the letter **B** (**G**) to present the data boldfaced. Also, select a light color in the **Fill** section (**H**) to highlight the data. Click on **OK** to close the **Style** dialog box, and then click on the **Apply** button in the **Formatting Rule** panel:

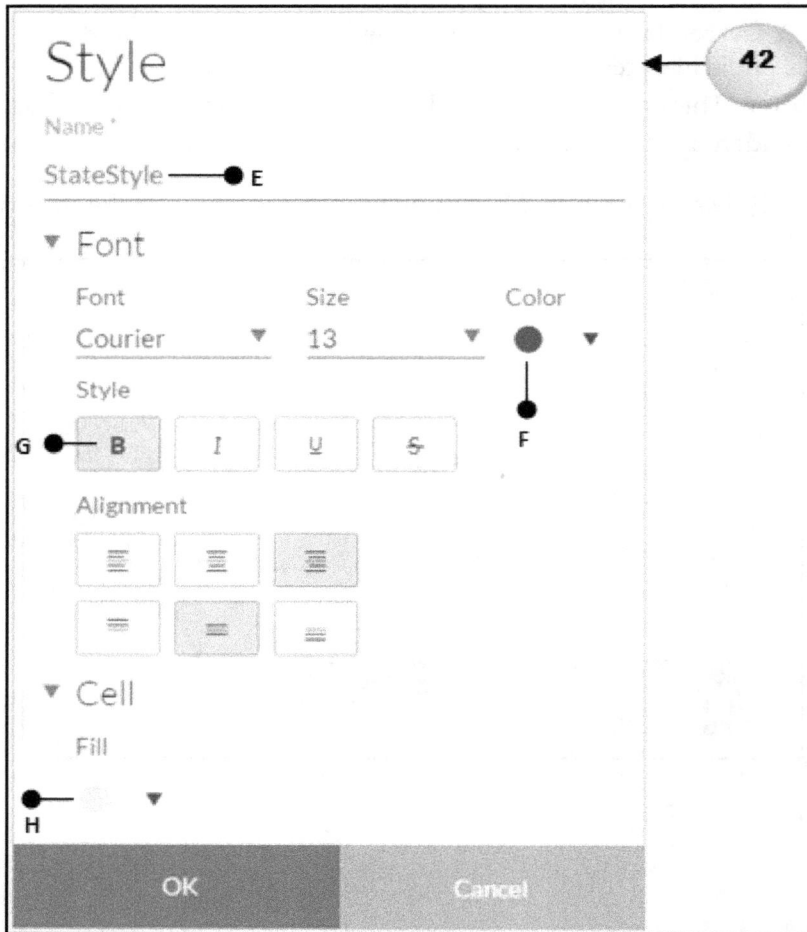

The output of the rule is illustrated in the following screenshot. The net revenue values for the three states are highlighted and are also presented in a different color to distinguish them from the rest of the table data:

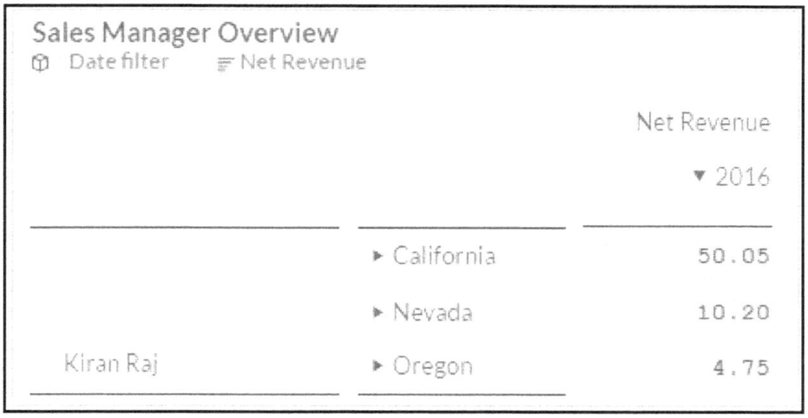

Sales Manager Overview
Date filter
Net Revenue
Net Revenue
2016
California
50.05
Nevada
10.20
Kiran Raj
Oregon
4.75

Now, expand the **California** state's node. The same rule is applied to the cities under this state, as shown in the following screenshot. This is because you selected **Self & Children** option in step 40-D.

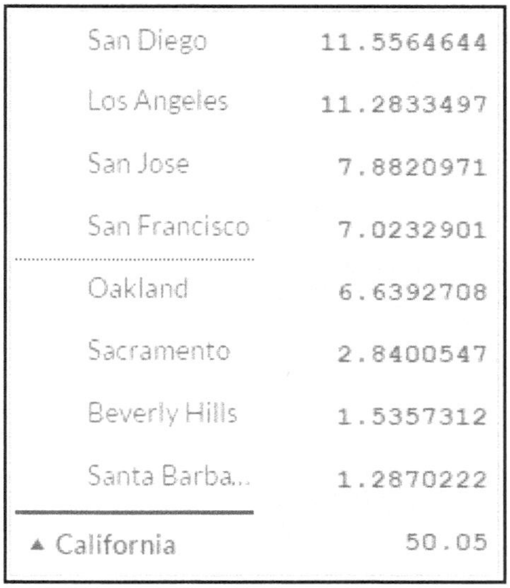

San Diego
11.5564644
Los Angeles
11.2833497
San Jose
7.8820971
San Francisco
7.0232901
Oakland
6.6392708
Sacramento
2.8400547
Beverly Hills
1.5357312
Santa Barba...
1.2870222
California
50.05

Let's create another rule in which you will set up another style to differentiate cities and states data. Here are the steps for this rule:

43. Select the table, and in the **Styling** tab, click on the **Add Formatting Rule** link in the **Formatting Rules** section. On the **Formatting Rule** panel, enter **City Rule (A)** for the rule name. Expand the **California** state node to view its cities. Click and hold the first cell showing **11.5564644 (B)** in the **Net Revenue** column and drag down to select all the cities in this state (**C**). Once again, the **Selected Content** section will be populated with the same dimensions and their members, as you saw in the previous rule. This time, accept all the default values appearing in this section, including the level **Self (D)**, set for the location dimension. By keeping the **Self** level, you specify to apply the rule to the selected data set, that is, cities in **California**, as shown in the following screenshot:

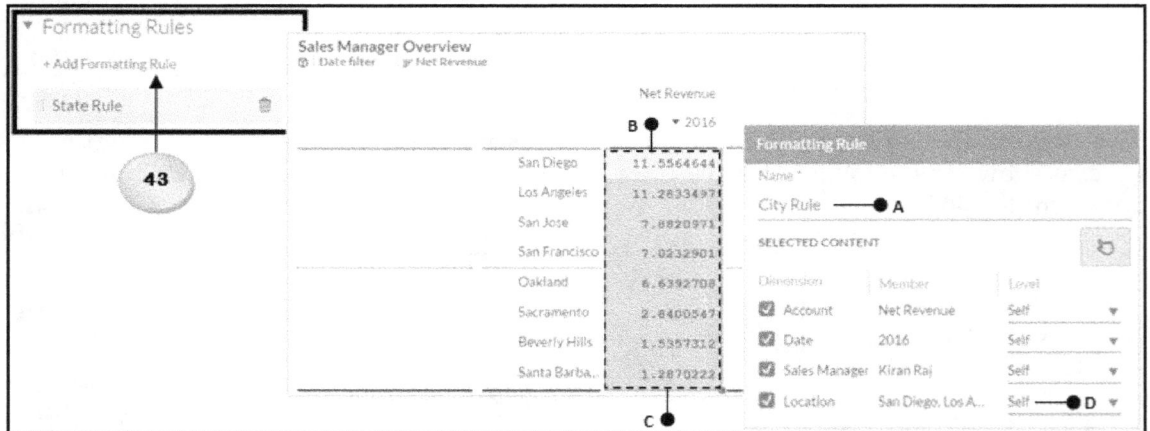

44. Once again, select **New Style** in the **Style** section to set up a new style for the **City Rule**:

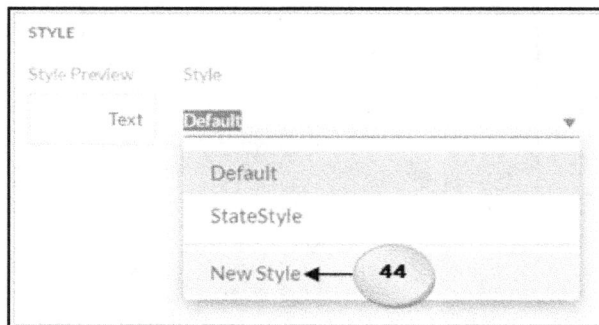

45. In the **Style** dialog box, enter **CityStyle** (E) for the name of the new style. In the **Font** section, select a font, size, and a different color (F). Make the text bold by clicking on the letter **B** (G). Also select a different color in the **Fill** section (H). Click on **OK** to close the **Style** dialog box, and then click on the **Apply** button in the **Formatting Rule** panel:

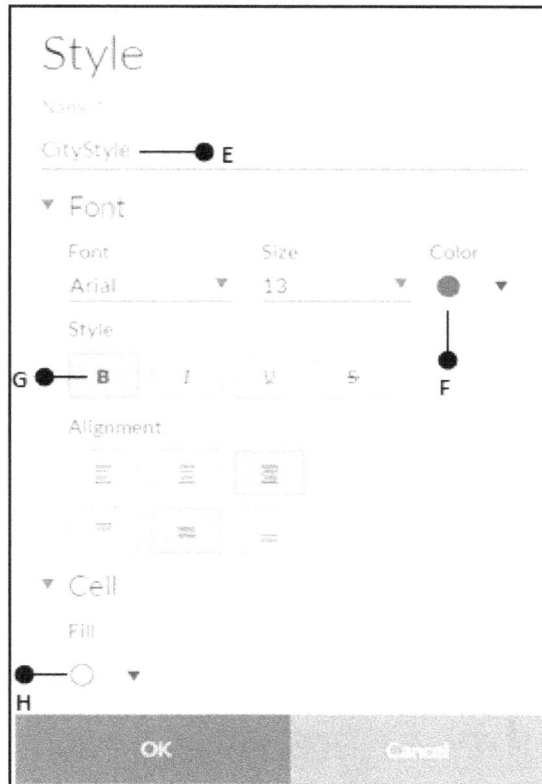

Here is the output of the rule in which cities data (**I**) can easily be distinguished from the state data (**J**):

```
Sales Manager Overview
  Date filter       Net Revenue

                                        Net Revenue

                                         ▼ 2016

                       San Diego         11.5564644
                       Los Angeles       11.2833497
                       San Jose          7.8820971
                       San Francisco     7.0232901
                       Oakland      ●─   6.6392708
                                    I
                       Sacramento        2.8400547
                       Beverly Hills     1.5357312
                       Santa Barba..     1.2870222

                     ▲ California          50.05
                     ▶ Nevada   J ●─      10.20
   Kiran Raj        ▶ Oregon              4.75
```

Setting visibility filters

In the previous chapters, you went through many techniques to filter the results delivered by your page objects. In those exercises, you applied conventional filtering options to control the display of dimension members. In this section, we will go through another type of filter called **visibility filter**. The main difference between a conventional filter and the visibility filter is that when you apply a conventional filter, the filtered-out members vanish from the scene and do not take part in the calculation, whereas if you apply the visibility filter to some dimension members, they also vanish from the page objects, but they still participate in the calculation. Let's go through an example to elaborate this concept. First, you will add a conventional filter, and then you will apply a visibility filter to observe the difference between the two.

Currently, the value of **Net Revenue** being displayed in the table object is 320.84 million (**A**), as illustrated in the following screenshot. Follow the instructions to first create a conventional filter:

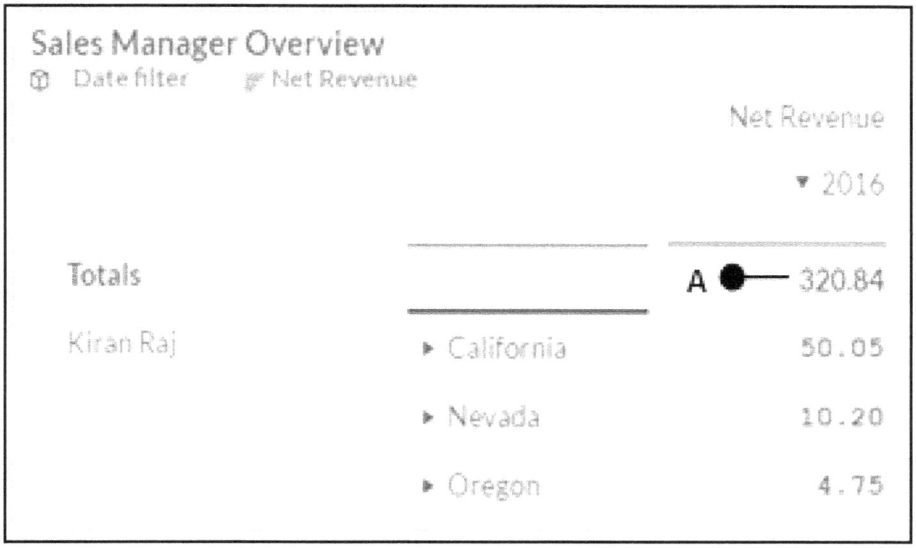

46. Select the table, and click on the Manage Filter icon (**B**) representing the **Location** dimension. In the **Selected filters for Location** dialog box, place check marks in the **Exclude selected members** option (**C**) and **Oregon** state (**D**) boxes to exclude this state's data from the table. Once you click on **OK** to get back to the page, you will notice that the **Oregon** state's data no longer exists in the table, as depicted in the lower view of the following screenshot. Due to this exclusion, the total value of the **Net Revenue** measure (**E**) is also affected.

Having seen the function of a conventional filter, let's see how the visibility filter works:

47. Once again, click on the same Manage Filter icon (**F**) representing the **Location** dimension. In the **Selected filters for Location** dialog box, uncheck **Exclude selected members** (**G**), and check **All Members** (**H**) to include all dimension members to the table. Then, click on the Set to invisible icon (**I**) next to the **Oregon** state to make this state's data invisible. Click on **OK** to get back to the page. Again, the **Oregon** state is not shown in the table, but its data contributes to the totals (**J**). Using the visibility filters, you can restrict your view to the areas you are most interested in without disturbing the overall aggregation:

Swapping the table axis

If you want to see the table results from a different perspective, you are provided with the swapping option, which converts the table rows into columns and columns into rows.

48. Select the table object, and click on the Swap Axis icon (**A**) in the **Builder** panel. The **Net Revenue** measure will be swapped to rows, and the two dimensions (**Sales Manager** and **Location**) will appear in the column position:

Freezing table rows and columns

You might have used the rows and columns freezing feature in a spreadsheet program, which allows you to focus on some specific data by keeping the rows and columns carrying that data always under sight. This feature is normally used with a large amount of data that scrolls down or across.

In SAP Analytics Cloud, you are provided with similar freezing features using which you can freeze specific rows and columns in a table. When you have a large amount of data in a table and you scroll down, the top rows of the table disappear.

Similarly, when you scroll towards the right, the columns on the left side hide. Usually, the top rows in a table carry header information, and the columns on the left side contain measures or dimensions. You cannot properly evaluate the data if this vital information goes behind the scene. For example, if you scroll down in the table you currently have on the page, you cannot tell which column is associated with which time period. Likewise, if you expand the time dimension and scroll across the table, you can no longer see which sale manager's data you are looking at.

Here are the steps to cope with this situation:

49. Click on the cell displaying **Date**.
50. Click on the more actions icon.
51. Select **Freeze** from the menu.

52. Select **Freeze up to row** from the sub-menu. A horizontal freeze line (**A**) will be added under the selected row. If you now scroll down in the table, you will observe that the top three rows in the table are static and you are able to see the headings even if you are at the bottom of the table. If you call the **Freeze** menu again, you will notice that the **Freeze up to row** option is replaced with unfreeze rows, allowing you to unfreeze all the rows you have previously frozen:

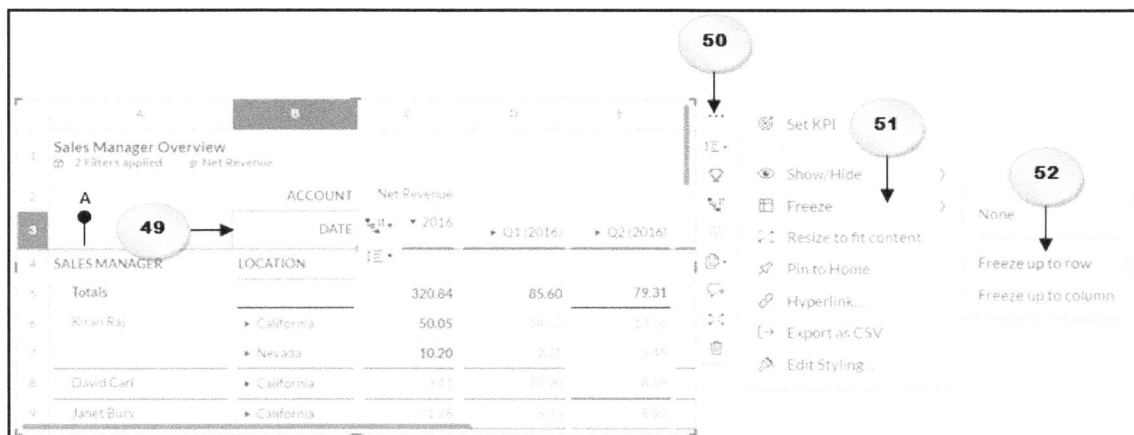

After freezing the headings, let's see how to freeze the columns on the left side of the table.

53. Click on the **Location** cell (**B**), and from the more actions menu, select **Freeze** (**D**) | **Freeze up to column** (**E**). This time, a vertical freeze line (**F**) will be added to the table. Scroll across the table, and observe that the two dimension columns remain visible even if you are looking at the last column in the table. This way, you can easily tell which rows belong to which sales manager. For example, in the following screenshot, you can tell that **David Carl** generated 12.49 million net revenue in the fourth quarter of 2016:

Note: If you want to hide the two freeze lines, click on more actions and uncheck **Freeze Lines** in the **Show/Hide** menu.

Using KPIs in a table

Key performance indicators (**KPIs**) indicate the status of a measure based on user-defined thresholds. You have already gone through some instances of KPI in previous chapters. Here, you will learn how to apply this success metric to a table. In this exercise, you will create a KPI to analyze the net revenue for 2016. First, you will define the KPI for a single cell in the table, and then you will apply the same KPI to a range of selected cells. Here's the procedure:

54. Click on the first record's cell in the **Net Revenue** column to select it.
55. Click on the more actions icon.
56. Select the first option, **Set KPI**, from the more actions menu.
57. In the **KPI** panel, which appears on the right side, click on the **Add KPI** link:

58. In the **Define KPIs** window, enter **Net Revenue 2016** for the KPI name, and create the three thresholds (OK, Warning, and Critical) along with respective values, as illustrated in the following screenshot. Use the + icon (A) to add additional thresholds. Once you are done, click on the **Apply Changes** button:

59. Dismiss the KPI panel by clicking on the **OK** button. The KPI will be applied to the selected cell, and the appropriate icon (**B**) will appear in front of the value--in this case, it falls in the **OK** range because the value is more than 50 million. If the backend value changes in the future, the KPI is re-evaluated, and a visual alert is generated using an appropriate icon. The **KPI** panel can be recalled using the same **Set KPI** option under the more actions menu. The Edit icon (**C**) in this panel can be used to modify the thresholds, and if you want to axe the KPI, click on the Delete KPI icon (**D**).

Let's extend the scope of this KPI to include other cells in the net revenue column.

60. In the selected cell (**C6**), press *Shift+Down Arrow* to select the other cells, and then call the **KPI** panel.

61. Click on the **Add KPI** link. The **Overlapping selection** dialog box appears.

62. Select the **Change scope of existing KPI** to **extend the scope of the KPI** option to your selections, and click on **OK**. Click on **OK** in the dialog box that asks "Do you really want to change the scope of the defined KPI Net Revenue 2016?" followed by the **Apply Changes** button in the **Edit KPI** window. Relevant icons appear for each selected cell. According to the KPI, the **John Minker** net revenue in **Nevada** is shown as critical because this value is less than the 10 million set for the critical threshold. The **Kiran Raj** figures in **California** are OK, whereas his net revenue figure (10.2 million) in **Nevada** is indicated as a warning because this values falls between the 10 million and 50 million threshold.

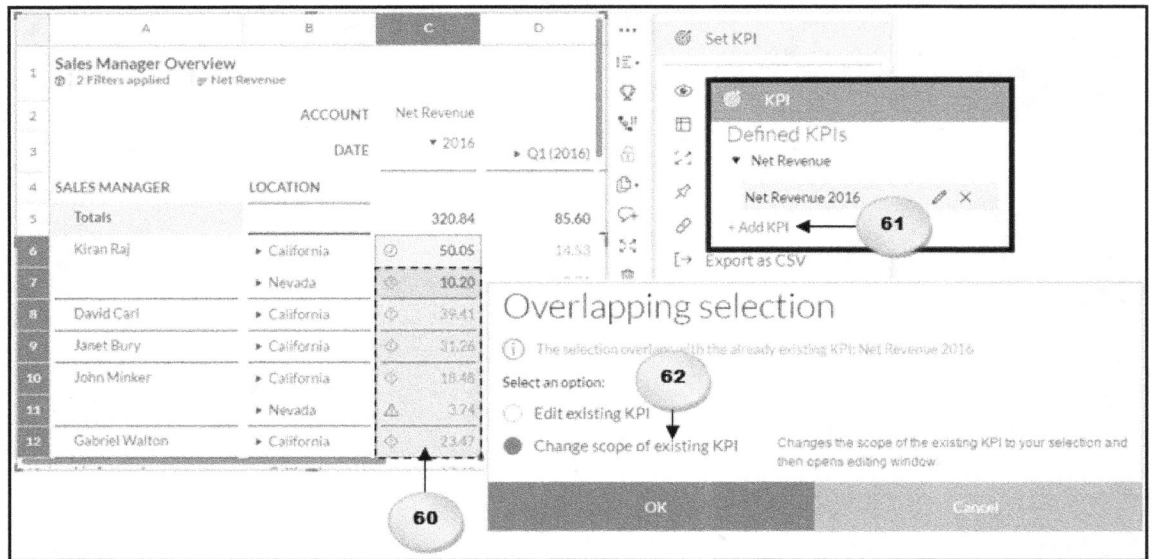

Working with grids

As mentioned earlier in this chapter, a grid is a spreadsheet-like object where you can create and work with formulas. Let's go through this object by adding one to our story:

63. Click on the Add New Page icon, and select **Grid** from the menu to create a grid page in your story:

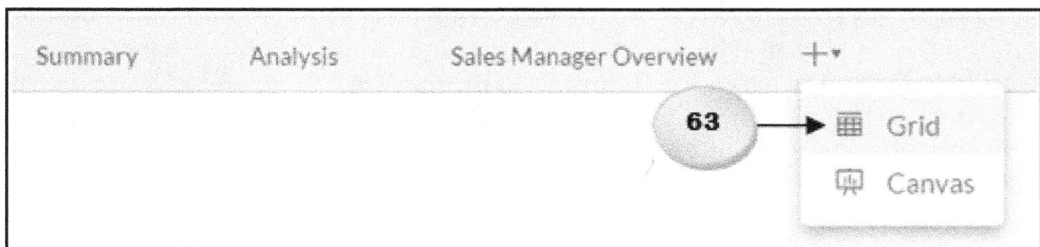

A new page will be created with a data grid covering the whole story page as illustrated in the following screenshot. Just like a spreadsheet, you can freely type or paste data into the cells (**A**) of a grid, create formulas that perform calculations (**B**), and apply formatting to the cells (**C**). This is one side of the grid where you work with it without connecting to a model. However, if you want to work with the data from a model, you have to add a table to the grid, as instructed in the following steps:

64. Click on the Add Table icon on the **Insert** toolbar.
65. The **Select Model** dialog box appears. Select the **Existing Model** option in this dialog box, and choose the **BestRun** model (**D**).

An outlined table is added to the grid page (**E**), and the data from the selected model is displayed in the table area. The model data in the table is not editable, but you can utilize the cells outside of the table area to add and manipulate your own data to perform analysis, which you will do next:

66. Type **Sales** in **A6**, **Discount** in **A7**, and **Net Revenue** in **A8**. Then, type **Actual** in cell **B5**, **Forecast** in **C5**, **1200** in **C6**, and **750** in **C7**. Note that all these text and numeric values are added to the grid outside the table:

	A	B	C	D	E	F
1	BestRunJuice_SampleModel in Million ↺					
2	ACCOUNT Gross Margin		Discount	Original Sales Price	Price (fixed)	Quantity sold
3		235.04 $	303.13 $	1,129.11 $	0.21 $	204.31
4						
5		Actual	Forecast			
6	Sales		1,200.00			
7	Discount		750.00			
8	Net Revenue					

67. Click on the **D3** cell carrying value **1,129.11** for **Original Sales Price**, and press *Ctrl+C* to copy this value to clipboard. Then click on **B6** and press *Ctrl+V* to paste the copied value. Similarly, copy the discount value from **C3** to **B7**, as illustrated in the following screenshot:

	A	B	C	D	E	F
1	BestRunJuice_SampleModel in Million ↺					
2	ACCOUNT Gross Margin		Discount	Original Sales Price	Price (fixed)	Quantity sold
3		235.04 $	303.13 $	1,129.11 $	0.21 $	204.31
4						
5		Actual	Forecast			
6	Sales	1,129.11 Million $	1,200.00			
7	Discount	303.13 Million $	750.00			
8	Net Revenue					

68. Next, click on the **B8** cell to input a formula that will calculate net revenue by deducting the discount value from the sales figures. Type the formula **=B6-B7** in the selected cell, and press *Enter*. The formula will derive the value 825.98M (**F**) for net revenue. If you want to modify the formula, double-click on the **B8** cell, or press the Formula Bar icon (**G**) to see the formula. The T symbol in the Formula Bar shows the cell value. To see the formula, click on this symbol. The T symbol will be replaced with **fx** (**H**), and the formula will appear in the bar.

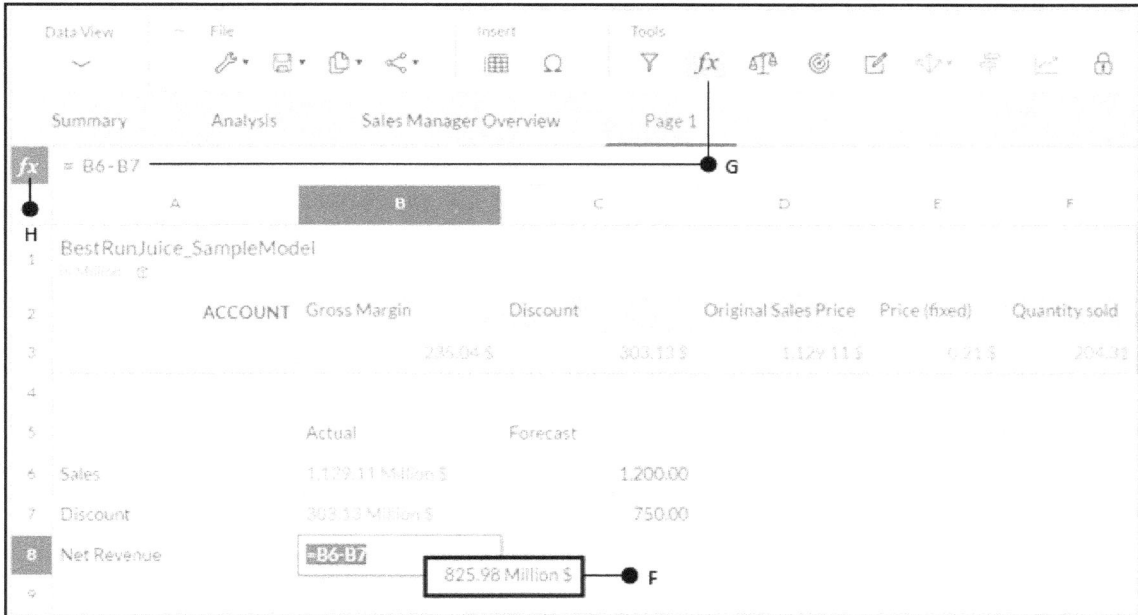

69. Just like a spreadsheet, you can also copy the formula from one cell of the grid to the others. Click on the **B8** cell, and press *Ctrl+C* to copy the formula. Click on the adjacent **C8** cell, and press *Ctrl+V* to paste the formula. The pasted formula appears in the Formula Bar with appropriate cell addresses (**I**), and the relevant forecast value for net revenue is displayed in the target cell (**J**). Alternatively, you can copy a formula by dragging the handle of the source cell (**K**) and dropping it in the target cell(s).

70. You can also style a grid as you style a table. Recall that you created two styles in a previous exercise for a table. In this step, you will utilize the same two styles to format the Actual and Forecast grid columns. Select the text **Actual** (B5), and drag the handle downwards to select the three values in this column. Then scroll down to the bottom of the Styling tab, and select **StateStyle** (**L**). The selected cells in the **Actual** column will be highlighted and presented in the color you set for the style. Repeat the same process for the *Forecast* column to format this column with the **CityStyle** (**M**).

71. In this step, you will create a couple of custom formulas in the grid. The values derived from these formulas will be formatted using the **Number Formatting** options available under the **Styling** tab. Input two pieces of text **Gross Margin** (**N**) and **Gross Margin %** (**O**). Click on the B10 cell and type **=B3/B8**. Copy this formula to **B11**. Select the **Gross Margin** value (**0.28$**), and then select **Currency** (**P**) in the **Number Formatting** section on the **Styling** tab. Click on the **Gross Margin %** value (**28.46$**), and select **Percentage** (**Q**) from the **Number Formatting** section. The **Gross Margin** value will be formatted to display a currency symbol, while the **Gross Margin %** value will be post-fixed with a percentage symbol.

Creating a blended table

A blended table is a table in which data is displayed from different models. You have already seen the use of linked dimensions to display data from multiple models in a single chart. Here, you will create a blended table to browse data from two models using the same linked dimension you created in Chapter 6, *Analyzing Data Using Geomaps and Other Objects*.

72. Click on the Add Page icon (**A**), and select **Grid** (**B**) to add a new grid page to the story. In the new grid page, click on the Add icon (**C**) to add a table to the grid. In the **Select Model** dialog box, select the existing **Planned_Events** model, and click on **OK**. A table (**D**) will be added to the grid containing the **Account** dimension (**No of Events for 2016**) from the **Planned_Events** model:

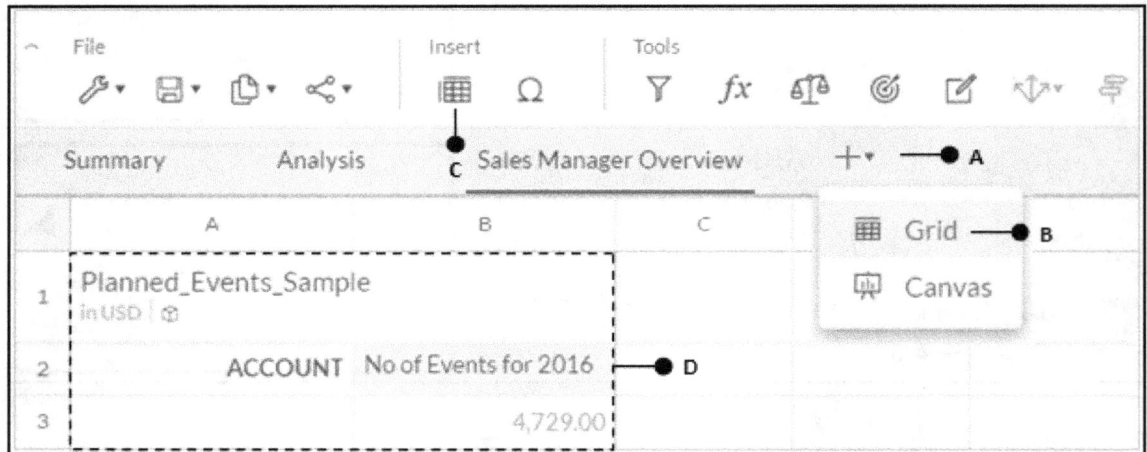

73. In the **Builder** panel, click on the link **Add Measures/Dimensions** in the **Rows** section, and select **City** from the list of dimensions. Click on the same **Add Measures/Dimensions** link, and select **Event** as the second dimension. The table will take account of these dimensions and will transform, as illustrated in the following screenshot, to display the number of events held in each city by event type:

	A	B	C
1	Planned_Events_Sample in USD		
2		ACCOUNT	No of Events for 2016
3	CITY	EVENT	
4	Las Vegas	Online Promotions	41.00
5		University Events	24.00
6		Instore Event	2.00
7		Flyers	87.00
8	Hillsboro	Online Promotions	47.00
9		University Events	24.00
10		Instore Event	13.00
11		Flyers	29.00

74. In **Data Source**, click on the link dimension icon (**E**), and select the **Best_Run** model (**F**). In the **Columns** section, click on the **Add Measures/Dimensions** link (**G**), and select the **Account** dimension (**H**). As you select this dimension, the table gets refreshed to show all the measures (**I**) from the Account dimension in the **Best_Run** model, as shown in the following screenshot:

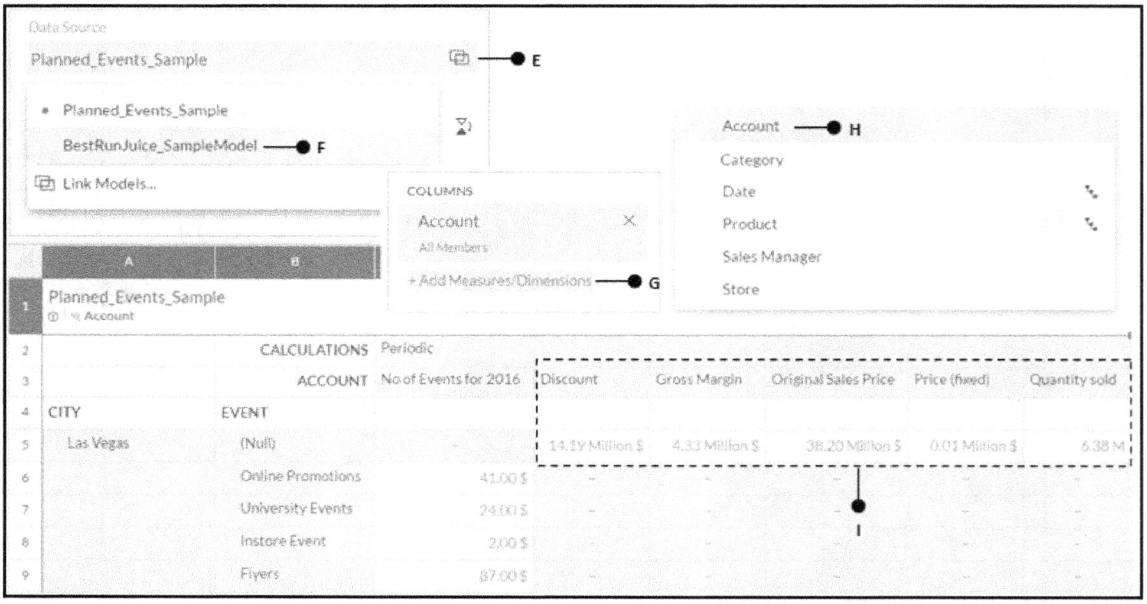

75. Click on the Manage Filter link (**J**) in the **Account** dimension, and select the **Best_Run** model (**K**) from the list. In the **Selected filters for Accounts** dialog box, select the **Discount** and **Original Sales Price** measures (**L**), and click on **OK** to keep these two measures in the table and remove the rest:

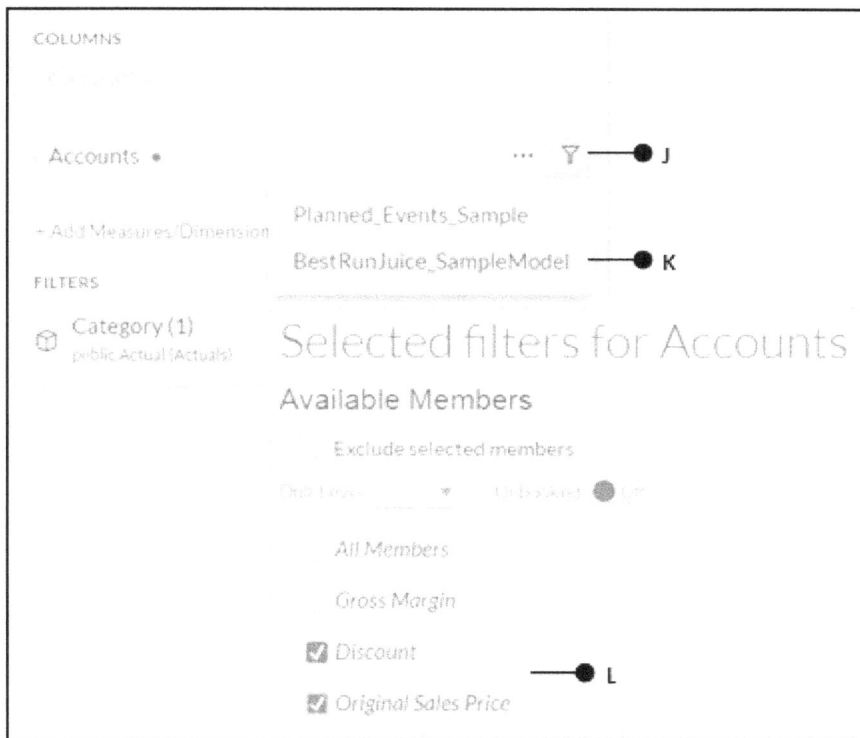

76. Type **Net Revenue** (**M**) in F3 and **=E5-D5** (**N**) in F5. By taking these two actions, you create a new column outside the table to show net revenue for each city, calculated by the formula you just specified. Copy this formula to F10, F15, and so on to show net revenue for each city.

The grid page contains a blended table carrying data from two different models and has also been augmented by a formula, which calculates the net revenue for each city. The analysis created on this grid page reveals the number of events by type held in each city and the amount of revenue earned in those cities.

	A	B	C	D	E	F
1	Planned_Events_Sample In USD ⊕ ☷ Account					**M** ●
2		CALCULATIONS	Periodic			
3		ACCOUNT	No of Events for 2016	Discount	Original Sales Price	Net Revenue
4	CITY	EVENT				
5	Las Vegas	(Null)	–	14.19 Million	38.20 Million	24.01 Million $
6		Online Promotions	41.00	–	–	●
7		University Events	24.00	–	–	**N**
8		Instore Event	2.00	–	–	
9		Flyers	87.00	–	–	
10	Hillsboro	(Null)	–	1.50 Million	5.13 Million	3.62 Million $
11		Online Promotions	47.00	–	–	
12		University Events	24.00	–	–	
13		Instore Event	13.00	–	–	
14		Flyers	29.00	–	–	

This concludes our efforts to create story pages in SAP Analytics Cloud. However, there are some more important areas you must be aware of. In the following sections, you will go through these areas to strengthen your knowledge further.

Copying objects, pages, and stories

In computing, copying and pasting are the most effective and widely used utilities, which enable you to replicate your work to save your precious time. SAP BusinessCloud also provides you with these utilities. You have already used this option at the beginning of this chapter where you copied objects from one page to another and on the same page of a story. In that section, you just copied a couple of page filters. However, you can copy any object, such as charts, geomaps, tables, input controls, images, text, and even shapes between pages or on the same page--also refer to the *Create Difference From Measure* section in Chapter 4, *Creating Stories Using Charts*, and the *Working With Story Pages* section in Chapter 6, *Analyzing Data Using Geo Maps and Other Objects*. In this exercise, you will learn how to copy a group of objects, complete pages with all objects, and the whole story.

Copying grouped objects

You have already seen the use of copying individual objects using menu options and keyboard shortcuts. Besides copying objects individually, you can group multiple objects and copy them in one go. Here's the process:

77. To create a group, press *Ctrl* and *click* to select multiple objects, or click and drag to use marquee selection.
78. Click on the Group icon to group the selected page objects. The collection of charts and other objects in a group is treated as a single object. For example, if you apply a background color to this group, the color is applied to all the group objects. After creating the group, the Group icon changes in the vertical toolbar and can now be used to ungroup objects.
79. Click on the Copy icon, and choose whether to copy this group to another page in the story or to a new canvas page:

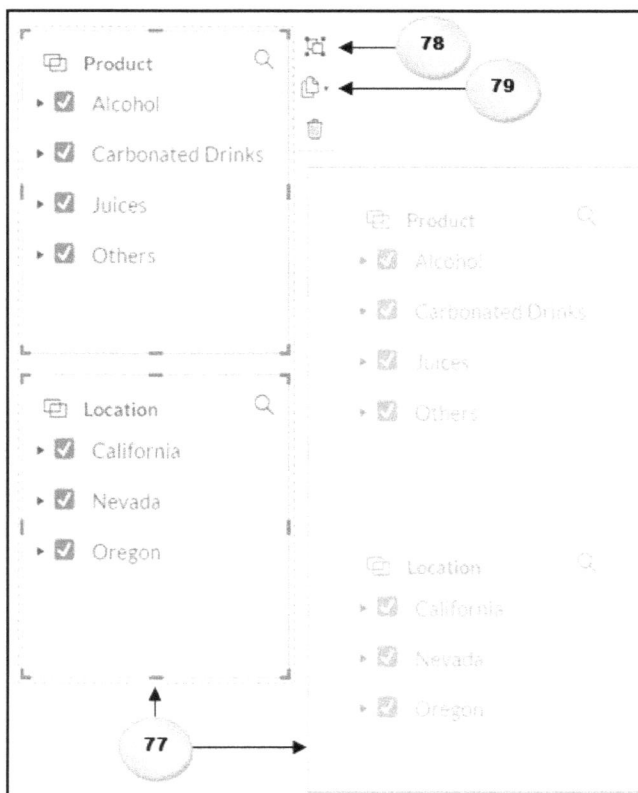

Copying pages with all objects

Here is the simple process to duplicate individual pages within a story:

80. Hover the mouse pointer over the **Summary** page title, and click on the tiny menu icon.

81. From the menu, select **Duplicate**. An exact copy (**A**) of the select page (with the same name having a post-fixed number) will be appended to the page tab, containing all the objects as the original, with the same format and layout:

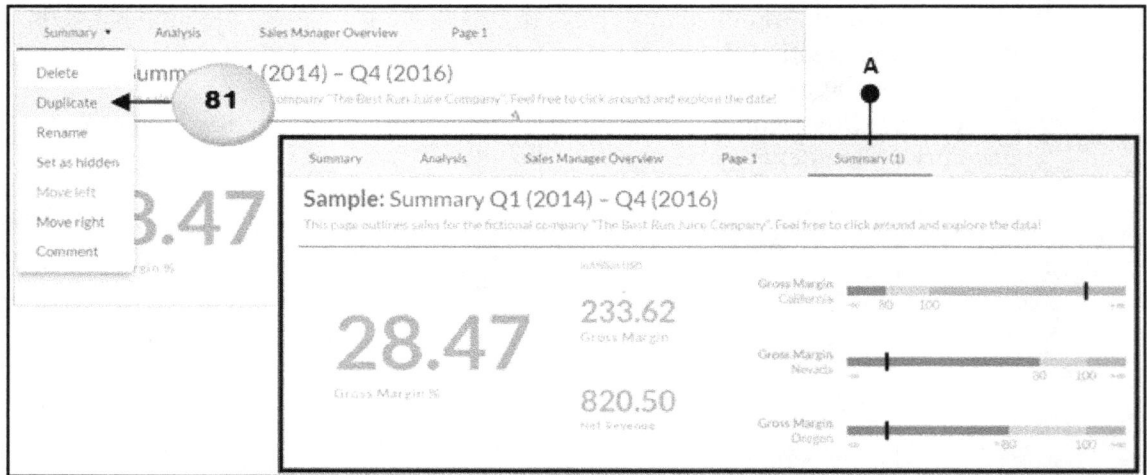

Copying an entire story

Here are the steps to make a duplicate of an entire story:

82. Switch back to the main list of stories by clicking on the **Stories** breadcrumb.

83. Select the story you want to copy.

84. Click on the Copy Selected icon.

85. Enter a name in the **Copy to Story** dialog box, and click on **OK**. The duplicate story will appear on your screen:

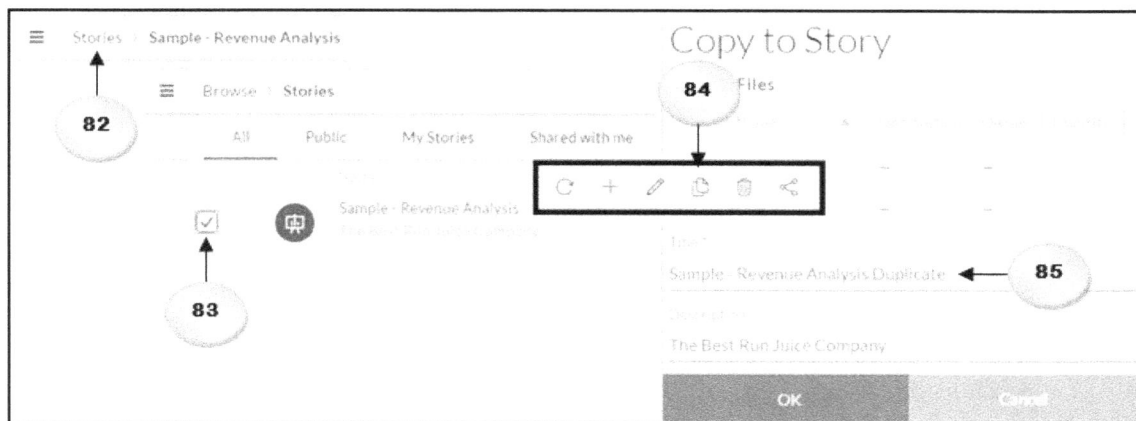

Saving a story as a PDF

Sometimes you need a hard copy to access your work offline. SAP Analytics Cloud lets you save your story in a **Portable Document Format** (**PDF**) file to meet your requirements. The option allows you save all the pages as well as some specific pages in your story. Here are the steps to create a PDF:

86. With your story open, click on the Save icon, and select **Save As File** from the Save menu. The **Save As File** dialog box pops up:

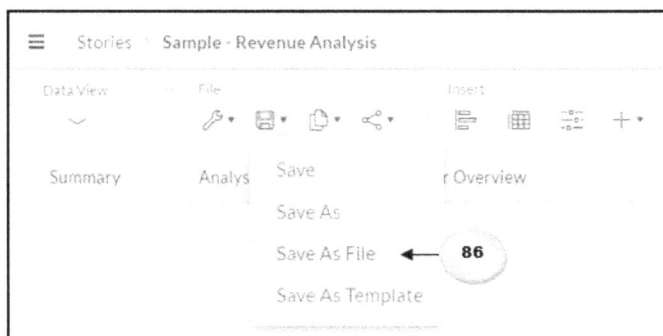

87. In the **Save As File** dialog box, select the **Range** option, and enter 1, 3, 7 in the adjacent box. The default **All** option (**A**) saves all the story pages, while, using the **Range** option, you can specify which pages to save. In my scenario, I have seven pages so I opted to save pages 1, 3, and 7. You can also specify a different combination of pages. For example, if you enter 1, 3-5 in the **Range** box, page 1, 3, 4, and 5 will be saved. Each story page is generated on a separate page in the PDF so you can modify it afterwards. If chosen, the **Insert Appendix** option (**B**) appends an appendix to the PDF to provide statistics about the filters applied in the selected pages.

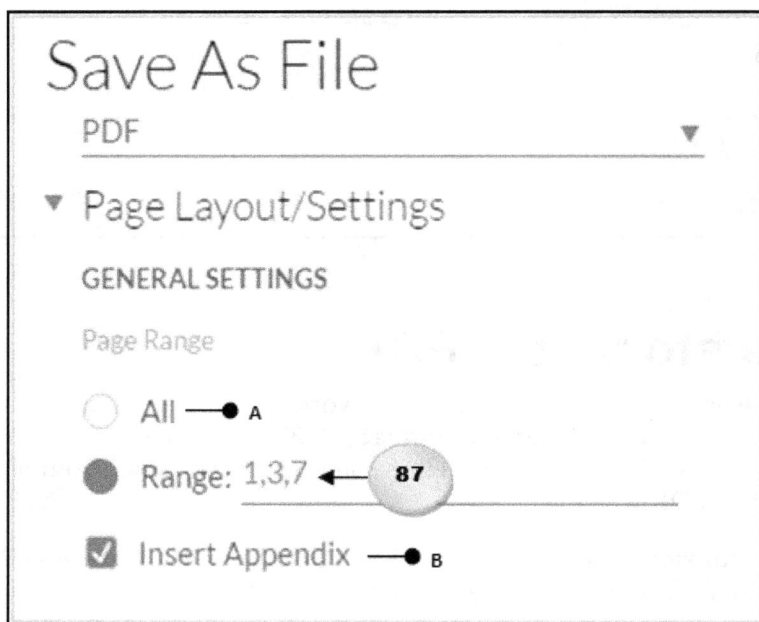

Save As File

PDF ▼

▼ Page Layout/Settings

GENERAL SETTINGS

Page Range

○ All —● A

● Range: 1,3,7 ◄— (87)

☑ Insert Appendix —● B

The **Grid Pages Settings** section is there to format your grid page in the PDF. The default **Use Whole Grid** option (**C**) saves the whole grid. Using the **Split Grid into Pages** option the grid can be split across multiple pages. Here's an example:

88. Select the **Split Grid into Pages** in the **Save As File** dialog box. Check the option **Use all Columns** (**D**) to include all the grid columns in the PDF. For **Rows**, enter 7 (**E**) to split the report after every seven rows:

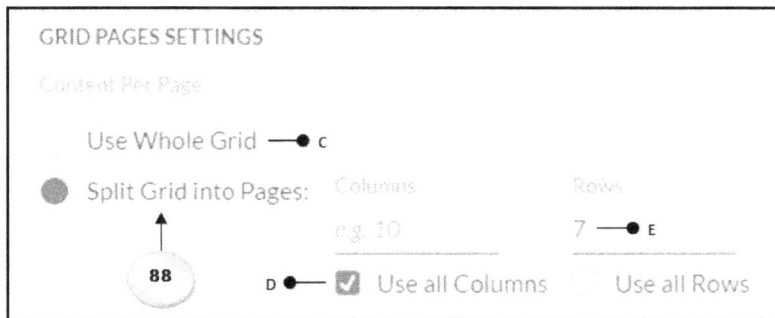

The following screenshot shows the grid page (**F**) and the PDF output (**G**) of your selections. As you can see, the PDF is split into two pages, each comprising seven rows:

Creating a personalized dashboard by pinning story objects

When you initially provide your sign-in credentials and are authenticated to access SAP Analytics Cloud, you see the Home screen, as illustrated in the following screenshot. The Home screen can be customized to create a personalized dashboard that contains objects from you stories, events and tasks, and notes. In this section, you will learn how to pin your story objects to the Home screen to create a personalized dashboard. By default, the Home screen displays a couple of objects from the sample story that you can remove by selecting the **Delete** option (**A**) from the **Tile Settings** menu.

Clicking on the first option in this menu takes you to the relevant story page, where the object exists. You can also remove the greeting bar and the **Recent Stories** tile by clicking on the respective Delete icons (**B** and **C**).

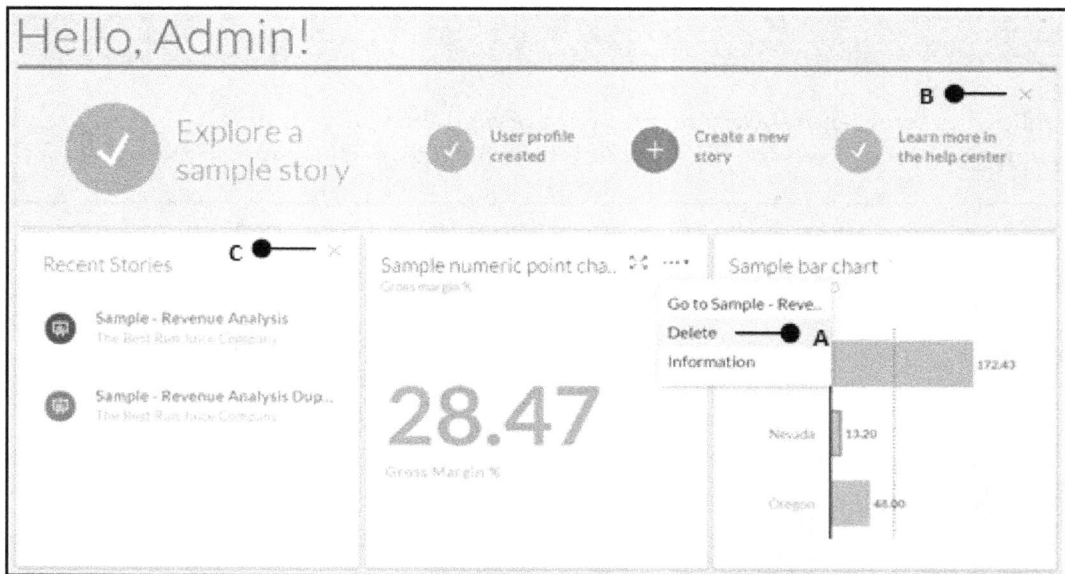

Pinning story objects

Here is the step to pin story objects to the Home screen:

89. Open your story, and select a chart. From the selected chart's toolbar, go to **more actions | Pin to Home**. The chart will be pinned to the Home screen. Repeat this step to pin more objects from other pages of the story:

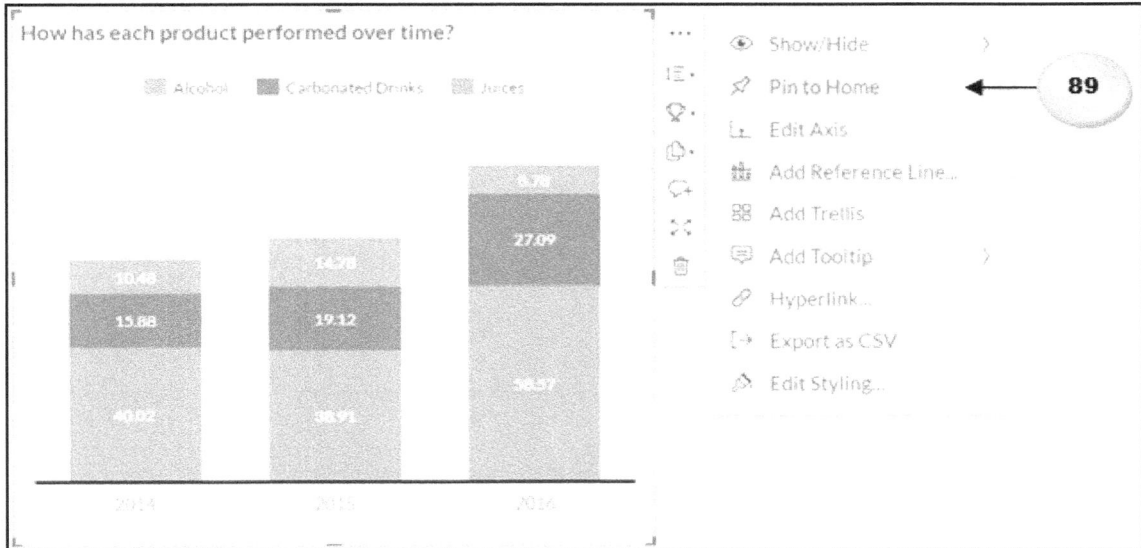

Note: You can pin objects from multiple stories on the Home screen. In addition to story objects, you can pin events and tasks from your calendar (discussed in the next chapter), and add static text notes (discussed next) to the Home screen. Your Home screen is private, and you can't share it with other users or add it to discussions. This also applies to the notes and tiles you pin there.

Adding text notes to the home screen

You can also add useful reminders, such as personal notes and upcoming events, to the Home screen. Here's the process to add text notes:

90. Click on the **Home** menu (**A**), and select **New Note** (**B**) from it. In the **New Note** window, type `Meeting Reminder` (**C**) for the note Title, and enter `Meeting with Nevada's regional manager on 15th July 2017 @ 3:30 PM` (**D**) in the **Note text** area. Click on **OK** to add the note to the **Home** screen:

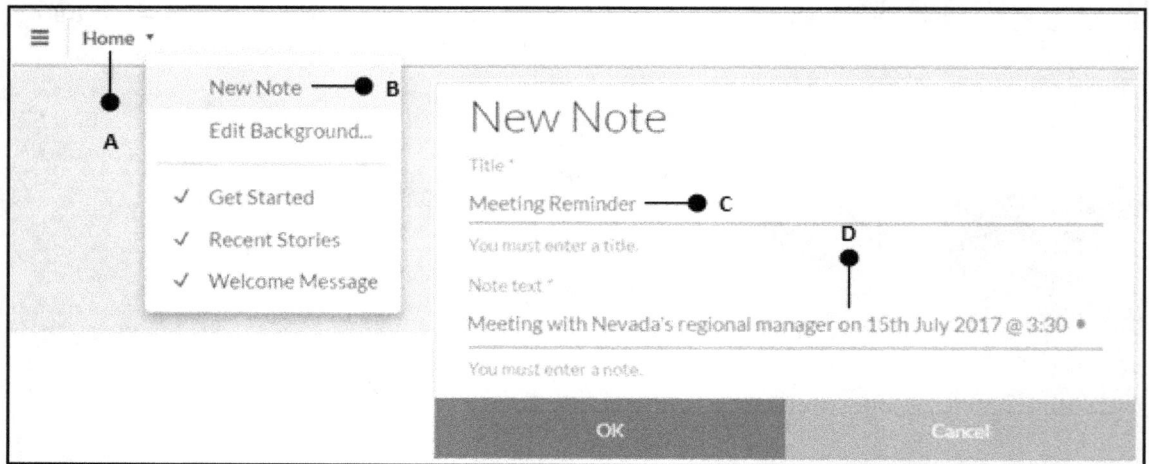

Here is the screenshot of my dashboard carrying multiple tiles of different objects from my story:

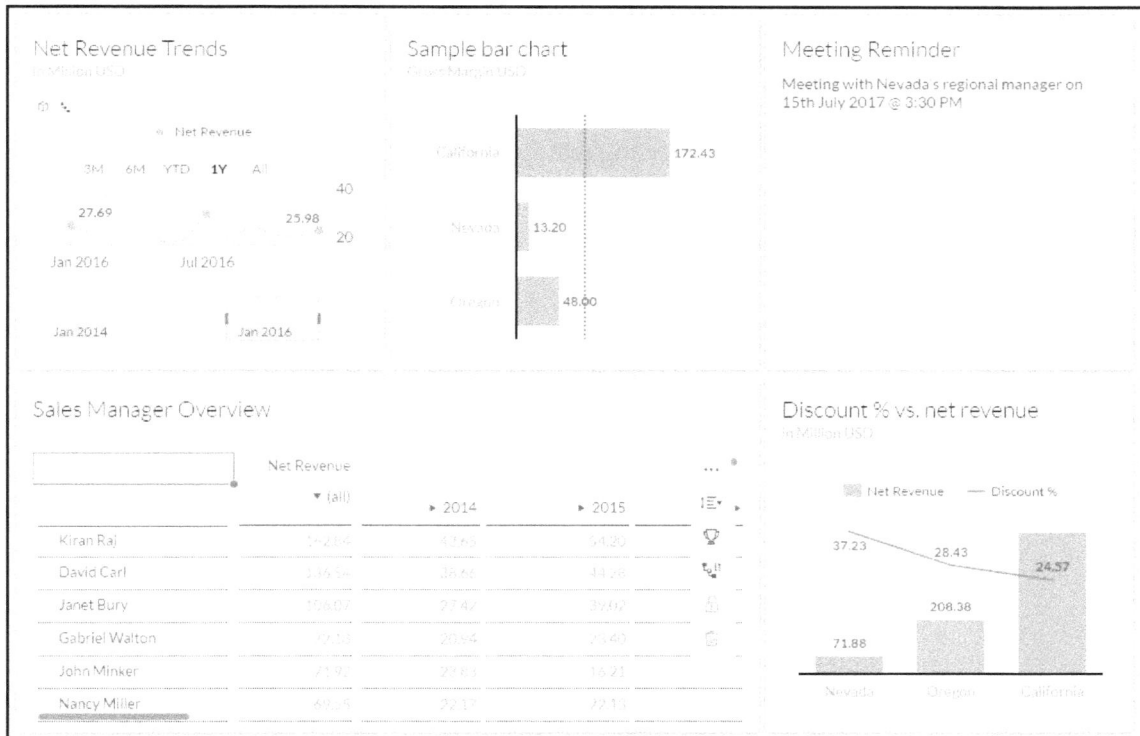

Summary

In this chapter, you completed the final page of your story. In these three pages, you learned the essence of SAP Analytics Cloud. You were taught how to create stories and pages and how to visualize data using different types of charts, geomaps, tables, and grids. In addition to demonstrating the use of different types of objects to analyze data, you were introduced to many options associated with these objects. For example, you learned how to copy objects between pages and on the same page, apply ranking and filters, show/hide object elements, sorting data, and more.

There is a long list of such options that you have already gone through, which doesn't need to be repeated here. In this chapter, you worked with tables and grid objects, which deal with text data. Besides the many features associated with the table object, such as setting visibility filters, swapping the axis, freezing rows and columns, and more, you learned the use of key performance indicators in tables. You added a grid page to the story in which you created your own formulas to analyze data. You also learned how to copy stories and objects and went through the process of creating a PDF of your story pages for offline access. Finally, you were guided on how to create a personalized dashboard, which provides a big picture of your story.

In the next chapter, you will learn how to manage planning and analytic activities by creating events and assigning tasks and how to monitor the task progress.

8
Collaboration

With the collaboration features available in SAP Analytics Cloud, colleagues can discuss business content and share information. Collaboration makes it easy to make decisions based on linked business content. Here is a list of features that allow group members to discuss stories and other business content:

- Creating a workflow using events and tasks
- Commenting on a chart's data point (refer to the *Pinning and Commenting on a Data Point* section in Chapter 5, *Extending Stories with KPI, Filters and other Handy Objects)*
- Commenting on a story page (refer to the *Adding Comments to a Page* section in Chapter 6, *Analyzing Data Using Geo Maps and Other Objects)*
- Producing a story as a PDF to share it with other users (refer to the *Save Story as a PDF* section in Chapter 7, *Working with Tables and Grids)*
- Sharing a story with colleagues
- Collaborating via discussions
- Sharing files and other objects

In addition to notifications, e-mails, and discussions channels, you can use a digital boardroom to collaborate with others in remote locations and on other devices in an interactive meeting room. With the SAP Analytics Cloud mobile app, you can collaborate with colleagues through the chat feature and view events and tasks anywhere and anytime.

Creating an events and tasks workflow

Collaboration is a joint effort of multiple individuals or work groups to accomplish a task. It directly impacts the outcome of a task or project. With SAP Analytics Cloud, you can use today's collaborative technology, such as tablets, and smartphones, that enable employees to work more flexibly from home and on the road taking advantage of the application's real-time collaborative capabilities to keep in touch with remote coworkers around the globe.

The events and tasks features in SAP Analytics Cloud are the two major sources that help you collaborate with other group members and consequently manage your planning and analytic activities. The chapter will demonstrate how events and tasks help in managing planning and analytic activities. After creating an event and assigning tasks to relevant group members, you can monitor the task progress in the **Events** interface. In this section, you will learn the use of these two features using the following workflow:

- Creating events based on categories and processes within categories
- Creating a task, assigning it to users, and setting a due date for its submission
- Monitoring the task progress

Creating an event

An event is a calendar event scheduled for a specific day and time. Meetings are good example of events. The events section in SAP Analytics Cloud is a calendar interface using which you can organize events and assign tasks to dedicated team members. Execute the following set of steps to understand the purpose of creating events and tasks in SAP Analytics Cloud:

1. Click the main menu icon (**A**) , and select **Events** from the menu:

The **Events** screen appears in which the current date (**B**) is highlighted. You can switch months using the two arrow icons (**C**) to view events and tasks in other months. You can view events and tasks by **Week** (**D**), **Month** (**E**), and **Year** (**F**). By default, you see the **Month** view:

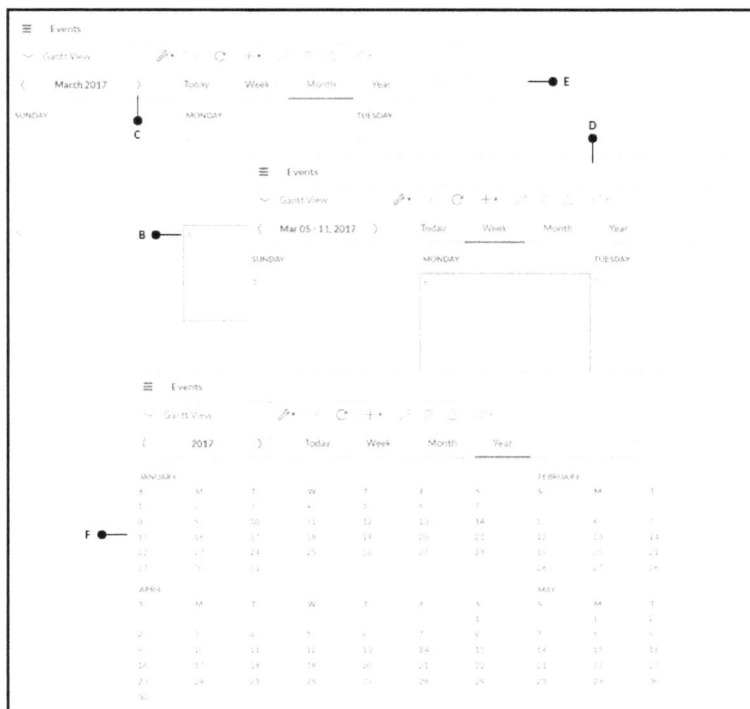

Before creating an event, you first need to modify the event categories and create processes within these categories. Event categories let you group your events in a way that makes sense to you. By changing the names and colors of event categories, you classify your event types.

2. Click on the Actions icon (**A**), and select **Edit Event Categories**.

   The **Edit Event Categories** screen (**B**) pops up containing category names that match the label colors. In the next step, you will provide descriptive names to some of these event categories.

3. Click on the first category name, and replace it with **Financial Planning**. Similarly, replace the second and third names with **Capacity Planning** (**C**) and **Global Planning** (**D**), as illustrated in the following screenshot. The preceding colors (**E**) let us identify the type of event on our calendar. You can also specify a different color from the color drop-list. If so desired, you can add new events using the + icon (**F**), and if you want to remove some of these categories, click on the delete icon (**G**). After providing the descriptive names to your events, click on **Save** to dismiss the **Edit Event Categories** screen.

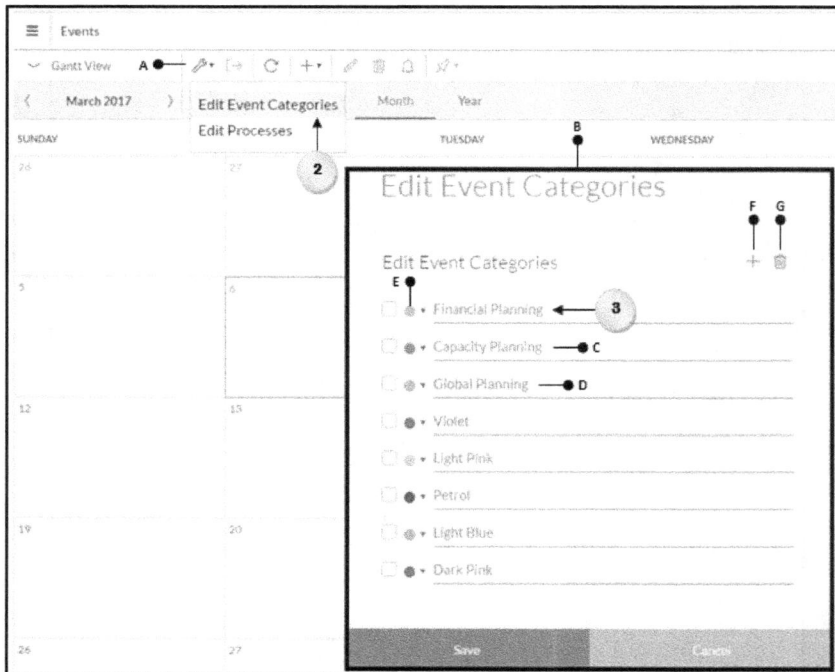

In the next two steps, you will specify the processes within the event category that you want to perform. You can create any number of user-defined processes for each event category.

4. Once again, click on the Actions icon, and this time, select the **Edit Processes** option.
5. Hover the mouse pointer over the **Financial Planning** category, and click on the New icon. A text area will be added just after the category name. Enter **Update Bocage First Quarter Data** (**A**) in this area, and click on **Save**. After creating a process under the event category, you can now add an event.

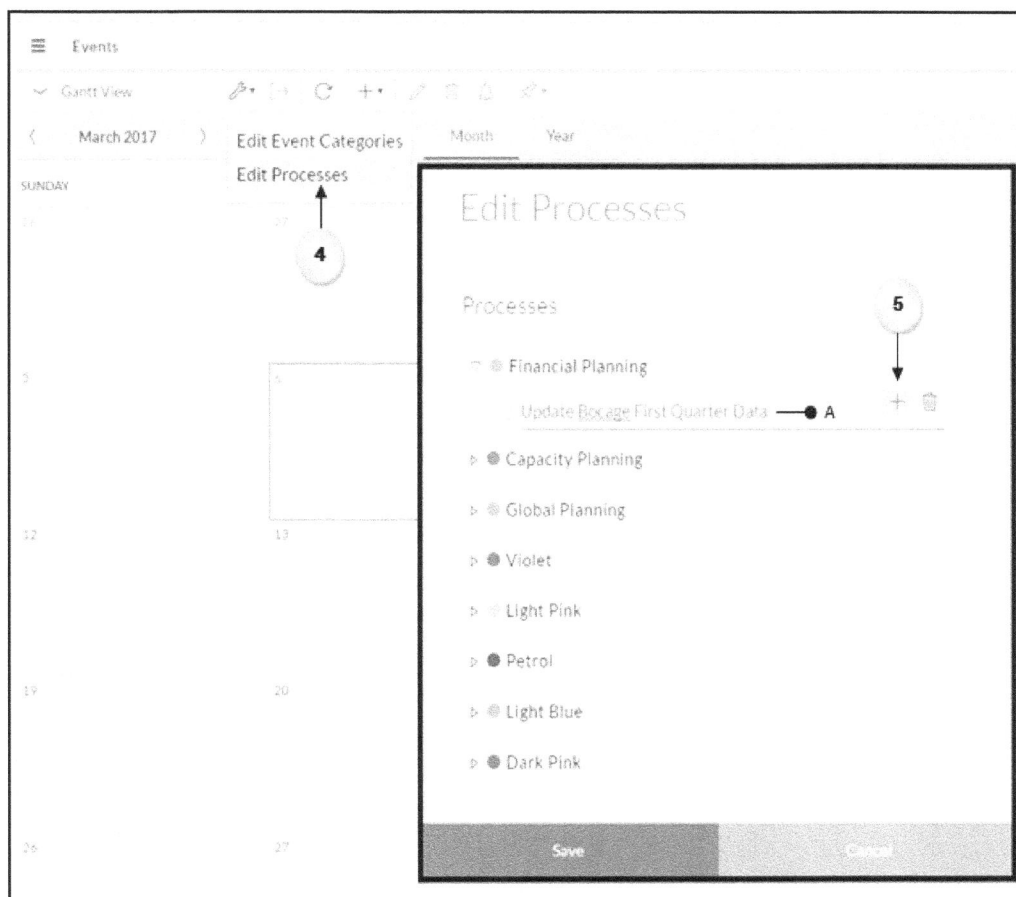

6. Click on the New icon (**A**), and select **New Event** from the menu. The **New Event** dialog box appears:

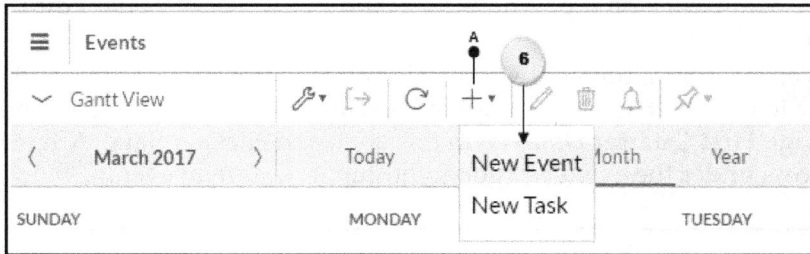

7. In the **New Event** dialog box, select **Financial Planning** from the **Category** list.
8. Select the process **Update Bocage First Quarter Data** from the Process list.
9. Enter **Update Q1 Data** in the **Title** field of the new event.
10. Using the calendar icons, select the start and due dates for the event. The due date must be chronologically after the start date.

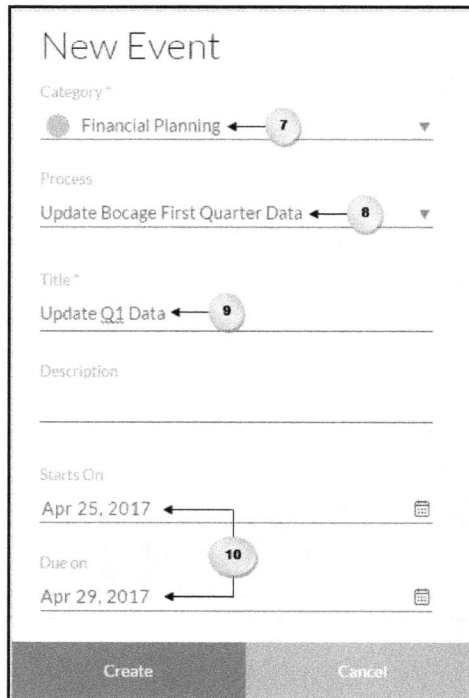

The **People** section in the **New Event** dialog box has two sub-sections: **Assignee** and **Owner**. In the **Assignee** sub-section, you can assign the event to one or more users. Subsequently, you can assign people from this group of users to individual tasks as you create the tasks. By default, the person who creates the event is set as **Owner** of the event, but this might be another person. So, you are provided with the option to change the event owner to ensure that the notifications are addressed to the right person--to the real task owner, not the creator.

11. Click on the Select Assignee icon, and select users (**A**) from the **Select Users** screen.

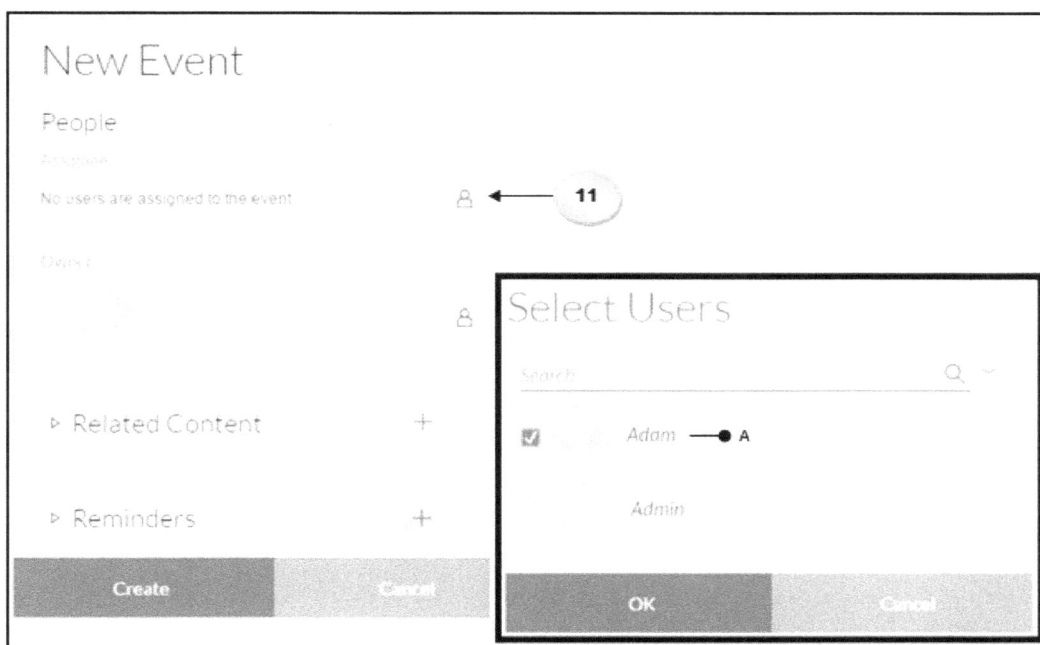

The **Related Content** area in the New Event screen allows you to add a link to an object, such as a story or a file.

12. Click on the Add Link icon, and type an alphabet (**A**) in the search box. A list of objects (**B**) will pop up. Select the desired object from this list. The selected object will be listed in the **Related Content** section (**C**). If you erroneously add an incorrect link here, you can remove it by selecting the object link (**D**) and clicking on the Delete Link icon (**E**).

In the **Reminder** section, you can create a reminder for the event, which is delivered automatically to the assignee. Reminder messages are sent to the task assignees the specified number of days before the due date. The messages can be sent as on-screen notification messages, e-mails, or both.

13. Click on the Add Reminder icon, which exposes the **Set Reminder** dialog box.

14. Enter 3 in the **Reminder Time** text area to deliver a reminder to the assignee three days before the due date. Check the e-mail box (**A**) to also send the reminder via e-mail associated with the account. Click on the **Set** button to set up the reminder, which is then placed under the **Reminders** section (**B**), as shown in the following screenshot:

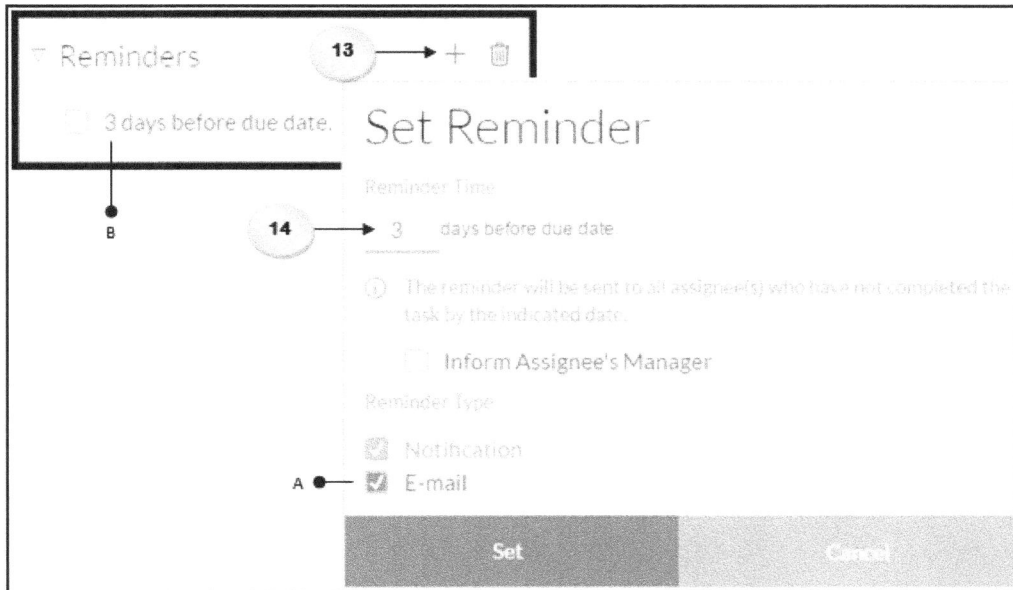

15. You must activate the reminder after its creation. So, check the reminder box to activate it. If required, you can modify the reminder using the edit icon (**A**) in this section.

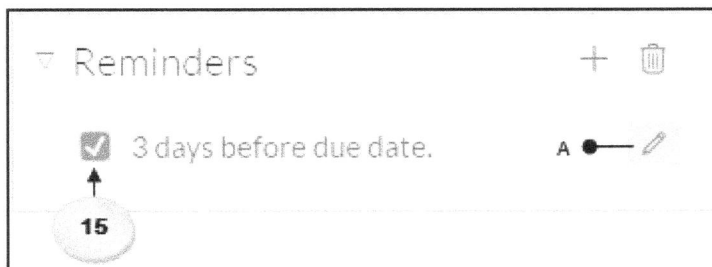

The event appears on the calendar in the due date cell. The color of the event in the calendar and in the **DETAILS** panel is the same you set for the **Financial Planning** event category in step 3. Click on the cell displaying the event to view its details in the **Details** panel, such as the start and due dates, related content, and the assignee. The options available in the panel provide you with the opportunity to start a group discussion about the event or add related tasks, which you will do next. The link provided in the **Related Content** area leads you to the content you selected in step 12.

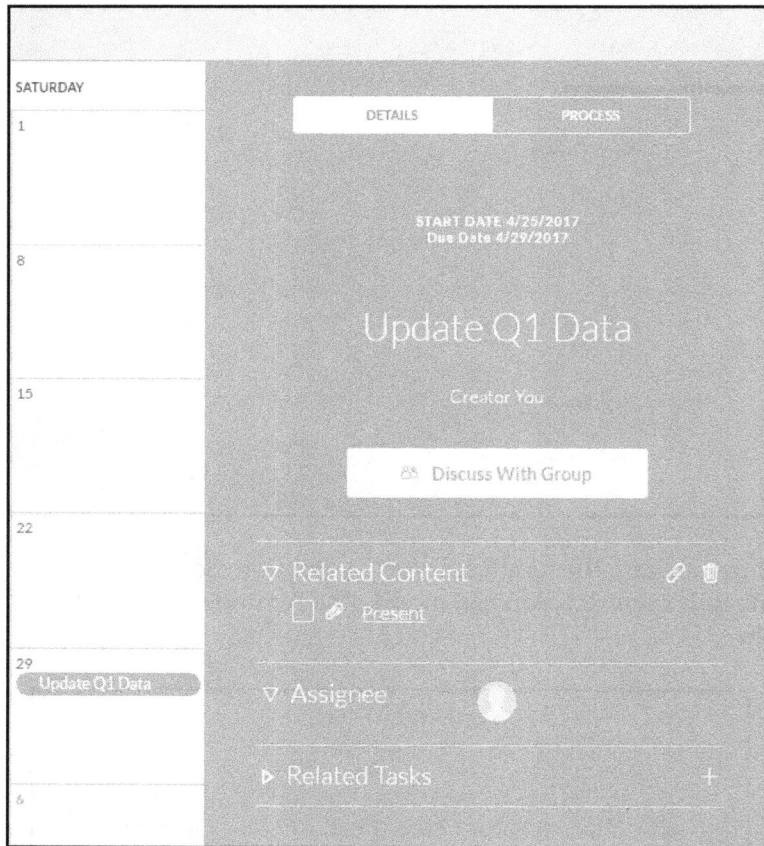

Here is the event notification that the assignees get when they log in:

All Types ▼   Search   🗑

☑   The event 'Update Q1 Data' will be due on
     2017-04-29.

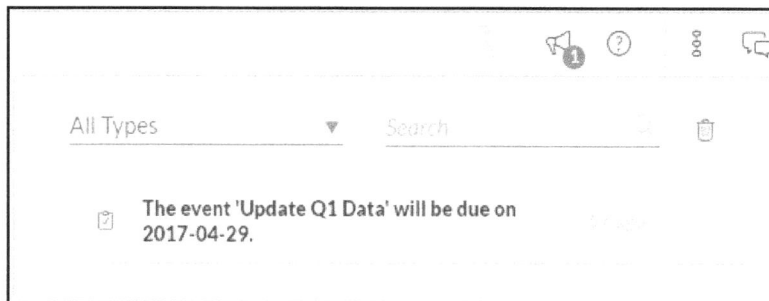

Creating tasks

After creating an event, you create tasks for the event and assign users to the task. A task is an activity not scheduled for an exact day and time. You can specify a due date for a task or there may not be a particular time or date that the tasks need to be completed by. In this section, you will create a task that will request the assignee to incorporate first quarter data to update the Bocage model. Here are the steps to create a task and assign users:

16. You can add a task either from the toolbar or from the **Details** panel. In the former case, click on the New icon on the toolbar, and select **New Task**. Alternatively, click on the Add Task icon (**A**) in the **Details** panel under the **Related Tasks** section. Either way, you will get the **New Task** window to set parameters for the new task.

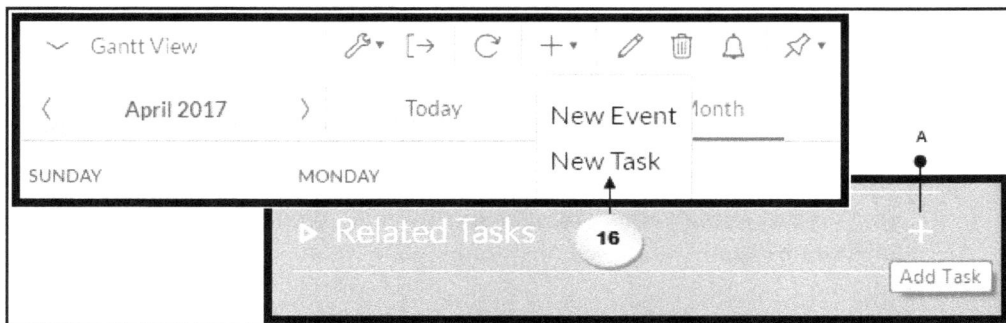

17. In the **New Task** window, enter the `Update Q1 data for West US in the Bocage` model as the title of the new task.

18. Set the start and due dates as illustrated in the following screenshot using the calendar icons:

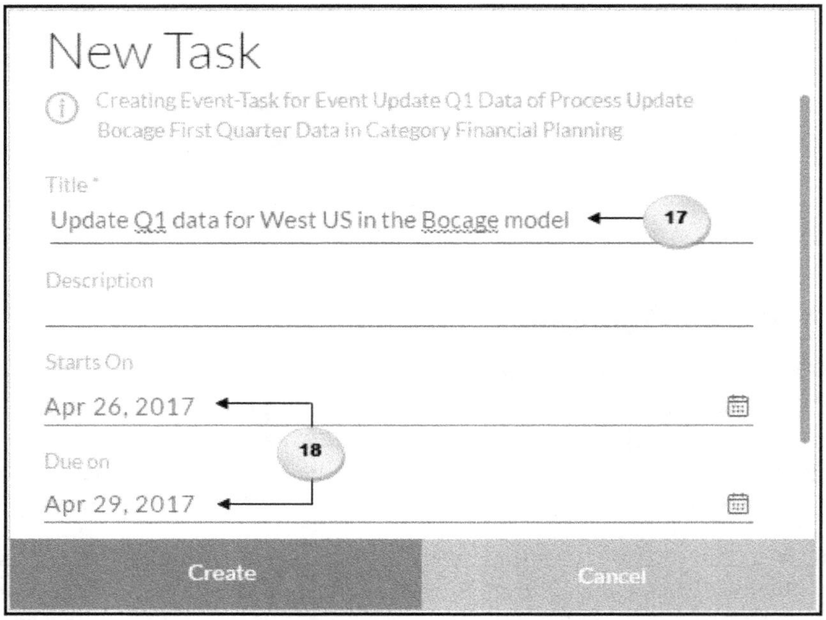

New Task

ⓘ Creating Event-Task for Event Update Q1 Data of Process Update
Bocage First Quarter Data in Category Financial Planning

Title *

Update Q1 data for West US in the Bocage model ◄─── 17

Description

Starts On

Apr 26, 2017 ◄────┐ 📅

Due on   18

Apr 29, 2017 ◄─── 📅

| Create | Cancel |

In the **People** section, you have to assign the task to at least one assignee and also have the options to nominate a reviewer and a final reviewer, if required. When you click on the Select Assignee icon, you see the users to whom you assigned the event in step 11.

19. Click on the Select Assignee icon, select the assignee from the **Select Users** screen, and click on **OK**.

As you did with events, you can specify related content and add reminders to the tasks as well.

20. Click on the Add Link icon in the **Related Content** section to see the list of available objects. Usually, you add the link of a story that needs to be updated by the assignee. The selected object appears under the **Related Content** section. Check the box (**A**) for this object, and click on Create:

The task is created and placed on the calendar under the event it belongs to. Both the event and task entries in the calendar as well as in the **Details** panel are shown in the same category color, but with different icons:

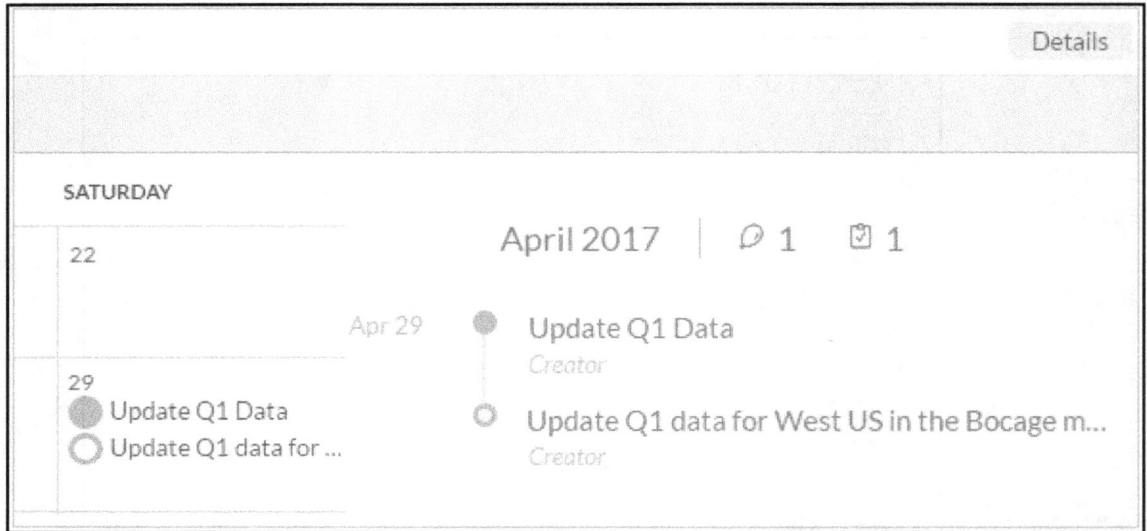

Displaying and monitoring events and tasks

To monitor is to check on how events and tasks are progressing. Using the monitoring feature of SAP Analytics Cloud, you can observe the activities taking place in the created events and assigned tasks. It helps you keep an eye on all aspects of the project. When it comes to displaying and monitoring the events and tasks you have created, SAP Analytics Cloud provides you with the following three options:

- **Calendar**: This is the default view in which the events and tasks are presented in a standard calendar layout
- **Gantt**: In this view, the events and tasks are presented in a bar chart with the start and due dates
- **Timeline**: This provides a linear view of the process

Click on the **Gantt View** option to switch to this view from **Calendar View**, which is set by default.

21. The **Gantt View**, as illustrated in the following screenshot (**A**), initially displays the event in a bar chart (**B**). Expand the **Update Bocage First Quarter Data** process node by clicking on the arrow icon (**C**) to also see the task (**D**), which is presented in dotted lines. The start and due dates (**E** and **F**) are also apparent in the chart:

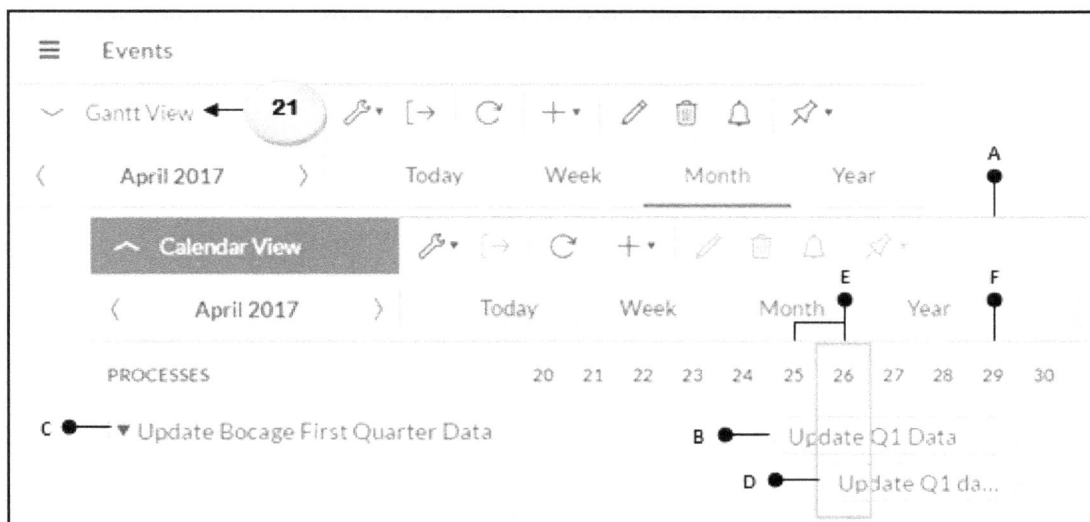

In addition to the Calendar and Gantt views, you can also view your events and tasks in a Timeline view.

You can configure the events timeline to show all of the events and tasks or a subset of them. Here are the steps to see the timeline view:

22. In the **Events** page, click on the Time Panel icon. The timeline view (**A**) will appear on the left side of the screen.

By default, the timeline shows all the events and tasks for the next ten days or less. You can modify both the number of days and the specific categories that you want to see in the timeline.

23. In the **Timeline** view, click on the Preferences icon.
24. Set the number of days to show from the **Number of Days From Today** list (for example, 5).
25. Select the categories that you want to see, for example, **Financial Planning**.

   Click on **OK** to apply your settings. The timeline view displays only the selected categories that fall within the specified number of days. Note that these steps will yield the result only when you have multiple events in different categories, spanning different timelines.

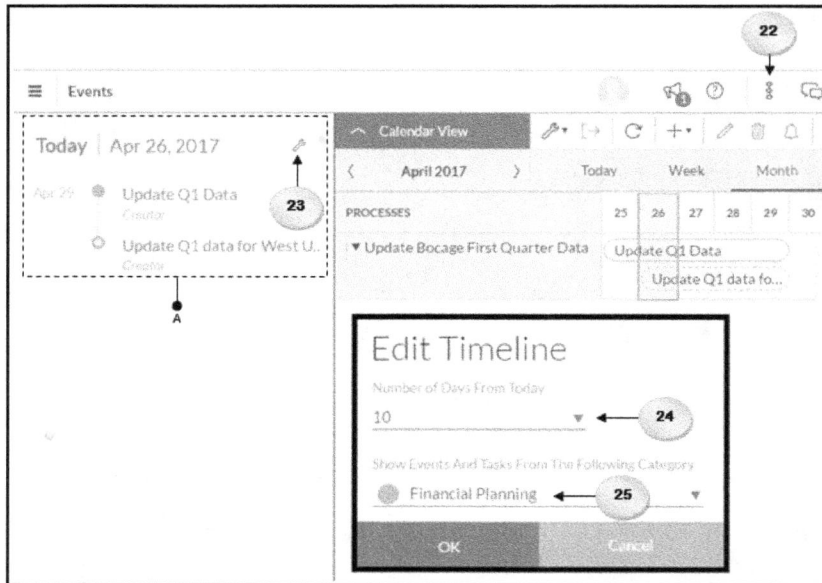

If you click on the task entry (**A**) in the Calendar or Gantt view, you see a section labeled **Assignees & Status** (**B**). This section displays the name of the assignee (**C**) and the status of the task, which should currently be displaying **Pending** (**D**). In the next section, we will see how the assignee views the task and event assigned to him.

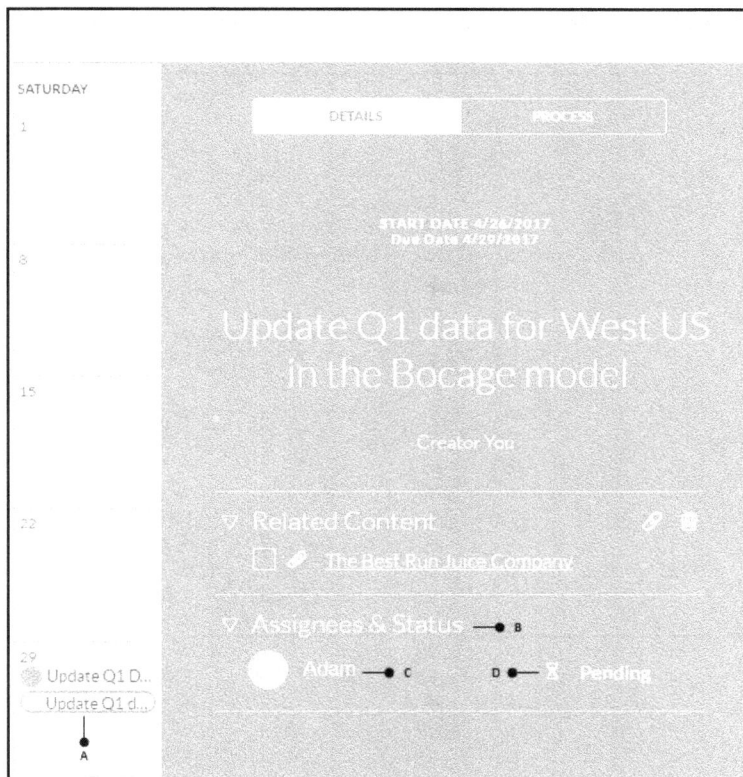

When the assignee logs in, the notifications area (**A**) alerts him that he has a couple of messages about the event and task assigned to him. Clicking on the notifications icon displays the messages. When he clicks on the event notification, the event screen pops up, where he can see the event's details. Among other details, he can find the task assigned to him in the **Related Tasks** section, which requires him to **Update Q1 Data for West US in the Bocage model**, as shown in the following screenshot:

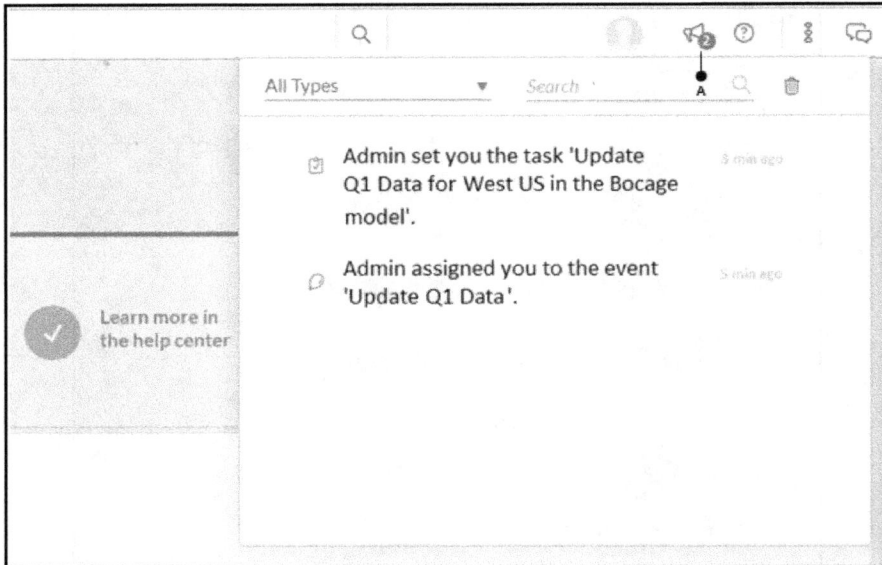

When he opens the task by clicking on the link in the **Related Tasks** section or by selecting it in the Calendar or Gantt views, he gets the following information in the **Details** panel. The two buttons at the bottom of this panel allow him to accept the task or decline it. The link in the **Related Content** area show the name of the story he needs to update. After completing the assigned task, he clicks on the **Accept Task** button in this panel, followed by the **Done** button.

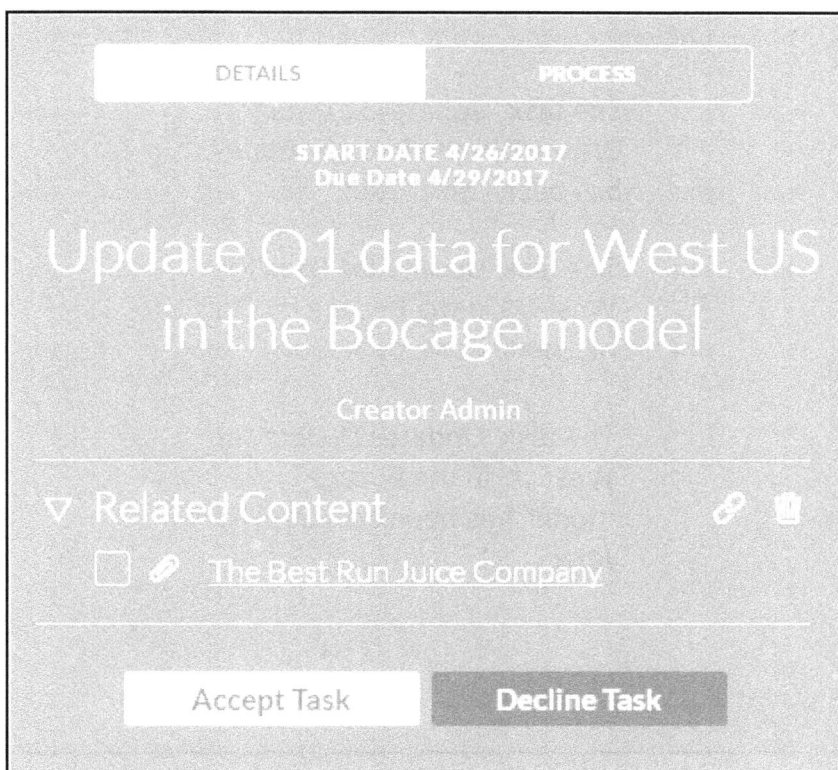

When the event and task creator logs in, he gets three notifications, as illustrated in the following screenshot. These messages inform him that the task was accepted and then completed by the assignee.

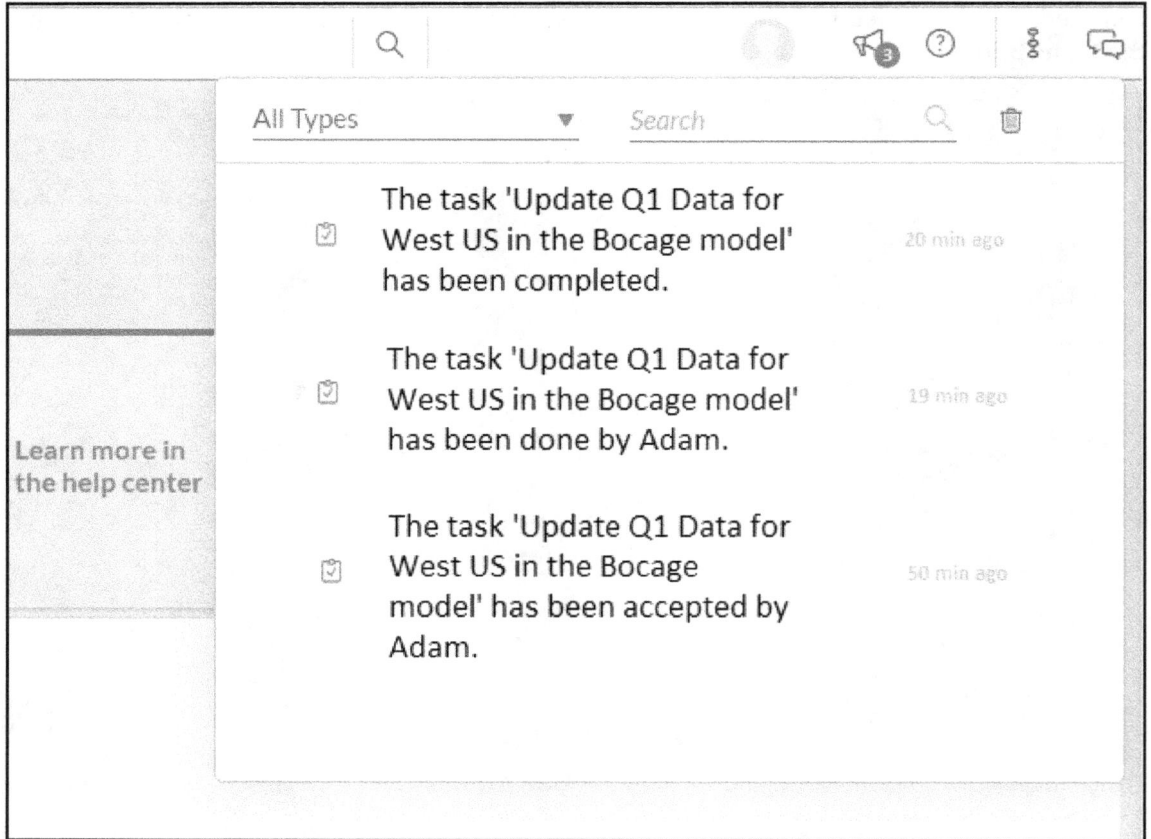

The completed event and the corresponding task are now presented in a dark color, and the statuses of both the event and the task are also marked as completed in the **Details** panel:

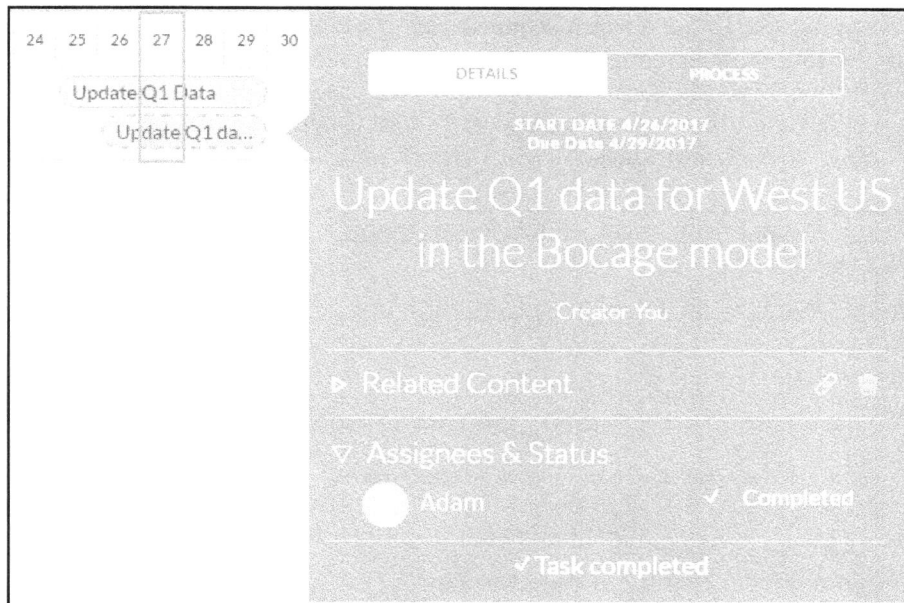

Events toolbar

You have already utilized some of the options available in the toolbar. Here are the briefs of the remaining options:

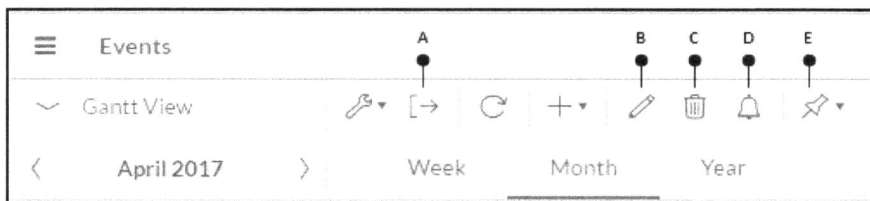

- **Export Event (A)**: When you select an event in the Calendar or Gantt view and click on this toolbar option, the event is exported as a `.ics` file. A file with the ICS file extension is an `iCalendar` file. It is a plain text file that includes calendar event details. In the current scenario, the file contains event details as illustrated in the following screenshot. You can open this file in Microsoft Outlook, Windows Live Mail, and IBM Notes, as well as in calendar programs, such as Google Calendar for web browsers, Yahoo! Calendar, Apple Calendar for iOS mobile devices and Macs, Mozilla Lightning Calendar, and VueMinder.

Update Q1 Data, event from SAP BusinessObjects Cloud
- Link -
  https://eu1.sapbusinessobjects.cloud/sap/fpa/ui/#;view_id=em;eventId=E85BFF58EF
- Description -
- assignees
  - Admin
- Tasks
  - Update Q1 data for West US in the Bocage model
    - Description -
    - Duedate - 2017-04-29
    - Reminder - reminder 3 days before

- **Edit Event/Maintain Task (B)**: This toolbar option can be used to modify the details of an event and the task as well. When you select an event in the Calendar or Gantt view and click on this icon, the **Edit Event** dialog box appears. When you select a task and click on this option, you see the **Edit Task** dialog box.

- **Delete Event/Task (D)**: Similar to the edit option, this one also toggles to delete the selected event or task.

- **Edit Reminders (E)**: This option is used to modify the reminders you have set for your events and tasks.

- **Pin to Home (F)**: You can pin your events and tasks to your Home screen using this option. For further details, refer to the *Pinning Story Objects* section in `Chapter 7`, *Working with Tables and Grids*.

Sharing a story with colleagues and granting access privileges

After completing a story, you save it and share it with other users. Sharing a story is a part of collaboration. The main purpose of sharing a story is to request others to provide their feedback, and based on their input further refine the story. You went through the saving process at the end of Chapter 5, *Extending Stories with KPI, Filters and other Handy Objects* in the *Save Your Story* section. To remind you, there are three options to save and share your work with colleagues:

- **Public**: You can share your stories by saving them to the Public folder, which makes them available to everyone
- **Teams**: This option grants the access of your story to specified teams
- **Private**: If you select the **Private** option, your story will be available only to users with whom you share it

You have a number of options to share your story with others. Here's the simplest route:

26. In your story, click on the Share icon, and select **Share Story** (**A**) from the menu:

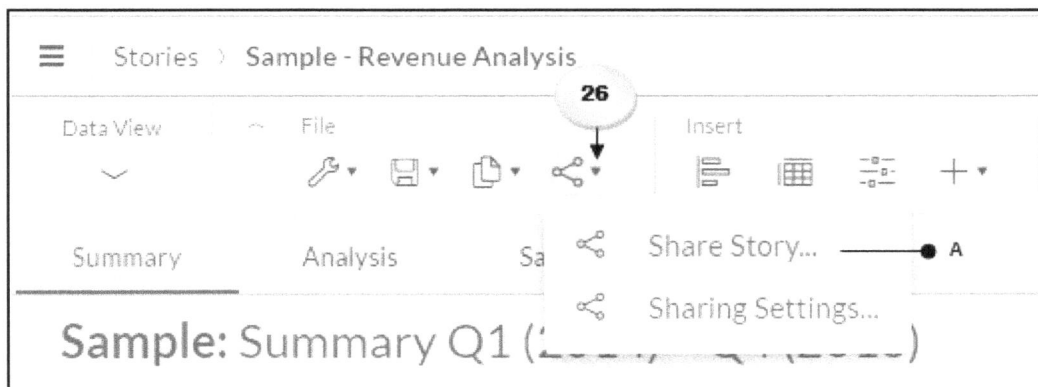

The **Share Story** dialog box pops up. You can send the link (**B**) in this dialog box to your colleagues to share the story with them.

27. To share the story with specific users or teams, click on the Add Usernames icon, which renders the **Select Users and Teams** dialog box from where you can select teams (**C**) or individual users (**D**).
28. From the **Access** list, you can provide the **Read, Update**, or **Full Control** rights to the selected people. For this example, provide the **Read** access right.

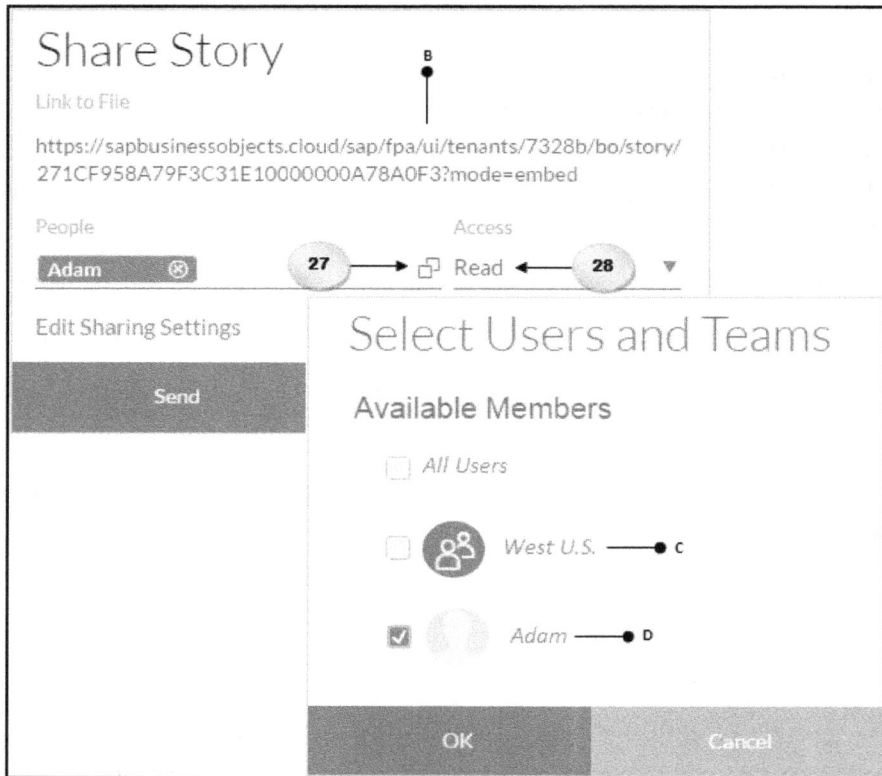

When the other users log in, they get a notification (**E**) about the share. Clicking on the notification opens up the story with limited access, in which they can see and utilize a subset of options in the main toolbar (**F**). The available options allow them to save the story with a new name, apply filters, and create their own formulas.

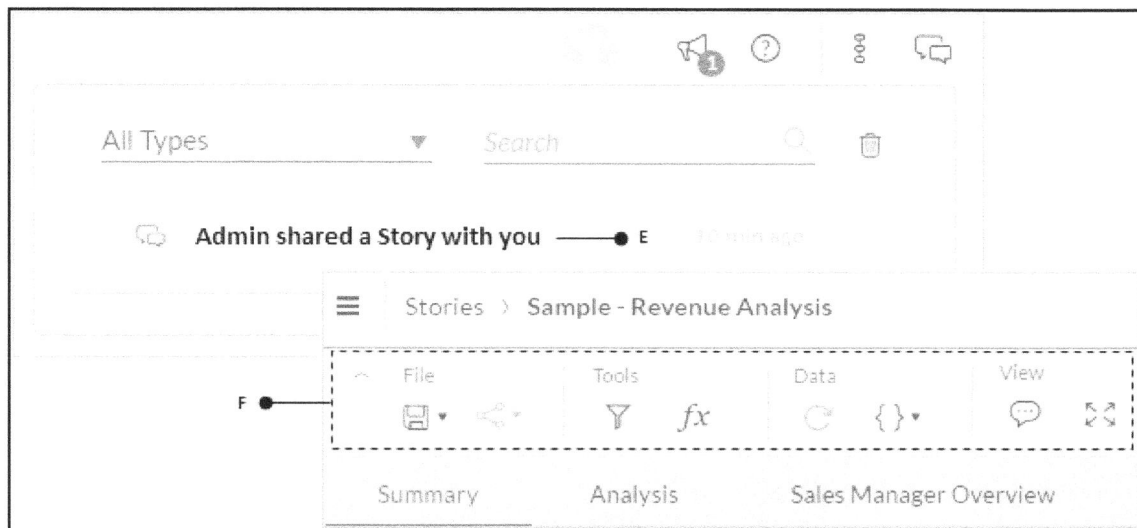

The other option in the Share menu is **Sharing Settings**. When you click on this option, you see the **Edit Sharing Settings** dialog box, as illustrated in the following screenshot. Here, you can adjust your story access privileges according to the users. As you can see in the screenshot, the dialog box allows you to grant full, read, update, and delete access to the selected members and groups. You can use different combinations for different people. For example, you can provide **Update Access** to some members so they can update the story, if required, and grant **Read Access** to others to prevent story updating. You can also add more users and teams using the **Add Users and Teams** button.

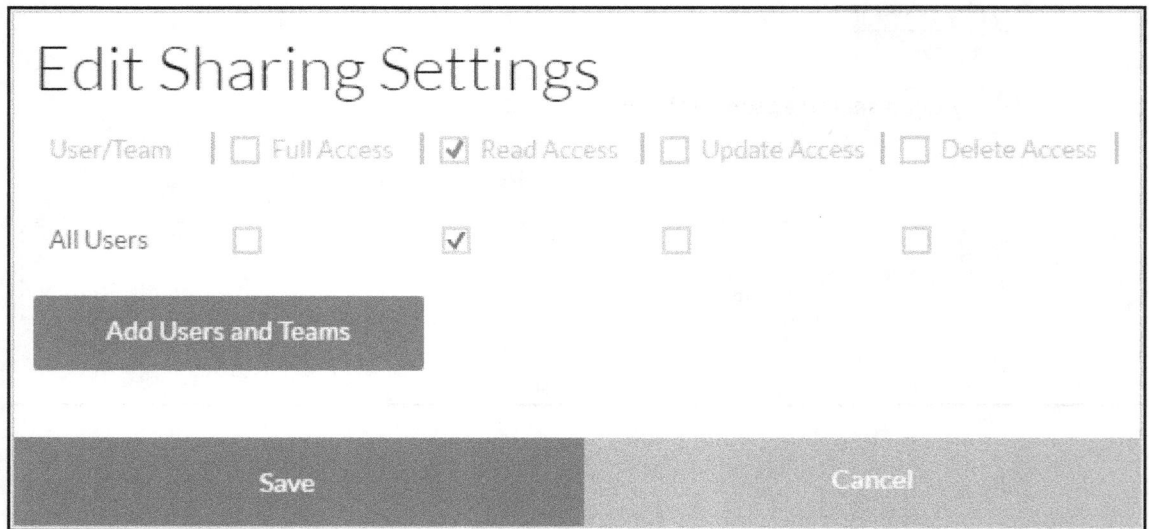

Edit Sharing Settings

User/Team	☐ Full Access	☑ Read Access	☐ Update Access	☐ Delete Access
All Users	☐	☑	☐	☐

Add Users and Teams

Save	Cancel

Collaborating via discussions

You can collaborate with colleagues using the discussions feature of SAP Analytics Cloud. The discussions feature enables you to connect with other members in real time. Here are the steps to utilize this feature:

29. Click on the Collaboration icon on the main toolbar to access the **Discussions** panel.
30. Click on the New Discussion icon. Use the left arrow if you want to switch back.
31. In **New Discussion**, click on the + icon to add participants
32. In the **Select Users** dialog box, select the users you want to add to the discussion.

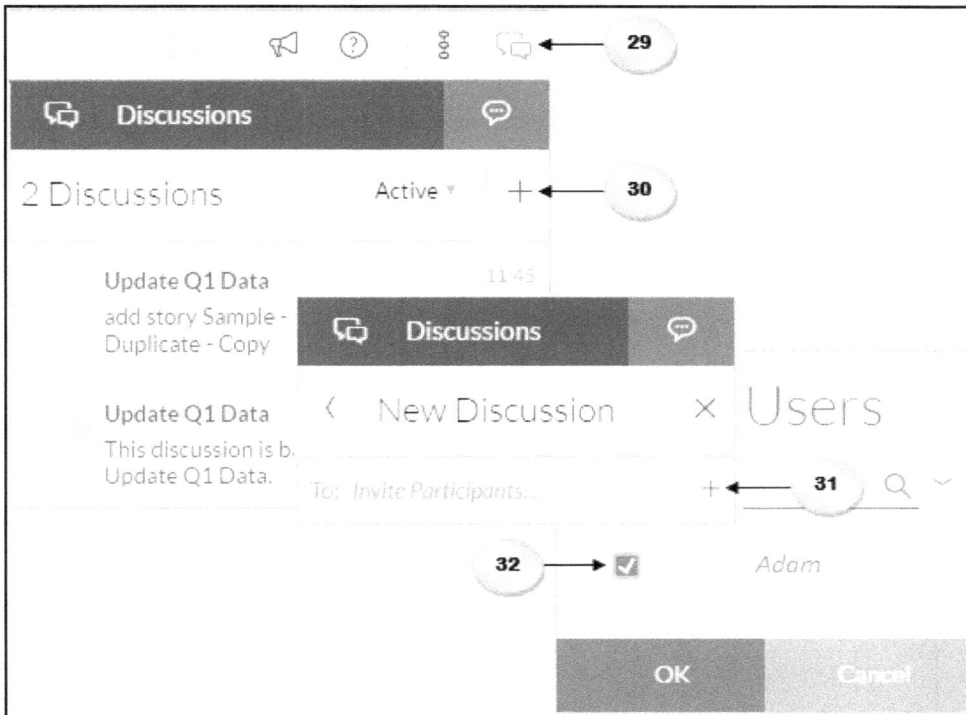

After inviting the participants, you can begin the discussion by clicking on the New icon (**A**) at the bottom of the **Discussions** panel. The button provides you with some collaborating options. If you choose the **Link Story** option (**B**), your story is added to the discussion panel. The **New Task** option (**C**) invokes the corresponding window you went through earlier in this chapter to create a new task. You can also send a text message by typing a message (**D**) and clicking on the send icon (**E**). The messages you send to the participants are also added to the discussion panel (**F**).

Clicking on the Manage icon (**G**) delivers a menu (**H**), which allows you to manage related content, manage users, archive the discussion for later reference, and delete the discussion. If required, you can access the archived discussion using the **Discussions** panel menu (**I**). The participants receive alerts about the discussion in the notification area. They can join the discussion by clicking on the relevant message in the notification area. Clicking on the collaboration icon shows a similar discussions screen, as illustrated in the following screenshot, from where they can access and respond to the shared content:

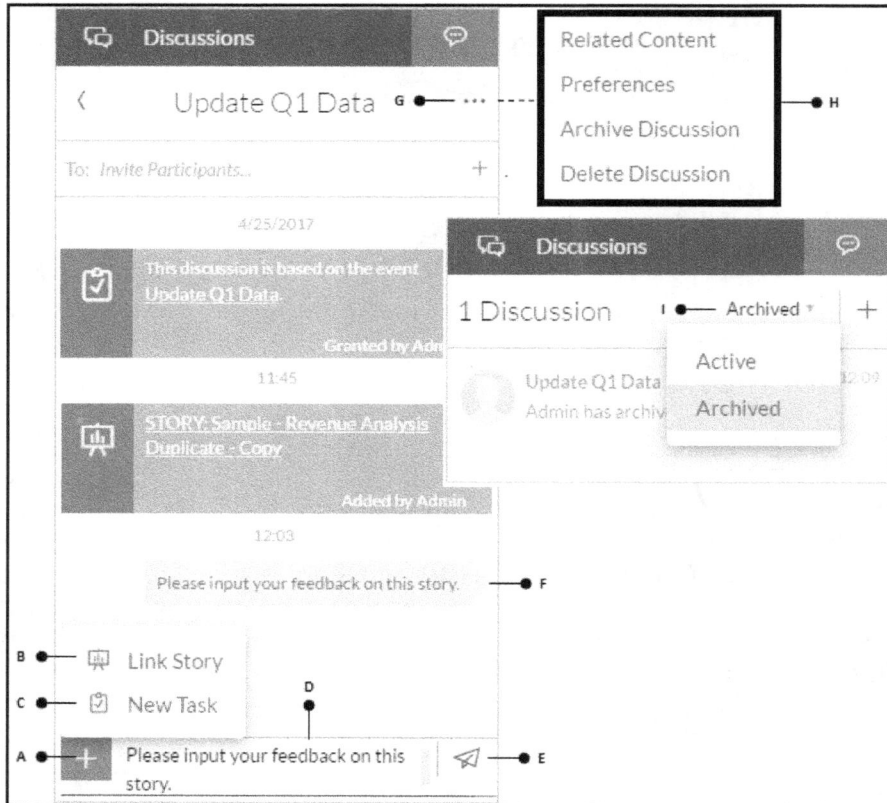

Sharing files and other objects

The stories you create and the files you upload are stored in the SAP Analytics Cloud repository. You can access and share these objects with other users from the **Files** page. The following are the main tasks that you can perform on the **Files** page:

- **Manage files and folder**: The main purpose of this page is to organize your stories, input forms, boardroom agendas, and uploaded files.
- **Upload files**: In addition to creating stories using different types of objects, SAP Analytics Cloud allows you to upload files from your own computer. You can store these files in the repository and share them with other colleagues.
- **Share files**: Using this interface, you can share your stories and other content with individual members or teams.
- **Change share settings**: Once you have decided to share your content with other people, you can define access privileges for the shared files or folders.

33. Go to **Main Menu | Browse | Files** to access the **Files** interface:

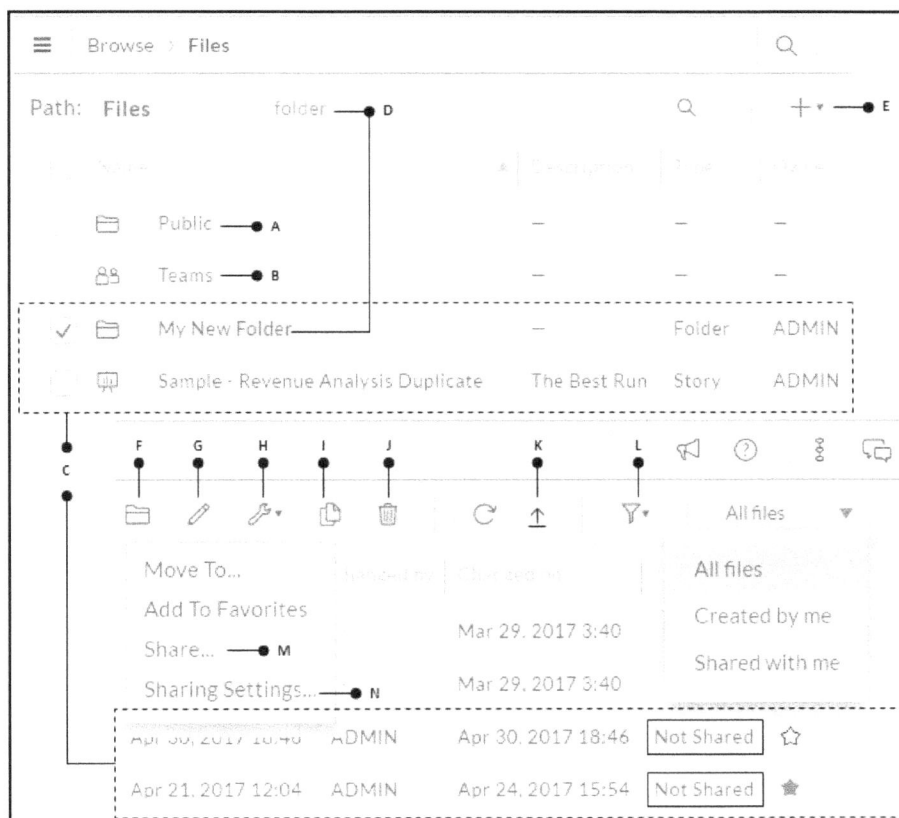

- The `Public` folder (**A**): Recall that when you saved your story in `Chapter 5`, *Extending Stories with KPI, Filters and other Handy Objects,* you were given three options: **Public**, **Teams**, and **Private**. The **Files** page organizes your content in one of these view categories. The `Public` folder contains a `Samples` subfolder, which holds sample templates, stories, and public files for which you are assigned full, read, update, and delete access privileges. Click on the `Public` folder link to see the `Samples` subfolder and the content it contains.
- The `Teams` folder (**B**): The **Teams** option grants the access of your story to a specified team and stores your story in the `Teams` folder.
- The `Private` files (**C**): The `Private` files are those files that are not shared with other users. The same rule applies to folders.
- **Search box** (**D**): You can find any content in the folders or subfolder by entering the keyword in the search box.
- **Create** (**E**): If you have appropriate permission, then the Files page also lets you create a Story and a Boardroom Agenda through the Create icon.
- **New folder** (**F**): Click on the New Folder icon to create new folders in the interface.
- **Edit** (**G**): Clicking on the Edit icon delivers another window in which you can modify the name and description of the selected file.
- **Manage** (**H**): The Manage option comes with a small menu. If you want to move the selected object to another location, select the Move To option from this menu. Mark files as favorites by selecting the star icon in the **Favorite** column. Or, you can select multiple files and select **Add To Favorites** from the Manage menu. The concept of sharing and the **Sharing Settings** options in this menu will be discussed in a while.
- **Copy To** (**I**): Choosing the Copy To option in the toolbar makes an exact copy of the selected object in the selected folder.
- **Delete** (**J**): Get rid of unwanted files or folders using the Delete icon on the toolbar. Depending on the access rights that have been defined for a file, the Delete option may be active when you select one or more files.
- **Upload file** (**K**): Use the Upload file icon on the toolbar to upload files from your own computer to SAP Analytics Cloud. Note that, at the time of writing this, you can upload PDF, text, and MS Office files, up to a maximum size of 250 MB.
- **Filter** (**L**): Select the filter icon on the toolbar to display certain file types. To further refine the list, select **Created by me** or **Shared with me** from the adjacent list.

- **Sharing Files (M):** Files and folders that are not shared with other users are shown as **Not Shared** on the **Files** page. You can share these objects with other users by clicking on the Share option in the Manage menu. For further details, refer to the *Sharing a Story With Colleagues and Granting Access Privileges* section in this chapter.

- **Change Share Settings (N):** By choosing the option **Sharing Settings** in the Manager menu, you see the same dialog box as you saw in the *Sharing a Story With Colleagues and Granting Access Privileges* section earlier in this chapter. Using the options provided in this dialog box, you can grant or revoke access permissions for a file or folder to and from other people or teams.

Summary

In today's fast-paced business environment, where things change very quickly, prompt collaboration among the workforce is imperative for any business to survive. SAP Analytics Cloud is a platform that delivers all the collaborating features necessary to cope with day-to-day business challenges.

This chapter provided an in-depth overview of these vital features. First, you went through the events and tasks features of SAP Analytics Cloud that come in handy in a collaborative environment, where each person is responsible for performing a job in a stipulated time frame.

Apart from that, you got hands-on exposure to these two vital features. Initially, you are required to set up event categories and add relevant processes to these color-coded categories. Then, you initiate an event by providing a title, specifying start and due dates and picking up users who will be assigned associated tasks in the next stage. Next, you create tasks and provide the same set of information you set for the event.

Once a task is created, you can monitor both the event and the task in a Calendar, Gantt, or Timeline view. The notification area keeps the task creator updated about the progress and, at the same time, generates alerts to inform the assignees about the tasks they need to complete.

Then you were shown how to share your story with colleagues and grant different access privileges on your story to different coworkers and teams. Next, you saw how to collaborate through discussions, which is a real-time way of sharing content and information. Finally, you were briefed about sharing files and other objects via the **Files** page.

The chapter provided you with a taste of different collaboration features in SAP Analytics Cloud. The next chapter covers yet another collaboration feature called the digital boardroom, which is used for remote collaboration.

9
Digital Boardroom

Why should I leave my traditional means of presentation? This is the first question that comes to your mind when someone recommends you switch to SAP Digital Boardroom. A short answer to this question is that SAP Digital Boardroom has revolutionized board meetings. This chapter is dedicated to exhibiting how the Digital Boardroom can revolutionize meeting experiences.

SAP Digital Boardroom is a next-generation visualization and presentation platform that enormously aids in the decision-making process and contextualizes the boardroom experience across people, places, and devices in real time. It transforms executive meetings by replacing static and stale presentations with interactive discussions based on live data, which allows you to make fact-based decisions to drive your business. By setting up the Digital Boardroom you can accomplish the following:

- Collaborate with others in remote locations and on other devices in an interactive meeting room
- Delve into the heart of your company to get insight into every process and data
- Analyze and plan your activities
- Answer ad hoc questions on-the-fly
- Visualize, recognize, experiment, and decide by jumping on- and off-script at any point
- Analyze financial processes in real time, generate sales forecasts, and understand employees
- Find answers to the questions that matter to you by directly exploring live data and focusing on relevant aspects by drilling into details
- Discover opportunities or reveal hidden threats
- Simulate various decisions and project the results
- Weigh and share the pros and cons of your findings

The Digital Boardroom is interactive, so you can retrieve real-time data, make changes to the schedule, and even run through what-if scenarios. It presents a live picture of your organization across three interlinked touch screens to make faster, better executive decisions:

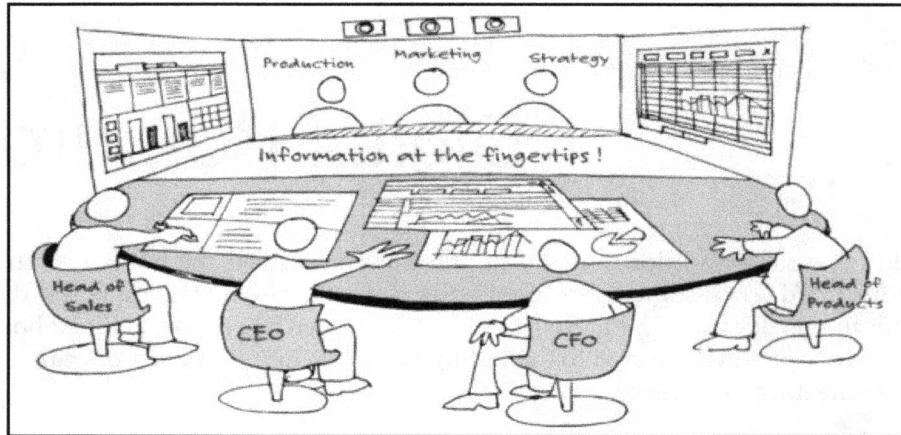

There are two aspects of the Digital Boardroom, using which you can share existing stories with executives and decision-makers to reveal business performance:

- **Creating an agenda**: First, you have to design your agenda for your boardroom presentation by adding meeting information, agenda items, and linking stories as pages in a navigation structure.

- **Starting a meeting to discuss the agenda**: Once you have created a Digital Boardroom agenda, you can schedule a meeting to discuss the agenda. In the Digital Boardroom interface, you can organize a meeting in which members can interact with live data during a boardroom presentation.

> Before you invoke the Digital Boardroom feature, make sure that your administrator has granted appropriate privileges to you and to all other members. You need the boardroom Creator role if you are creating the agenda. Other participants who will access the agenda must be granted the boardroom Viewer role. Creation and assignment of roles is covered in the next chapter.

In this chapter, you will be briefed on the following segments of SAP Digital Boardroom:

- Customizing the environment by setting display size, enabling data exploration, setting navigation targets, enabling touch cell input, and setting miscellaneous preferences to change the look and feel of your Digital Boardroom
- Creating an agenda
- Creating agenda sub-items
- Starting an online meeting
- Inviting people to the meeting
- Adding annotations during presentations
- Stopping an online meeting

Optimizing the display

As just mentioned, you first need to create an agenda for the Digital Boardroom meeting. But before that, you have to optimize the display and navigation for Digital Boardroom.

Execute the following steps to set up the stage:

1. With your story open, click on the **Styling** tab in the **Designer** panel.
2. Turn on the **Fix Page Size** switch.
3. Set **Width** to 1920 pixels. This is the optimal width for each story page displayed in the Digital Boardroom.

4. Place check marks in the two checkboxes to select the **Continuous Height** and **Snap to Nearest Grid** options:

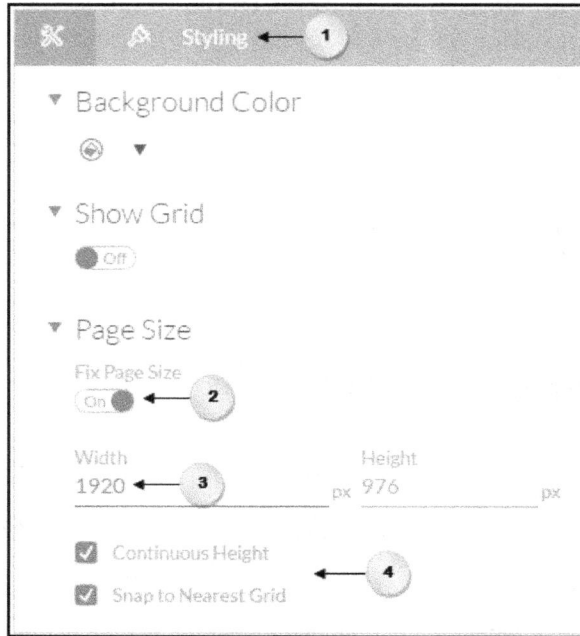

Creating an agenda

After adjusting the page width, you are ready to create an agenda in which you can add meeting information, agenda items, and link story pages for your boardroom presentation. Here are the steps to create an agenda:

5. Go to **Main Menu** | **Create** | **Boardroom Agenda**:

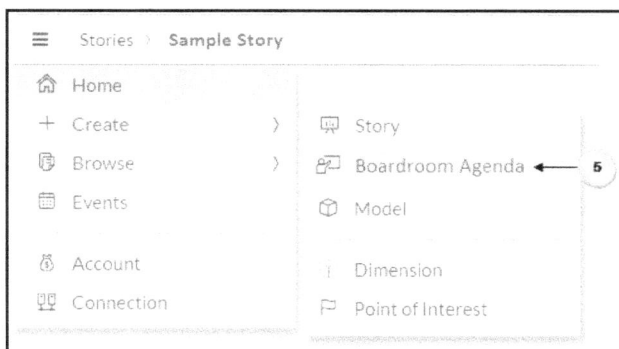

The **Create Agenda** dialog box comes up. Just like stories, an agenda can also be marked as **Public**, available to specific teams, or kept as private.

6. For now, select **Public** from the **Path** list.
7. Enter `Annual Board Meeting` as the agenda name.

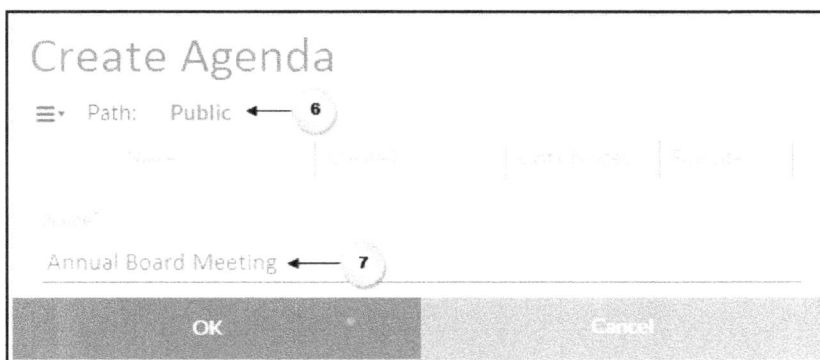

An interface to create a new agenda will be displayed, as illustrated in the following screenshot, where you can input title, date, location, and create agenda items for your presentation.

8. Click on the New icon to add an agenda item (**A**). An agenda consists of one or more agenda items that break up your presentation into different topics. Agenda items break up your presentation into parts so different presenters can cover specific topics, each with its own stories and data.
9. Enter a title, date, and location for the meeting. You can select a date from the date picker.

10. Enter a title and sub-title for the agenda item.
11. From the **Story** list, select a story that is to be discussed.
12. From the **Page** list, select the story page that will serve as an overview summary for the agenda item. The content of this page will be shown in the left overview screen.
13. Enter the presenter's name.
14. Type the presenter's job role.
15. Set the scheduled time for the agenda item.

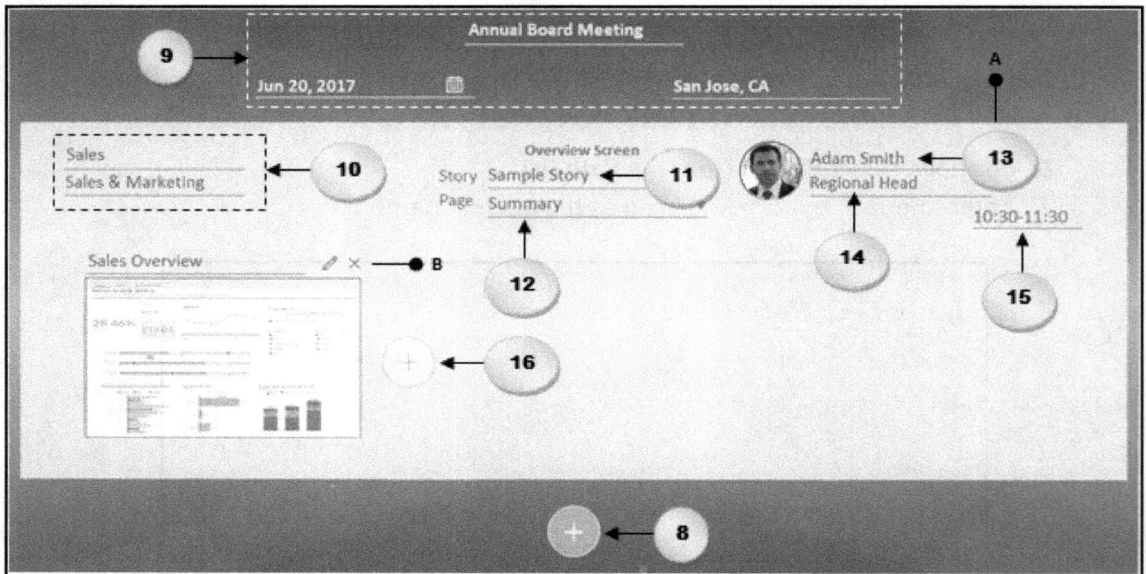

You can add more agenda items by clicking on the same New icon. For example, you can create one agenda item to discuss sales and another to talk about finance

Creating agenda sub-items

After providing details for the agenda, you add sub-items to it (refer to **B** in the previous screenshot). You add sub-items to an agenda item to link additional story pages to the three-screen display. Note that you can reorder both agenda items and sub-items by dragging them to a new position.

16. Click on New (refer to the previous screenshot) to add a sub-item. The **Agenda Sub Item** dialog box is displayed in which you specify the three story pages you created in the previous chapters.
17. In the **Agenda Sub Item** window, enter `Sales Overview` for **Title**.
18. Select **Sample Story** for all three screens.
19. Select the **Summary**, **Analysis**, and **Sales Manager Overview** pages, as illustrated in the following screenshot.

Select **Ignore Boardroom Formatting** if you want to preserve the formatting of a story page as set in the **Story**. Click on **OK** to save agenda sub-item:

With this setup, when you create your agenda, the **Summary** page will be shown on the left screen, the **Analysis** page on the **Content** or **Center** screen, and the **Sales Manager Overview** page on the context or right screen. The **Story** page you select from the **Overview Screen** drop-down list appears on the left screen. This is a story page that best summarizes the sub-item, such as a visualization that provides a summary view of the data. The page you specify for the **Content** Screen is shown in the **Center** screen. It links a story page to drive the main point of discussion for that sub-item. The page you select for the **Context** Screen is displayed in the right screen. Usually, this is a page that provides context for the data in the **Content** screen, where details can be drilled into.

You can also add a thumbnail of the story to the sub-item. Click on the sub-item rectangle box, and select a story image from your computer.

If needed, you can add more agenda items (**A**) and sub-items to the same interface. For example, if you have planned to present the financial status of your organization in the same meeting, then repeat steps 8 to 20 to add a new agenda item and a sub-item mapped to a different story containing pages revealing the financial status.

After setting up all relevant items, you need to save your agenda so you can give it a test-run in boardroom mode.

20. On the toolbar, click on the Save icon (🖫) to save the agenda.
21. To test your presentation, launch boardroom mode by clicking on the boardroom icon (🖳) appearing on the right side of the toolbar.

22. Click on the arrow icon to expand the agenda item, and click on the thumbnail to open the story, as shown in the following screenshot:

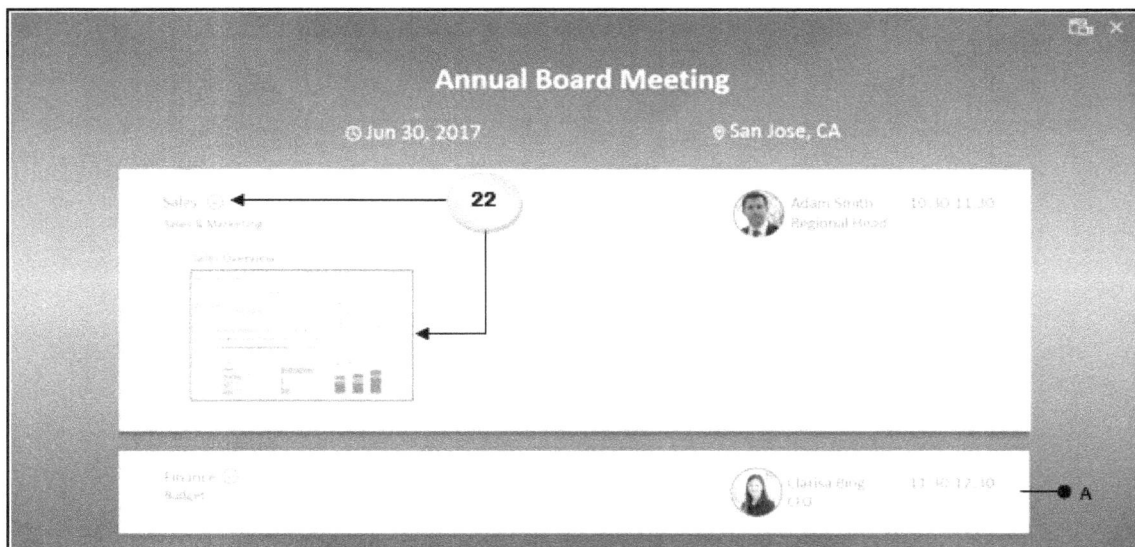

According to the preferences you set up in the previous steps, the **Summary** page of the story opens in the left **Overview** screen (**A**), and the other two pages are shown as thumbnails to its right (**B**). You can use the close icon (**C**) to switch off boardroom mode. To start an online meeting, click on the Start Meeting Room icon (**D**) for an online presentation and recording. Currently, you will be testing your presentation in a single-screen mode, so you will be navigating between the three screens instead of viewing them all at once. To see the other two screens, click on their thumbnails. If you want to go full screen, click on the full-screen mode icon (**E**).

In this mode, the selected page covers the full screen, and the two thumbnails disappear. Use the page controls that appear at the sides of the window to navigate to and fro.

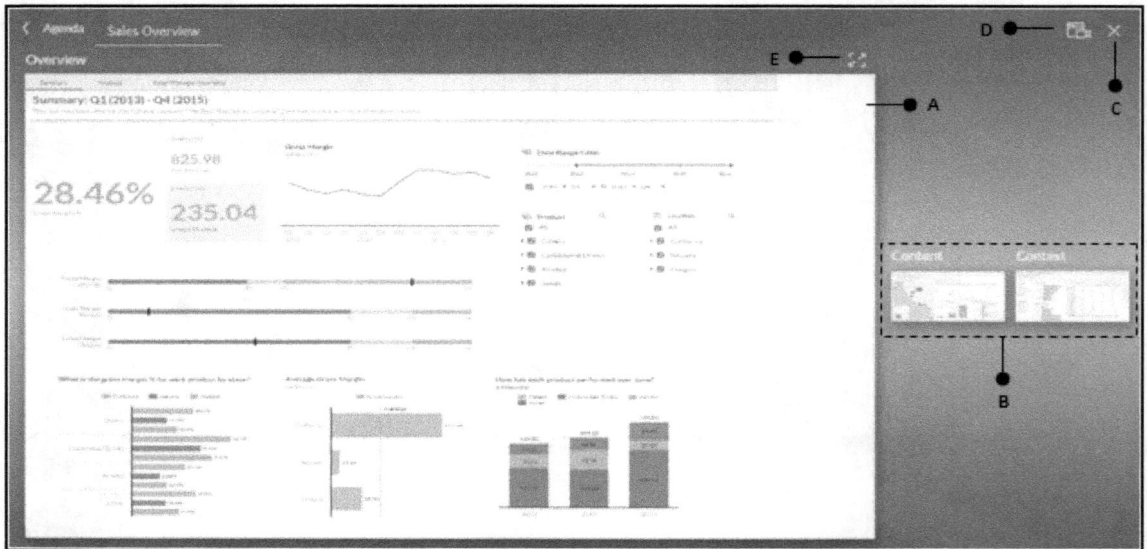

Enabling data exploration

While presenting a story tile in the Digital Boardroom, you sometimes need to change measures, dimensions, and chart types to analyze the data from a different perspective. For this, you have to enable data exploration on the desired story object. So, when you are presenting the story in the Digital Boardroom, you can open the chart in Explorer mode to make the alterations. Here's the step to enable data exploration:

23. With a chart tile selected in a story page, click on the **Styling** tab in the **Designer** panel, and then select **Open in Explorer** in the **Widget** section.

After configuring a chart in your story to act as a widget, you see an additional menu (**A**) on the chart when you are working in boardroom mode. When you click on this menu, you see the **Open in Explorer** option (**B**). Clicking on this option opens the **Widget** in Explorer, where the participants in the meeting can change its measures (**C**) and dimensions (**D**) to get a different view. You can also enable the sorting (**E**) and ranking (**F**) options for boardroom by checking the relevant options on the **Styling** tab, as shown in the following screenshot:

Setting navigation targets

The Digital Boardroom is capable of displaying different story pages across three screens. Since your story may have more than three pages, you can navigate to additional pages by turning on the Navigate to feature.

Enable the Navigate option by placing a check mark in front of it. Then, click on the tiny pencil icon beside it (refer to the previous screenshot).

In the **Navigation Target** dialog box, you are provided with a couple of navigation options. Select **Navigate to Agenda Sub Item** (**A**) to create a link to access any agenda sub-item. Otherwise, deselect this option, and specify the story pages for the three screens (**B**) in boardroom mode to be presented by your link.

In the boardroom mode, when you click on the selected widget's More Action menu, you are taken to **Agenda Sub Item** or to the alternative path you specify here. For example, if you have four pages in your story, you can specify the fourth page here for the **Context** page instead of the **Sales Manager Overview** page. When a chart is configured for navigation and you click on the More Actions menu in the boardroom mode, you see a link displaying the name of the fourth page. When you select this option, the **Sales Manager Overview** page is replaced with the fourth one, and the corresponding page's thumbnail appears in the **Context** section.

You can also set the display behavior for a single-screen display by picking an option from the single-screen mode drop-down list (**C**). It allows you to define how the story will be presented in single-screen mode when you are using this view.

Navigation Target

Label

Sales Manager Overview

☐ Navigate to Agenda Sub Item ——● A

Agenda

▼

Agenda Sub Item

● B

▼

Overview Page	Content Page	Context Page
Sample Story ▼	Sample Story ▼	Sample Story ▼
Summary ▼	Analysis ▼	Sales Manager Overview ▼

In single screen mode, scroll to

Left Screen ——● c

▼

OK	Cancel

Enabling touch cell input

The Digital Boardroom can be used with both touch and non-touch displays. You need the touch capability in your meetings to modify numbers in a table cell on a story page. Here are the steps to turn on this feature if it is not already turned on:

24. Select a table object on your story page.
25. On the **Styling** tab, set **Boardroom Cell Input** to **On**.
26. Specify the minimum, maximum, and step size values for the slider of the touch keypad.
27. Save the story. The touch keypad will be enabled and can be used to modify numbers in a table cell during the boardroom presentation.

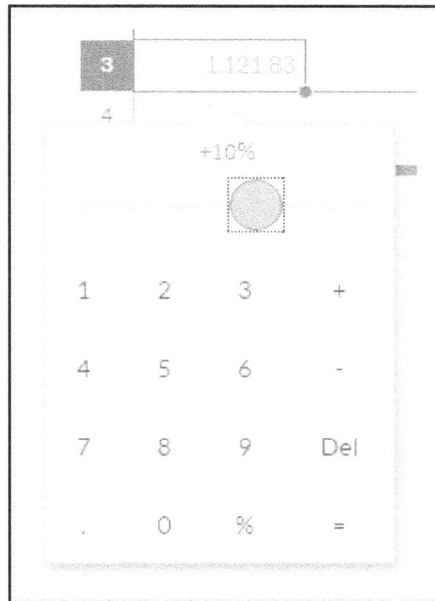

Setting preferences

You can change the look and feel of your agenda by applying custom formatting attributes through the **Preferences** dialog box, which you can access by clicking on the Preferences icon (🔧) on the toolbar.

In the **Preferences** dialog box, you can change the name of your agenda (**A**). The name you set here is referenced throughout the Digital Boardroom. You can also add a thumbnail image (**B**) for visual recognition.

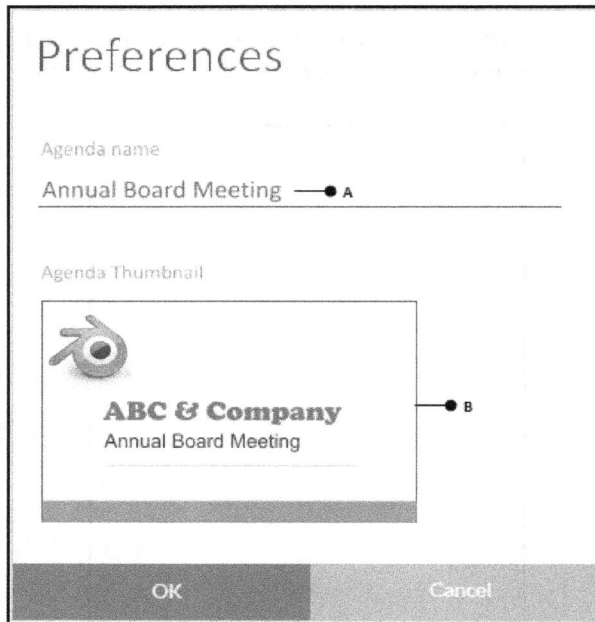

In the **Meeting Settings** section, you can set the **Presentation Mode** by selecting whether to show the agenda or jump right into the first sub-item. From the **Online Meeting Session** list, you can choose whether to start the meeting in the same window as the Digital Boardroom or in a new window.

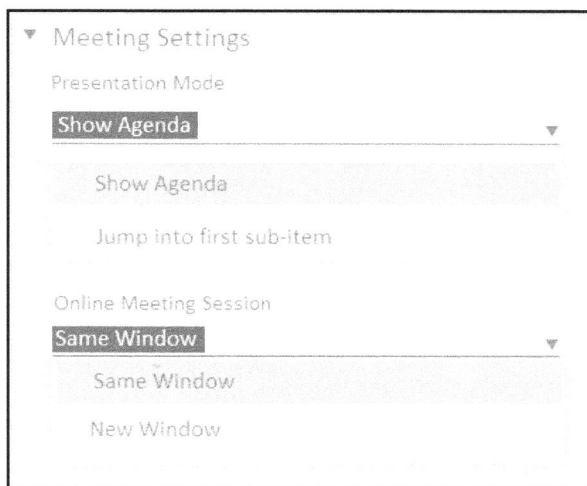

The options provided in the **Boardroom Background** list let you select one from the predefined background for the meeting, upload an image that will serve as the background, or select a **Solid Color**. By selecting the **Ignore Story Background** option, you opt to hide the background of story pages when they are rendered during the presentation.

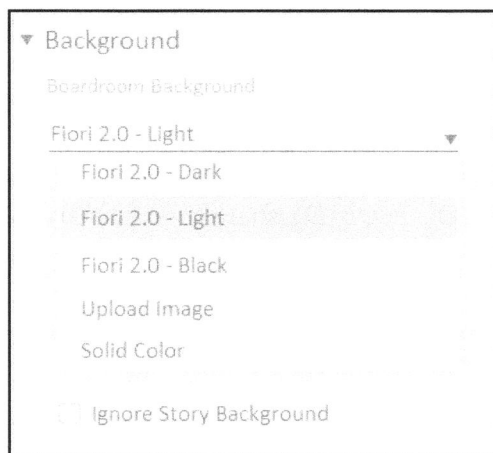

By now, you are very much familiar with the **Font Styles** section. Here, you are provided with some more options using which you can set the font style for your content using the styles set in your stories, keep the default formatting, or specify your own styles. The options provided in the **Text Element** section cover almost every element in your content, which means that you can apply a separate customization to each option available in the list.

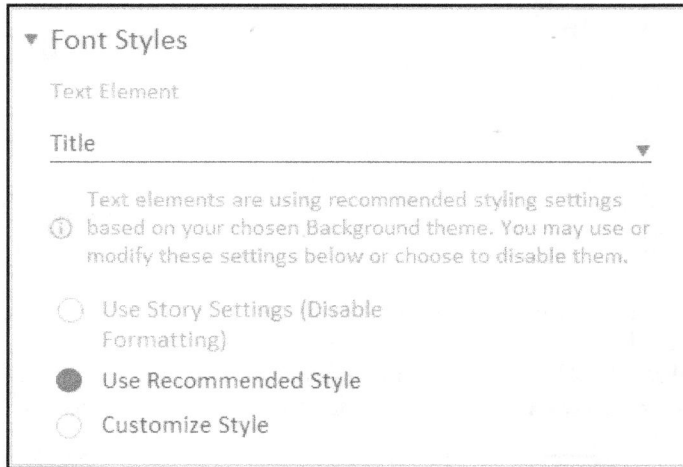

The Digital Boardroom page

The **Digital Boardroom** page lists all of your agendas. Just like stories and models, you can add (**A**), present (**B**), modify (**C**), delete (**D**), share (**E**), and start an online meeting (**F**) from this interface. To perform these operations, you have to select an agenda (**G**) from the list, as shown in the following screenshot:

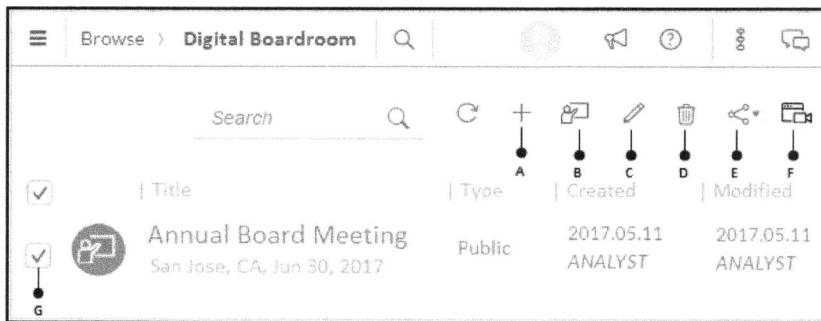

Starting a meeting

Once you have created an agenda, you are ready to conduct a meeting to present the performance of your organization. The online meeting feature of the SAP Digital Boardroom is a great solution for organizations whose board members are located in different parts of the world and cannot participate in person. By scheduling an online meeting, you allow these people to connect with each other from remote locations and discuss the agenda using their own devices. Here are the four alternate methods to start an online meeting:

- On the **Digital Boardroom** page, select an agenda, and choose **Start Online Meeting** (refer to **F** in the previous section).
- Open the agenda from the **Digital Boardroom** page, and click on the Start Online Meeting icon on the agenda page.

When you start a meeting, you act as its organizer (**A**) and are provided with extra privileges that other participants don't have.

When you initiate a meeting, screen sharing starts automatically along with annotation, which is needed to highlight specific areas during the presentation. You get separate notifications (**B**) at the bottom of your screen about the launch of these features. A presenter panel (**C**) appears at the top of the screen, using which you can start the presentation or add annotations. Another panel called Meeting Widget (**D**) is displayed on the right side of the screen. The features provided in this widget are discussed in subsequent sections.

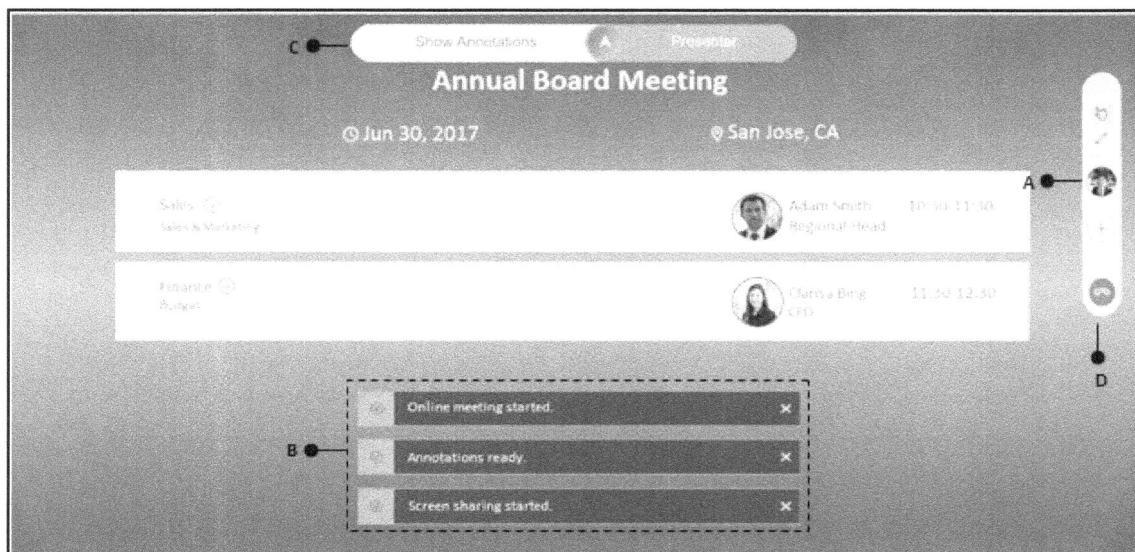

Inviting people to the meeting

After initiating the meeting process, you invite other members. As the meeting organizer, you have the privilege of inviting people to join the meeting. Here are the steps to do so:

28. On the meeting widget, click on the Invite icon.
29. The **Invite Participants** dialog box appears. Select the users you want to add to the meeting, and click on **OK**. Click on **OK** again in the **Invite Participants** dialog box to send the invitations. At the time of writing, the maximum number of users you can invite to a boardroom meeting is 20.

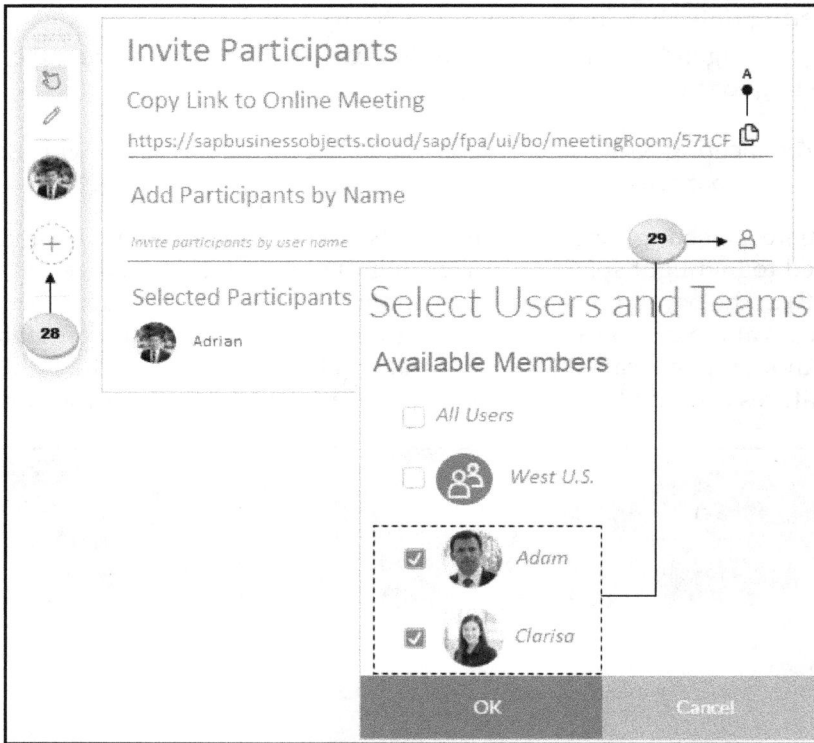

In addition to adding participants by name, the **Invite Participants** dialog box contains a link to the online meeting being organized by you. As an alternate method of invitation, you can copy the URL (**A**) and send it directly to the invitees.

All the members you selected in the previous step will see a splash notification (**B**) on their screens when they access SAP Analytics Cloud, asking them to join the meeting. They can accept the invitation by clicking on the **Join Session** link in the notification. A similar message is placed simultaneously in the notifications area on the toolbar (**C**). In addition to the notification, an e-mail (**D**) is also sent to the e-mail addresses associated with their profiles. When the participants accept the invitation, either through the notification or the e-mail link, the meeting interface opens in a new tab, where they can see the organizer's screen shared with them, and they can open the agenda item to access the underlying story, as shown in the following screenshot:

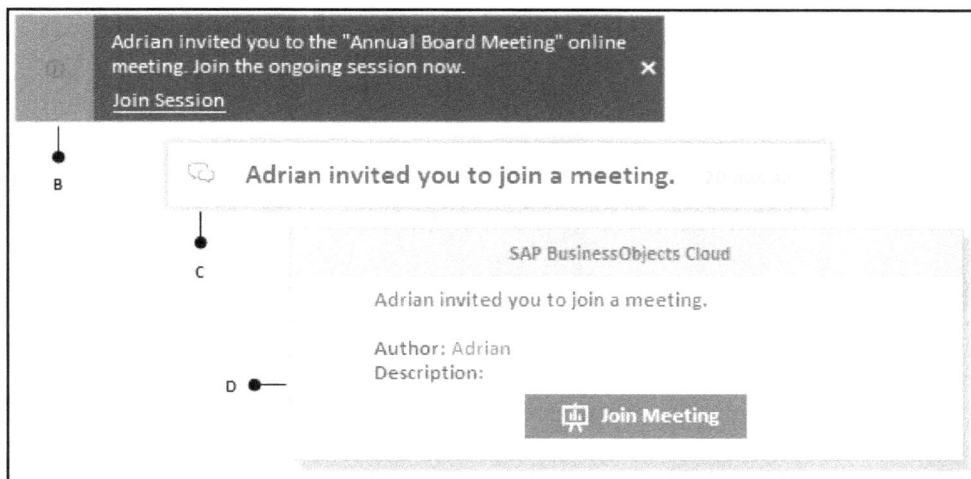

Once the participants accept the invitation, the Invite icon (**E**) changes to indicate the number of people who have joined the meeting. If you click on this icon, you will see all participants in a separate window (**F**). If needed, you can invite more people from this window.

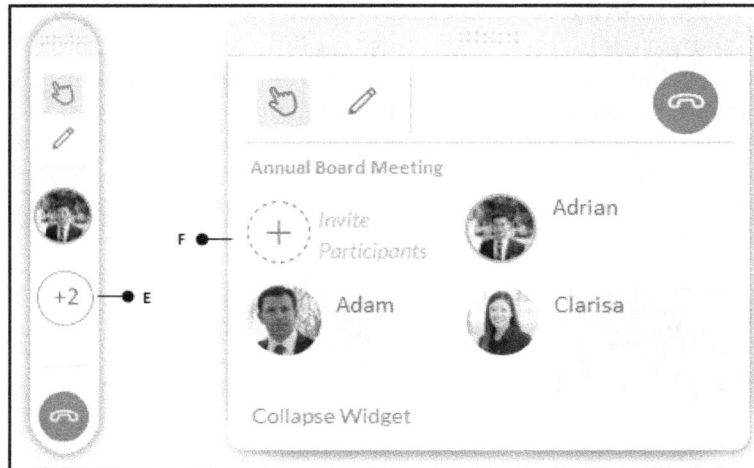

Starting a presentation in a meeting

After joining the meeting, the participants can become presenters to share their agendas with others in a boardroom meeting and annotate the screen with text and drawings. As a meeting organizer, you have the default presentation and annotation rights during the boardroom meeting. Participants can request permission from the organizer to share their screen or enable annotations. When participants request permission to present or annotate, you receive a message where you can choose **Accept** to grant control.

Once participants are granted the necessary permission, they can drill-down into hierarchies, apply filters, and navigate between story pages in the agenda to present their point of view to other board members.

You can take back control from a participant at any time by selecting the present or annotation buttons on the meeting widget. Note that only one participant at a time can present or annotate.

Execute the following steps as a participant to start presenting:

30. On the meeting widget, click on the present icon. You will see a message informing that you currently have no presentation rights.
31. Click on the **Send Request** link in the message to request presentation rights from the organizer or the current presenter.
32. The organizer or the current presenter receives the request through a notification and can accept or reject it, as shown in the following screenshot:

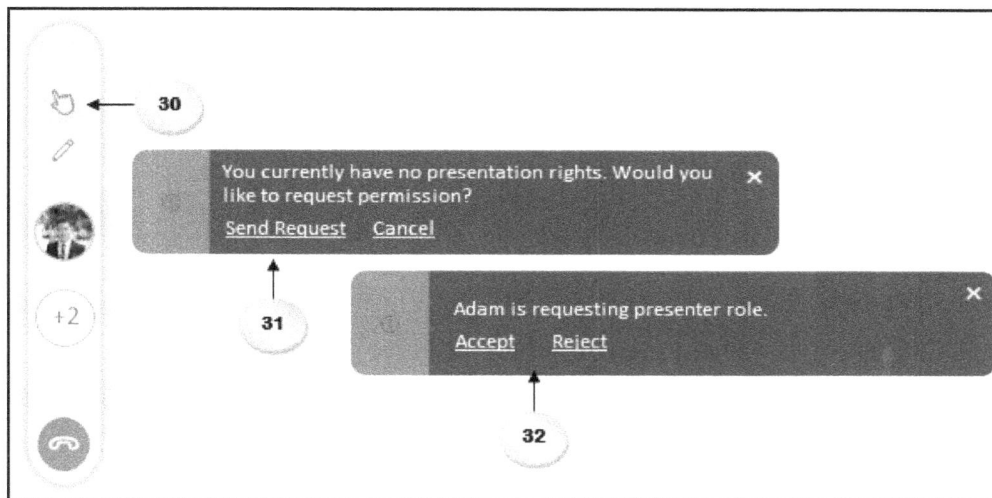

After getting approval from the organizer or current presenter, you get control of the boardroom agenda screens and can navigate to different agenda items. A presenter panel (**A**) at the top of the screen is displayed, which shows you are the current presenter. After completing your presentation, select **Stop Presenting** in the presenter panel to return control of the presentation:

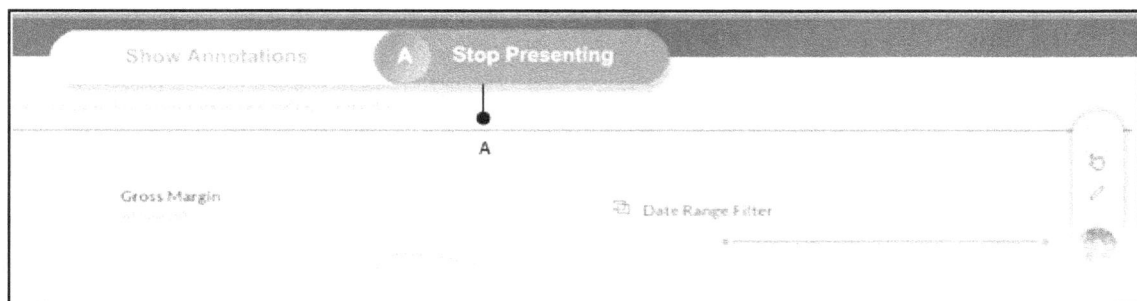

Adding annotations

Participants can add annotations to the story pages to highlight key information, provided they have been granted annotation rights. The current presenter can switch to annotation mode by selecting **Show Annotations** from the presenter panel. This action will switch the panel to annotation mode, where the presenter can mark up the current agenda page with freehand drawings and text comments. While adding annotations, the presentation is put on hold to focus on the current page and prevent navigation. In order to mark up the current agenda page, the participants need the annotation role. Here is the process to acquire this role, which is similar to the one you executed in the previous section to request presentation rights:

33. On the meeting widget, click on the Annotate icon.
34. Click on the **Send Request** link to request annotation rights from the current presenter.

Once the request is approved by the current presenter, you can draw freehand (**A**) or add text comments (**B**) on the boardroom screens to highlight specific areas. The toolbar in the annotation mode allows you to erase (**C**), undo (**D**), redo (**E**), and delete all annotations (**F**).

Annotations are color-coded by participants, which means that each participant is assigned their own color to identify their annotations. There is a maximum of nine colors that can be assigned to participants. Once all colors are assigned, additional participants cannot annotate.

After delivering your presentation, click on **Stop Annotating** in the presenter panel at the top of your screen to return control to the presenter.

Stopping an online meeting

Once all the participants have presented their agenda items, the organizer can stop the online meeting by clicking on the Hang Up icon (**A**) in the meeting widget. After clicking on the **Proceed** link (**B**) in the notification to confirm the conclusion, a message is displayed on each participant's screen, informing them that the organizer has ended the online meeting and they can close the Meeting tab.

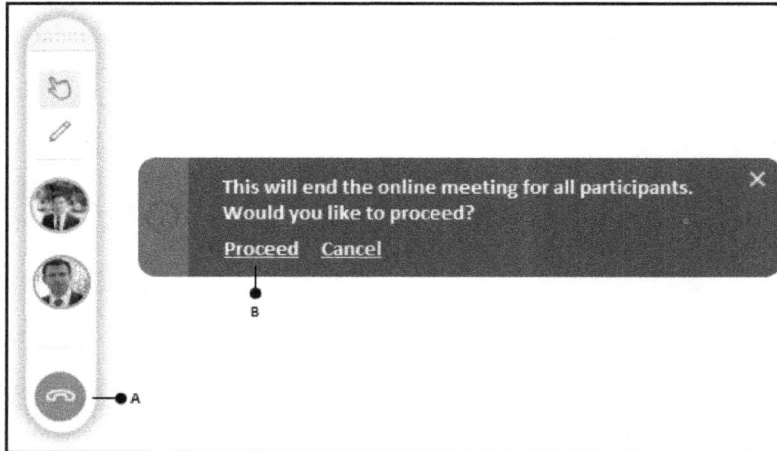

Summary

The Digital Boardroom has set a new trend for board meetings. Not only does it support the traditional presentation method in which board members sit together in a meeting room to analyze business performance and set future directions, it also has the potential to go beyond the corporate boardroom to allow members sitting in any part of the world to attend the meeting online. Just like local participants, these remote members can actively participate in the discussion and play with live data by setting filters, changing dimensions and measures, drilling into details, and more, using their own devices.

This chapter briefed you on two aspects of the Digital Boardroom: creating agendas and setting up an online meeting. In the Digital Boardroom agenda, you provide some basic information, such as the name, date, and venue for the meeting. Then you add sub-items, which are stories you want to discuss in the meeting. You also separately specify the presenter name and the duration for each sub-item presentation.

Next, you initiate the online meeting as its organizer and invite participants, who get notifications in their SAP Analytics Cloud sessions or through emails, to join the meeting.

The participants accept the invitation and make a request to the organizer to allow them presentation and annotation rights. After the organizer's approval, the participants can start their presentations and annotate key information with the help of text and freehand drawings.

The Digital Boardroom is a flagship solution provided by SAP to cope with the needs of today's fast-moving digital economy. This engaging and collaborative technology is applicable to all team meetings and is not just limited to the boardroom. It has the potential to answer both today's and tomorrow's expectations. So, why not take your boardroom to the next level?

Now that you have gone through all the features offered by SAP Analytics Cloud, let's move on to the final chapter, where you will learn how to administer and control your SAP Analytics Cloud environment.

10
System Administration

System administration is a key task in computing which includes upkeep, configuration, and reliable operation of the system. Uptime, performance, resources, and security of the system are the major responsibilities of a system administrator. In SAP Analytics Cloud, a system administrator takes care of the following segments:

- Creating users and setting their passwords
- Importing users from another data source
- Exporting users' profiles for other apps
- Deleting unwanted user accounts from the system
- Creating roles and assigning them to users
- Setting permissions for roles
- Forming teams
- Setting security for models
- Monitoring users' activities
- Monitoring data changes
- Monitoring system performance
- System deployment via export and import

Creating users

When a new user joins a company, the system administrator has the privilege of creating the account of this user in SAP Analytics Cloud. This task is performed through the **Users** page. Here are the steps to add a new user account:

1. Go to Main Menu | **Security** | **Users** to access the **Users** page.
2. On the **Users** page, choose New (+) on the toolbar. A blank row will be appended to the user management table, where you can input the credentials of the new user.
3. Enter an ID for the new user, which should be unique. Note that spaces are not allowed in this field. You can use uppercase letters, digits, underscore, hash, and ampersand in user IDs.
4. Enter the user's first, last, and display names in relevant cells.
5. In the **E-Mail** address cell, enter the user's email address. After creating the account, a welcome email with login information will be sent to this address.
6. If the user is a subordinate, then select **Manager**, who will approve requests from this user for access rights. Roles will be discussed in a subsequent section. After providing this information, click on the Save icon (**A**), as shown in the following screenshot:

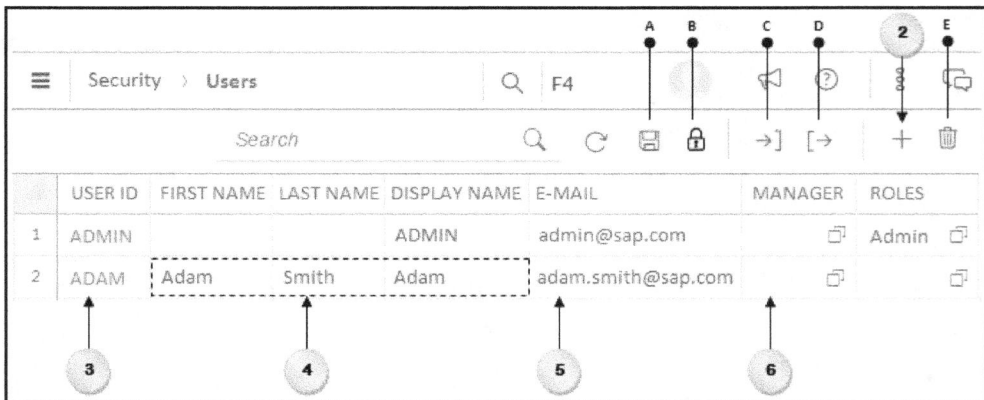

The icons provided on the toolbar allow you to create and delete (**E**) user records. You can also import (**C**) user data from another system using a CSV file. Likewise, you can export (**D**) your SAP Analytics Cloud user data to a CSV file to use this information in some other system. Using the lock icon (**B**) on the toolbar, you can reset users' passwords. The following sections provide sequential instructions to perform these tasks.

Setting a user password

When you click on the Save icon in step 6, the **Set Password** dialog opens to set an initial password for the new user. If you do not use SAP Cloud ID, a temporary password must be set for all new users.

7. Enter a password, and then confirm this password in the second text box. Passwords must be at least eight characters long and should have uppercase and lowercase letters and digits. After entering the passwords, click on the **Set Password** button in the dialog box.

A welcome email including first-time login credentials will be sent to the user. The user will be prompted to change the temporary password when s/he logs in with these initial credentials:

Changing passwords

As a security measure, users often need to change their passwords. There are two ways to change a password: an administrator can change a password for users in the **Users** list, or users can change passwords in their user profile. Users that connect using the SAP Cloud platform **Identity Authentication service (IAS)** can select **Forgot password?** on the login page to create a new password. As an administrator, you can execute the following steps to create or change a password:

8. On the **Users** page, select one or more rows in the users list.
9. Click on the Set Password icon (🔒) on the toolbar.
10. Enter a password, and then confirm it.
11. Click on the **Set Password** button to end the process. If valid email addresses exist for the users, the system automatically sends emails containing the user name and new password to the users.

Importing users

If you have to create a few user accounts, you should use the steps mentioned in the Create **Users** section. However, if the users list is large, you can use the import utility, which fetches user data from a CSV file into SAP Analytics Cloud. Here are the steps for this process:

12. On the **Users** page, click on **Import Users from File** (→]).
13. In the **Import Users** dialog, choose **Select Source File** to upload your CSV file.
14. Map your user data from the CSV file to the fields in user management by selecting **Define Mapping**.
15. The **Map Source to Target** dialog appears, where you have to select the appropriate entries for **Header**, **Line Separator**, **Delimiter**, and **Text Qualifier**.
16. Check the preview of the mapped data. If the mapping is correct, click on the **Define Mapping** button.
17. Click on **Import** in the **Import Users** dialog to upload data from the CSV file.

Exporting users

In addition to importing user data from other sources, you can use SAP Analytics Cloud user data in some other systems with the help of its export utility.

18. Click on the Export icon ($\rightarrow$) on the **Users** page. The user data will be exported to a CSV file, which you can find in the default download folder set in your browser.

Deleting users

You can delete the accounts of those employees who have left your company. This privilege is specifically allowed only to administrators, and any private data associated with the user will also be deleted when you perform this action. So, make sure that you have archived that user's private data before removing the account.

19. In the user's management table, select the user ID you want to delete by clicking on the user number in the leftmost column of the table. This selects the complete row.

20. Click on the Delete icon (🗑) on the toolbar.

21. Click on **OK** to confirm the removal.

Assigning roles

After you create user accounts, you must assign roles to the new users, which will determine what a user can or can't do in an application. It doesn't matter whether you create users first or roles first. A default role is applied if no role is assigned when users are created or imported. As a system administrator, you usually handle two situations in which you assign roles to users. In the first situation, you assign one role to multiple users, and in the second one, you update the role for individual users. The steps to handle both these situations are listed next.

Assigning a single role to multiple users

Here is how assign a single role to multiple users:

22. Go to Main Menu | **Security** | **Roles** to access the **Roles** page.
23. On the **Roles** page, click on an existing role to call its definitions page.
24. On the selected role's definition page, click on the Assign Role icon ($\mathcal{P}$), and select one or more users from the users list. The selected role will be assigned to all the selected members, as shown in the following screenshot:

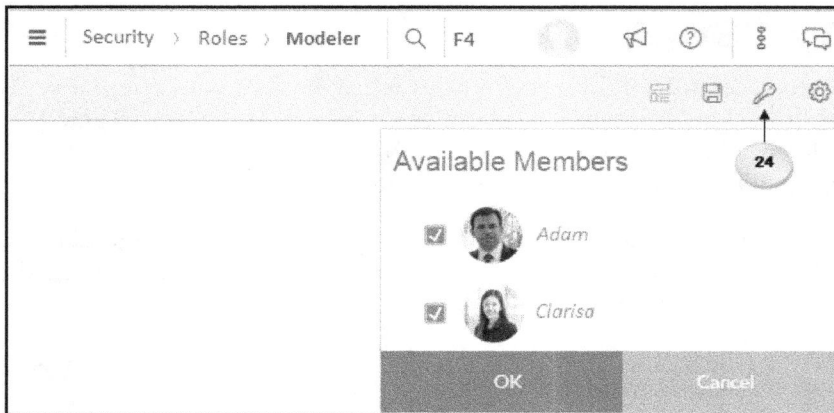

Assigning or updating an individual user's role

The following steps can be used to assign a role to a new user or to update the role(s) of an existing user:

25. Go to Main Menu | **Security** | **Users** to access the **Users** page.
26. On the **Users** page, find the user to whom you want to assign roles.

27. In the selected user's row, click on the Copy icon (⧉) in the **Role** column. This time, you will see a list carrying all roles.

28. Select one or more roles, and click on **OK** to assign the chosen role(s) to the selected user.

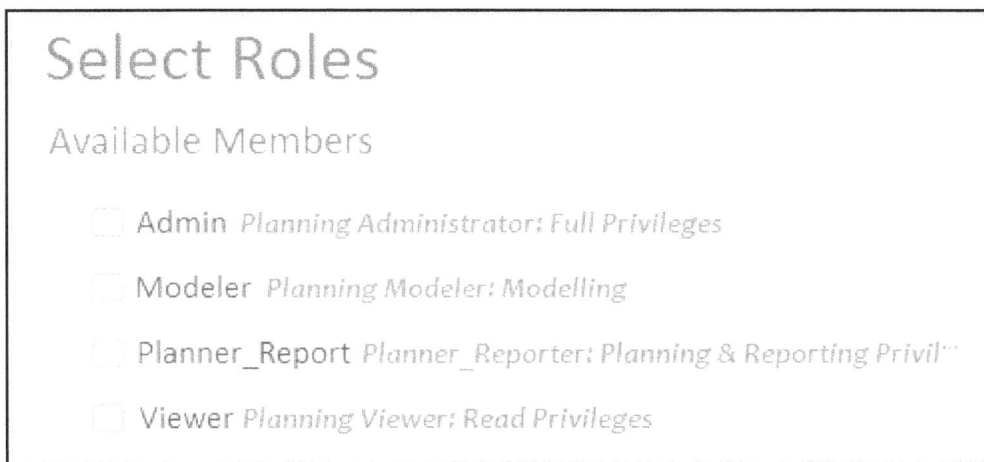

Select Roles

Available Members

Admin *Planning Administrator: Full Privileges*

Modeler *Planning Modeler: Modelling*

Planner_Report *Planner_Reporter: Planning & Reporting Privil…*

Viewer *Planning Viewer: Read Privileges*

Built-in roles

SAP Analytics Cloud comes with some out-of-the-box roles. In addition to assigning these built-in roles directly to end users, you can use them as a template for defining new roles.

The following table lists these roles:

Role	Description
System owner	Full privileges At the top of the role hierarchy is the system owner. This is a mandatory power-user role, which must always be assigned to a user who (after being assigned the role) possesses unrestricted access to all the areas of the application.
Admin	Planning administrator: full privileges This role includes all task authorizations available in SAP Analytics Cloud. The person who is assigned this task acts as the system administrator and is made responsible for setting up roles, creating users, and perform system transports via import and export.
Modeler	Planning modeler: modeling privileges The holders of this role possess all authorization needed to manage models and dimensions. With this role, they have the authority to create and apply changes to models and dimensions.
Planner reporter	Planner reporter: planning and reporting privileges This role is usually assigned to users who are responsible for planning and budgeting.
Viewer	Planning viewer: read privileges This role includes read-only privileges, and the users who are granted this role can only read the data.
BI admin	Business Intelligence administrator: full privileges The person who is granted this role can perform all task authorizations, except those related to planning. The person acts as the Business Intelligence administrator and is made responsible for setting up roles and users.
BI content creator	Business Intelligence content creator: create and update privileges The possessor of this role has the authority to create and modify non-planning models and dimensions.
BI content viewer	Business Intelligence viewer: read privileges This is a read-only role for non-planning data and is assigned to users who only want to view data

SAPCP content creator	SAP Cloud Platform creator: create and update privileges This provides all authorization to the assigned users for managing non-planning models and dimensions. This role is associated only with the SAP Cloud Platform (SAPCP) data source.

Along with these, the following are some more that are important:

SAPCP content viewer	SAP Cloud Platform viewer: read privileges **This provides read-only access privileges for non-planning data whose source is SAP Cloud Platform (SAPCP).**
Predictive analyst	Predictive analyst: automated discoveries privileges This includes all authorization that is required to manage non-planning models and dimensions.
Boardroom creator	This includes all authorization to create, edit, share, delete, and view boardroom agendas in the Digital Boardroom area.
Boardroom viewer	This provides the read-only privilege for the Digital Boardroom area and is assigned to users who are only allowed to view boardroom agendas.

Creating a new role

As a system administrator, you often encounter situations in which you have to create some special roles. For example, you might be asked to create a role for a new employee who is authorized to access just one planning model. Note that you can create a new role from scratch or use the built-in roles as a template for creating a new role. Here are the steps to create a new custom role:

29. Go to Main Menu | **Security** | **Roles** to access the **Roles** page.

30. On the **Roles** page toolbar, click on the New icon to add a new row to the roles management table.

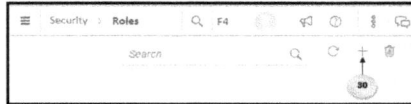

31. Type a unique name (for example, `Sales_Marketing_Plan_Role`) for the roles name in the **Create New Role** dialog, and click on **OK**, as shown in the previous screenshot. Note that blanks are not allowed in the role name.

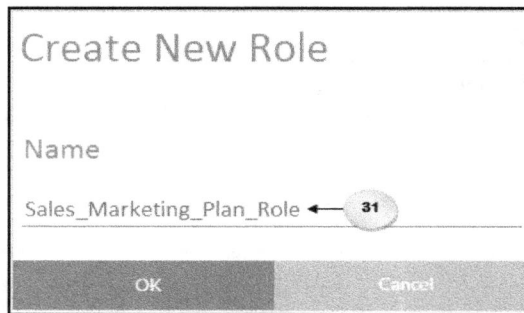

The role is created, and its permission page (discussed in a subsequent sub-section) is displayed, where you can define the permissions for the new role for every activity, either for all objects of a business object type or individually for every existing business object. In the current scenario, for example, you are creating a role for a user who is allowed to access just one model.

The hierarchy on the permissions page contains a large list of objects. You can specify permissions for all of these objects manually, or you can base the new role on a template, which is more convenient because using this approach, you need to make a few changes from an existing role.

32. If you want to define permissions based on a built-in role, click on the Select Template icon (⊡≡) on the **Permissions** page toolbar.

33. In the **Select Template** dialog box, select a role (for example, **Planner_Reporter**).

Select Template

Search 🔍

Admin

Modeler

Planner_Reporter

Viewer

BI_Admin

BI_Content_Creator

The permissions of the selected role will be copied to the new role. If required, you can modify these permissions to meet your specific business needs.

34. To define that the user should be allowed to read only a specific model, remove the global read settings for **Planning Model**, which would have allowed the new employee to read all models. Then expand the **Planning Model** node, and set the indicators in the **Read and Update** columns of the **SalesMarketingPlan** model.

35. Click on the Save icon to save the role.

36. If you have already created users that should be assigned the new role, choose **Assign Role**, select one or more users in the **Assign Role to User** dialog. All users that are currently assigned the role appear in the **Selected Users** list along with any new users you select. Click on **OK** to dismiss the **Assign Role to User** dialog. Permission to read and update the selected model will be granted:

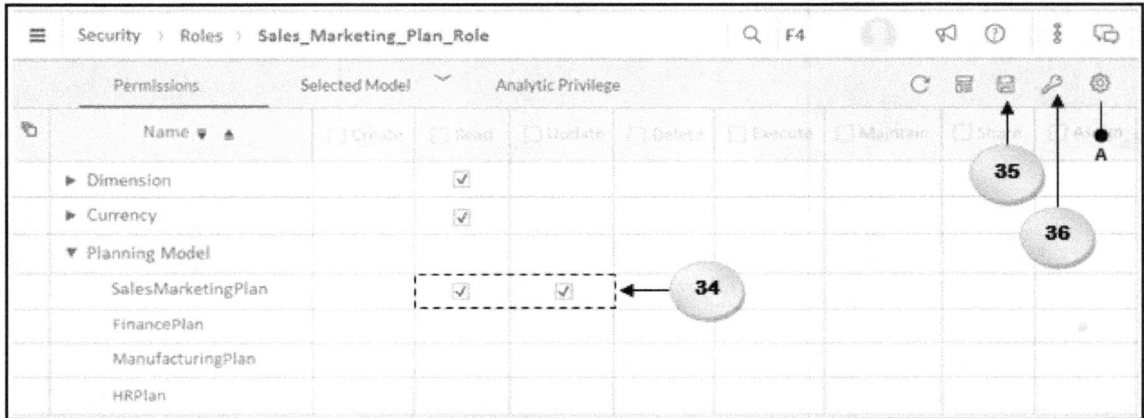

Role settings

The Settings option in the toolbar lets you review the role settings. Click on the Settings icon (**A**), which displays the following options in the Settings dialog:

- **Enable Self-Service**: If you activate this option, any business user can request this role for himself using the **Request Roles** option (**B**). Once the approver is notified that a role assignment has been requested, he goes to **Security ǀ Requests** page from the main menu and approves the request by selecting **User ID** and then choosing **Approve**. After confirmation, the requested roles are immediately assigned to the user. The request can be rejected in the same manner. A dialog is displayed where the approver enters a reason explaining why the request was rejected.
- **Use as Default Role**: The role is assigned by default to all new users if no role is specified when users are imported or created.
- **Full Data Access**: This option should be used carefully because users who are assigned this role can see all the data of any model regardless of how the data access for the model is defined.

The two options provided in the **Approver** section determine who is authorized to grant the role:

- **Manager**: If you select this option, the manager of the requesting user will be authorized to approve the role request. Note that the manager is assigned to a user on the **User** page in the user management area.
- **Other Users**: A specific user that you select from the dialog must approve the request.

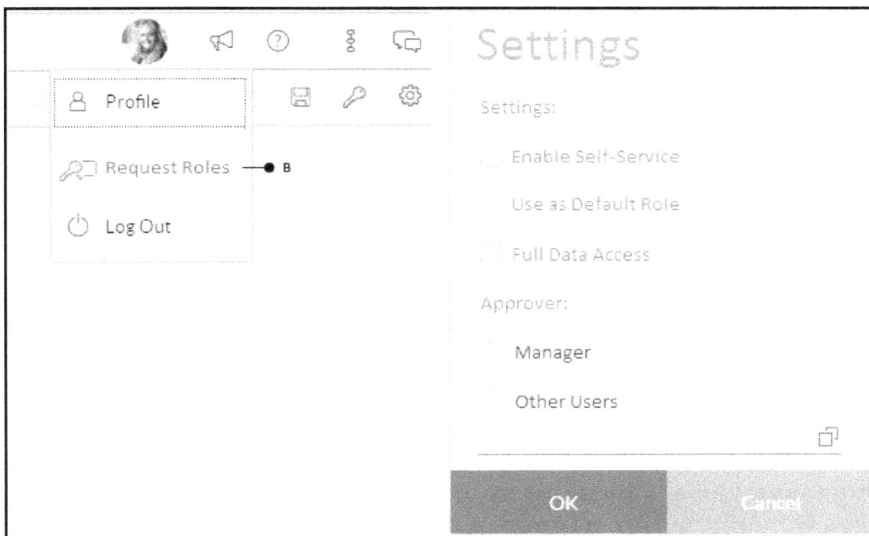

Permissions

When an administrator creates a new role or modifies one, he is greeted with the **Permissions** screen, where he can view or edit the permissions associated with that particular role. The following table describes the basic permissions you can assign to different file types and other items. It is recommended you create and edit custom roles rather than editing the default roles since default roles are reset during updates:

Permission	Description
Create	Create new instances of the selected item type and modify its contents.
Read	View the listing of an item and its content.
Update	Modify and update existing items, including the structure of models and dimensions.
Delete	Delete items.
Execute	Execute the item to run a process. For example, acquiring data from a data source.
Maintain	Allows the maintenance of data values, for example adding records to a model, without allowing changes to the actual data structure.
Assign	Permits assigning users or teams to roles, and approving role assignment requests from users.

The basic permissions that you can set for each type of item are listed in the following table, which is taken from an SAP source. Some of these items, such as **Dimension**, **Currency**, **Planning Model**, **Analytic Model**, **Data Change Log**, and **Value Driver Tree**, can be assigned permissions globally for all items of that type or individually on specific items. Recall how you went through an instance of this scenario in a previous section, where you removed global permission from the **Planning Model** permission and assigned read-and-update permissions on a single model.

> Some permissions require other permissions to be active first, and may be automatically set. For example, setting the **Delete** permission on Public Files will automatically set the **Read** permission as well.

The following screenshot will give you an understanding of the permissions:

Name	Create	Read	Update	Delete	Execute	Maintain	Share	Assign	Notes
Dimension	X	X	X	X		X			Set the Maintain permission to permit adding members to a dimension without being able to change the actual definition. Set Update to allow changing the dimension definition itself.
Currency	X	X	X	X					
Planning Model	X	X	X	X		X			Set the Maintain permission to permit adding records of data to a model without being able to change the actual structure. Set Update to allow changing the model structure itself.
Analytic Model	X	X	X	X		X			Set the Maintain permission to permit adding records of data to a model without being able to change the actual structure. Set Update to allow changing the model structure itself.

The following set of permissions are important as well:

Name	Create	Read	Update	Delete	Execute	Maintain	Share	Assign	Notes
SAP Cloud Platform Datasource					X				
Other Datasources					X				Set the Execute permission for users to see the **Connnections** menu.
KPI	X	X	X	X	X		X		
Role	X	X	X	X					
User	X	X	X	X				X	
Team	X	X	X	X				X	
Activity Log		X		X					
Data Change Log		X		X					Provides access to the **Security	Data Changes** area.
Lifecycle		X				X			Provides access to the **Deployment	Export** and **Deployment	Import** areas.
Event Category		X	X						
Event Process		X	X						
Connection	X	X	X	X		X			You must also set the Execute permission on Other Datasources for users to have access to the **Connnections** area.

Note the permissions about the following aspects:

Name	Create	Read	Update	Delete	Execute	Maintain	Share	Assign	Notes
Public Files	X	X		X					Permits access to public files.
Private Files	X	X		X					By default, the Create permission is granted to all roles except the Viewer, BI Content Viewer, and SAPCP Content Viewer. Without this permission users cannot create stories, upload data into a story, or upload other local files from their computer.
Ownership of Content					X				Users with this permission can transfer the ownership of content to another user when a user is deleted.
System Information		X	X						Set Read to provide access to the **System | Monitor** area. Set Update to additionally provide access to the **System | Administration** area.
Allocation Step	X	X	X	X	X				
Allocation Process	X	X	X	X	X				
Pool Mapping	X	X	X						

And the following screenshot completes our list:

Name	Create	Read	Update	Delete	Execute	Maintain	Share	Assign	Notes
Explorer					X				Set Execute to provide access to the **Data View** mode in a story.
Personal Data Acquisition					X				
Value Driver Tree	X	X	X	X	X				
Automated Discoveries					X				
Boardroom Agenda	X	X	X	X			X		

Test role permissions

When you create the account of a new user and assign her relevant roles, the user receives an email that provides her the username, initial password, and a link to access SAP Analytics Cloud. When she successfully logs in, she is prompted to reset her password. After fulfilling these formalities, when she goes to the **Models** area, she gets the following screen. Note that the only model she can access is **Sales Marketing Plan** due to the permissions assigned to her in the previous section:

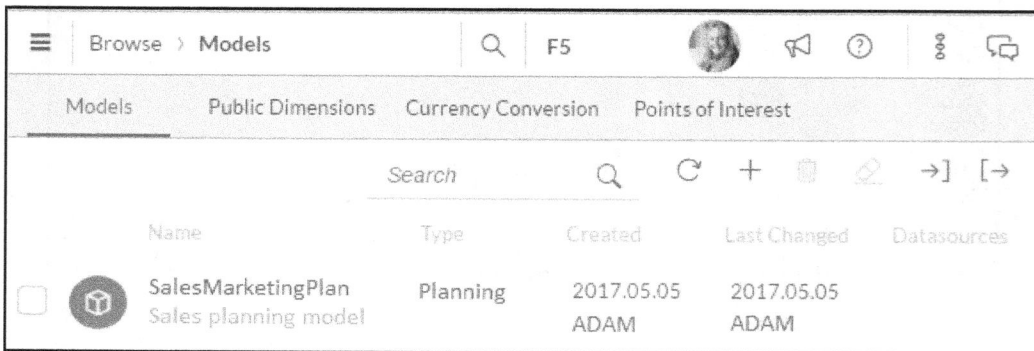

	Name	Type	Created	Last Changed	Datasources
☐	SalesMarketingPlan Sales planning model	Planning	2017.05.05 ADAM	2017.05.05 ADAM	

Browse › Models · F5 · Models · Public Dimensions · Currency Conversion · Points of Interest · Search

Update user profile

Users can update their own profile, which includes adding a picture, entering **Job Title**, **E-mail** address, and **Function Area**, as shown in the following screenshot. Users can access their respective profiles by clicking on their default picture icon and selecting **Profile** (**A**) from the menu:

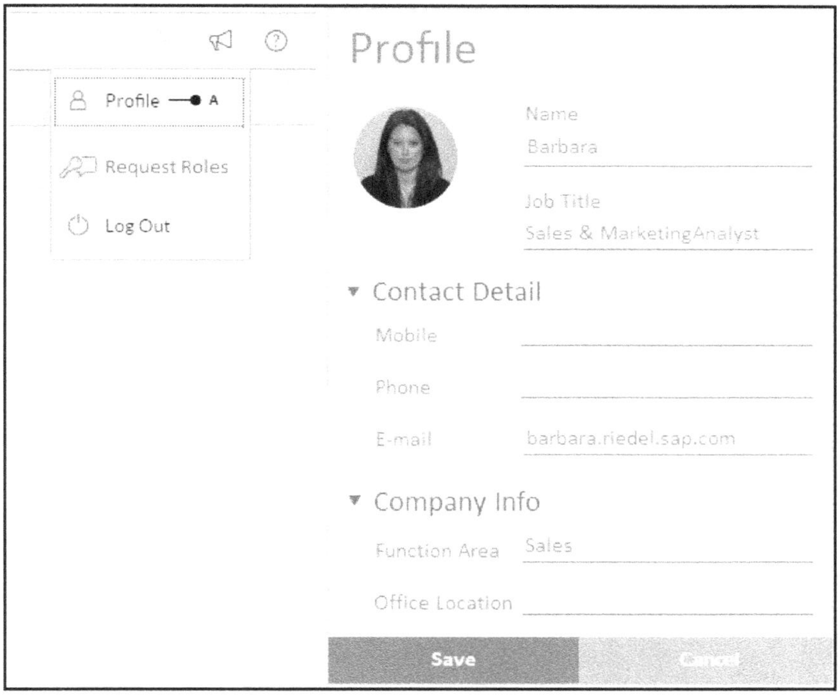

Forming teams

A team is a group of users who perform a similar type of task. In SAP Analytics Cloud, you can group individual users together to create teams. There are many benefits to forming teams. For example, you can share a story with all the members of a team without having to select users individually. Similarly, you can create a role and assign it to a team. If you make any changes to the permissions set for the role, the changes are inherited to the team and consequently to each member of the team. Here are the steps to create teams:

37. Go to Main Menu | **Security** | **Teams** to access the **Teams** page, as illustrated in the following screenshot. The **Teams** page lets you add, modify (**A**), and delete (**B**) a team.

38. Click on the Create Team icon on the toolbar to form a new team.

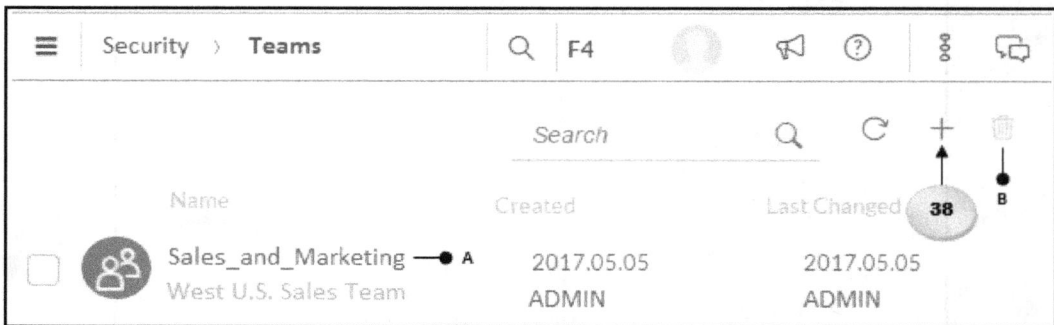

39. Enter a unique name in the **Team Name** box. Spaces are not allowed in the team name. You can use uppercase and lowercase letters, numbers, underscores, hash mark, and ampersand.

40. If required, enter a **Description** to further elaborate the team.

41. Click on the **Add** button to select the team members from the ensuing **Select User** dialog (**A**). When you are done, choose **OK** to return to the **Create Team** dialog.

The control provided in the **Members** area can be used to add or remove users from the list. Use the **Search** control to find a particular user if your list is long. Click on the **Create** button to finish the team creation process.

Now the members of the team can share their stories and files with each other by selecting the team name in the Select Users and Teams dialog instead of individual members. The team members can find the shared story under the Shared with me tab on the Stories page. For further details, refer to the *Sharing a Story With Colleagues* section and *Sharing Files and Other Objects* section in `Chapter 8`, *Collaboration*.

Transferring the system owner role

One user must always be assigned the system owner role. The user who possesses this role can access all areas of the application without any restrictions. This role is transferable. If, for any reason, you want to transfer this role, you can do that. You must be logged in as a user with the system information update privilege. By default, the system information update privilege is enabled for **Admin**, **BI Admin**, **System Owner**, and **BI System Owner**.

Here are the steps to transfer this role:

42. Go to Main Menu | **Security** | **Users**.
43. On the **Users** page, select the user you want to assign the system owner role.
44. Click on the Assign as System Owner icon (⇌) on the toolbar. The **Transfer System Owner Role** dialog appears, which shows the selected user as the new system owner and also displays the name of the **Previous System owner** section.
45. Under New Role, click on the icon to open a list of available roles. Select one or more roles for the previous system owner, and click on **OK** in the **Select Roles** dialog:

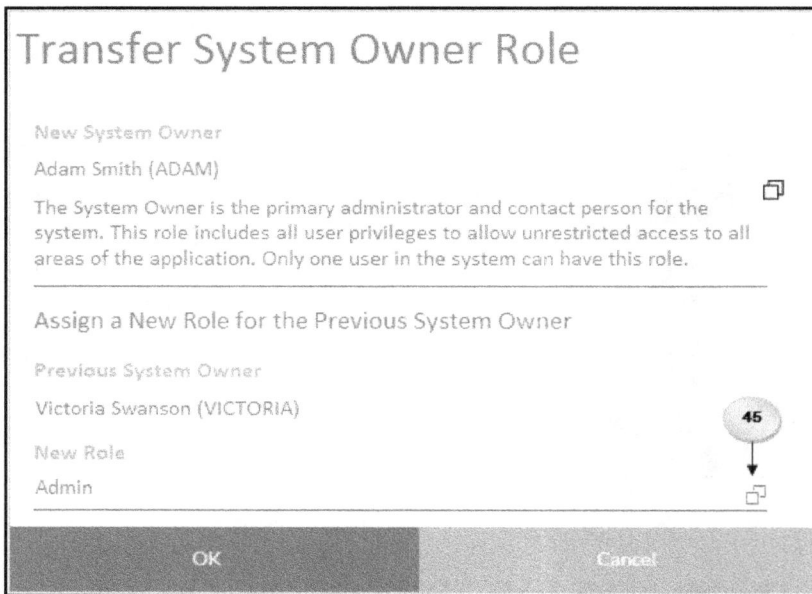

46. Click on the **OK** button on the **Transfer System Owner Role** screen to complete the process.

The user you selected is assigned the system owner role, and the previous owner is assigned the role you selected:

	USER ID	FIRST NAME	LAST NAME	DISPLAY NAME	E-MAIL	MANAGER	ROLES
1	ADAM	Adam	Smith	Adam			
2	VICTORIA	Victoria	Swanson	Victoria	v.swanson@sap.com		Admin

Setting security for models

You can also make your models secure. The following options are available for this purpose:

- **Model security**: You can make your model secure by turning on the **Privacy** option (**A**) in model preferences. When this option is turned on, the model is accessible only to the owner and other users who are explicitly granted access through roles by the administrator:

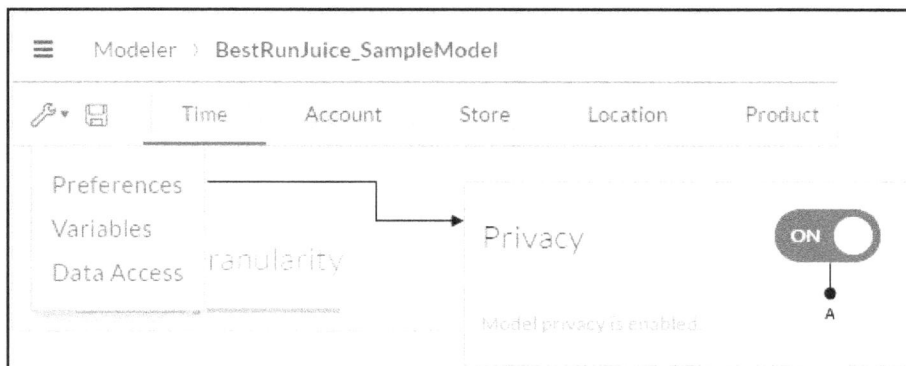

- **Dimension security**: You can also apply security at the dimension level by enabling **Data Access Control** (**B**). With this type of security, access to individual values in the model output can be restricted to specific users. You can apply this security to a new dimension (**C**) or to an existing dimension by selecting it and clicking on **Preferences** (**D**). When you enable **Data Access Control**, the **Read** and **Write** columns are added to the dimension. Using these columns, you can specify the users you want to grant permission to in order to read or write the values for that dimension:

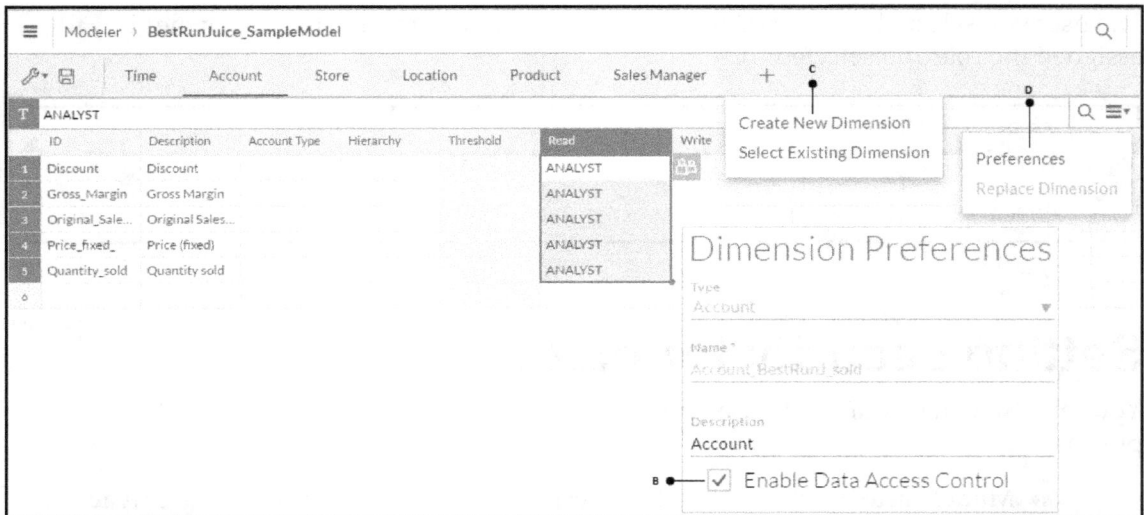

- **Roles-based security**: You have already applied role-based security in the previous section through permissions. When you access the definitions of a role, you see the **Permissions** screen, where you can grant permission to access specific functional areas of the application including models. In addition to providing permission on individual items, you can grant read or write access to selected models and model dimensions using the same interface. For models that have the **Privacy** feature enabled, you can apply some more granular security features.

Here are the steps:

47. Click on the **Select Model** menu, and choose the **Select New Model** option.

48. In the **Select New Model** dialog, choose a model with privacy enabled. The name of the selected model will appear on the second tab, and the screen will be transformed to define permissions for the model. You have the option to grant **Full Access** or **Limited Access** to the role. After selecting an option from this radio group, you have to click on either the **Define Read Access** or **Define Write Access** buttons. Clicking on any of these buttons displays another window, where you can specify a detailed set of permission rules based on all members and categories of the model. For example, you can add an entry that provides read access to the role only for the **Actuals** category of the model.

Keep a vigilant watch

Keeping an eye on the system is indeed the most important task of an
administrator, especially in a multi-user environment. In SAP Analytics
Cloud, you, as an administrator, can monitor users activities, data
changes, and system usage.

Monitoring user activities

SAP Analytics Cloud logs all activities performed by users on business objects, such as models, dimensions, KPIs, stories, and discussions. For example, if a user makes any changes to a model, the activity is logged by the system for auditing. Here are the steps to monitor users activities:

49. Go to Main Menu | **Security** | **Activities** to access the **Activities** page.

    On this page, you can see object type, object name, user name, activity, transaction type, status, and timestamp. The navigation control (**A**) provided at the top of the page lets you page through the activity records. The search box that you have seen on every segment page comes in handy for this segment of the application, which carries thousands of records. In addition to the search utility, you can apply filters to locate specific types of activities, such as restricting the list to view the activities of a particular user:

☰	Security › **Activities**					🔍 F4		📢 ⑦ ⁞ 💬

⏮ ‹ 1 2 3 4 5 › ⏭ ──● A				Search	🔍 C ▽ ↓ 🗑

Object Type	Package	Object Name	User Name	Activity	Transaction Type	Status	Time Stamp
Story	t.2	Transactions	CLARISA	Update	Unknown	Succeed	2017.05.22 13:25:15
User		ADMIN	ADMIN	Update	HANA Cloud Platfo...	Succeed	2017.05.23 15:31:13

50. Click on the filter icon to see the **Set Filters** dialog. In this dialog box, you can select one or more parameters to filter the activity data using the options provided in the **Available Filters** list. When you mark a column in the **Available Filters** section, the **Active Filters** section on the right side shows the selected filter and prompts you to input a value for it.

51. To see the activities performed by Adam, select the **User Name** column in the **Available Filters** pane:

52. Type Adam in the value box in the **Active Filters** pane, and click on **OK**. The log will be filtered according to your selections:

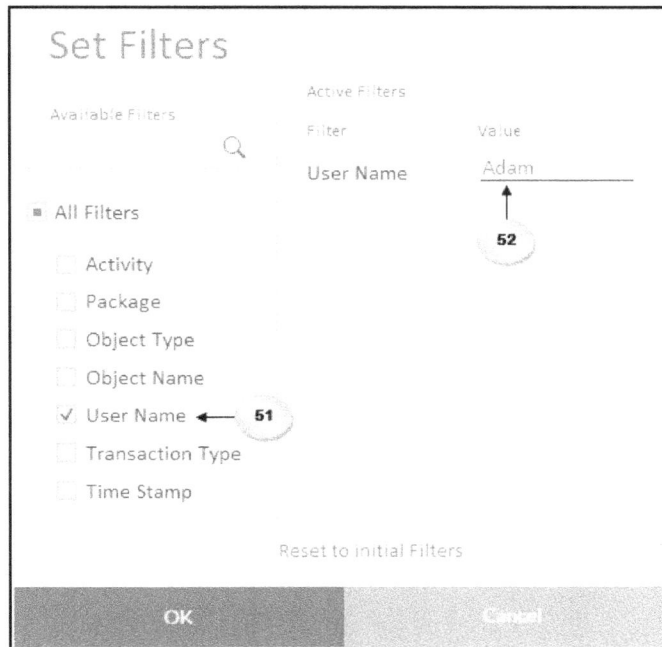

Monitoring data changes

You can also monitor changes made to the transaction data in your models. To perform this monitoring activity on a model, you have to activate the data auditing settings in the **Preferences** dialog of that model. Once you turn on the **Data Audit** feature, SAP Analytics Cloud logs all changes to the transaction data of that model, and you can review the data changes using the following step:

53. From the main menu, go to **Security | Data Changes**.

The **Data Changes** page appears in which you can see the logs of all the changes to the transaction data for the models that have data auditing enabled. Note that the audit data is logged only when data is published from a private version, and all the changed cells in the published version will be audited. When you select a model from the **Select Model** list, you see the audit information in a table for each changed cell. The table shows the date and time of the change, the user who made the change, the value that prevailed before the change, and the new value.

Using the options provided on the toolbar, you can search for specific items, select the desired columns (**A**), and restrict the results by applying time filters (**B**). You can also archive the **Data Changes** log as a CSV file by clicking on the Download icon (**C**) and delete the data change data for the model by clicking on the Delete icon (**E**). A normal user must have the **Read** and **Delete** permissions on the **Data Change** log for the appropriate model to perform these operations:

Monitoring the system

Another important task that an administrator performs is system monitoring. By monitoring the system, administrators can identify the key areas of usage and performance. Using this information, they can evaluate the current state of the system and can also go back in time to compare the current state with historical information. Here is the step to access the monitoring screen:

54. From the main menu, go to **System | Monitor**. The **Monitor** page appears, comprising the following four tabs:
    - **Overview**: This is a dashboard that shows basic system information, such as licenses in use, number of active users, number of logins, and memory usage.
    - **System Usage by Memory**: This tab has two charts that display **Memory Use by Model** and **Memory Use by User**. Hover the mouse pointer over the data points to view the respective details. Both the charts are also equipped with the **Sort** buttons to order the data.
    - **System Usage by User**: You can see **Transaction Count** and **Storage Usage** metrics report for each user on this tab. A drop-down menu is provided in the header of each column to sort and filter values.
    - **Trace**: If you want to see any error messages that were generated in the system, then the **Trace** tab is the place to look for those error messages. Here, you will see the date and time values for each message, trace level, username, component, and message. The **Trace Level** column categorizes log messages on the basis of the severity level. The default entry (Error) in this column can by changed by the administrator from the **System Configuration** interface, which can be accessed from Main Menu | **System | Administration**.

Deployment

The system administrator also takes care of deployment, which includes creation and management of exports and imports of content. The **Export** option in the **Deployment** menu item lets you export the following components, while the **Import** option reinstates these components in the system:

- Dimensions
- Models
- Currency tables

- Roles
- KPIs
- Events
- Event categories
- Event processes
- Allocation steps, processes, and pool mappings
- Value driver trees
- Files, including folders, stories, and boardroom agendas
- External connections, including import data connections and live data connections

The export process

The main advantage of the export process is that it backs up the current state of your objects and data that can be used to revert in the future. To export objects from SAP Analytics Cloud, execute the following steps:

55. Go to Main Menu | **Deployment** | **Export** to access the **Export** page.
56. On the **Export** page toolbar, click on the New icon (+) to create a new export.

The left pane on the New page lists all the object categories that you can export. You can export all the objects of any category or expand the list to select individual components. Note that when you select an option from this list, all dependent objects are selected automatically. For example, if you select a story (**A**), the underlying model and dimensions (**B**) are also added to the export. However, if you do not need these dependencies, you can exclude them by removing checks from their relevant boxes.

The **Data** option (**C**), which is checked by default, allows you to export dimension, model, and currency data:

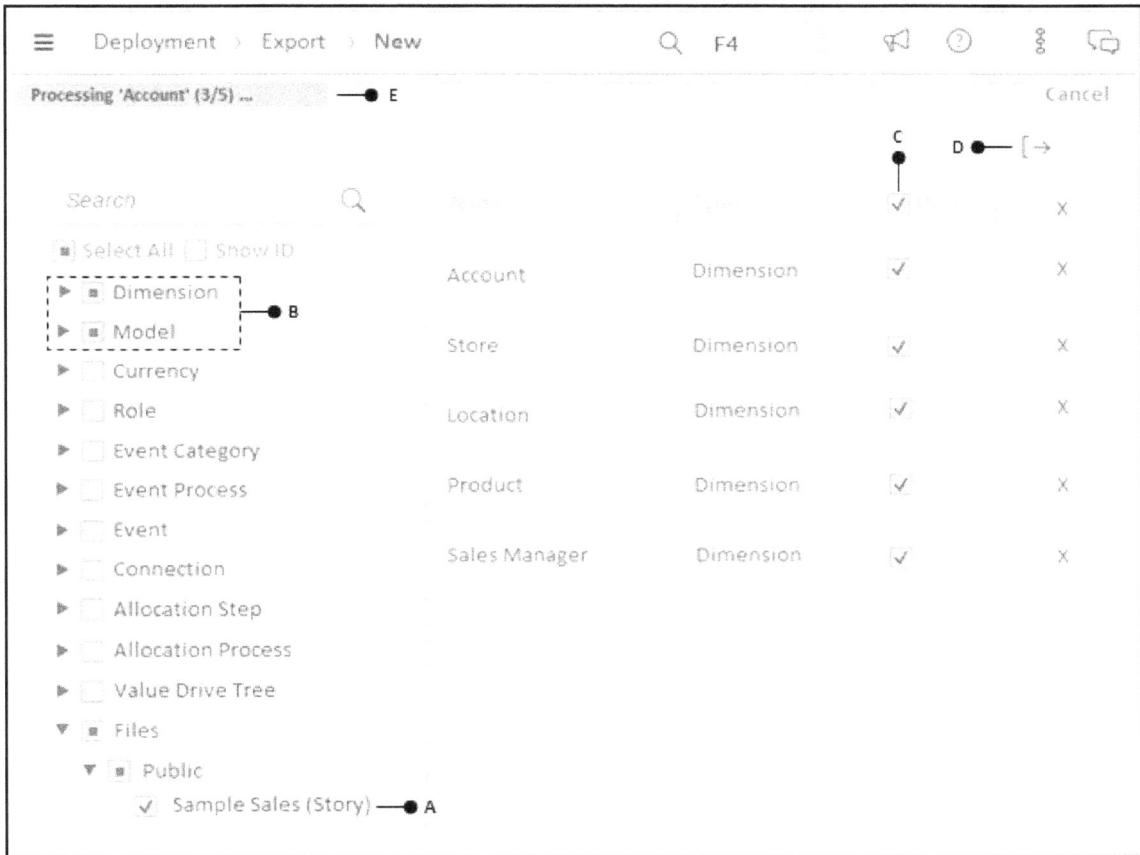

After making your selections, click on the Export icon (**D**). The **Export** dialog comes up, where you can select either to export the objects to a local file or to export them for transport. You are required to provide a suitable name to the export unit. The first option saves the file on your local machine, while the second one saves the export unit within your system. When you click on the **Export** button, the export process starts with a progress bar (**E**) at the top, which indicates the export status.

Export

◯ Export to Local File   ⦿ Export for Transport

Name

SampleSales

The name may have maximum 20 characters: upper-case and lower-case letters (A-Z, a-z), numbers (0-9), or underscores(_)

☐ Include Audit Data

OK	Cancel

The exported content can be imported back to the same or next version of SAP Analytics Cloud only.

The import process

You can upload an export unit that you saved on your local machine, or you can import one that was saved within your system. Here are the steps for this process:

57. Click on the Main Menu icon, and go to **Deployment | Import**.

58. Execute this step if you are uploading the export unit from your local drive. On the **Import** page, click on the Upload icon on the toolbar. In the **Upload** dialog, choose **Select Source File**, and pick the file from the saved location:

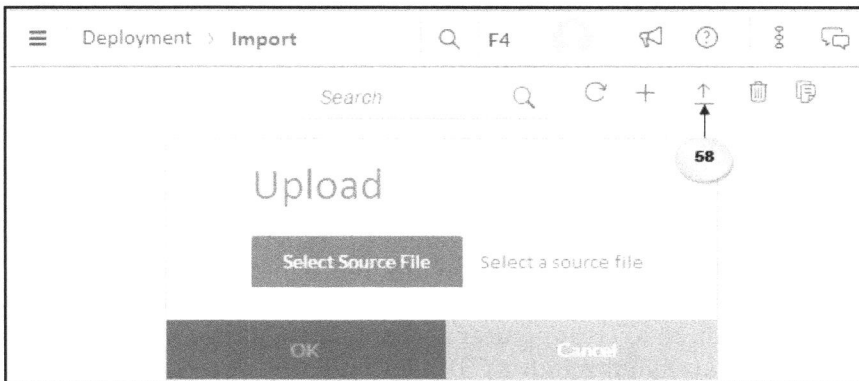

59. To import objects and data from an exported unit saved in the system, click on the New icon (+) on the toolbar. From the list of exported units, pick one to import (**A**). You will be presented with a preview of all the objects in the export unit from where you can select or deselect items. After picking your objects, click on the Import icon at the top right of the screen. A small window appears, which provides you with the following options: **Update existing object**, **Import data only**, and **Drop dependent objects**. After taking these inputs, the import process starts with a progress bar at the top of the window, which shows how the import is being processed:

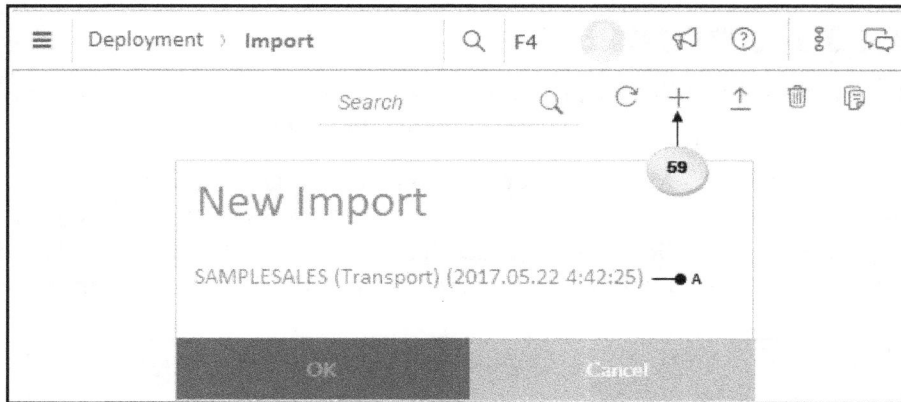

Summary

System administration is the most important area in computing, especially in a large multi-user environment. The chapter briefed you on different aspects of this key area with respect to SAP Analytics Cloud. You were guided on how to add users to the system and how to set their passwords. In addition to creating user accounts manually, you can also import bulk user data from another system through a CSV file. Similarly, you can export user profiles from SAP Analytics Cloud to a CSV file that you can use in another system.

Next, you learned how to assign roles to the system users. You can assign a single role to multiple users or multiple roles to a single user. To save your time, SAP Analytics Cloud comes with some built-in roles, which you can assign directly to your users. You can also add new roles to the system and define custom settings and permissions for these new roles. You also learned how users can make changes to their own profiles. Next, you went through the process of forming teams, which is a group of users who perform similar tasks. You were also guided on how to transfer the role of a system owner and set up security for models. You learned how to keep an eye on the system by monitoring user activities and data changes and monitoring the system itself to evaluate how it is performing. Finally, you got step-by-step instructions to deploy the system via export and import utilities.

Congratulations! If you have come this far, you deserve a pat on the back for accomplishing the quest. In this expedition, you learned about SAP Analytics Cloud, which is a one-stop-shop for end users for anything in the field of BI & Analytics. The book tried to help you learn how the tool can be used to visualize, analyze, and share data for all your business intelligence and planning needs.

SAP Analytics Cloud is a new generation of **Software-as-a-Service** (**SaaS**), which brings BI, planning, predictive analytics, governance, and risk together in one application. It provides access to all the possible data so that the user can visualize, plan, and predict in real time.

As you have experienced, the product is extremely easy to use. Users also benefit from the embedded collaboration and alerting facilities. The agility to generate analytics without any additional infrastructure is a plus.

Take advantage of the modern, intuitive user experience and save time by planning, analyzing, predicting, and collaborating. The world is going cloud, and while many enterprises run a lot of other applications in the cloud, why not run your BI and analytics in the cloud too?

Index

G

geomap
  about 21
  creating, with choropleth layer 212, 214
  filter, applying to 216
Google Drive
  connecting, to import data 16
grids
  about 252
  working with 284, 285, 286, 287, 289
gross margin numeric point chart 106
gross margin percentage numeric point chart 109
grouped objects
  copying 295

H

hierarchies 42
Home screen, SAP Analytics Cloud 10
home screen
  text notes, adding to 302
hyperlinks
  creating 180

I

Identity Authentication service (IAS) 366
images
  about 21
  adding, to story page 178
import process 395
imported data
  refreshing 17, 18, 19, 20
input control
  calculated measures, creating with 128
  creating 130
  restricted measures, creating with 128
  values, adding to 132
intersecting data example 223

J

join types 222

K

key performance indicators (KPIs)
  about 145

using, in tables 281, 282

L

line chart
  creating 229
linked analysis
  creating 168, 170
location clustering
  in geomaps 208, 210
location page filter
  adding 165

M

main menu, SAP Analytics Cloud 11
measures 34
model data
  clearing 51
  viewing 51, 54
model security 385
model, viewing in modeler interface
  about 45
  account dimension 46
  private dimensions 47
  time dimension 45
modeler 370
models
  about 8, 12
  analytics models 12
  browsing 48
  copying 49
  deleting 50
  linking 217, 220

N

numerical data
  viewing 55

O

objects
  copying 294
  copying, between pages 245, 246
  copying, to same page 250, 251, 252
  pages, copying with 296
  sharing 332, 333, 334

P

page filters
  about 146
  adding 158
  adding, for products 162
  effects, testing on table 261, 262, 263
pages
  copying 294
  copying, with objects 296
  objects, copying between 245, 246
passwords
  changing 366
permissions 376, 377, 378, 379
personalized dashboard
  creating, by pinning story objects 300
Planned Event model
  about 88, 93
  model, selecting of story 96
  numeric point, creating to show net revenue 97
  story, creating 93, 95
planner reporter 370
planning model data
  visualizing 70, 72, 74, 76
planning model
  about 35
  creating 60, 63, 65, 67, 68, 70
Portable Document Format (PDF)
  story, saving as 297, 298, 299
pp
  signing, for trial version 29
predictive analyst 371
predictive forecasting
  using, through trend time series chart 232
presentation 27
private versions
  creating 83, 84
products
  page filters, adding for 162
public versions 83

R

ranking
  applying 246, 247, 248, 249
reference line

adding, to chart 150, 152, 154, 155
remote systems
  connecting, to import data 15
restricted measures
  creating 135
  creating, with input control 128
role settings
  reviewing 374, 375
roles-based security 386
roles
  assigning 367, 368
  creating 371, 373
  single role, assigning to multiple users 368

S

SAML Single Sign-On (SSO) 12
SAP Analytics Cloud
  about 7
  anatomy 8, 9
  Home screen 10
  main menu 11
SAP content viewer 371
SAP ERP Central Component (SAP ECC) 17
SAP HANA
  direct live connection, creating to 14
SAP high-performance analytic appliance (HANA) 35
SAPCP content creator 371
security 28
shapes
  about 21
  adding, to story page 176
spreading operations 80
stacked column chart
  creating 122, 124, 126
static text
  about 21
  adding, to story page 174
stories
  about 20, 87
  copying 294
  creating 22
  entire story, copying 296, 297
story filter
  about 145

www.ingramcontent.com/pod-product-compliance
Lightning Source LLC
Chambersburg PA
CBHW080651220326
41598CB00033B/5169